BANGS

Joey Bangs (kneeling, foreground) and Bobby Spencer (center background, in sunglasses) responding to riots at Carson Beach (1976).

BANGS

A POLICEMAN'S GUIDE TO CORRUPTION

How one cop's crimes destroyed
Boston's Metropolitan Police

D.B. FLOWERS, JR.
WITH CAMERON DEAVER

Library of Congress Control Number: 2014910664
Bella Productions, Inc., Palm Springs, CA

ISBN-13: 978-0-692-23552-2
ISBN: 0692235523

DEDICATION

To the hardworking men and women of the Metropolitan District Commission Police—past and present—who faithfully served to protect the people of the greater Boston area.

To the memory of an honest cop and all-round respectable human being—retired MDC patrolman, the late David B. Flowers, Sr.

And to our wives, always, for everything.

CONTENTS

ACKNOWLEDGMENTS

Sincere thanks to Joey Bangs and family, Deborah O'Malley, Brother O'Leary, Elaine Spencer, and above all, our families.

PREFACE

I GREW UP IN THE WINTER HILL NEIGHBORHOOD of Somerville, Massachusetts, a few miles northwest of Boston proper. Until recent gentrification, Somerville was a crime-ridden, blue-collar quarter dubbed "Slummerville," more or less affectionately, though any affection for the area existed primarily in the wistful remembrance of those who had long ago quit its confines.

Our family lived on Walnut Street, just blocks away from the Bangs family home on Tyler Street, and I recall vividly the first time I met Joey Bangs.

He came to our home early one morning to meet my father and some of Dad's police buddies, who were headed out on a deer-hunting jaunt. All the men were excited to meet the upstart my father had invited, and Joey certainly knew how to turn on the charm.

Being very young, I was frightened by Bangs, even though I had grown up around the outsize personalities in Dad's police cohort. As a child, I never got over my initial misgivings, mostly because Joey took intense pleasure in teasing me. Whenever someone else was around, Joey was kind and playful, like the uncle every kid wants. But once we were alone, he mussed my hair, pinched my arm, roughed me up, called me names ("pussy," "little faggot," and "motherfucker" were favorites), and did anything else he could imagine to torment me. He was making me tough, he said, getting me ready for the world. And although the slaps and hits have long since ended, the banter has continued throughout our adult life.

Once I decided to write this book, I met with Joey frequently and got him on the phone every day for more than a year, torturing him with questions about the rumors I heard growing up. He was surprisingly candid and entertaining, and his stories equally hard to believe.

But the tales told here are true, and the characters are real people, even if in some instances I've omitted or altered a name in deference to the innocent, who are often the families of the not-so-innocent. Despite their absurdity, these accounts were all corroborated by other sources, including news reports, police records, court transcripts, Joe's cronies—or foes—and my own observations. I've tried to strip embellishment from truth and get down to facts in my sources, but alas, I've learned that memories are slippery beasts—and the motivations of those who give them life are rarely pure.

Unless otherwise noted, footnotes offer my personal observations of or reactions to events.

DBF, JR., JUNE 2014

Joey Bangs with his first gun (1948)

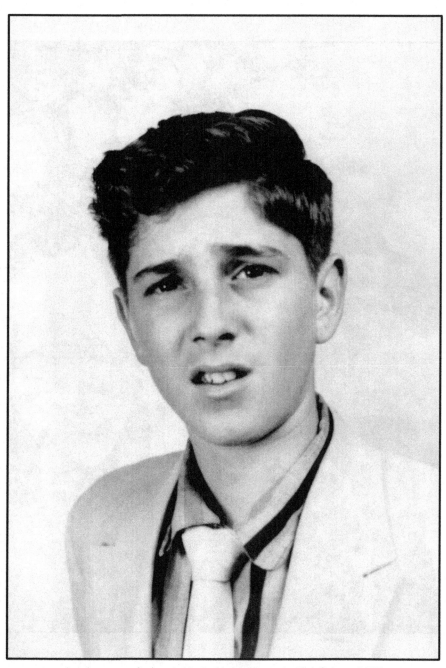

Joey in a new suit given to him by his favorite uncle, Nick Salerno (1955)

Joey's first crew

PROLOGUE

*"The world is full of people whose notion
of a satisfactory future is, in fact,
a return to the idealized past."*

~ ROBERTSON DAVIES

Medford, Massachusetts ~ October 16, 1984

JOEY STOOD NEXT TO THE CONSOLE TV in the dim living room, flipping channels while he waited for Debbie, who was bickering in the bedroom with her teenage daughter, Kelly Ann.

Harvey Leonard babbling the weather forecast—clear, with an overnight low of 45 and a high of 60. Perfect fall weather.

A clip of last week's debate between President Ronald Reagan and hopeless contender Walter Mondale. Polls indicate, according to the commentator, that Reagan will win 49 states.

Arnold Schwarzenegger chattering about his upcoming film, The Terminator, *as images of mayhem and violence pop across the screen, resolving strangely on a photo of Arnold shaking hands with Reagan at an event a few weeks earlier.*

The phone rang—odd for this hour—and Joey debated answering, but anything was better than the squawking in the hall. The alcohol from dinner still swirled in his head.

'Hello—What the fuck do you want at eleven o'clock? . . . It better not be less than twenty grand, Tommy, or we're done and you're fucked. Deb and I are headed out—I'll stop by in five."

A door slammed, and Debbie bustled into the room, a flurry of complaints about raising teens and hair and makeup and tomorrow's luncheon. A radio blasted in Kelly Ann's room, only slightly muffled by the door—Stevie Wonder's "I Just Called." Maybe the squabble was better after all.

Joey took a hit from his cocaine pipe and handed it to Debbie— something in her mouth for a moment of calm—and she inhaled deeply, passed the pipe back and slumped into the couch. Joey sat next to her and took another long drag. The room came into focus, Joey's heart found its rhythm. Eddie Murphy's hammy interview on TV pulled a sweet chuckle from Debbie.

"I'm walking across the street, and then we'll go," Joey said.

Debbie bristled but Joey shushed her as he slipped on his favorite leather jacket. He loaded his pockets with wallet and keys from a tray on the credenza, pausing to straighten the police commendation that hung on the wall next to medals and photos from Vietnam. The new issue of *Time* sat with the mail: "Crackdown on the Mafia." *Fucking morons.* Debbie was now fully enthralled with coke and Eddie Murphy—Joey slid out the door into the silent night.

As Joey clicked down the steps, the cool air whipped into his lungs and drew his attention tighter to the task at hand. He scanned the dark streets, flipped open the trunk of his new Cadillac, and rummaged through the trove: an array of weapons, a satchel of jewelry and gems, briefcases, folders, envelopes of cash, a kilo of cocaine. He put a tiny amount of coke into a glassine bag—a teaser for Tommy, in case he didn't really have the money—and then picked up a revolver and checked the cylinder—*Fuck it*—before slipping it back into the holster and locking it in the trunk.

Joey quickstepped across the street toward Tommy's windowless, barn-style garage, his new Italian shoes skipping around the mud that had puddled in the driveway. No lights, no voices, no cars outside. He surveyed Tommy's house next door—the same. Joey yanked on the door of the barn.

"What the fuck!" he bellowed. "I got no time for fucking games, Tommy. Unlock the door, goddammit!"

A moment later the deadbolt clanked and the door eased open. Joey flung it wide to find Al standing inside, clenching a massive monkey wrench. Joey glared and shoved past him, demanding to know where Tommy was hiding. "Upstairs," Al grunted, pointing to the metal spiral staircase.

Fuck it! Joey thought. *I'm done with this cocksucker.* He flew up the stairs and through the open door at the top landing, stormed down the hall, and yanked hard on the door to the office—locked again. Joey pounded on the door, yelling for Tommy to open. The lock engaged, and the door opened slightly, then exploded outward as a shotgun blast shredded the air with nine pellets the size of .33-caliber bullets. The impact to the right side of Joey's chest spun him around and drove him down the hall. *Motherfucker! He shot me!* Another blast ripped through his upper left torso from the back.

He felt no pain, but the alcohol and coke, the adrenaline and betrayal, all stunned his senses. His mind rang with echoes from ambushes in Vietnam, from the night he stood in a storm of bullets in a backwoods cabin, from deadly shootouts between cops and criminals.

The acrid swirl of gun smoke, blood, and singed leather and flesh stung his throat and stole his breath. He stumbled toward the stairs, his legs shaking under the weight of his heaving torso, limp arms, and the hot, sticky blood that soaked his clothes. *FUCK!*

He had stared down death before but never imagined it like this. He could still get out—he knew it. He had always gotten out before.

PFC Bangs in Germany, age 18 (1961)

PFC Bangs in Germany (1961)

Landing in Vietnam
(October 1965)

Base camp (1965)

Partying in Saigon (1966)

Photos for Army recruiting posters

Joe Faces War

Army orientation courses taught Sgt. Joseph P. Bangs, son of Footwear's Margaret Bangs, D 830, Prep, about the birds and the bees, but it took a new dimension when this jungle parrot alighted on his helmet and made a home for itself. This photo of Mrs. Bangs' son on patrol duty in Vietnam appeared in many of the nation's newspapers. The picture was loaned by a Boston paper.

Bangs was a squad leader in the 1st Battalion, 2nd Infantry of the 1st Infantry Division, which was seeking Viet Cong between South Vietnam and Cambodia. Here, he's holding an enemy rifle captured with hundreds of tons of supplies. This AP photo ran in papers across the country on May 9, 1966.

Bangs as a young GI enjoying a few beers

Joey and his first wife, Judy

BACK ON THE BLOCK

IN SEPTEMBER 1967—AFTER SEVEN YEARS IN THE ARMY that included two combat tours in Vietnam as a recon scout squad leader—Staff Sergeant Joseph Bangs returned to his hometown of Somerville, Massachusetts, with a handful of medals and commendations and no idea what to do for work. The only thing he knew how to do was be a soldier—and he was a damn good one, at that. But by October he had begun working for Buddy Toomey—an old-time gambler and bookie who had an office in Melrose—supervising various construction projects and specializing in home improvement—aluminum siding, roofing, gutters and such. Just twenty-four years old, Joey didn't mind the work: the physical activity kept him in shape, and the busy schedule kept him out of trouble. And as grumpy as Toomey often was, he gave Joey a decent paycheck and stayed away from the work sites, preferring to spend his afternoons hiding out from his wife at one of the local bars.

One day after work, Bangs stopped in at his Uncle Nick's Villanova Lounge to grab a cold beer and chat with Nick about family holiday plans. Toomey had been there for hours and was in no condition to walk, much less drive, so Nick asked Joey to make sure the old man made it home safely. Bangs dutifully loaded Toomey into the back seat of his Buick, where Buddy could stretch out, and headed toward Toomey's residence.

"Where the fuck you taking me, Joe?" Toomey mumbled when he saw where Bangs was going.

Joey peeked at Toomey in the rearview mirror. "I'm taking you home, Buddy," he said firmly.

"You gotta save me, Joe—I'm in no condition to see that harpy, and if I come home without the car again, she'll rip my eyes out and squawk all night."

"Can't let you drive. You know that."

"Then just let me sleep it off in the car. Just stop off first so I can grab a coffee and some sliders."

Joey was in no mood for an argument tonight and simply wanted to get home early—he had promised his wife, Judy, dinner out for the first time in weeks and knew she'd fuss more than Toomey's old lady if he were late. So he did as Toomey asked and pulled into the parking lot at the White Tower restaurant. Toomey stumbled from the car and staggered inside.

Checking his mirror occasionally for Toomey's return, Joey spun the radio dial, searching for something other than the rock-and-roll that had come to dominate the airwaves in the years he was away. He glanced up again.

Son of a bitch! Those motherfuckers!

Bangs spotted four thugs giving old man Toomey the business. Sure, Toomey could be a fresh prick when he was on a toot, but at nearly seventy years old, he didn't deserve this kind of treatment, no matter what he may have said.

Having survived the bloodbath of Southeast Asia, Bangs had no qualms about doing what needed to be done in any given situation. He snapped into action, reached into the glove box for a .38 Special revolver and a handful of bullets, and slammed the door as he exited the vehicle. He stalked across the parking lot, loading the handgun without looking, eyes fixed on the mayhem ahead.

By this time, Toomey was being struck and tossed about like a rag doll, and he spewed an absurd stream of drunken profanity that matched his ludicrous attempts to fight back, flailing and kicking at empty air.

Bangs closed in on the four thugs, who were laughing and rifling through Toomey's pockets, showing no signs of letting up. Revolver trained on the ringleader, Bangs accosted the ruffians and ordered them against the wall. The criminals sensed their assailant was not fucking around, and after a beat, turned to face the building.

"Shoot the cocksuckers, goddammit!" Toomey sobbed.

Bangs cocked the hammer. He had no taste for killing, but Vietnam had seared into his nerves the mettle needed to pull a trigger with ease. At this moment, however, his mind shot to Judy, the woman he had married just two years before, and Jody, their newborn daughter. He reset the hammer, glanced at the piss-and-blood-covered Toomey crumpled against the wall, and began to pistol-whip the living shit out of the hooligan quartet.

Each thug collapsed at the first crack, but something inside Joey wouldn't let up. He struck again and again, and when the force of the blows cracked the grip on his revolver, he began taking the boots to the muggers.

Unnoticed by Joey, a patron exited White Tower, saw the chaos and pulled the lever on the police call box at the corner of Broadway and McGrath. McGrath Highway was considered a throughway, so the alarm sounded at the nearby Lower Basin Station of the Metropolitan District Commission Police (MDC), and it took only a minute for the "Mets," as they were known, to arrive. Bangs had barely noticed the approaching sirens, yet somehow managed to make his way back to his vehicle, toss the bloody weapon onto the front passenger seat, and get the car into drive before a police cruiser blocked his exit.

David B. Flowers, Sr. (1932-2005)

Officer Bobby Jones checked on Toomey and the thugs, who were all still writhing on the pavement, while Officer David Flowers, Sr., flashed his light at Joey to signal him to roll down his window and put his hands on the wheel. Jones interviewed the muggers, who appeared to the cops to be the bloodied victims, and Flowers cautiously approached Bangs, who had turned off the engine and was sitting dead still in the old Buick.

"I need to see your license," Flowers ordered, as he surveyed the car and driver.

Bangs just stared ahead, still catching his breath, feeling the shadows around him deepen as the sunset's glow evaporated. Despite knowing that this moment might cost him everything he had worked for for almost a decade, all Joey could think about was being late for dinner. He'd never hear the end of it from Judy, and he now felt Buddy Toomey's domestic anxiety all too keenly.

The beam from Flowers' flashlight sparkled across Joey's chest. The officer directed the light into the vehicle and saw the real story: Joey's torso and hands spattered with blood and a gash on his palm from the cracked handgun that lay on the seat next to him.

"Is the gun loaded?" Flowers asked.

"What gun?" Bangs tried first. Then, a beat later: "I don't know—it's not my gun."

Flowers circled to the passenger side of the car, opened the door, and reasoned with Bangs: "Play it straight with me, I'll play it straight with you."

Flowers seemed sincere. Bangs dropped his guard and explained how the thugs had been smacking around the elderly goodfella. Flowers, who lived just around the corner, confided in turn that he also knew and liked Toomey. Bangs played along, opening up about his infant daughter and recent military discharge.

"How long you been out of the Army?"

"Couple months."

"You gotta be shitting me . . . ."

Flowers could relate to Bangs' predicament: he was also a recent dad and a veteran of foreign war, having served honorably in Korea on the USS *Leyte* CV 32—a fact he was very proud of. Flowers nodded and moved to lift the weapon from the seat with a ballpoint pen.

Realizing he had an ally, Bangs grabbed Flowers' arm and fessed up: "It's loaded—all six chambers."

Feeling for the sticky situation, Flowers glanced over his shoulder as he let the bullets fall from the weapon's cylinder into his hand.

"You must be mistaken, son," he informed Bangs. "This gun's empty."

Flowers wrapped the revolver in a handkerchief and replaced the bullets in the box of cartridges he had discovered in the glove compartment.*

---

* Everyone knew Flowers as a solid cop who followed protocol; even so, Bangs claims that Flowers unloaded the weapon. Flowers passed away on April 24, 2005, and this story could not be verified.

Bangs smiled at the thought that people like Flowers still existed in this crazy world. He and his colleagues were a generation of cop's cops, street-savvy World War II and Korean War vets who might pull over a working stiff for having too much to drink and send him home in a cab or take the keys and let him sleep it off in the vehicle. Sometimes, if it wasn't too far, they might even drive him home in the police cruiser. Cops like Flowers weren't just shit-bum headhunters out to make a collar or cause people trouble simply because they could. They were cops who wanted to make a difference, Joey thought, make lives easier, not more difficult.

Bullets or no bullets, because of all the eyewitnesses, Flowers arrested Bangs for illegal possession of a firearm and assault and battery with a dangerous weapon, both felonies. But he reasoned that if the case were to go to trial, the simple fact that the gun was not loaded might make a difference for the young Bangs.

"When you get to the police station," Flowers instructed Bangs, "whatever you do, don't make any additional statements whatsoever. Just keep your mouth shut and you'll be out before the ink dries on my paperwork. Do you know a good lawyer?"

"McKenna has done some work for my family," Joey replied.

U.S. Senator Dennis McKenna was also a dear friend of Flowers', and Flowers reassured Joey that he'd be just fine, as far the law was concerned. But another matter bothered Flowers more.

"You need to know, Joey, that those punks you pistol-whipped work for Howie Winter of the Winter Hill gang. Expect a call." Flowers needed to say no more.

As promised, Bangs was booked at the Lower Basin Station and bailed out immediately after Flowers finished the paperwork. Joey hopped a ride back to his car and headed home to face Judy's wrath.

❧ ❧ ❧

Early the following day, Bangs was summoned to Winter Hill, in Somerville, to meet with Boston's formidable Irish mob boss, Howie Winter. The Winter Hill gang had just concluded a bloody, five-year gang war with the notorious McLaughlin brothers from neighboring Charlestown. During the fighting, the Winter Hill gang's founding father and local hero, James Joseph McLean

("Buddy"), was assassinated by Stevie Hughes, a McLaughlin henchman, just two blocks from the White Tower Restaurant where Joey had been arrested.

Howie Winter

The McLean–McLaughlin feud had been the bloodiest gang war in U.S. history, a conflict in which nearly one hundred men lost their lives. Thus, when Howie Winter learned that a Vietnam vet was running around Winter Hill with a loaded weapon and pistol-whipping his street soldiers, it did not sit well. Howie sent word to Joey's uncle, Nick Salerno—a loyal Winter Hill ally and bookie—that he wanted a sit-down with the brash young war hero. Nick agreed to set up the meeting on the condition that it be peaceful.

Come meeting day, Winter kept his word. However, unbeknownst to Howie or the half-wit henchmen who patted down Bangs, Joey managed to enter the sit-down with two guns—one in his ankle holster and another in the small of his back. Two guns had become Bangs' signature, along with a pair of pineapple hand grenades, which Joey, respectful of the circumstances, left in his car for this particular meeting.

Bangs and Winter met in the backroom of Pal Joey's Barroom— also known as The 318 Club—and Winter read Bangs the riot act, making it clear that the only people who carried guns in Somerville were cops or people who worked for him. "Carry a gun in *my* city," Winter told Joey, "and you're fucked."

Winter reassured Bangs he had nothing to worry about concerning the pending court case, whereas the so-called "victims" would be no-shows. Winter also informed Bangs that he now owed him a favor. Bangs agreed, of course, and during the proceedings that followed at Somerville District Court, the case was ultimately dismissed, given that the victims, as expected, were nowhere to be found.

As the arresting officer, Flowers encountered Bangs at various court appearances and got to know Joey better during the proceedings. Once the judge released Bangs, Flowers noticed the smirk that broke across Joey's face.

"I don't believe you had anything to do with that," Flowers advised. "And I don't think about it too much, either." Bangs smiled, put an arm around Flowers' shoulder, and insisted, "I believe I owe you a drink."

Joey knew he had dodged a bullet, thanks partly to Flowers' kindness, and he happily picked up the bar tab. He had found a fellow veteran, an ally, and a lifelong friend.

In the following weeks, Bangs and Flowers became friendly. Having seen how Bangs handled himself in high-stakes situations, Flowers encouraged him to register for the police department's upcoming entrance exam. However, Joey believed that because he had been arrested for such a serious crime, he would be ineligible. But Flowers explained that since there had been no conviction in the case, it was as though it had never happened. Flowers liked young Bangs and didn't want to see him step in any more shit. He figured that a police job would set the kid straight, and his pitch was convincing.

In December 1967, Flowers and his police buddies were in the thick of deer-hunting season. In an effort to wrangle Bangs into the police fold, Flowers invited Joey to join them on a big excursion to New Hampshire. Joey arrived at Flowers' home on the appointed day and was introduced to Flowers' family, as well as to the orange-vested, rifle-toting cops, including Frank Thorpe ("Crazy Indian") and MDC Sergeant Gerald Clemente ("Jerry"), whose fate would soon become inextricably entwined with Joey's.

Holed up in a backwoods cabin, the men enjoyed drinking, telling tall tales, and, occasionally, chasing deer. Thorpe in particular drew Joey's attention: Frank was as ruggedly handsome as his relative, the great Olympian Jim Thorpe, and his athletic presence won him the respect of his colleagues and the admiration of the ladies. Even though Thorpe was an honest and hard-working cop, he regaled the men with tales of romantic prowess and fantastic accounts of on-duty escapades, especially his aggressive, but effective, driving. In fact, he was assigned the state's first battering-ram-equipped cruiser in the early 1960s—"nothing but the best for the Mets, be it push-bars or pussy," Frank always boasted, with a wink.[*]

Once the stories ran out and the men grew drunk, all bets were off concerning the dares they would offer each other. Most challenges

---

[*] Frank Thorpe was also a dear friend to my father for decades and as much of a second father to me as anyone in my life.

involved physical stunts, like smashing through the woods on snowmobiles while blindfolded or sliding down the snow-covered hills outside the cabin using a garbage can lid for a sled, broken bones from colliding with trees be damned.

Welcomed as he was by the family of cops, Joey nevertheless grew bored sitting around the fireplace of a rented backwoods cabin drinking beer, shooting the shit, and playing cards. So he decided to liven things up a bit and tossed a handful of live ammunition into the roaring fire. As the ammo exploded and sprayed the cabin with hot lead, the cops hit the floor in panic, while Bangs, the recent combat veteran, stood in the middle of the room and laughed.

The relationships spawned that weekend would lead to the biggest scandals in Massachusetts state history, but for the time, Joey respected the old-time Met cops, and they enjoyed the younger Bangs' sense of humor, no matter how twisted it was. That first weekend showed omens of things to come, though no one had the foresight to read the signs or a crystal ball to predict the future.

▾ ▾ ▾

In 1968, Bangs struck out with an ambitious plan to build his own home improvement enterprise, forming JBK Corporation with childhood friend Robert Kotowski. An MDC patrolman in 1968 made a mere hundred dollars a week, give or take, and most cops worked a second job to make ends meet, so Flowers began moonlighting for Joey's home improvement company on his days off, taking on whatever projects came around.

JBK kept its overhead minimal because Joey stole most of his building materials. He regularly backed a flatbed truck—also stolen—into Lynn Lumber Company and cleaned out the yard, hauling off thousands of dollars of building supplies at a clip. At the same time, Joey won the trust and goodwill of the community with his generosity; he offered to re-side friends' homes at deep discounts or used "upgraded" material for special customers.

Unaware of how Joey was sourcing his supplies, Jerry Clemente convinced Bangs during one hunting excursion to re-do the gutters on his home in Medford—for a discounted rate, of course. After Jerry ground the shit out of Joey's price, Joey and partner Bobby Kotowski replaced the gutters just in time for the unforgiving winter storms to hit.

Joey was amazed during his first inspection of Jerry's home. Clemente had hundreds of law books, and anyone who knew Jerry knew he had read them all. Clemente's basement revealed that he was also a pack rat, albeit an excruciatingly neat one.

Jerry Clemente

Gerald William Clemente was a classic tall, dark, clean-cut, and handsome Italian, with a Roman nose and high cheekbones, who was always in tremendous shape. Born on March 2, 1932, and christened "Edigio," Jerry was brought up in East Boston until the age of ten, when the family settled in Medford. Son of Ida, a homemaker, and Gerald, a carpet installer, Jerry was older brother to Bobby, nicknamed "Blackie," who also became an MDC police officer, and Richard, who worked for an electronics firm. Clemente wed a sweet southern girl, Mary, who kept an immaculate house, doted on Jerry with cheer, and gave him a beloved son, Barry, who made his father proud by becoming a Medford police captain.*

The Clementes were a top-notch family from generation to generation, but Joey was particularly impressed by Jerry's father, who seemed to work without pause, always with infectious good cheer and an undeniable gusto for labor, whether laying carpet or running the bowling alley in Malden that he owned for a time.†

Joey often joked that Jerry Jr. was so tight his ass squeaked when he walked. Fishhooks in his pockets, squeezing a buffalo nickel 'til it shit—however they described him, everyone knew that Jerry worshipped money and that if he did you a favor, he expected it back tenfold.

---

* I have fond memories of Jerry from my childhood. I spent time in his Medford home with him, Mary, and Barry. Jerry is a class act, as is Barry.

† I also remember Jerry's father well, especially from the time he spent installing carpet throughout our two-story home in Somerville. Jerry Sr. struck me, even when I was a child, as a good man with a pleasant disposition.

Clemente was also a "sneak thief," as Joey described him—a cop who always committed crimes while in uniform, to avoid scrutiny. He stole notebooks and pencils for his son to take to school and gave the kid slugs for vending machines. Clemente himself kept a bag of slugs for tollbooths and pay phones and even used them to buy cigarettes—though he didn't smoke—which he then sold at half-price for a profit. He even got Bangs to start using slugs around town and kept him well supplied, a favor Joey very much appreciated.

Bangs was fascinated by Jerry, and he did anything and everything for him short of washing his car—although he did drive one into the Boston Harbor for him. Jerry was the number one son of an Italian father who had provided him with whatever the fuck he wanted, and Jerry was still all take and no give.

Clemente dutifully entered the Army on March 20, 1953, and was honorably discharged on February 10, 1955. Just before entering the Medford Police in 1959, Jerry used his G.I. Bill funds to finance a locksmith course, a trade he used for good and ill for years to come.

In 1960, Clemente received the Medford Police Department's highest award for valor after being shot at while apprehending two armed liquor store bandits. For his trouble, Jerry received a meager $50-a-year bonus in his already less-than-adequate paycheck, but he didn't complain, given the grief that Italians suffered at the hands of the predominantly Irish Medford police force.

Instead of investing the money in something constructive, however, Jerry purchased tools that he used to break into various stores around the MDC Police Department's Fellsway Division, located at Wellington Circle in Medford. His targets included Zayre's Department Store, Child World, laundromats, liquor stores, dry cleaners, and any place else that seemed easy prey. Jerry stole washers, dryers, television sets, stereos, toys, clothing, anything his family required, and then some. He provided well for his family, and what they and his friends and colleagues didn't know wouldn't hurt them.

In 1963, Jerry left the Medford Police Department to enter the ranks of the MDC because the Mets offered additional pay and there was a much better chance for advancement. Jerry didn't waste any time and took full advantage of the MDC's education incentives, studying criminal justice at North Shore Community College on the department's dime, eventually earning an associate's degree. Additional education, after all, meant higher rank and increased pay and, in Jerry's estimation, less work.*

Joey had found his tribe—Flowers and Thorpe were respectable, trustworthy men of action whose beacon would always signal Bangs' distance from shore. And Captain Clemente had figured out how to navigate the world—how to build a faster ship, so to speak, and plunder better ports. Little could Joey envision at that moment, however, the vast treasures and deep waters that he and Jerry would encounter together.

Members of the MDC Underwater Recovery Team in 1963.
Jerry and Mary Clemente (furthest left), Frank and Trudy Thorpe (third from left),
David and Chickie Flowers (fourth from left).

---

* Clemente grudgingly hacked his way up the ladder, joining the Underwater Recovery Team in 1963 and then moving from the Lower Basin to Revere Beach in 1964, where he remained until a transfer to the Fellsway Division in 1965. Jerry returned to the beach as a sergeant in 1967. In 1972, he made lieutenant, was transferred to the Blue Hills Division and later returned to Revere Beach in 1973. In 1977, Clemente was promoted to captain and became watch commander of the entire MDC police department.

David Flowers, Sr., with members of the MDC Underwater Recovery Team (1963), including Frank Thorpe and Jerry Clemente (standing, first row, second and third from right, respectively).

Flowers, a fast-pitch softball pitcher for the MDC, helped raise thousands of dollars for charitable organizations such as the Jimmy Fund.

BLACK IN BLUE: THE CAPITOL POLICE

DURING THE WINTER OF 1968-69, when the home renovation business took a dip, Bangs began collecting street loans and gambling debts for reputed *La Cosa Nostra* associates. Once a scrappy inner-city kid, Joey lived by the rules of the street and the protocol that justice demanded. He soon carved out a place as confidante to some of Boston's most ruthless gangsters, especially those in the Italian North End, who dubbed him a *uomo di onore*—a man of honor. The Italian women just called him *la piovra*—the octopus—for his incessant groping.

Bangs never asked what the debt was for or why it hadn't yet been paid. By the time a marker made it to Joey, all amounts were immediately payable in full, and one way or another, Joey balanced the books, usually with the assistance of a sawed-off shotgun dubbed "Myrtle," he explained, after a high-priced French call girl who had once given him the bang of his life.

One of Joey's favorite collection spots was King Arthur's Lounge, a popular strip joint in Chelsea. In addition to the good food and fine scenery, Joey found that the debtors he cornered there usually had cash in their pockets and their heads in someone's tits. They were soft targets who never made a fuss in public, and Joey usually enjoyed the remainder of the poor bastards' lap dances after he roughed them up and chased them away.

Bangs also specialized in "making things right" in situations that didn't involve money, such as morons who dared mess around with a connected man's wife. In the case of one high-priced, philandering lawyer, Joey made an appointment under a phony name, claiming he had been in a serious car accident and needed legal representation. He arrived at the law office with a phony neck collar and cast, and once he was alone with the attorney, he made it known exactly who he was, informing the man that his fling was officially over.

"The neck collar looked better wrapped around that attorney's neck than mine," he loved to recount. "They always got the message."

Bangs extended his network exponentially while working collections, often bringing in his childhood friend Brother O'Leary to provide backup. The duo made themselves at home in the North End, where they mingled with the Mafia's movers and shakers. Joey and Brother were an infamous team known around town as men you could rely on if you needed something—anything—done.

∨ ∨ ∨

Bangs was born in Somerville but moved at an early age to Cambridge, where he met Francis Xavier O'Leary—the character who would become his better criminal half and life-long best friend—at Saint Mary's grade school. "Brother" was accorded the nickname because he had an angelic appearance—the true baby face and innocent smile of an altar boy—and an older sibling who was in the seminary.

Brother was born in Cambridge just four months after Joey and was the second youngest child in a working-class family with four children. He was physically large for his age, but not overly bright, slipping from grade to grade until he finally had to repeat the sixth.

Even as a kid, Brother was an incorrigible prankster and a funny bastard who craved attention and thrived on laughter. O'Leary's mischievous disposition naturally led to a lengthy arrest record for various assaults and thefts and an eventual appearance before the juvenile board, which remanded him to serve several months at the youth service facility at 100 Canterbury Street in Boston. Brother had balls of brass, as did Joey, and the two became fast friends. The boys held court at Senate Park, where they formed the Senate Park Gang, which included fifteen or so hardened inner-city English, Irish, and Italian petty-thief derelicts. Gang feuds were not uncommon, and Joey and Brother saw more than their fair share of street violence.

The boys were infamous around Cambridge for breaking into boxcars at a nearby railroad depot. On one occasion they managed to steal a cow from a cattle car coupled at the John P. Squire Slaughterhouse and Packing Company. But Joey soon discovered that he had nowhere to fence the beast after his local butcher told him to get lost. So young Bangs kept the cow as a pet until someone spotted him walking down the street, cow in tow, and turned him in to local authorities.

v v v

As adults, the men expanded their illegal activity well beyond collections and rough-ups, most notably forging driver licenses and stealing credit cards— and making a mint in their spare time.

Bangs had befriended a mail carrier—who also carried a significant gambling debt that he needed to satisfy—and arranged to "borrow" new credit cards before they were delivered. Bangs and O'Leary then took orders from buyers for all kinds of products—from clothing to cigarettes to appliances to toys—purchased the items with the cards, and resold the goods to their buyers, usually for fifty cents on the dollar. With an average of fifteen to twenty credit cards per week, Joey and Brother each netted thousands in profit while providing families with discounted goods and helping a sad-sack mailman dig out of debt. Fancying themselves modern-day Robin Hoods, they calculated that those who could afford credit could share a few dollars. On other occasions, they simply sold credit cards for half of the predetermined credit line.

Since returning from the military, Joey had unwittingly begun laying the foundation for a new dream city, built to his specifications, that brought under one roof all the sources he needed for money, influence, pleasure and power—except one. He needed a façade of legitimacy and respectability.

v v v

After months of nudging from Flowers and friends, Joey finally took the civil service entrance exam in 1968 and received the call to join the MDC police force, although he turned down the job simply because they didn't pay enough at the time. Construction was booming, and Bangs was making $400-500 a week from his mob collections—the equivalent of a month's salary for a policeman. Policing could be just as dicey as collecting, and Joey was under no illusion that he would enter the force for the common good: he only wanted the access and cover of legitimacy that a badge and gun provided, for whatever purposes he decided to pursue in life.

The following year, Flowers convinced Joey to take the exam again, and of course, Bangs mastered the test. In fact, Joey scored the top grade and advanced to the number one slot on the lengthy disabled veterans' waiting list, which he qualified for because of the skull fracture he had sustained in the Army. Bangs was offered a job with the Capitol Police, a small department of fewer than a hundred men and no women, charged with protecting the state capitol and other government buildings in the Capitol Hill area. Since the force didn't have its own academy, recruits attended the MDC Police Academy, the Medford Police Academy or the State Police Academy in Framingham. Joey chose the Medford Police Academy because of its convenient location and awaited the start of the next training session.

Despite the success of his home improvement business and profits from numerous illegal activities that had not yet come to light, Bangs joined the ranks of the Capitol Police in October 1970 and easily finished training at the academy. After life on Boston's streets, two tours in Vietnam, and a healthy dose of the "business" world, police classes with a bunch of candy-asses was a breeze.

However, Joey's police career was nearly stillborn when he found himself in the crossfire of a double murder investigation. Someone took a shot at "Chocolates"—a local hustler and nightclub owner known for his sweet tooth, natch, as well as for hijacking candy trucks—but missed by inches, killing Chocolates' associates, Deacon Doyle and John Mills, as the men confabbed outside the Pony Room Lounge, on the corner of Creighton Street and Massachusetts Avenue, in North Cambridge.

Given that Bangs had a propensity for violence and lived just up the street, Cambridge Police questioned him, but he was cleared of any involvement in the case.

However, police later arrested the proprietor of the Pony Room, Paul Walker. Walker was the retired teamster-turned-bookie everyone referred to as "The Mayor of Cambridge," not only because he held most of the loansharking and gambling action in town but also because he did, in fact, govern the community's affairs, legitimate and otherwise. Walker also owned and operated the Shamrock Lounge, located in Cambridge's Inman Square—another favorite location to hold high court.

Walker was investigated and eventually cleared of any wrongdoing after police determined that he, Doyle, and Mills were close friends.

˅ ˅ ˅

Still hunting the killer, Walker called for a sit-down with Bangs. Several years Joey's senior, Walker and Bangs had grown up on the streets together. Joey had always admired and respected Paul, a steely inner-city kid who had never lost a fight, and Paul had a good sense of Bang's personality and capability, with or without a weapon. But now that they were adults and men around them were dead, the conversation ratcheted up.

Walker asked what Bangs knew about the murders: whoever did the shooting, Walker asserted, knew what the fuck he was doing with a high-powered rifle like the one that killed Mills and Doyle. Joey had heard no rumors in advance and no whispers in the aftermath. And even though he clashed with Chocolates—just a personality thing, he explained—he considered Mills and Doyle friends and admirable goodfellas.

Walker scrutinized Bangs' gaze—if he had doubted before, now face to face, he believed him. Paul and Joey traded suspicions about the killing and landed on the same name. Walker warned Bangs to keep his distance from this acquaintance, who would shortly thereafter receive his comeuppance.

Bangs was again in the clear, and the meeting with Walker was the beginning of a relationship that would pull mightily against Joey's new career in public service and test his friendship with Brother O'Leary.

Walker recognized the lifelong bond that Joey and Brother shared, but he thought that Brother was too unfocused and erratic to do the work that men like Walker and Bangs had to do. In fact, Brother's uncle, Channing Smith—known about town as "Smitty the Carpenter"—booked and loansharked for Walker, another reason that Brother got a pass with Paul. Nonetheless, Walker advised Bangs, "Pick your allies wisely—O'Leary will bring you down if you're not careful."

˅ ˅ ˅

Francis "Brother" O'Leary

A chain-smoker who sported an unkempt Fu Manchu mustache, Brother indeed had a growing reputation for getting drunk and committing all kinds of childishness. He thieved for a living—which provided a comfortable two-story home on Trull Street, just outside of Magoun Square, in Somerville—and lived to be a jokester, always finding his way effortlessly to the center of attention. It was impossible not to laugh once Brother got on a roll, and unless you were the direct target of one of his legendary practical jokes—and even sometimes when you were—he always left you wishing you could do funny like he did.[*]

Bangs had been on the Capitol Police less than a year when he joined O'Leary at a gin mill on McGrath Highway in Cambridge for a beer after work one evening. As expected, one drink turned into one too many until they stumbled out at closing, drunk but orderly and without incident. Brother stood in the middle of the sidewalk and looked up and down the street at the surrounding stores. He picked up a brick, hefted it in his hands and nonchalantly tossed it through the plate glass window of a lamp store. The bell alarm screamed; Brother carefully reached through the shattered pane, grabbed a lampshade for his head and a lamp for each hand, and started to dance down the street. Joey wasn't amused: he slid into his car and sped away, leaving Brother standing in the middle of the road, shit-faced and looking ridiculous.

Bangs stopped not far away at a friend's after-hours joint for last call. He had barely gotten his drink when an acquaintance strolled in and advised him that Brother was walking down McGrath Highway with a lamp in each hand and a shade on his head. *Fuck it*, Joey sighed. He gulped

---

[*] Brother is one of the most outrageously funny people I know, and it's always a riot to be in his company. While nothing is sacred in Brother's world, he is also optimistic, friendly, and—if you're even minimally kind to him—generous and willing to help in any way he can.

his drink, hopped into his vehicle, drove back down the street, and wrestled Brother into the backseat, tossing the stolen lamps and shade to the sidewalk before he sped away. Moments later, the Cambridge police arrived on the scene.

A couple days later, the police tracked Brother to a local watering hole, served a warrant and arrested him on the spot. They prodded him for hours for details of the incident and his accomplice, but Brother refused to give up his childhood pal Joey.

Unbeknownst to Bangs, earlier that evening, O'Leary had run into a couple local thugs who asked if he needed a ride. Brother assured them that his partner, who was a cop, would be back to pick him up. When Joey returned to the scene, the cop-hating thugs took down the license number of Bang's car and reported it to the Cambridge police. With a questioning session on the horizon, Joey knew he was in trouble; even a misdemeanor could cost him his job on the Capitol Police.

Scrambling for answers, Joey enlisted his uncle, Eddie Bangs, to concoct a scheme. Uncle Eddie was a no-nonsense teamster and business agent for Local 25, who had a penchant for shoving troublesome drivers out the window of his office at union headquarters. Eddie persuaded a teamster friend who looked like Joey to say he was with Brother that evening. The Cambridge detectives didn't bite, and they eventually arrested Joey while he was on duty at the Capitol Police's office in the State House. Joey did a simple "walk-through"—photographs, fingerprints and an immediate release.

Capitol Police Chief Paul Doherty, whom Bangs admired for his intelligence and fairness, and Superintendent of Police George Luciano both told Joey that they wouldn't do anything to hurt his career if he were found not guilty. However, if he were found guilty, they warned, they'd have to "shit-can his ass." Shortly thereafter, Bangs found himself in front of an East Cambridge District Court judge, and luckily for him, the charges were dismissed.

The Cambridge detectives knew the case had been fixed, so they went over the head of the district court judge to a Middlesex County grand jury for an indictment. Their strategy worked, and Bangs was again arrested while on duty, did yet another walk-through, and was suspended with pay pending the outcome of a jury trial. The case had become a vendetta for the Cambridge police, who spared no expense to have Joey Bangs—someone they knew only too well—convicted and fired.

But Joey and his defense team—State Senator McKenna and famed defense attorney Ralph Champa, who was at the top of his game—were ready to play.

Police Chief Doherty believed at the time that Bangs was a solid cop and stuck his neck out to vouch for Joey. Doherty's credentials were impeccable: he was known publicly as a savvy yet fair official, taught criminal law at Suffolk University, and was serving at the time as president of the Massachusetts Chiefs of Police Association.

Then Bangs' longtime friend, an MDC Patrolman Joey affectionately referred to as Donnie, testified that he had taken Bangs to Wonderland Dog Track that evening and further impressed the jury by claiming he had studied to become a Jesuit priest before joining the police department.

Joey knew that Brother would be called to testify, and he feared what O'Leary might say in jest and how his previous felony convictions might influence the jurors. When Brother finally took the witness stand, he flashed a twisted grin at the room as the state prosecutor began questioning.

"What do you do for a living?"

"I'm a thief," Brother smiled.

"Why are you in prison?"

"Thievery," Brother replied.

"Well, you're not very successful at it, are you?"

"To the contrary, my good man," Brother retorted. "I'm quite good at it! I've probably committed a hundred, but you've only caught me thrice."

The courtroom roared with laughter, and Brother's candor won over the jury, who believed him when he stated that Joey Bangs had not been present during the lamp store burglary. After just two hours of deliberation, the jury returned a verdict of not guilty.

❤ ❤ ❤

The truth of the matter was that both Donnie and Brother were compromised witnesses who owed Joey big favors. A year earlier, Donnie had dropped off his wife at Downtown Crossing in Boston to do the family Christmas shopping while he slipped over to the Combat Zone for a quick blowjob.

As the story goes, Donnie picked up a hooker who went by the name "Brandy," with the intent of scoring a quickie, but found that his guilt kept him from getting a nut. Donnie infuriated Brandy by refusing to pay, and she threatened to call the police. Donnie in turn flashed his MDC badge and threatened to arrest her for prostitution. Undeterred, Brandy jumped out of Donnie's car and went straight to MDC headquarters to report the incident. Facing a departmental hearing for conduct unbecoming an officer and with his job and marriage at risk, Donnie approached Bangs for help, believing that Joey's miscreant past might hold a magic bullet. Joey called a Boston police sergeant pal named Joe Cavanaugh, who reached out to a couple of vice cops he had in his pocket, and assured Joey that Brandy would be a no-show for the scheduled hearing. Indeed, she failed to appear, Donnie walked, and Bangs added Donnie's name to his list of favors to be repaid.

As far as O'Leary was concerned, he had previously agreed—and rightfully so—to take the entire beef. He was already a full-time resident at Walpole State Prison for the lamp store larceny, as well as for breaking and entering a private residence, a move that would become his forte. After Bangs' trial, O'Leary was promptly returned to Walpole, although it was not long before he was out on regular weekend furloughs.

One Sunday evening during such a release, Bangs and O'Leary crawled their favorite pubs, finding themselves finally at Ralphie Chong's bar in the North End, where they knew they could drink after hours. After downing a few too many beers, Brother leaned in close to Joey, wrapped a sweaty hand around the back of Joey's neck, and tried to blink away the haze of inebriation.

"Joe," he pleaded, "I can't go back. So I need you to do something for me."

Bangs had never seen Brother so sober. "What do you need, Brother?"

"Run me over with your car."

Bangs stared at O'Leary for a long moment and then drained his glass in one deep draught. Without speaking a word, Joey snatched a set of Cadillac keys that the drunk patron next to him had left on the bar when he went to take a piss. He dragged Brother outside by the collar, planted him in the middle of the street, and walked away.

"Where the fuck are you going, Joe?" Brother whined.

"Borrowing a car."

Bangs scanned the street. He found the Caddy and started it up.

Brother stood in the middle of the road, wearing a twisted smile and waving a handkerchief as if giving Bangs the "Go" signal. Joey revved the engine, threw the transmission into Drive, and hit Brother so hard he smashed the hood and windshield, nearly totaling the car, before flying up and over the roof and crashing to the ground more than twenty yards away.

As the paramedics loaded him into the ambulance, Brother came to his senses for a moment and yelled for Joey. Bangs rushed to the gurney and leaned in close to shush O'Leary, fearful that he might reveal their ruse.

"Joe! Where am I? What happened, Joe?"

Joey relaxed; Brother was playing out the charade, a twinkle in his eye.

"Listen, shithead," Bangs picked up, "you called me for a ride, and when I got here, you jumped in front of me, half in the wrapper. I hit you so hard, they picked you up in China for speeding!"

Brother spent the next few weeks in a highly medicated state of euphoria in a cushy Massachusetts General Hospital bed, where Bangs saw to it that he received visits from various flask-toting prostitutes who made his stay even more comfortable.

Once O'Leary had recovered, Bangs helped him secure an early parole through a good friend, Joe Devlon, who was President of the Corrections Officers Union. Bangs had met Devlon, an ex-professional fighter, while working on Capitol Hill, and Devlon was happy to arrange a meeting for Joey with another distinguished gentleman who served on the state's stringent parole board. A month later, Brother O'Leary was back on the streets.

▾ ▾ ▾

Bangs usually worked days from 8:00 a.m. to 4:00 p.m., Wednesday through Sunday, and even if he enjoyed the notion of being a police officer, he detested his daily duties, mainly directing traffic and writing parking citations. Bangs had obtained his GED in order to join the police force, and in the fall of 1971, he received federal funds to enroll at Suffolk University as a part-time student majoring in criminal justice.* Bangs

---

* In 1970, the Massachusetts legislature passed the Police Career Incentive Pay Program, also referred to as the "Quinn Bill," to provide incentives to officers to continue their education: a 15% raise to police officers who completed an associate's degree, 20% for a bachelor's degree, and 30% for a master's.

studied diligently and excelled in college, eventually receiving associate's and bachelor's degrees (1978) in criminal justice from Northeastern University, then a master's degree from Anna Maria College in Paxton, located in the rural western part of the state.

Working around the State House gave Joey the chance to become friendly with a variety of politicians, including U.S. Senator Ted Kennedy; U.S. Speaker of the House Tip O'Neill and his aide, Tommy Mullen, whom everyone addressed deferentially as "Mr. Mullen"; Massachusetts governor Francis Sargent; Boston mayor Kevin White; longtime President of the State Senate Billy Bulger; and many other state representatives.

Despite his disdain for many of his assignments, Bangs worked conscientiously on tasks he deemed important. In fact, he received accolades for disarming a knife-wielding mental patient from the VA hospital who crashed state offices intent on assassinating Governor Sargent. Before allowing Joey to lock the door on his holding cell, the paranoid-schizophrenic vet instructed Bangs, "Whatever you do, don't look in the trunk of my car." Of course, that was like telling a hungry grizzly bear to stay away from the honey tree.

Joey lifted the suspect's keys from the evidence room, ran the vet's license and located the registration to his automobile. Keys in hand, Bangs searched every street surrounding Capitol Hill. As far as Joey was concerned, there very well could have been a pile of money in the trunk— or a body, for that matter. But Bangs never located the vehicle in question.

∨ ∨ ∨

In spite of the security a police job provided, Joey wasn't yet ready to abandon his lawlessness, and he and Brother O'Leary still enjoyed pulling gaffs together, both for pleasure and profit.

Brother had his own favorite gaff, a con he had perfected over the course of several years. He ran personal ads in the Boston *Phoenix* and other local papers, searching for "love and companionship." A typical ad might read: *6'4" tall, athletic, blond hair, blue eyes, financially successful, loves animals and children, in search of a soul-mate. Are you that woman?*

O'Leary likewise scoured the papers for ads posted by others and answered dozens every week; grifting was a numbers game, in more ways than one.

It was easy enough to find willing companions, given that there was no shortage of women who thought they were too old, too heavy, or too unattractive to attract honest suitors. Brother didn't care what they looked like; it was a short game. He would fool around for a week or two until the woman was comfortable enough that he could snoop through her apartment without raising suspicions, and once he had collected all the checkbooks, cash, jewelry, and credit cards he could find, he disappeared from her life.

Brother also loved to regale Joey with his more kinky searches in the alternative lifestyle section—sometimes for money, sometimes not. *Will do anything! In search of a sex slave! Bark like a dog for me!* O'Leary spun the tale of an encounter with a couple of free-spirited, hippie girlfriends who belonged to a swingers club and lived in Stoughton, on the South Shore. Brother said a girl by the name of Sandy would sometimes perform unnatural acts on her thoroughbred boxer, Buster, who had what O'Leary described as a "lively libido," even for a dog. Joey never knew quite what to make of Brother's stories. On the one hand, he knew Brother was crazy enough to do half the shit he talked about; on the other, he hoped to God he didn't.

▾ ▾ ▾

As time passed, Brother and Joey grew even more brazen in their moneymaking schemes and started playing a twist on the dating con that resulted in a much quicker score. For a first or second date with a woman of obvious means, Brother asked her to put on her best dress and jewelry so that he could take her out for a romantic, candlelit dinner at a fancy restaurant. If they had a table in a private area of the restaurant, Joey would show up during the meal and threaten Brother, brandishing a revolver and making a scene, as if O'Leary owed him money for a gambling debt or street loan. For his part, Brother played the terrorized victim so convincingly that his date unfailingly offered up everything she had in her purse, plus the promise of more if Joey would let Brother walk.

On other occasions, Brother would take his date to a swanky restaurant in Boston's historic Waterfront District, where he parked in a dark and distant section of the parking lot—perfect for an ambush by the ski-masked Bangs, who would strip Brother's date of her jewels and purse.

Whatever the case, the men would reconvene after Brother had taken his date home and comforted her—and gotten laid, if he was lucky—to divvy up the loot and plan their next assault.

These fleece jobs went on the entire time Bangs was a Capitol police officer, from 1970 to 1973, and half the time, Joey pulled the stunts simply concealing his uniform beneath an overcoat and using his service-issued revolver to assist in the robbery.

Brother pulled his share of solo stings during this time as well. However, O'Leary was eventually caught, convicted, and sentenced to five years in Walpole State Prison. Nonetheless, Joey pulled a few strings, and within two years, his sidekick was once again trolling the personal ads.

Joey always knew that he was walking a fine line by mixing himself with Brother's unpredictable, mischievous mind. Brother was often careless in concealing his identity and sloppy in cleaning up after his crimes. In fact, Bangs frequently discovered stolen credit cards and other items beneath the passenger-side floor mat of his sedan, stashed there by Brother for safekeeping when Joey would drive him home after a night of debauchery and raiding women's purses. Brother was usually too drunk to remember what he had done, and Joey never bothered to remind him. Bangs just pocketed the cash, sold the credit cards, or fenced the stolen items through his uncle, Red Delaney, as he once did with a clutch of traveler's checks worth eight hundred dollars, making sure that Uncle Red got a taste. *Second thief, best thief*, as the saying goes. But soon enough, Brother's impetuosity would cost Joey dearly.

▾ ▾ ▾

Shortly after O'Leary's release from prison, he and Bangs were having a drink with a couple of nice honeys at a bar in Cambridge when the waitress brought them an unexpected round of drinks: "Chum" Leonard, one of the detectives who had arrested Joey and Brother for the lamp store robbery, had seen them come in and wanted to provoke a confrontation. Bangs wanted none of it; he scribbled on a napkin and asked the waitress to deliver the note to Chum: *Go fuck yourself.*

Joey and Brother spit in the cocktails so Leonard would still have to pay for them and sent the drinks back. Too drunk for his own good, Chum downed the drinks, flashed Bangs and O'Leary a grin, and flipped them off. Joey knew this situation could quickly get out of hand, so he wrangled Brother and the girls and slipped out to the parking lot before they found themselves in deep shit.

As they approached Joey's vehicle, a vanity license plate caught Brother's eye: "CHUM." That was all Brother needed—he found a brick, smashed all the windows in the sedan, and slashed the tires for good measure.

The next morning Joey received a phone call he would rather not have had: it was Paul Walker. Walker instructed Bangs to get his ass to the Pony Room Lounge on the double, and always respectful of The Mayor, Joey dropped everything and left for Cambridge.

Walker shredded Bangs, not allowing him a word of explanation, and warned him again to stay away from Brother. Walker then demanded that Bangs summon O'Leary to the lounge, and within an hour, the jovial Brother bounced through the door, oblivious of the reason for the meeting.

Walker laid down the law: "O'Leary, if I catch you hanging around with Bangs again," he ordered, "I'll break your legs—and his, too! And you're gonna pay for new tires and glass on Leonard's vehicle."

"It wasn't me," Joey protested.

"You were stupid enough to be out with this asshole, so for my aggravation, you no-good cocksuckers are gonna paint my house, trim and all! I'll see your sorry asses on my front porch tomorrow morning at eight. And let this be a lesson to you!"

There was no use arguing; Walker's word was law in Cambridge. Joey and Brother knew the games were over.

Walker had a hunch that Bangs was about to resign from the Capitol Police, where his authority was somewhat limited, in order to be appointed to the MDC Police, where his influence could be endless. So Walker didn't want anything to interfere with Bangs' advancement, especially any of Brother's antics. Walker was a consummate businessman, a professional who was well aware of the potential money he and Bangs could earn together with Joey operating as his mole inside the ranks of the powerful MDC.

▾ ▾ ▾

When Joey and Brother left the Pony Room, they looked at each other and knew there was only one thing to do—get plastered. Unfortunately, they had been banned from most of the bars in Cambridge, and, to their dismay, they discovered that neither of them had enough cash on hand to do any worthwhile drinking. So they did what they did best: they drove around town looking for a score.

As Joey rolled to a stop at an intersection a few blocks away, Brother threw open his door, leapt out, and dashed around the corner. Bangs made a quick turn and followed O'Leary down the residential street, trying to determine what had possessed him, but he lost sight of his friend when Brother ducked in between two garages. Bangs circled the block, scanning the yards and driveways, until O'Leary charged into the street and banged on Joey's hood.

"I've got it!" Brother exclaimed, as he bounced into the car. Then Joey saw it: Brother was clutching a filthy, foul-smelling puppy beneath his coat.

"What the hell are you going to do with that mangy mutt?" Joey blurted.

"Watch and learn, my good man, watch and learn," O'Leary trumpeted. "I'm gonna sell the little bastard, and tonight we shall drink and make merry!"

Joey burst into laughter—the day could not become more absurd. Brother directed Joey back to a bar they had passed—an establishment under new management that didn't know either of them. Brother staggered into the gin mill with the pooch in hand and Joey still laughing, close behind.

Brother put on his best dog-and-pony show: he sidled up to the bar and laid out a story to the owner about the purebred dog he had just bought for his children, only to discover, after paying for all its immunizations, that his asthmatic wife was allergic to the animal. It broke his heart—and his kids' hearts—to get rid of the pup, but he had no choice.

"I paid $200 for the little guy," he chimed, "but I can't take him back home. I'll let him go for $50 and bring you the registration papers tomorrow."

The bar owner considered for a moment and was sold when the dog nuzzled his hand. Fifty dollars agreed—plus he'd buy Joey and Brother a drink.

Bangs and O'Leary settled at a table in the corner and watched as the owner poured a dish of milk for the mongrel and tussled the fur on his neck. The man was so taken by the animal that he let Joey and Brother stay for several hours, with drinks on the house.

About three months later, when the puppy had grown a bit, it became obvious that there was no pure blood in the mutt, and the proprietor put the word out that if he ever ran into either Joey or Brother again, he'd shoot them on the spot. By that time, however, the scammers were long gone and onto their next gaff.

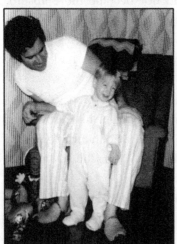

Above: Bangs with his daughter, Jody,
and his nephew, Paul (1971).
Top left: With his nephew, Paul.
Bottom left: With his son, Joey, Jr.

Bangs with his daughter, Jody (1972)

Left: O'Leary, after being released from prison, no worse for the wear.
Above: As a high school sophomore (top). His grandfather, an MDC patrolman (bottom).

Brother O'Leary and his wife, Margie

❧ ❧ ❧

Although Bangs didn't get along with many cops, as time passed he became friendly with co-worker Dick Madden, who resided in Dedham. Before Bangs entered the Capitol Police, Jerry Clemente had told him to look up Madden and vouched that Dick could be trusted. Many Boston cops loved Big Dick—and knew better than to make fun of his nickname—as well as Madden's cousin, Jimmy Crocker, who also got a pass on the name. Crocker was a stand-up MDC sergeant, narcotics officer and prosecuting cop at the Chelsea District Court House, and the family relationship entitled Madden a lot of drag with the Mets as well.

Heavyset and about six-foot-three, Madden was an amiable sort and a true gentleman. He was a gung-ho cop who always carried a revolver, even when off duty, and proudly went out of his way to make sure everyone knew he was packing. Dick loved vodka, and even though he was generally a happy drunk, his alcoholism took its toll on his health and relationships. Dick often talked out of school when he was feeling good, mainly about other people, so Bangs knew better than to tell him anything important. Madden worked midnight to eight in the morning while on the Capitol Police force and slept away most of his uneventful career.

Madden had started with the Capitol Police as a part-timer, but eager to land a secure full-time job, he allegedly schemed to have another officer fake a late-night robbery and shoot him in the process. Everything went as planned—phony break-in, superficial bullet wound, commendation for courage under fire, and permanent appointment to the Capitol Police Department.

Because Bangs worked days and Madden nights, the two never became close, but they exchanged pleasantries as they crossed paths during shift change each day and grabbed drinks together on their occasional shared days off. As Bangs now got to know Madden personally, he discovered just how close Clemente and Madden were. Given that Joey and Jerry had maintained their hunting relationship and become very good friends, Bangs now felt he had formed an inner circle that would protect and empower him.

▼ ▼ ▼

In the winter of 1972, Joey received an urgent call from the MDC station at Revere Beach: it was Jerry Clemente, and he wanted to see Joey immediately. When Clemente arrived at the Capitol Police's office, he peppered Bangs with questions: *Where is the civil service department located?* Here in the State House. *Can you get us in?* Of course. When Joey asked why, Jerry informed him that he was interested in getting his hands on a few police entrance and promotional examinations—for reference.

Joey and Jerry prowled the State House on numerous occasions over the next year, but they failed to locate the exams. However, Clemente never gave up hope, and in 1975-76, after Joey had transferred from the Capitol Police and forfeited his extensive set of keys, Jerry found an opening. He tracked down the exams with a hand from Dick Madden and another accomplice he had engaged, Medford Police Sergeant Thomas Kevin Doherty ("Tommy"). Madden gave Clemente unrestricted access to the State House property and the newly opened John McCormack Building, while Doherty gave Jerry ample encouragement and backup in his misdeeds.

Everybody in Boston knew the John W. McCormack Building located on Beacon Hill at One Ashburton Place, which served as the headquarters for the Massachusetts Department of Personnel Administration. But nobody would come to know the property as intimately as Joey Bangs, Jerry Clemente, and Tommy Doherty.

▼ ▼ ▼

Both of them residents of Medford, Clemente and Doherty first met at Mister Doughnuts Coffee Shop, a favorite cop stop on Mystic Avenue, while Clemente was officer-in-charge at Revere Beach. The pair seemed made for one another—loners with families at home and girlfriends on the side, heads full of plans to plunder the town under the protection of a badge.

Short and stocky with a mop of blond hair and a happy-go-lucky disposition, Doherty was born of thick Irish blood on December 16,

Tommy Doherty

1941, and raised in Medford. Exceptionally skilled with his hands and capable of puzzling out any mechanical problem, Tommy worked during his youth at Hurley's Dodger Cars (bumper cars) and at the Medford Bowl, which hosted demolition-style car racing. From there, his life followed a trajectory typical for the young men around him: marriage (to Carol Graham in 1961), military (three and a half years in the Navy with an honorable discharge as a Vietnam vet), and Medford, where he eventually settled, buying up properties on Pleasant Street for members of his family to occupy.*

Doherty was an unassuming man—Bangs often quipped that he looked like the Pillsbury Doughboy's Irish cousin—and his typical outfit of flannel shirt, blue jeans, and work boots did nothing to smooth his rough demeanor. Doherty rarely drank and was always in control. In fact, if Tommy indulged in a libation, he would limit himself to a beer or two on hot summer days or a single mixed drink on social occasions.

Always mischievous, Tommy himself often boasted that he had been a thief his entire life and that he'd steal an airplane if he had a runway to stash it on. In fact, there seemed to be a compulsion or fatal lack of awareness in many of his actions. For example, he had joined the ranks of the Massachusetts State Police in 1964 but was forced to resign in 1966 because he had "borrowed" a vehicle from the motor fleet to commute between work and home. When he was called on it, he could see nothing wrong with the unauthorized use of a state-owned vehicle.

Within months of his dismissal, Doherty finagled an appointment to the Medford Police with the help of some string-pulling by dear friends of his deceased father, mainly then-Chief of Police Charles Donovan ("Red"). Doherty came from a long line of copper buttons that included not only his father, Francis Patrick Doherty, a well-liked and respected Medford police detective who died while on the force, but also his grandfather, Patrick Francis Doherty, who was a Massachusetts state trooper, and his great-grandfather, who was a policeman in Ireland. But by the time Tommy brought his shenanigans to law enforcement, the family line had lost its genetic predisposition to serve and protect the community.

---

* Doherty surrounded his children, Michael and Karen, with extended family, including his mother (Mary), brothers (Brian and Allen), and brother-in-law through marriage (Jackie Gillen).

Now, it would be another relative, brother-in-law John J. Gillen ("Jackie"), who would subsequently end Tommy's police career.*

Not long after he was promoted to sergeant in 1972, Doherty found himself in a bit of hot water when Jackie, a former Marine and petty thief who had never in his life pulled off a crime without getting pinched, was charged with illegal firearm possession. Doherty made the mistake of trying to sandbag the case.

MDC Patrolman Frank McDonald was working out of the Fellsway Division one evening when he notified the Medford Police Department that he had just arrested Gillen for the burglary of the Woolworths Store located at Wellington Circle Shopping Plaza in Medford. Gillen and his accomplice were sitting in the front of a stolen station wagon when McDonald rolled up on them to see why they were at the store after hours. Before Gillen noticed him, McDonald was standing beside the car, eyeing the burglary tools and loaded .45-caliber automatic handgun on the front seat and a Wurlitzer Organ, stolen from a nearby warehouse, in the back. Doherty, who was the Medford Police desk sergeant at the time, intercepted the incident call and showed up on scene before any other patrol car was dispatched.

According to McDonald's report, Doherty asked him to ignore the weapon charge and give him the handgun—after McDonald already had Gillen in custody for the offense. When McDonald balked, Doherty protested that he had given the gun to Gillen and was the responsible party. Nonetheless, McDonald held fast and refused to drop the charges against Jackie. In fact, he went a step further and reported Doherty to the city manager's office.

McDonald also alleged that weeks after the incident, none other than Lieutenant Jerry Clemente approached him during his overnight shift at the Stoneham Zoo and asked him not to lie but to "create an air of doubt" about his recollection of the events. The slick Clemente allegedly told McDonald, "If you cooperate, I can ensure you will be made sergeant." Again, McDonald stood his ground, rejected the request to drop the charges, and later testified in the disciplinary hearings that resulted in Doherty's firing. Doherty was ultimately dismissed for interfering with an arrest, just days before the Civil Service Commission heard his appeal. In 1973, however, Doherty succeeded in having the judgment overturned

---

* In my interactions with Doherty, he was always a perfect gentleman and extremely charismatic. Tommy was a good guy who unfortunately made some bad decisions.

when the civil service commissioner—the only one with the power to do so—changed the punishment to a one-year suspension from the Medford Police Department and a reduction in rank from sergeant to patrolman.

Doherty returned to work a year after the initial incident and used stolen promotional exams to rise once again to sergeant in 1980 and lieutenant in 1983. During this time, Frank McDonald suffered the consequences of his honest actions. He was ostracized by many on the MDC force, and for reasons he couldn't understand, he failed the sergeant's promotional exam twice, by just a few points each time. The answer, of course, was that Clemente and Doherty gained entry to the State House and compromised the exam results, lowering McDonald's grade for spite.[*]

According to Bangs, McDonald was a "Dirty Harry" wannabe—and actually looked a bit like Eastwood in the right light. One of the most physically fit officers in the department, McDonald was a gung-ho working cop, a genuine "headhunter," as Bangs and others referred to them, meaning a cop who loved to bust people. While working at the Fellsway Division, Joey heard McDonald's voice over the radio nearly every night making some kind of arrest. McDonald ran with his own clique of Met cops—who eventually encountered troubles of their own—and Joey remained careful around McDonald, making sure to steer wide where McDonald couldn't possibly hurt him. Bangs didn't necessarily dislike McDonald; he was just indifferent to him, mainly because McDonald would bust Joey's balls if he asked for a favor, like burying a ticket for a friend. Joey didn't need one more asshole in his world of fools.

▾ ▾ ▾

After making small talk over coffee and doughnuts, Clemente and Doherty learned they had a mutual acquaintance, Billy McGovern, whose brother, Freddie, owned and operated a fleet of tow trucks that were often dispatched by the City of Chelsea. In fact, Billy himself occasionally worked the tow trucks and was well known as a car thief and truck hijacker. Unlike

---

[*] By law, police officers who were wrongly passed over for promotions could file suit and seek monetary damages from the individual officers who obtained advanced copies of promotional exams, but not from state or municipal entities, unless they could prove negligence on their behalf. However, McDonald finally passed his third sergeant's promotional exam in April 1985, finishing at the top of the list—most likely because for the first time in more than a decade, Clemente and Doherty were unable to tamper with scores.

Clemente and Doherty, Billy was a ladies' man who played hard and lived large, and as time passed, the three colluded to form a stolen car ring. Jerry used his locksmith training to make keys and create fake vehicle identification number tags for the cars McGovern stole, and Doherty helped fence them, providing buyers with custom-ordered autos—make, model, year, options. Besides a steady supply of cash, the operation provided each of the men with a new car of their choice, which Doherty was brazen—or foolish—enough to register in his own name. Clemente, however, regularly used his father's name for illegal transactions such as this.

Clemente and Doherty also engaged in all sorts of other petty crimes to supplement what they considered an inadequate police salary. While many cops worked legitimate second jobs to make ends meet, Clemente and Doherty invested their energies gaming the system. Clemente figured out how to rig utility meters and taught other cops the trick—for a small price, of course. When Clemente and Doherty needed shoes for the family, they broke into Thom McAn. On Valentine's and Mother's Day, they found their way into local flower shops. Come September, they made after-hours trips to school supply stores to steal pencils, pens, paper, and notebooks for their kids who were returning to school. They also went so far as to drop off film to be developed or clothes to be dry-cleaned under an assumed name, and later break in and grab the finished items at night. Groceries and cigarettes, gas and electricity, anything from dishes to furniture to appliances—if they could use it or sell it, Clemente and Doherty found a way to steal it, rationalizing that their work as protectors of the city earned them the right to partake freely of its bounty.

Clemente wanted to introduce Bangs and Doherty, but he sensed that the two might prove a combustible mixture. There were too many pots boiling to risk a scuffle in the kitchen—keep working each side, he figured, and it'll come together when it's right. He knew there was a job brewing that not even he could envision right now, and he knew that given their personal histories on both sides of the law, he, Bangs and Doherty would find the recipe. They essentially had master keys to the entire City of Medford—although Jerry often chose to pick locks to keep his locksmithing skills sharp—and an unassailable disguise that emboldened their mischief. When they all finally came together, they would doubt no scheme and fear no man.

Doherty shortly after becoming a state trooper (1964).
Inset: His father, Frank, a sergeant in Medford.

Doherty as a sergeant in Medford.
Inset: His grandfather, Patrick, an MDC patrolman.

METROPOLITAN DISTRICT COMMISSION POLICE

IN 1892, AS URBAN CENTERS BURGEONED and the modern century loomed on the horizon, the Governor of Massachusetts appointed a commission to preserve natural areas across the state as recreation spots for the Commonwealth's citizens, and the following year, the Metropolitan Police was established to patrol the parks.

As the Commission built new parkways and accumulated open areas over the next twenty years, the Mets expanded their jurisdiction, updated their technology and reorganized as the Metropolitan District Commission (MDC).

When other Boston police forces went on strike in 1919, Massachusetts Governor Calvin Coolidge ordered the Mets to patrol the city in their stead, giving rise to the bad blood between the organizations that would persist for decades.

Over the course of the century, the Mets expanded their reach, eventually covering 53 cities and townships, as well as 311 historic sites, recreational facilities, parks, waterways, and beaches visited by 25 million people annually.

They also proved their worth repeatedly during tumultuous periods such as the labor riots of the early twentieth century, the violent protests against the Vietnam War in the 1960s and against forced bussing in the 1970s, and the never-ending drug and gang problems that plagued the state for decades.

The MDC was also known for its unparalleled organizational and technological innovation, and by the 1980s, it had become the most highly regarded, full-service force on the east coast, boasting a state-of-the-art mobile command center and aviation unit, maximum-security motor escorts, and the nation's top homicide, narcotics, firearms, immigrations and customs task forces. Two units in particular exemplified the MDC's standard of excellence: In 1963, the MDC assembled the first underwater recovery unit in the state, with Bangs' pals Jerry Clemente, David Flowers, Sr., and Frank Thorpe as charter members. And in the mid 1970s, the commission formed, the Traffic-Oriented Patrol Squad. Although TOPS appeared to be a motorcycle patrol squad, it was actually a select fifty-man tactical unit that had been established for riot and crowd control, similar to Special Weapons and Tactics (SWAT) teams later organized around the country.

For Bostonians, the rich tradition of the Mets represented the best their city had to offer, but once Joey Bangs pinned on the MDC badge, the department—and the city it served—would never be the same.

Leadership of the MDC Police (clockwise from upper left): Superintendent William Bratton, Superintendent Thomas Keough, Commissioner William Geary, Superintendent John McDonough

Early MDC officers. Above, in
winter uniforms (1912-1915).
Right, at Riverside (1900).

MDC officers in riot formation during the busing protests (1975-1976).

On duty in the 1970s

On duty in the 1970s

Top photo: Bangs (L) with Kevin Layden
Bottom photo: Bangs (C) with Bobby Spencer and Kevin Layden

Fellsway Division: Getting His Feet Wet

Fellsway Division Station

From the moment he first considered joining the police force, Joey Bangs felt ambivalent about a career in law enforcement. He thrived on the discipline and adrenaline of military service, but police work, from what he could observe, seemed to be a never-ending cycle of boring beat patrols and mind-numbing paperwork, biding time and accumulating service years until retirement brought drunken weekends on the couch watching football.

Nevertheless, a paycheck was a paycheck, Joey thought. Just get in and get rolling, and as soon as something better comes along, get out and get on with life. Bangs signed on first with the Capitol Police, even though he had planned to join the Metropolitan Police, where he already knew a handful of people. But the MDC had restricted hiring for nearly two years during the pendency of a lengthy affirmative action lawsuit against the Commonwealth, and at the time, he could earn more on the Capitol. So Bangs worked the Capitol Police for three years, until October 1973, when he finally received a call to join the MDC, who were by that time paying substantially more.

Although he had already been through the academy for the Capitol Police, Joey entered the MDC's more rigorous training program shortly after his appointment. The MDC academy operated like a military institution, and cadets trained under the direction of the Federal Bureau of Investigation. Joey completed the twelve weeks of training just before year-end and began what would become a storied career at the Fellsway Division in Medford.

Newcomer Bangs was already vouched for by hunting buddies Clemente, Thorpe, Flowers, and Joe McCoy.* From the get-go, Joey didn't care much for most of his other co-workers, whom he considered

---

* Bangs and Flowers never actually served together on the Mets. By the time Bangs joined the department, Flowers had sustained a broken vertebra in his neck while in the line of duty and subsequently suffered a heart attack, retiring under the state's "Heart Bill."

judgmental prigs more interested in self-promotion than building comradeship with their fellow officers. Thorpe was a different matter; Joey unabashedly called him the best cop he ever knew, better even than famed top cop, Lt. Detective Tommy Spartichino. There was rarely a case that Frank couldn't solve, big or small, and he had won the MDC's highest award for valor after just six months on the force—an incredible recognition of his dedication to police work. Frank took Joey under his wing and became one of Bangs' closest friends and confidants, both on and off duty. The job of breaking Joey in, however, fell to two old-timers, "Bob" and "Jack," longtime partners who took Bangs on ride-alongs for his first two months in the department.

According to Bangs, the first essential lesson addressed on-the-job drinking techniques. Since Jack didn't drink, he drove Bob and Joey to either Ma's Cafe or the Highland Cafe in Malden, made sure they donned civilian jackets over their uniforms, and then headed to his home not far away to relax until his partners had drunk their fill or they received a dispatch. If they happened to get a call to duty, which they rarely did, Jack would swing by to pick up Bob and Joey, and off they went. Such was Bangs' training every day for two months. In fact, Bangs recalled receiving only one dispatch the entire time he was stationed at the Fellsway division—a bizarre incident that could have gone seriously awry.

It was a fall day at the outset of rush hour. Jack was home napping when he received an urgent dispatch, swung by the bar to collect Bob and Joey, and headed to the scene on Mystic Valley Parkway, by the Mystic Lakes. When the officers arrived, they discovered an adult male German shepherd that had been struck by a car and lay howling in agony in the middle of the busy road. The dog needed to be put down, but Joey and Bob were in no condition to be seen in public, much less wielding a weapon and doing police work. But the inebriated Bob stepped over the animal and fired a single round from his service revolver. Unfortunately, his impaired vision caused him to miss the dog completely.

By this time, a thick crowd of sympathetic on-lookers had amassed, and the dog's yelping had intensified. Joey's head spun from the alcohol and howling and yelling and freezing wind. *Fuck it*, he thought. *I can't do any worse.* He staggered toward the dog, grasped his revolver tightly with both hands to steady it, leaned down to get a bit closer to the animal, and squeezed the trigger. Gun blast, skull crack, silence. Jack cleared the crowd, and Joey staggered to the cruiser, crawled into the backseat, and wiped the blood from his shoes. His training days at the Fellsway Division were complete.

Revere Beach Station: Revenge Is a Bitch

Revere Beach Station

In the 1960s and 1970s, Revere Beach was a dreadful place to work, especially if you were a cop. "The Beach" was a hangout for reputed gangsters such as the most infamous assassin in New England history, Joseph "The Animal" Barboza; his equally dangerous associate, Vincent James "Jimmy The Bear" Flemmi; or any of the other monsters in the menagerie of cold-blooded killers and hustlers. The Beach was also a notorious biker hangout for gangs such as the Lynn Chapter of the Hell's Angels, the Devil's Disciples, and Headsmen, and not a weekend passed without a barroom brawl or bloody altercation. It took a particular type of cop to work the battlefield at The Beach—someone who was not squeamish about mayhem, mauling, and death: The Met cops at Revere Beach Station were the stuff of legend.

Known on the street as "The Black Glove Gang," the Revere Mets relished a fight as much as the thugs they confronted. The cops wore black leather gloves with fine, sifted sand padding the knuckle area to protect their hands from bottles, rocks, and debris thrown at them during riots, and to beat down suspects while breaking up brawls or, even better, simply picking a fight. The Black Glove Gang also wielded their nightsticks with impunity, "splitting unruly punks' heads wide open and bludgeoning them from asshole to elbow," as Bangs loved to tell it.

Unlike many other police stations, Revere Beach used several walking beat cops in addition to squad cars, given the heavy traffic flowing from the sea of dark, seedy barrooms, the swarming crowds at the popular amusement park, and a terrific takeout restaurant by the name of Kelly's Roast Beef, which piled the sandwiches a little higher for the cops.

After only a few weeks at Revere Beach, Bangs already had a growing reputation among fellow officers as the man to fix the toughest problems, and he never failed to rise to the occasion, meeting force with force, if warranted, and doing whatever it took to accomplish the job.

While on duty one evening, Bangs was approached by a fellow patrolman named "Billy," who was doubling as an inside deskman. Billy casually asked Bangs to get rid of his civilian car for him so he could use the insurance money to get out of a financial pinch. Joey was never one to turn down such a request—and earn a favor in return—so he took Billy's vehicle north on Route #1 to a spot in Saugus, near the Kowloon Chinese Restaurant, which was famous for its themed dining rooms and spicy Scorpion Bowl. Bangs somehow managed to get Billy's vehicle wedged on the edge of the cliff where he tried to dump it, and despite all his efforts to shake it loose and push it over, the damn thing wouldn't budge. Left with no alternative, Joey made his way back to the station and nonchalantly informed Billy, "We have a little problem."

Billy panicked, but being the experienced thief he was, Bangs calmed Billy and laid out a plan: All they needed to do was borrow a paddy wagon and give the car a little shove. Desk Sergeant Phil Moore was sound asleep on a cot in the backroom, so Bangs and Billy snatched a vehicle and made their way back to the cliff. They lined up the wagon and Billy's immovable sedan, gave it a nudge, and watched it tumble down the hillside into a ravine. As Joey saw the car sink out of sight, he realized how Billy could pay him back.

Sergeant Moore reviled Bangs and had a hard-on for bringing him down—of course, the feeling was mutual. Nearly every night, Moore dispatched Bangs to walk the beat at Revere Beach, in all kinds of inclement weather, from midnight to eight in the morning. Come hell or high water, this vigil became Patrolman Bangs' only duty. To find shelter during the brutal winter, Bangs began ditching his patrol to keep his ass warm and dry in one of The Beach's many watering holes, usually Sammy's Patio, Bill Ash's or Buddy's Cafe, Joey's personal favorite and the hostelry of choice for most Met cops. In fact, some were there so often that Captain Collins—a real working cop who firmly believed that guns and booze didn't mix—threatened to place the saloon off limits.

Arriving at work around eight in the morning, Collins often noted either the civilian or duty vehicles of most of his officers still lined up in front of Buddy's place from the night before, many of them double-parked or facing the wrong direction on the sidewalk. Collins finally declared he would bring his men up on departmental charges for "dereliction of duty" if he saw any more cars belonging to cops parked in front of the cafe. The boys heeded the warning, and from that day forth, parked their vehicles around back.

A favor turned is a favor earned, so each night when Bangs walked his beat, he gave inside deskman Billy the phone number of whichever watering hole he was whetting his whistle in. If Sgt. Moore awoke and decided to make his rounds, Billy gave Bangs a quick heads-up and Joey hustled back to his beat, acting for Moore as if he were merely doing his job. If it was storming, Joey went as far as to sprinkle snowflakes on his reefer jacket for added effect.

The only thing that made Revere Beach tolerable for Bangs was the fact that Jerry Clemente was the lieutenant in charge. Clemente was overly cautious about the way he pulled his shenanigans while stationed at The Beach because there were some real gung-ho cops who undoubtedly would have taken pleasure in dropping a dime on him.

Nonetheless, Clemente's rank as lieutenant had just enough drag to keep Joey out of the shit and in good standing with the upper echelon. In fact, Lieutenant Clemente even kept Patrolman Bangs from being fired on numerous occasions when Sergeant Moore attempted to stick it up Joey's ass. Clemente always went to bat for his hunting pal and got him off the hook. But Joey hated asking Jerry for favors, because asking him for one meant paying back two. For example, if you asked Jerry for a day off from work, he'd ask you to get rid of a car for him, or something similar. Clemente always had to come out on top, and because he was a lieutenant, he usually did.

What Goes Up Must Come Down

During the months to follow, Moore took every opportunity to give Bangs grief, but Joey eventually puzzled out ways to beat his nemesis at his own game, tit for tat, sometimes with stunning theatricality.

By the early 1970s, the Revere Beach amusement park was little more than a graveyard for boardwalk attractions and carnival rides. The area was haunted most by the skeleton of The Cyclone, a fabled wooden rollercoaster that languished in disrepair at the edge of the ocean, providing an irresistible gathering place for drug dealers and other riffraff. For half a century, The Cyclone had been the world's largest and fastest coaster, but since 1969 it had suffered fires and vandalism that left it in a precarious state.

Moore decided to place a security detail at the base of the coaster every night to prevent further arson attempts, and he usually assigned Bangs to cover the miserable eight-hour shift in the unforgiving arctic weather blown in from the North Atlantic. Very soon, the four "B's"—boredom, booze, broads, and bullets—consumed Bangs' attention, and the devil himself found a playground in Joey's idle mind.

To keep occupied, Bangs took target practice by shooting at water rats and pigeons, adjacent streetlights or neon signs, just to keep himself from going mad. Booze and broads—or rather the lack thereof—became an aggravation for Bangs, since there were no cozy barrooms in that particular area, and Moore had begun checking up on him nearly every hour.

Before long, Joey could take no more. At the end of March 1974, after working the four-to-midnight shift, he hung around during roll call for the night shift, noting, as he had hoped, that they were short-handed and didn't have a patrolman to guard the rollercoaster. Joey left the station and headed to Sammy's Patio for a drink to steel his resolve: *No more rollercoaster, no more guard detail. I'll just burn the motherfucker to the ground!*

Around 2:30 a.m., the tipsy Bangs stumbled from the bar and drove to his home in Burlington, about thirty minutes northwest of Revere. He grabbed a five-gallon container of gas from the garage and made the long drive back to the amusement park, where he ringed the base of the rotting wood structure with fuel, lit a book of matches from Bill Ash's, and burnt the beast to the ground. The ride was razed the following month, as Bangs watched with glee during his beat on the boardwalk.

In his gut, Sergeant Moore knew that Bangs had had something to do with the five-alarm blaze, but he could never prove it, and the incident only provoked him to make things more difficult for the rogue patrolman.

▾ ▾ ▾

Life at The Beach had occasional bright spots. Revere Beach Station is where Bangs met MDC Patrolman Bobby Spencer, who became not only Joey's partner on the job, but also his partner in crime and one of his closest allies and confidants through the years, even when their plans went to shit and long after the job had ended for both men. Just as Brother O'Leary had shaped the first act of Joey's life, Spencer would shape the next.

Spencer had had his share of trouble. In 1969, before being hired by the MDC Police, he was charged with larceny, but the charges were later dismissed and he was allowed to join the department, probably in part thanks to the influence of his uncle John Spencer ("Jack"), a popular Malden city alderman.

Bobby Spencer and his mother

A few years younger than Bangs, Spencer was a big, strong kid and a perfect gentleman, even if a bit vain and fastidious about his appearance. He dressed impeccably in expensive suits he stole or bought cheap from local hijackers, stayed scented with fancy colognes, and wore a thick, perfectly kempt mustache. Although Spencer had no prior military service, Bangs saw that he was a stand-up guy with a crazy streak and big balls. Bobby was not a big drinker and would only sometimes sip on a beer or strawberry daiquiri. In fact, when ordering such a "lady's drink," the hyper-masculine Spencer simply stated, "Give me my usual," rather than speak the name of the drink. Just like Joey, Bobby was a big flirt and womanizer who always had a girlfriend or two, although he and his wife—his childhood sweetheart, Elaine—never divorced.

Spencer's only dangerous vice was cocaine, which he broke out for two- or three-day binges on weekends, yet somehow he remained a reasonably well adjusted husband and family man, rearing his three children in the city of Medford, just a half mile from Jerry Clemente's family home.[*]

Spencer loved his bikes. Above, in 1998. Inset: Spencer in 1980.

---

[*] Sadly, Bobby Spencer died from cardiac arrest during the writing of this book.

One of Bang's best friends, Spencer was well liked and respected both on and off the force. Above, Spencer (second from right) receives a recognition from MDC Police Superintendent Larry Carpenter (second from left).

Chain of Causation

Although Bangs was stationed at Revere Beach only for a short stint, he remained long enough to break in the rookie Spencer from the summer of 1974 to 1975. The men had been working together just a short time when they received a dispatch describing a vehicle leaving the scene of a home invasion robbery. The call warned that the car's occupants were armed and dangerous. As soon as Bangs and Spencer received the call, the vehicle in question sped past them, driving north on Revere Beach Boulevard. Spencer hung a U-turn and floored it: The chase was short and sweet, and Bangs and Spencer stopped the suspects a few miles away by the Point of Pines.

Guns drawn, Bangs and Spencer ordered the four occupants out of the vehicle without incident, and then separated them for a divide-and-conquer interrogation, peppering them with questions to extract information about the recent heist. But Bangs was more concerned about the thousands of dollars in loot and jewelry stashed in the vehicle than about the weapons beneath the front seat.

"Was anyone hurt during the robbery?" Bangs asked the driver. "Were any weapons discharged?"

All four men swore that no one had been hurt and no weapons had been discharged during the robbery.

"How much money did you boys take?" Bangs pried.

Oblivious of his intent, the men answered honestly that they had no idea. *Beautiful,* Joey mused.

Lieutenant Clemente rolled up on the scene, and as Bangs knew too well, Jerry could smell money. Following protocol, Bangs explained the situation to his supervisor and emphasized—as any pal would—that the suspects had no idea how much money and jewelry they had stolen. *Beautiful,* Clemente winked, and he, Bangs, and Spencer—as many cops would—helped themselves to the booty, divvying up the cash and jewelry right there at the scene, on the hood of Clemente's cruiser.

When they returned to the station, the officers again patted down the suspects, and this time Bangs discovered a small amount of marijuana in the driver's pants pocket. A nearby narcotics detective took note and brightened: "Now that brings *us* in on it!" he informed Bangs.

Bangs cornered Clemente to warn him: "Whatever you do, Jerry, make sure none of these goddamn greedy vulture detectives get involved."

Bangs wasn't afraid the narcotics detective would learn that stolen items were missing: he knew that once they took over the case, they themselves would loot the remainder of the evidence and compromise the trial.

Nevertheless, Clemente put his foot down and kept the detectives away from the investigation. The marijuana was smoked behind the station by another reefer-loving cop, Bangs and Spencer got the collar, and everyone lived happily ever after—with a little extra jingle in their pockets.

Mr. Pottle

While working Revere Beach, Bangs rode with a number of colorful characters, including George Pottle, a former Marine, Korean War veteran, and one-time Chelsea police officer. Most people who had the pleasure of making his acquaintance called him "Mr. Pottle"—Joey dubbed him "Big George."

Big George Pottle (standing) with Al Falcone

At six-foot-six and nearly three hundred pounds, George was the unrivaled giant of the MDC Police, and rumor had it he could tear a phone book in three. Although not much of a people person, Pottle instantly befriended the young and ambitious Bangs, and Joey in turn took an immediate shine to the larger-than-life Pottle.

"Big George is no slouch," Bangs always warned people, "and he's not a 'bashful boy' either, if you catch my meaning."

One evening while working the 201 route—and after a few too many drinks—Bangs and Pottle decided to stop at the drive-in movie theatre located at Wellington Circle in Medford to watch a rerun of the Academy Award-winning film *Patton*. Being diehard patriotic veterans, when George C. Scott as General Patton stood in front of the immense American flag to deliver his celebrated speech, Bangs and Pottle stumbled from their cruiser, placed a hand over their heart and stood respectfully at attention.

Before the feature ended, Big George and Joey fell asleep in the MDC station wagon and awoke the next morning to find themselves surrounded by a sea of curious bargain hunters who had arrived for the weekly flea market in the theatre's lot. Several shoppers snapped photos and hoisted up their kids to have a peek inside the vehicle, where Pottle lay sprawled out like an accident victim on a stretcher in the back and Joey slumped against the passenger window up front. A light sleeper from the Vietnam years, Bangs started awake and reached back to shake Pottle, but the big man could not be bothered.

"What the hell are so many people doing at the drive-in this early in the morning?" Joey asked.

Pottle peeked outside and moaned. "You gotta be shitting me!"

"Get up and let's get outta here," Joey pleaded.

"I don't know about you," Pottle grumbled, "but I'm just gonna lay here. Outta sight, outta mind."

Pottle buried his face in his jacket, and Bangs crawled to the driver's side, cranked the wagon, waved one last time for the cameras, and steered the cruiser slowly through the mass of laughing onlookers.

Bangs drove straight to Chelsea and pulled in front of Pottle's favorite watering hole. He popped the blue light and hit the siren once— the signal for the barkeep to bring out their favorite beverages, disguised in a soda cup with a straw, of course. Joey drank beer with ice, and George downed plain-old rotgut whiskey. Like old-timers everywhere, Big George and Bangs started almost every day this way, and more often than he should have, Pottle kept the fires lit well into the evening.

Sammy's Patio at The Beach, a lounge noted for its quality live entertainment and spirited stream of customers, was a favorite stop for cops and late-night holdover patrons. Sammy "The Armenian" Faysal, the owner and operator, took good care of the Mets and vice versa—on the weekends, when his place was over legal capacity and there was no parking, the cops allowed patrons to double park or even angle cars onto the sidewalk. In fact, for a price, the officers would act as valets. Sammy in turn allowed the policemen to drink on the house, or better, run tabs he never got around to collecting.

A few months after the drive-in incident, Bangs received an urgent call from Faysal in the middle of the night. Since Sammy had drag with the Mets, he was able to get Joey's home phone number from a mutual friend working at the Revere Station. As soon as Bangs picked up, Sammy started chattering in a state of sheer panic.

Bangs deciphered that Pottle had become extremely drunk, lost his senses, and locked Sammy, his bartender, and all his patrons out of the lounge. George was just sitting inside Sammy's joint, pouring himself whatever the fuck he was drinking at the time. Sammy begged Bangs to help and threatened to call headquarters to turn in "Mr. Pottle" if he didn't come down and remove the big man from the establishment.

Bangs reluctantly agreed to sort out the situation, but he admonished Sammy: "Whatever you do, stay the fuck away from Mr. Pottle when he's like this. Under no circumstance whatsoever do you attempt to fuck with him!"

Not only big and tough, George could be a mean son-of-a-gun when he was drunk. Joey told Sammy to go have breakfast and promised he'd be there by the time Sammy returned.

Bangs entered the lounge from the back service door and found Pottle in a drunken stupor. Joey sidled up to Big George at the bar and poured himself a drink. And another, and another, not saying a word for the longest time. After an hour of heavy drinking, Bangs finally convinced Pottle to move the party to Buddy's Cafe.

Big George acquiesced, with a warning: "If I see Sammy over at Buddy's, I'm gonna beat the shit out of him."

"And if that Armenian's got the balls to show up there," Joey chimed in, "he'll deserve it."

Of course, Sammy didn't show, and Pottle never mentioned the incident again.

▾ ▾ ▾

The following week, while again on the 201 route, Bangs and Pottle decided to take in another flick at the Medford Twin drive-in, this time to see *Walking Tall*. Lounging comfortably in their police cruiser, they stuffed themselves with buttered popcorn and cotton candy and reveled in the violent justice meted out by Sheriff Buford T. Pusser. When they received a dispatch about a stolen car, Big George wanted to stay and finish the film, but Bangs convinced him to take the call. Pissed at the interruption, Pottle sped out of the lot, screaming repeatedly that there would be "goddamn hell to pay!"

Everyone who knew Joey agreed that he couldn't drive worth a shit, so this night Big George was at the wheel, and he was flying. Moving at close to a hundred miles per hour, Pottle lost control of the cruiser near the Everett Football Stadium on Revere Beach Parkway and flipped the car onto its roof. Joey never let him drive again. In fact, no one let him drive again, and due to broken vertebrae and other severe injuries sustained in the accident, Big George retired shortly thereafter.

▾ ▾ ▾

Most MDC cops were battle-tested veterans of foreign war and hardcore drinkers, and at Christmas time, the preferred gift was undoubtedly booze—bottles for some, cases for others. Fix a ticket, receive a bottle of your favorite hooch for your trouble. Bag an arrest, receive a case. Bar owners sent cases of alcohol to their local police stations every holiday, and in return cops allowed them to stay open after hours or permitted double-parking or parking on the sidewalk out front. On the other hand, if a cop wasn't feeling festive and had vehicles towed, towing companies sent booze in appreciation, in addition to a small cash reward in an unmarked envelope—sixteen dollars per car towed to be split between the lieutenant in charge and the ticketing officer. Construction companies, cab companies, any enterprise affiliated with the Mets in any way sent alcohol and an envelope for every conceivable holiday. Especially at Christmas, the officers had trouble walking into the Revere Beach Station because of the cases of liquor piled high near the entrance. "Don't forget—Christmas is for cops and kids," Joey remarked each holiday season, as he made the rounds of local proprietors, reminding them not so subtly about the expected payment for continued cooperation. It was the way of life back in the day. Indeed, the job had its perks.

▼ ▼ ▼

During the holiday season, Sergeant Moore became even more intolerable. Although Clemente had Bangs' back, after a year of Moore's constant torment, Joey had had all he could take and requested a transfer. Moore didn't trust Bangs. Bangs trusted Moore even less. And Moore more often than not rode Joey to the point of no return.

Years later, after Bangs became a sergeant, Moore congratulated him on the promotion. Respectfully, Joey told Moore, "Go fuck yourself." Only Moore's advanced age saved him from the justified comeuppance of a backhander.

Just before his reassignment to the MDC Lower Basin Police Station, Bangs' law enforcement career was marred by controversy when a detainee was discovered unconscious in his cell. Joey claimed the arrestee had been pounding his head on the cell wall and must have beaten himself to death. Bangs was transferred shortly thereafter, but not before being questioned by the FBI and cleared of any wrongdoing. MDC Police Sergeant David Walsh had pointed the finger at Patrolman Jackie Ginelli, claiming he was the last one to be seen with the suspect, but the case was never solved, since the only eyewitness to the vicious beating was hit by a speeding car a few months later and never recovered from a vegetative state. Bangs always maintained that he never struck a man in handcuffs, but he was quick to add that a few bad apples did not operate with the same integrity.

Bangs fought force with force, but he always fought fairly. If necessary, he was the first to use his nightstick to break up a barroom brawl or riot, but one on one was a different story. On occasion he removed his gun belt and badge and locked himself in a cell with a loudmouth arrestee to "set the story straight" and "make things right." And he didn't always win—in fact, his nose was broken five times, all while on official police duty.

The Beach had given Bangs the experience and contacts he needed to work his way up the force. The only other thing he wanted to add to his record before transferring was a commendation, especially one from Lieutenant Richard Feeney ("Dick"), a master with the pen whose official reports made his men look like goddamn mythological heroes, when most of the time they had actually done nothing at all. Bangs got his wish during a three-alarm house fire in Revere.

Feeney showed up on the scene to find a slew of his men standing around waiting for the fire department to arrive—"roasting hot dogs and marshmallows," Joey joked. As local newspaper and television reporters arrived, Feeney suggested that Bangs and the others wipe soot from the fire on their uniforms. But Joey had not only refused to go into the burning structure, he also balked at the thought of the soot: He and all the other Met cops watched the structure burn to the ground and applauded when it finally crumbled.

The legend of Feeney's subsequent report grew as word spread around the department, until the tale recounted the thrilling heroics of the brave patrolman: as flames engulfed the three-story structure, the men disregarded blinding smoke, searing heat and their own injuries to storm the inferno and carry scores of inhabitants to safety, stumbling out with the last survivors just as the building crashed around them. And just like that—commendations for everyone.

The Lower Basin: Let It Be

In 1975, Bangs transferred to the Lower Basin Station located adjacent to the Museum of Science on the Charles River in Boston. Bangs knew before he ever joined the force that being a cop was just a job like any other job. He had learned this lesson the hard way in Vietnam, where his ass was left hanging in the breeze on many occasions and he saw many young men perish from friendly fire or because an officer was trying to make a name for himself. His time as a cop thus far had further fueled his desire to do whatever the fuck he pleased and make money while he was at it.

Lower Basin Station

Bangs enjoyed his short stint at the Lower Basin. Just like at The Beach, he and his cop buddies often got drunk and took target practice, shooting at the packs of longhaired water rats and pigeons in the area, and if they happened to bag a duck, they'd take it home to roast. This took place mainly at the Esplanade, home of the Boston Pops Orchestra's famous Hatch Shell. In those days, MDC officers had private access to the Esplanade's pool near the Lower Basin police station, after it closed to the public. And in the hot summer months, many of the Mets congregated at the pool, even while on duty, to get shit-faced, strip bare-ass naked, and go swimming.* On many occasions, they arranged "picnics" with female companions, a blaring radio, and coolers brimful of cold beer and sandwiches—sucking the city for every perk and benefit they could finagle.

At the end of a long Fourth of July celebration, Captain John O'Brien caught more than fifty cops cooling their heels in the Lower Basin pool with an equal number of scantily clad or naked women. O'Brien, who was well liked and had a reputation as a womanizer himself, gave the drunk Mets a stern lecture on the dangers of mixing alcohol, women and guns, especially as on-duty police officers. After he left, the cops looked at one another for a moment, then did what they had been trained to do best—they continued to party. Everyone knew that had it been fifteen years earlier, O'Brien would have been the first one in the pool, even though now, with his mature physique, he was wise to keep his clothes on.

While stationed at the Basin, Bangs discovered one of the paddy wagons had broken down, so he removed the carburetor to keep the vehicle inoperable and converted it to a card room—complete with a well-stocked,

---

* When Bangs was a kid, he spent many summer days at this pool, which was referred to on the streets as the "West End" pool.

fully operational bar, with beer on tap and top-shelf booze—and placed an unpickable Medeco lock on the doors to keep the superiors and snoops away.

In fact, Bangs and his fellow officers had so much fun that they did the same thing to a wagon at the Old Colony Station in South Boston when he transferred there several months later. The converted police vehicle soon became his go-to place for the legendary high-stakes card games he organized for fellow MDC officers and other big gamblers from Boston. Games including three-card monte, stud, and blackjack began on Friday night and often ran the entire weekend. Joey supplied food, booze, and, on occasion, top-notch hookers, and as the "house," he took a generous cut from each player.

Weekends in the wagons were so profitable for Bangs that he ran them as a business, and as the enterprise grew, he eventually hired Bobby Spencer to assist him. After nearly being discovered on more than one occasion and having made some decent cash from their gaff, Bangs and Spencer eventually rented an apartment in Everett, a more comfortable and appropriate setting to host their games with a bigger, better-stocked bar and, of course, more working space for high-priced call girls.

Bangs often snapped Polaroids of his cop friends in compromising positions as a gag, but the photos also provided currency to buy future favors he might need or keep lips sealed about his numerous gaffs.

Daily police work at the Lower Basin was more about traffic control than anything else. The cops there had more than their share of domestic bullshit, especially during the Vietnam-era riots, but all in all, they mainly directed traffic and responded to the frequent accidents that occurred on Storrow and Memorial Drives, the Southeast Expressway, and the Tobin Bridge.[*]

∨ ∨ ∨

When Bangs first entered the force, the Mets were trained in life-saving techniques and were allowed to transport victims to the hospital in their cruisers, if contracted ambulances were too far from the scene of the accident. However, because of lobbying from for-profit ambulance companies and misdirected complaints from grieving families, the legislature

---

[*] Technically, the Tobin Bridge itself—but not the onramps—fell under the jurisdiction of the State Police, but the MDC officers were usually first responders to accidents or incidents on the bridge.

eventually passed a bill preventing police officers from transporting victims. Later, another bill was passed that prohibited cops from providing medical service of any kind, although most Metropolitan officers had been trained as first responders and EMTs, a certification they had to renew each year.

While working at the Basin, Bangs responded to an accident where a man had suffered a heart attack while driving along the Southeast Expressway and arrived on the scene to discover the man slouched over his steering wheel. The car doors were locked, but when Bangs used his nightstick to try to smash the side window, the sturdy glass wouldn't break. Bangs grabbed an axe from a fire truck that had just arrived, smashed the glass, and attempted to resuscitate the man, but the driver had already expired.

A few days later, Bangs was summoned to the Lower Basin Station where the grieving family was waiting to greet him. Joey thought the family was there to thank him for trying to save their loved one's life, but instead the family demanded to know whether he had proper CPR training and had done everything possible for the man. In Joey's mind, the icing on the cake was when they asked who was going to pay for the vehicle's smashed window. This and similar incidents turned Bangs sour on the public, to whom he had never refused anything, and gave rise to a fierce *fuck it* attitude toward his work as a servant of the people.

However, this was not the case when it came to children. Although not very paternal, Joey loved kids. On one rainy afternoon, he received a radio dispatch regarding an accident on Memorial Drive in Cambridge. It was a deadly pileup that began with a head-on collision and involved more than a dozen vehicles. Bangs was the first patrol officer to arrive on the scene, where he found bodies strewn everywhere, the smell of blood, fire, and death thick in the air. In a strange way, it was a flashback to Vietnam. But Bangs held it together and first attended to two very young, critically injured children, a boy and a girl, whose parents had been killed in the crash.

With no time to lose, Joey moved from one child to the other in an attempt to resuscitate them both at the same time. He succeeded in saving both children, but again the joy of the moment was soured for him when his actions were not acknowledged by his superiors or even by the children's extended family. A cop could more easily get an official commendation for shooting someone or making an arrest than a pat on the back for saving a life. The moral mathematics of the world had never made sense to Bangs and never would.

Indeed, for what was generally touted as a cushy traffic-cop gig, working the Lower Basin was often dangerous, and Bangs got sucked into the first of many shootouts during his career while directing congested traffic by the Massachusetts Bay Transit Authority, located at Lechmere Station. Standing in the middle of a busy intersection, white gloves waving furiously and whistle blasting, Bangs heard what sounded like the pop of small-arms fire. Almost instantly, Patrolmen Bobby Mannke and Joe McCoy drove up and hustled Bangs into the cruiser—there was a robbery in progress at a meatpacking plant near the Lechmere up-ramps for the MBTA Green Line.

Upon arriving at the scene, the cops spotted two armed individuals attempting to start their getaway vehicle. Bangs double-checked his weapon to be sure it was loaded and slid silently from the cruiser to corner the criminals. The suspects spotted the police cruiser and began firing at it, before fleeing the scene to an adjacent railroad yard, where, after a vicious exchange of gunfire with Bangs, Mannke, and McCoy, they were able to elude capture among the many boxcars. One of the knucklehead bandits, however, had left his wallet in the getaway car, and he and his partner were later captured without incident. After the event, while filing his reports, Bangs noticed that a .38-caliber bullet had pierced his police hat, and from that day on, he wore the damaged hat as a reminder to keep his goddamn head down.

Old Colony: New Tricks

Old Colony Station

Patrolman Bangs had been stationed at the Lower Basin just a few months when riots erupted over desegregation and forced bussing in the South Boston public school system. Since Southie's Old Colony Police Station was overwhelmed by the tumult,

Bangs was transferred and inducted into TOPS. Little did Bangs imagine when he arrived at Old Colony that he would be stationed there for five years, from 1975 to 1980, but the transfer opened doors to him that would change the course of his life.

Although not politically inclined, Bangs disagreed with recently passed desegregation legislation, and, in anticipation of its taking effect, he had already relocated his family from Cambridge north to the serene suburbs of Burlington. He had even been able to score a two-week vacation—paid, of course—in order to find a home, pack, and transfer the Bangs clan, bag and baggage.

Against their desires, Boston's African-American communities were forced to have their children bussed into the South Boston school system, by order of federal judge Paul Garrity. Because of the consequent turmoil, the MDC police maintained a heavy presence during school days, escorting busses filled with African-American students into predominantly Irish-Catholic neighborhoods. Disorderly Southie residents hurled bricks and bottles and debris at the unwelcome bus caravan from the rooftops of adjacent housing projects. And on the weekends, bloody rioting broke out across greater Boston, particularly at the popular Carson Beach, in close proximity to the MDC's Old Colony police station.

Bangs' Revere Beach partner, Bobby Spencer, had also transferred to Old Colony by this time, and Bangs called in favors in order to be assigned to ride with him. The partners spent their first weeks atop the flat, rubber-covered roofs of the housing projects, where they were assigned to monitor the mischief in the streets with binoculars. Most days, however, they just sunned themselves on deck chairs, wearing nothing more than flip-flops and sombreros, and, of course, a gun belt and badge, just in case. While on duty, the partners also frequently barbecued and downed margaritas with the friendly local Irish girls who were also easily inclined to supply sexual favors of most any kind.

Joey Bangs (kneeling, foreground) and Bobby Spencer (center background, in sunglasses) responding to riots at Carson Beach (1976).

Details, Details

The daily perils of the police profession struck Bangs and many of his colleagues as a steep exchange for a mediocre paycheck and job security, so they often resorted to various schemes to pad the nest and secure a few eggs for the future.

In his first years at Old Colony, Bangs enjoyed a run of easy gigs and lucky scores. While deployed with TOPS in April 1975, he was chosen by the Secret Service to escort President Gerald Ford, who was visiting Boston to inaugurate the nation's bicentennial celebration. Bangs lucked into the detail because he was one of only thirty MDC police officers with the necessary military experience and top-secret clearance, but he knew he could work the opportunity to his advantage: a few days away from the routine of the station, maybe a fine meal with the president's entourage, a story he could milk for years to come, and—who knows?—a chance to rub shoulders with the Secret Service and maybe finagle his way into a new job.

On April 18, Ford arrived from New Hampshire by helicopter at the Boston Coast Guard Station, where he was greeted by Mayor Kevin White. As the motorcade made its way through the North End, crowds thronged the streets, waving Italian flags to welcome the president, with the exception of scattered individuals protesting desegregation and bussing. "ROAR," the signs read—Return Our Alienated Rights.

Just after sunset, the escort arrived at the Old North Church on Salem Street for a lantern lighting ceremony to commemorate Paul Revere's ride two centuries before. President Ford spoke to a capacity crowd of more than 500, with hundreds more standing outside, many of them trying to disrupt the proceedings with chants against the war effort in Vietnam, which would collapse in chaos within days. Police removed a few demonstrators from the area, but overall the event unfolded smoothly and the crowd remained friendly and enthusiastic for the celebration, throwing out a cheer when Ford lighted a third lantern in the church's steeple to mark the start of the nation's third century.

The following day, the president traveled to the North Bridge in Concord to lay a wreath and deliver a short speech marking the 200th anniversary of the first battle of the Revolutionary War—and "the shot heard round the world," memorialized by Emerson in his "Concord

Hymn"—and then to nearby Lexington Green for another brief ceremony. By 11:30 a.m., President Ford was safely cocooned in *The Spirit of '76*, as Richard Nixon had dubbed Air Force One, and Joey's national security assignment was history.

The events stirred the memories of Joey's time as a soldier in Vietnam— the adrenaline and smell and danger of war, the camaraderie and patriotism, that ineffable aliveness that made his prick hard. But the charge dissipated quickly, and Bangs was back on the street, parked in the cruiser, camped on the roof, trying to cover his own ass while he protected the city's.

❯ ❯ ❯

A short time later, Bangs drove another official escort, this time from Hanscom Air Force Base in Bedford to Stoneham Zoo, to accompany two baby gorillas that had just arrived from South Africa. The gorillas had been purchased and donated to the zoo by the generous Peter Fuller, proprietor of Peter Fuller Cadillac.

On this auspicious occasion, Bangs was ordered to be in his best dress uniform and had his photo printed on the front page of the *Boston Globe*. While casing the airfield, Bangs acquired some silverware— candlesticks, teapot and cups—which he learned much later had once belonged to the Queen of England and was to be displayed at a local museum. But Bangs fenced the silverware to a hustler who melted the items within a matter of seconds, like butter on a hot skillet. Even more impressive than the smelter, however, was the high price the silver commanded. Guarding the gorillas, Bangs contended, was a much better gig than escorting the president because the gorillas were sedated, leaving Joey free to stop for drinks or attend to other business.

❯ ❯ ❯

All the while, Bangs continued his moonlighting activities, above all making mob collections with Spencer—for a flat fee, not a contingent percentage—and they never failed to get paid. Bangs' mob contacts gave him an envelope with the relevant details about the debt and debtor, and while on duty, Bangs and Spencer tracked down and stopped the mark under the guise of writing a traffic citation. But instead of roughing up the man, they took his cash and jewelry and released him, with a warning. If they couldn't obtain a full and final payment on the spot, Bangs and Spencer would drive the mark to another location and hold him, threatening his family or associates, until he made a call and secured the funds. After giving the sap a beating for their hassle, they would toss him in a dumpster or the harbor, however the whim struck them.

Sometimes Bangs could be persuaded to work without cash payment, if the return favor were enticing. Jerry Clemente once recruited Bangs to get rid of his used Cadillac for the insurance money. Following captain's orders, Bangs did what any obedient patrolman would have done for his superior: he drove Jerry's car to the Boston waterfront and dumped it into the murky harbor water. The job well done, Bangs phoned Clemente at the station and informed him that they were golden.

Jerry thanked Joey and told him that, of course, he now owed Joey a favor. But Jerry's idea of returning the favor surprised even Joey. Clemente informed Bangs that if Joey ever located "a suitable place to break and enter in the city of Medford," he would assist in any way he could. It was about this time that Bangs discovered a television warehouse with an outdated bell alarm system that was ripe for the picking. But for now, they put the score on ice.

That same week, Boston Police Sergeant Joe Cavanaugh introduced Bangs to the infamous Brinks heist bandits, Jazz Maffi and Sandy Richardson. Joey was fascinated by their story and relished drinking with these old-school thieves and gleaning valuable tips along the way. Best of all, Joey knew that if you had the good fortune to drink with Jazz, a prominent Boston bookie, you never paid for a drink. Jazz would lay down a C-note on the bar and that was that. At the time, Hollywood was filming *The Brinks Job*, starring Peter Faulk, who was utterly fascinated by Bangs. And Jazz and Sandy were thrilled to death that Hollywood was portraying their lives and lining their pockets with a little cash for their time as technical advisers. In Bangs' eyes, Jazz Maffi and Sandy Richardson were true gentleman, and the Brinks job gave Joey insight and some big ideas.

Boys Will Be Boys

During his time at Old Colony, Bangs and his cohorts took advantage of every opportunity for mischief and high jinks. On Saint Patrick's Day, the entire TOPS riot squad was on standby alert behind the Old Colony Station, restless with the slow day of calls. Bored to tears, Bangs dared one of the motorcycle cops, who was passionate about his bikes, especially his department-issued Harley-Davidson 1200, to ride naked along the Day Boulevard parade route, a major thoroughfare in Southie.

The cop cowboyed up: "I'll do it, but not completely naked—I never ride without my helmet and boots. That would be illegal."

Neither Bangs nor any of the other officers believed their colleague would actually do it—but the cop was half in the wrapper and knew that if anyone claimed to have seen an MDC motorcycle cop riding bare-assed on the thruway, more than fifty policemen would swear it wasn't true. The officer had nothing to lose: he stripped out of his uniform, kicked the cycle to life, and roared up and down the crowded boulevard, weaving in and out of the midday parade traffic. Bangs nearly lost his lunch on one of the passes when the cop rose up off the seat and flashed his hairy ass.

As much as Bangs loved harassing the motorcycle cops, he had a soft spot for one in particular: Bobby Powers, who was in fact a very skilled motorcyclist. On one occasion after the end of a shift, Lieutenant LoConte couldn't locate Powers—who hadn't checked out—and instructed Bangs to track him down. Bangs agreed only on the condition that if he found Powers intoxicated, LoConte wouldn't file disciplinary charges. LoConte[*] reluctantly assented, and off went Bangs with his partner Spencer.

Powers wasn't much of a drinker, but now and then he made his way to Revere Beach to tie one on. Bangs and Spencer probed the usual gin mills along the beach—and grabbed a drink or two as they went—but Powers was nowhere to be found.

---

[*] Anthony LoConte ("Tony"), who later became a captain, was one of the most respected and well liked cops on the force. Because of his ability to rally the troops, LoConte often took on the task of planning most major events for the MDC Police.

Bangs assumed Powers was lurking somewhere nearby, and on a hunch, he headed to the Ebb Tide Lounge, a bar owned and operated by *La Cosa Nostra* associate Richie Castucci. Before entering through the back entrance, as he so often did, Bangs noted a narrow, sixteen-foot plank running up a steep set of stairs to the door. He scampered up the board and bounded into the kitchen, where he found Powers' Harley parked smack in the middle. The scene amused Bangs, even though he hated babysitting his friends and coworkers. In fact, when he tried to remove Powers from the premises, Bobby became belligerent and refused to budge from his table unless Joey agreed to have not one, but two drinks with him. Arm sufficiently twisted, Bangs pulled up a chair to share some cheer with his intoxicated friend.

Spencer eventually caught up with the pair, and being the only one sober, he rode the Harley back to South Boston with Bangs and Powers following slowly in the cruiser. Upon entering the station, the shit-faced Powers spotted Lieutenant Dick Feeney—someone he had a long-standing grudge with—and attempted to draw his weapon to shoot him.

After a brief struggle, Bangs disarmed Powers and handcuffed him to an old steam radiator. Feeney was screaming to have Powers arrested, but Bangs advised the lieutenant to leave the building and not return until the next day. Bangs left Powers on the floor to calm down while he discussed the situation with LoConte, who, true to his word, did not discipline Powers. Powers was in no condition to drive home, but once again Bangs had to promise they'd stop for two drinks before Powers agreed to let Joey taxi him to his house that night and bring him back to work the following morning.

❣ ❣ ❣

Other slow days on the TOPS squad were filled with less dangerous shenanigans, such as the "bucket bet." The men circled their chairs around a bucket filled with ice water, anted up $10 a piece, and took turns plunging an arm into the freezing container. Whoever held his hand in the longest won the pot. The game was always great fun, especially when the guys were a little buzzed—until, that is, one winner actually lasted so long he damaged the nerves in his hand and lost feeling in his arm. Tragic, but good for a laugh and an early retirement.

Backhoe, Anyone?

During his years with TOPS, Bangs kept close tabs on his childhood pal, Brother O'Leary, with whom he still did odd jobs now and again. Although Joey had outgrown Brother's antics, O'Leary was a loyal friend who could be trusted, and the men remained close allies through thick and thin.

So it was that Joey reached out for Brother after he was approached by a general contractor acquaintance who was building a condominium complex off Storrow Drive on the Charles River, along the Cambridge–Watertown line. The contractor asked Bangs if he could get his hands on a backhoe.

"I'm a cop, I can get anything," Bangs replied nonchalantly. The streets of Boston were Joey's oyster.

Joey called Brother. "We have another order to fill," he explained, as O'Leary laughed at the outrageous shopping list.

At the time, Brother worked for the City of Somerville and knew how to operate heavy machinery. He also knew there was plenty of equipment at a construction site across the street from the Seven Sons Diner on Washington Street in Somerville, and Brother was convinced he could hotwire a backhoe. Bangs and O'Leary made a few dry runs past the site to be sure the coast was clear and the backhoe ripe for the taking. They planned to come back one night when Bangs was on duty with a cruiser in order to escort the backhoe on the main roads.

The following Sunday night, Bangs was working alongside partner Spencer when he told Bobby he had an errand to run. As he always did in a situation like this, he dropped off Spencer at his home in Medford and said he'd pick him up if they received a radio dispatch.

Bangs drove the police cruiser to Somerville to pick up O'Leary at his home, and the men made their way back to the Washington Street construction site, where Brother struggled for more than an hour to hot-wire the backhoe, with no success.

Bangs had already cut the deal—for four grand—and had called to inform the general contractor that he would deliver the goods within the hour. The contractor replied that he'd be unable to meet Bangs, but he told Joey where to stash the backhoe. He also assured Bangs there would be a money envelope waiting the following day.

Joey pressured Brother to hurry, but O'Leary was unable to get the damn machine started. Brother nonetheless promised Joey that he'd get his machinery in time. In fact, Brother knew another place where they could thieve one, even closer to the locale where they had been directed to deliver the cargo. All they would need, Brother continued, was a pair of bolt cutters.

"I keep a pair in the trunk of the cruiser for just such an occasion," Joey offered, and they were off to Fresh Pond, where the City of Cambridge kept most of their trucks and heavy equipment.

Upon arriving, Brother snipped the padlock on the front entrance of the city yard, opened the fence for Joey to drive through, and replaced the loose chain and broken padlock so the gate would appear locked. It only took Brother a moment to locate a backhoe, with the keys in the ignition, of course, and he started the machine and followed Joey's cruiser back to the surface streets.

As if it were nothing more than a legitimate police escort, Bangs led O'Leary onto main thoroughfares and through town en route to the delivery location, blue lights flashing as citizens drove by, honked, waved, and thought nothing of it.

When they arrived at the construction site, Bangs guided O'Leary to the hiding spot, and they secured the backhoe, taking the keys as insurance against payment. Joey quickly scouted the site and noted that the costly condominiums, about three-quarters built, were left wide open: the large crates on the first floor beckoned.

Joey and Brother lit up when they discovered that the crates contained top-of-the-line HVAC units. The plan was hatched, but they needed more manpower, so they sped back to pick up Spencer, who was napping at home in Medford.

Bangs hadn't told Spencer about the backhoe deal—as Joey reasoned, Bobby was just another mouth to feed. However, Joey now informed Bobby that he and Brother, a man Spencer didn't care for, had located a shitload of heating and air-conditioning units and needed his box truck and muscle to pilfer them. Bangs also told Spencer they needed to change out of their uniforms because after days of rain, the unpaved construction site was covered in mud.

Bangs and Spencer quickly changed and picked up Bobby's box truck, which he stored at the Sunoco gas station on Mystic Avenue, just outside of Medford Square and across the street from the police station. O'Leary then drove the truck to the construction site, escorted all the way by Bangs and Spencer.

Before leaving home, Spencer made a quick call to an affluent heating contractor and distributor who was more than interested in the stolen units and had a sizeable warehouse in Medford where they could store the hot merchandise. Spencer instructed his contact to leave the main gate and cargo door open, and they'd be in touch the next day to finalize the deal.

Midnight was fast approaching, the deadline by which Bangs and Spencer had to return the cruiser to Old Colony in South Boston or risk that the watch commander would send a posse to find them. The three thieves worked furiously to load the HVAC units, transport them to the warehouse, and return for more. They made multiple trips and by the end of their shift had scored thirty units, another thirty grand in "overtime" to go with the $4,000 for the backhoe.

Although his life of crime was paying off in spades, Bangs was still cashing paychecks from the Commonwealth of Massachusetts, which meant he had a job, and that job was usually a pain in the ass. But for every pain in the ass, Joey knew he could learn a trick or make a contact or steal some goods, so he sucked it up and soldiered on.

Blizzard of `78

In February 1978, New England was hit with a devastating nor'easter still referred to today as the "Blizzard of '78." Bangs and Spencer were deployed to their old stomping grounds at Revere Beach, where the ocean waves were crashing over the sea wall and snowdrifts rose thirty feet in some areas, completely covering businesses, homes and vehicles of every kind. Just prior to the storm's hitting, Bangs and Spencer received a call from Sergeant Daniel Gately ("Danny"), who informed his men to grab an early dinner, since they expected a lot of automobile accidents and other emergencies due to the extreme weather conditions.

Moments after Gately's call, Bangs and Spencer received a radio dispatch regarding a heart attack victim. Joey and Bobby responded to the call and arrived at a two-story home. They made their way to the second floor and discovered an unconscious elderly woman. Bangs grabbed the woman and carried her down the narrow staircase, Spencer guiding him and assisting as best he could. Once outdoors, Bangs was blasted by a wet wind and knocked to the ground. As he scrambled to cover the old woman, the wind buffeted again, and Joey realized it was salt water— blown from the waves breaking a mile away. Another massive storm was barreling in not far off shore. Bangs performed CPR on the dying woman until the paramedics arrived and then helped load her into the ambulance.

A more powerful second storm pounded New England later that night, causing burglar and fire alarms all over the state to go off and crushing commercial and residential roofs beneath the immense snowfall's weight. Bangs and Spencer returned to the station to fill out their reports and put chains on their cruiser's tires before being dispatched to save other lives.

Over the following three days, Bangs and Spencer personally evacuated dozens of people, taking them to shelters scattered across the greater Boston area. And true to form, once things settled down, they took advantage of the emergency situation to help themselves to all kinds of goodies—cleaning out stores such as Bob's Discount Warehouse and carting off televisions, stereos, VCRs, and other expensive electronics— before the National Guard arrived to secure the streets.

Dead Men Tell No Tales

"Selective enforcement" was the assignment every officer angled for every shift: with selective enforcement came free reign to patrol wherever the fuck they pleased—a dangerous permission to grant men like Bangs and Spencer.

On blistering summer days, for example, Joey and Bobby often opted to head north to Nahant Beach to check out the honeys in their bikinis, an oldie but goodie for the duo in those days. It took approximately twenty- five minutes to get to Nahant Beach from Southie, but it was always well worth the trip. Plus, selective enforcement usually meant a quiet shift— perfect for catching up on some much needed sleep.

But selective enforcement wasn't always a cushy gig—officers had to deal with problems whenever and wherever they found them. On one freezing cold evening in December, Bangs and Spencer were ordered to cover the Lower Basin's 401 squad car while working selective enforcement. They received a dispatch that a man appeared to be dozing in his vehicle on Memorial Drive, a busy thoroughfare. They surmised it was most likely an intoxicated fellow sleeping it off, but when they arrived, Joey checked the man's pulse and realized he was dead.

Every cop knows the amount of work involved in reporting a death—form after form, filled out in triplicate, filing a death certificate, calling the meat wagon, contacting the coroner, the photographer, maybe some reporters, onlookers, and on and on—"a real pain in the prick," Joey frequently complained. It was no secret that paperwork didn't sit well with Bangs and Spencer. In fact, they dodged it to the point of jeopardizing their jobs. And now Joey had to find a way out of this night's hassle.

Bangs peered up the road and realized that the deceased was only thirty yards or so from another traffic route, where another set of cops would have to handle the situation.

"Fuck it!" Bangs told Spencer. "I'm going to drive this dead asshole across the intersection into the other route."

Bangs turned the ignition key, but the car wouldn't start.

"Goddammit!" he yelled to Spencer. "You push the car with the cruiser and I'll steer the motherfucker." Joey eased the dead body aside to get to the steering wheel and wedged himself onto the seat.

Spencer had just begun pushing the vehicle when he heard a grinding noise and stopped; the bumpers weren't lined up, and the contact was damaging the cruiser.

"Fuck this!" he shouted at Bangs.

Spencer hopped out of the cruiser and pushed the vehicle by hand across the busy intersection and oncoming traffic and into the next police route, amid the angry shouts and honking of dozens of peeved commuters.

Once across the intersection, Bangs reset the body to an upright position, while Spencer caught his breath and radioed for the 415 squad car, which was the supervising sergeant's vehicle. Minutes later, the sergeant arrived on the scene and made a mental note of the situation before calling for the 402 squad car to take over the investigation. When the 402 car arrived, Bangs played it perfectly:

"Geez, fellas, we'll be more than happy to help you guys out. If you want us to do the paperwork, we will."

"Don't worry about it," they replied. "We have it."

"Well, at least let us buy you guys a cup of coffee," Bangs offered, since he knew they were going to freeze their asses off for the remainder of the shift. Plus, cops like Bangs and Spencer never paid for coffee and doughnuts anyhow.

So Bangs and Spencer returned to the scene a while later with fresh doughnuts and hot java and thought that they had once again beaten the system, when they received a dispatch from the supervising sergeant ordering them to get their asses to the station on the double.

Bangs and Spencer knew from the tone of the sergeant's voice that something was up. When they arrived at the station, the sergeant didn't waste a moment.

"You two motherfuckers! I got a call from a lady who said she saw two MDC policemen pushing a car across an intersection. You wouldn't happen to know who these two cops are, do you?"

Bangs shrugged; Spencer stood silent.

"Then who, may I ask, do you think would be pushing a car around our fair city with a dead body in it?"

Bangs shrugged again. With no real proof, the sergeant dismissed Bangs and Spencer from his office without further discussion.

What's Up, Doc?

Bangs and Spencer's endless exploits became legendary in law enforcement circles. On occasion, the partners stopped at the Lower Basin station to gas up their personal vehicles. On this night, around 11:30 p.m., they had stopped to gas up their police cruiser when a dispatch crackled on the radio for them to meet another patrol car near the Museum of Science, just blocks away.

When Bangs and Spencer arrived at the scene, they found two MDC colleagues in a cruiser positioned directly behind an idling vehicle with "M.D." (medical doctor) plates. The driver was passed out drunk at the steering wheel. This was the perfect moment for a common police maneuver.

Bangs and Spencer won the coin toss to determine who was going on "vacation," that is, who was going to get time off for injuries sustained in the line of duty—after the accident that was about to occur. Joey and Bobby carefully repositioned their cruiser twenty yards in front of the snoozing doctor's vehicle, and then backed into the car at a high rate of speed. The stunned doctor, drunk as he was, stumbled from the wreck, and the "injured" patrol officers, Bangs and Spencer, radioed for an ambulance and a tow truck. After everyone had been treated at the scene, Bangs and Spencer accompanied the doctor to the station and began to book him for driving under the influence.

Bangs pulled the doctor aside and acted as if he were doing him a favor.

"Look, Doc," he confided. "Let's sweep this under the rug. If you sign this statement, admitting responsibility for the accident—how you took your eyes off the road and rear-ended us—I'll call you a cab and cut you loose, or else you're fucked."

Of course, the inebriated doctor agreed, signed the document, and thanked Joey profusely. Because of injuries sustained in the line of duty, Spencer was out on paid leave for eight weeks. Later, he also sued the doctor's insurance company and received a healthy settlement to boot.

High-Speed Pursuits

Upon returning to work on a wet and miserable fall evening in 1979, Bangs and Spencer were patrolling the Dorchester area along Morrissey Boulevard, when Joey decided he needed a cup of coffee. About a quarter mile from the Old Colony police station, a Lincoln Continental sped past the cruiser in the opposite direction, and Bangs recognized the driver as the black teenager he had arrested for grand theft auto the week before. Joey had something of a hard-on for this kid since that incident because he had ripped a brand-new pair of police pants on a chain-link fence while pursuing the felon on foot. Bangs had been tempted to bust the kid's head, but had restrained himself and just stewed about it all week.

"Hang a U-turn and go after that cocksucker!" Bangs ordered.

On this night, Bangs and Spencer were assigned an SUV complete with a metal push bar used to move stalled vehicles out of traffic. Spencer hesitated— he wasn't up for paperwork tonight—but Joey explained how this punk had caused him to rip a new pair of pants. And to add fuel to the fire, he told the macho Spencer that the kid purposely sped past them to instigate the situation, to see if Bobby was up for a chase. In reality, once the teen spotted Bangs, he tried to duck down in the driver's seat to avoid a confrontation, and by the time Spencer agreed to give chase, he was nearly out of sight. *Fuck it*, said Spencer— he flipped on the siren and lights and set the wheels of justice in motion.

After a high-speed pursuit of four or five miles, Spencer finally caught up to the teenage driver and his three joy-riding companions, who were by now going more than eighty miles per hour and slaloming through traffic on the 35-mph boulevard.

The young car thief darted in and out of Dorchester side streets in an attempt to elude capture and was winning until he made a fatal error and turned down a dead end. As the stolen sedan made its way toward the end of the street, it began to slow. Bangs and Spencer spotted the brake lights and saw that the vehicle's four occupants were about to bail out. But Spencer would have none of it: he rammed the Lincoln and locked the SUV's push bar onto its bumper.

The force of the impact flung all four teens back into the vehicle as the cars' tires screeched and smoked and the screams of the terrified teens ripped the air. Spencer didn't let up—he pushed the stolen vehicle through a chain-link fence and onto the front porch of a single-family home, where it finally came to rest in the living room. The home's elderly owner—who had dozed off drunk in his recliner—sat stunned and silent, covered in dust and debris, his eyes blinking slowly as he tried to understand what the fuck had interrupted his nap. Bangs finally stopped laughing long enough to help his partner capture the driver, while the other suspects escaped on foot through the demolished dwelling.

When the teen's day in Dorchester District Court arrived, the judge was infuriated to lay eyes on the juvenile, who had become a frequent visitor in his courtroom.

"I thought I told you I never wanted to see your face again," the judge exclaimed.

"I told that to the policemen, but they arrested me anyhow," the kid replied, trying to be cute. The courtroom erupted in laughter, and the judge gaveled for silence.

As expected, the boy protested his involvement in the theft and claimed that Spencer had tried to kill him, but the judge ignored his plaint.

The judge ordered the teen to be transferred from the Boston City Jail, aka "The Tombs," where he was being held in lieu of bail, to the Billerica House of Corrections to serve a one-year sentence.

For Bangs and Spencer, a court appearance meant overtime, a minimum of three hours at $30 per hour. A little payback, a chance to gloat, an extra paycheck—not a bad arrest, even if Joey and Bobby did receive minor injuries in the collision.

A similar incident occurred on the southbound side of the Southeast Expressway, just outside the Dewey Tunnel. Bangs had a terrible hangover and wanted a nice, easy night, but the coffee-stoked Spencer tossed that idea out the window after a Corvette flew by. Ignoring his partner's pleas, Bobby hit the lights and siren and went after the Vette with a vengeance. Bangs told everyone that Spencer was the best driver he knew, and tracking down the Corvette was no problem. But what happened next surprised even Joey.

Spencer took it upon himself to ram the vehicle at better than a hundred miles per hour, and the impact ejected the driver from the vehicle, head first through the windshield. Bangs, who received minor injuries in the collision, felt in his gut that this guy was dead. As Bangs and Spencer approached the victim, they noted he was still breathing and radioed for an ambulance.

"You did it this time, Bobby, you did it this time," Bangs repeated over and over. Bangs had no doubt the driver would never make it to the hospital, and he was concerned about the implications for both officers. However, after running the victim's identification through NCIC, Bangs established that they had an escaped convict on their hands, and what had appeared to be the start of a difficult road turned into a pat on the back and three days' vacation.

Bangs soon learned that the convict—a lifer and trustee—had escaped from Norfolk State Prison while on a weekend furlough, per Governor Michael Dukakis' controversial work-release program. Coincidentally, instead of Spencer standing in front of a judge for using excessive force, he soon found himself standing tall in front of the entire TOPS squad and MDC brass, where he received an official commendation for bravery, a recognition that Bangs had nudged his superiors to award his beloved partner.

▼ ▼ ▼

Not long after this incident, the shit hit the fan for Spencer, who nearly lost his police job when he was arrested for trespassing and larceny. Spencer had started a side business supplying wooden pallets to a shipping company in South Boston. Of course, the gig was illegal—he picked up pallets he saw while on patrol in his police cruiser, loading them in the trunk or tying them to the roof, and then resold them for a decent price.

One afternoon while on duty, Bobby changed out of his MDC jumpsuit, picked up his box truck, and began stealing pallets from various locations along the South Boston waterfront. A port security guard for one of the companies spotted him and jotted down his license plate number. Spencer was arrested and did a walk-through, similar to the ones Joey had done while on the Capitol Police. However, Spencer was later exonerated when the terrorized security guard failed to show in court. It was obvious to everyone that somebody had paid the guard a visit, but Bobby had never asked, and Joey had never offered, and no one else had anything to say about it.

Two in the Bush

During the 1960s and 1970s, the Boston Esplanade was a notorious gathering place for the city's homosexual community. The cops were not sent there to harass the gay men, per se, but to keep them from being robbed, since the Esplanade was also a hot spot for muggings. But Bangs did arrest men—everyone from priests to doctors to lawyers and other prominent citizens—for lewd and lascivious behavior, mainly for performing oral sex or sodomy behind the Esplanade's dense shrubbery.

One unlucky arrestee happened to be the general manager of the Kentucky Fried Chicken in North Cambridge. After being booked and fingerprinted, he dropped dead of a heart attack in his cell. Joey surmised on the one hand that maybe the guy had eaten too much fatty food at work, but reasoned on the other that the man couldn't bear to reveal his behavior to his wife and five children. Unfortunately for all involved, the family discovered the truth the hard way.

Watch commanders and sergeants alike knew very well that the homophobic Spencer and Bangs loathed dealing with the growing gay community. So one night, after they were caught drinking on duty—as they had done on many nights—Joey and Bobby were assigned to patrol the Esplanade nightly for a month. This detail was one they couldn't ditch, because it was much too easy for their supervising sergeant to check up on them.

Sunday nights were what Bangs and Spencer referred to as "visiting night": most weekends they ditched work and spent time with their extended families. Spencer dropped off the married Bangs at his girlfriend's condominium or at Twigs Restaurant in the North End, where Joey had a stash of civilian clothes to wear over his police uniform. Spencer was separated at the time, yet still visited his estranged wife, Elaine, each weekend. Bobby hid the police cruiser in Elaine's garage and ran a speaker wire from the cruiser radio to the house so he could hear any dispatch calls that might come in.

On a blustery Sunday night, after Bangs and Spencer had rendezvoused with their wives, the partners were drinking beer in their cruiser while watching football on a portable television. Joey had a hundred dollars on the Patriots, who were not worth a shit in those days, and of course he lost the bet. The game threw him into a less than congenial mood, which in turn soured Spencer's disposition.

Bangs always drank his beer icy cold, so every now and then he exited the cruiser with flashlight in hand to grab a handful of clean snow to chill his brew. And Joey and Bobby were always careful to drink alcohol from a paper cup with a straw to disguise their beverages in the event one of their superiors happened to roll up on them.

On this particular night, while Bangs was out of the cruiser, he heard what sounded like moaning coming from a nearby hedge. He alerted Spencer, who shined the cruiser's spotlight at the source of the sound: two men engaged in sex. Taken aback, the patrolmen approached the couple, whose pants were still down at their ankles.

"What the hell are you doing?" Bangs demanded of the man on top.

"Just pissing," came the quick reply.

"You weren't pissing!" Joey snapped. "You were fucking him in the ass!"

Joey and the "alpha gay" argued back and forth until Spencer couldn't take any more and told the men to pull up their pants. Bangs and Spencer huddled in conference. Bangs didn't want to arrest the men because he didn't want to do the paperwork, naturally. Spencer almost gave in, but his homophobia just couldn't let it go. He again accosted the more masculine of the men.

"You better tell me the truth or I'm locking up your perverted ass! Tell me you were fucking him in the ass, and I'll let you go!"

Once again, the gay man denied they were having sex and insisted they were merely taking a piss. Bangs found the exchange amusing, but Spencer was infuriated.

Spencer gave the man one final chance to come clean. This time the gay man confessed: "Okay…I was fucking him in the ass." Then, as if to temper Spencer's wrath, he added, "But I didn't have it all the way in!"

Amused as he was, Joey was getting a chill in the freezing weather and had had enough of the bullshit.

"Make 'em promise they won't come back and let's get outta here," he told Spencer.

Spencer harangued the men with the dos and don'ts of respectable public behavior and then joined Bangs in the warm cruiser. The partners were about to drive off when Bobby heard a light tap on his window. Spencer turned to the sound and found himself face to face with the gay man, who was standing outside, a scowl on his face. Bobby cranked down his window to ask what the fellow wanted.

"Don't tell me you two drive together all night and don't touch each other!" the man hissed.

Infuriated and half intoxicated, Spencer jumped from the cruiser, grabbed the man by the seat of his pants and collar of his jacket, and carried him twenty yards to the edge of the partially frozen Charles River. He found his footing on the slippery bank, reared back and tossed the man into the gelid water. While the man screamed and splashed about in the icy river, Spencer smirked—a job well done. Realizing he may be next, the other gay fellow dashed off into the night.

Meanwhile in the warm cruiser sat Joey Bangs, nearly pissing his pants in laughter, until common sense set in and he grew concerned not only for Spencer's job but also his own. As soon as Spencer returned to the car, Bangs ordered him to hightail it out of there before anyone could jot down the number of their cruiser.

Spencer drove to the other end of the Esplanade and into Brighton, nearly five miles away. With the coast now seemingly clear, they cleaned the beer cans and trash from their cruiser, locked the portable television in the trunk, and bought a box of breath mints at a local convenience store.

As he thought about the incident, Joey began to worry that hypothermia may have caused the wisecracking gay man to drown. But not fifteen minutes passed before Bangs and Spencer heard a dispatch on the police radio. The watch commander began calling squad cars into the station one at a time, beginning with the 401 squad car, the 402 squad car about ten minutes later, and so on.

"Here we go, pal," Bangs said grimly. "They're calling everyone in. We're fucked now!"

The watch commander finally reached the 406 squad car, which was the last of all the Lower Basin cars on duty.

Then Bangs remembered they were driving the 17-4 car on selective enforcement for TOPS out of South Boston. A glimmer of hope lit his face. But once all the Lower Basin cars had reported to the station, one last call came over the dispatch: "17-4 selective enforcement squad car, report to the station."

"Keep out of sight while I go in," Joey ordered Bobby when they arrived at the station. Apparently, the gay man, who was tightly wrapped in a pile of police blankets, had informed the watch commander—who also happened to be the lieutenant in charge—that the two cops responsible for throwing him into the river had mustaches. Fortunately for Bangs and Spencer, most cops had mustaches or facial hair at the time. The gay man added that "one cop was big, and the other not so big."

Bangs entered the station and asked the lieutenant what the problem was. Before the man could get a good look at Bangs, the lieutenant shuffled Joey into his office.

"I know it was you, you no-good motherfucker!" he whispered angrily.

Joey played the part. "What are you talking about, lieutenant?"

"I knew it was you and Spencer the moment that sopping-wet fairy walked through the front door!"

"I haven't the slightest idea what you're talking about, lieutenant."

By this time, Spencer had slipped into the office, careful to go undetected by the shivering gay man. Bangs had now had his fill of the lieutenant and was tired of taking the heat for Bobby, so he decided to break Spencer's balls a bit.

Joey came clean: "It was Spencer."

The lieutenant was shocked: he would have sworn it was none other than the mischievous Joey Bangs.

Bangs went on to explain how the gay men were committing lewd acts—a felony—in the bushes at Esplanade and how he and Spencer were inclined to allow the homosexuals to walk before the gay guy in question made a wise-ass comment to Bobby.

"So what do we do now, lieutenant?" Bangs queried.

The lieutenant asked Bangs if the man had gotten a clear look at him. Joey answered that it was dark and Spencer had done most of the talking, yet it was impossible to say for sure whether he'd be recognized. The lieutenant laid out his plan.

"I'm going to tell him that yours is the last squad car we have on duty and it had just one man in it. Spencer, you stay put, and I'll bring Bangs for identification."

The lieutenant and Bangs confronted the vindictive man—Joey was careful not to make eye contact. Spencer peeked at the scene through the mini-blinds in the lieutenant's office and tried to provoke Bangs to laughter by making lewd gestures and absurd faces.

The lieutenant asked Bangs if he had seen the man before. Calm and polite, Bangs altered his voice slightly and denied ever seeing him. The lieutenant then asked the man if he could identify patrolman Bangs as his assailant.

The gay man studied Bangs carefully. Realizing that Joey felt uncomfortable with such scrutiny, he examined Bangs again, with an ambiguous glint in his eye. The lieutenant noticed the game, informed the shivering man that patrolman Bangs was the last officer he had on duty that night, and confounded him by asking if he was positive it was an MDC patrolman and not an officer from the Boston police, which also patrolled the Esplanade.

The lieutenant then explained that if he happened to locate the officer who had allegedly thrown him into the river, and the officer stated he was a fugitive from justice guilty of any illegal acts or crimes, he could still be charged with a felony. The lieutenant also suggested that an officer's report might indicate that the man had fled the scene and may have accidentally fallen or even jumped into the river in an attempt to elude arrest.

In the end, the gay man was so confused he didn't know whether to shit or wind his wristwatch. The infuriated gay man informed the lieutenant he wanted to drop the matter, and he stormed out of the police station, forgetting to leave behind the MDC blankets wrapped around his shoulders. The cops promptly apprehended the man, who was now in possession of stolen state property, and booked him on a misdemeanor, for spite.

Bangs and Spencer knew that they had dodged a bullet and that the lieutenant had gone out on a limb for them. The lieutenant sent them away with a stern warning—"If you shitheads ever pull a stunt like this again, you're on your own"—and Joey and Bobby knew he meant it.

Damned If You Do

The lieutenant's admonition did little to deter Bangs and Spencer's mischief. While drinking in South Boston's Teachers Union Hall—as they did regularly—Spencer nudged Bangs to get back to work. They were under scrutiny, it was nearing midnight, and they needed to write at least one ticket to show they were actually working. Peeved by the interruption, Bangs nevertheless conceded that Spencer was right.

Normally, in these instances Bangs and Spencer simply grabbed a phone book and copied names and addresses for a few warnings, but the brass had become suspicious about why they weren't writing any actual complaint citations. So Bangs agreed to find someone they could write up.

While en route to Revere Beach, an expensive sedan flew past their police cruiser doing better than ninety miles per hour on the Southeast Expressway, just before the Dewey Square Tunnel.

Already agitated, Bangs was now pissed off. "Get that motherfucker!" he bellowed at Spencer. Spencer was a maniac behind the wheel, but he was also extremely skillful, and they quickly tracked down the vehicle and pulled it over. Tension was high between the longtime partners, and unfortunately the speeding driver had no idea what he was in for.

The driver, a resident of the South Shore, was a "belligerent cocksucker," according to Bangs. Before Joey could utter a word, the driver began ranting about how he was an honest taxpayer who paid the patrolmen's salary out of his hard-earned money—the same bullshit the cops heard all too often. Most cops would go soft on someone who was in a situation they could relate to—a domestic squabble, stress at work, financial troubles—but this kind of piss and vinegar stuck in Bangs' craw.

"License and registration," Bangs barked.

"For what?" demanded the driver.

"'Cause I said so!" Bangs snapped. The alcohol was starting to talk and Joey's patience was running thin. The driver continued to bicker while he pulled out his wallet.

"Strike one," Joey warned him.

Bangs examined the license and noted that the driver was from a small South Shore town he had never heard of—this guy didn't know anyone. *Strike two*, Joey thought to himself, as he glared at the driver. The driver continued to badger Bangs with expletives and threats.

"Strike three, motherfucker!" Joey exploded. "Let me explain something to you, pal—you're not in East Bumfuck, Mass., no more!"

The driver now sat silent, and Bangs smiled as he tossed the driver's license over the Expressway Bridge.

On the other side of the car, Spencer popped his head into the window: "License and registration."

The driver babbled something about how Bangs had just thrown it off the bridge.

"Come on," Spencer replied. "You expect me to believe that crock of shit? I've heard it all before, pal! Do you have his license?" Spencer queried Bangs.

"Nope," Bangs answered flatly.

The driver knew he was in a sticky situation now, and he began addressing Joey and Bobby as "sir" and "officer." He rummaged through the glove compartment in search of his registration.

By this time, the driver had found his registration and thrust it into Spencer's hand. Bangs popped his head into the window.

"Registration, please!" he demanded.

"I just gave it to the other officer, sir!"

Bangs and the driver peered at Spencer, who was stuffing the crumpled registration into his mouth. He flashed his empty hands, swallowed, opened his mouth wide, and stuck out his tongue.

"This guy thinks we have his license and registration. He must be drunk," Bangs said.

Joey opened the car door and instructed the driver to step outside for a field sobriety test, which in this case became a circus sideshow as the officers put him through ridiculous exercises, including an attempted handstand. The driver of course failed miserably. Bangs informed the alleged "drunkard" that if he made just one more obscene remark, he was going to throw *him* off the bridge after his license.

"You can't do that!" the driver squealed.

"Listen, pal," Bangs explained calmly as he began writing the citation, "you're in South Boston, it's pitch black . . . we can do whatever the fuck we want."

The driver quieted and craned his neck to see what Bangs was writing: no license or registration, failure to stop, speeding, disorderly conduct, obstructing traffic. Bangs and Spencer were tempted to cite him for driving while intoxicated, but doing so would have meant more paperwork, so they gave the driver a pass.

Bangs had learned from the best and had become a master with the pen, writing all the citations and police reports for both himself and Spencer, alternating citation books and pen colors so it looked like each officer was doing his fair share of the work. Bobby of course signed the tickets in his own book.

The speeding driver's ticket would ultimately result in hundreds of dollars in fines, plus a suspension, a hefty price to pay for having a big mouth.

But they weren't off the hook yet, because as soon as they cut the speeding driver loose, he drove straight to Old Colony to file a complaint. When Bangs and Spencer ended their shift and returned to the station, their exasperated sergeant was waiting for them. He called the patrolmen into his office, slammed the door, and began grilling:

"Did either of you clowns threaten to kill someone tonight?"

Whereas it was technically after midnight, Bangs got cute and replied: "No, sir, not tonight we didn't." Spencer snickered.

"How about last night?" the sergeant fired back, unamused.

"Come on, sarge," Bangs deadpanned, "we threaten to 'kill' somebody *every* night. So what?"

The sergeant caught a familiar odor and began to sniff at Bangs like a K-9.

"Do I smell booze?" Joey shook his head no and tried to hold his breath until the sergeant backed away.

The sergeant laid into Bangs and Spencer about a disgruntled citizen who claimed a patrolman named Bangs had thrown his driver license off a bridge and then threatened to throw him off after it. Joey shrugged and started in on a story about how the vindictive, cop-hating driver was looking for revenge because of his numerous citations. As usual, Bangs did all the talking, and Spencer merely nodded and punctuated the tale with *Yes* and *That's right*. The sergeant warned Bangs to make certain he filed a proper report to cover his ass, and Bangs—as much as he hated the task—wrote a masterpiece.

The driver protested the citation and filed for a hearing on the matter, and about two months later, Bangs received notice to appear in Boston Municipal Court. The driver didn't want just revenge, he wanted blood. The way Joey figured it, this clown probably had to miss a day's work, lose a day's pay, and drive God-knows-how-far just to be in court, believing he could get Bangs and Spencer in trouble for threatening his life. He took the stand and told his story to the judge. He admitted speeding, but explained that Bangs threw his license off the bridge and Spencer ate his registration, before Bangs threatened to throw him off the bridge as well. The Boston cops awaiting their cases tried to stifle their laughter, and the judge finally interrupted the driver:

"Son, I've been sitting on this bench for an awful long time, and I know these policemen have a difficult job. I also know they get frustrated at times, but I have never in all my days on the bench heard of a policeman throwing away a license or eating a registration, much less killing someone for speeding!" The man protested, but the gavel shut him off: "Guilty! Next case!" As Bangs and Spencer exited the courtroom, they met a small throng of laughing cop fans who shook their hands in congratulation.

First Commendation

In addition to regaining the adulation of his peers, near the end of his tenure in South Boston, Bangs received a Certificate of Commendation for Bravery, the first of two such awards he would receive from the Metropolitan District Commission's TOPS. The Certificate of Commendation recognizes work performed in an outstanding manner, with courage and devotion to duty in accordance with the highest tradition of the Metropolitan District Commission Police.

On a rainy winter evening, Bangs and Spencer were working selective enforcement in the 17-2-3 car, a two-division squad car that patrolled both the Revere Beach and Fellsway Divisions. They were permitted to travel anywhere throughout Greater Boston, as the need arose—and of course, to do whatever they wanted, whenever and wherever they wanted.

During this particular shift, they received a dispatch regarding an armed robbery in progress at a convenience store in Revere. Perfect—they happened to be drinking at Buddy's Cafe. The All-Points Bulletin advised that shots had been fired between police from Revere and Winthrop and an armed suspect, so Bangs and Spencer hesitated a moment, contemplated, downed their cocktails, and high-tailed it to the scene.

The partners soon found themselves involved in a high-speed chase that ended right back on Revere Beach Boulevard, where the cops were able to stop the suspect's vehicle. Once again, Revere police jumped from their cruisers and exchanged gunfire with the armed robber, as did Bangs and Spencer.

Under cover of pitch darkness, the desperate bandit hopped the seawall, ran onto the beach, and plunged straight into the frigid North Atlantic Ocean in an attempt to evade capture. Bangs took control of the scene, as he usually did, and ordered the other policemen to stop shooting. The air fell silent except for the driving rain and pounding surf; Bangs strained to listen for the suspect.

"Come out of there, you motherfucker!" Bangs ordered.

"You'll kill me if I come out!" the suspect replied.

A backup patrol arrived with a floodlight that allowed Joey to scan the icy waves, and he finally spotted the fugitive drifting about fifty yards away from the shore. Bangs feared that if the man happened to drown, the cops might be held liable in a civil lawsuit—not to mention the paperwork involved.

Bangs could see that the criminal was struggling to stay afloat, so he ordered one of the Winthrop officers to radio for a boat. Bangs stripped down to his skivvies and socks—and gun belt, of course—and dove into the gelid surf.

The water hit like a sledgehammer to the face, and Joey fought to catch his breath and get his bearings. He felt his arms and legs tighten and go numb as he approached the semi-conscious suspect.

"You better not shoot me, you motherfucker!" Bangs stammered through the cold. The suspect was unresponsive, held from disappearing underwater only by the air trapped in his oversize coat. When Bangs reached the body, he saw that the suspect was just a youth, a gaunt African-American kid maybe fifteen years old.

Goddammit! Bangs thought. "Don't die on me, kid!" he yelled as he shook the teen to rouse him. Bangs cradled him by the shoulders, keeping his head above water, and began the agonizing swim back to the beach.

The tide had carried them nearly a half mile from their original point of entry, and by the time Bangs made it to shore, both he and the boy had ice crystals dangling from their hair, nose, and ears, and hypothermia had begun to set in.

Lieutenant LoConte arrived on scene to witness Joey's heroic action and watch as the other officers pulled Bangs and the criminal from the waves. Spencer wrapped Joey in a woolen police blanket and shuffled him toward the warm cruiser.

"You're one crazy son-of-a-bitch," LoConte muttered to Joey, both incredulous and admiring, as Bangs and Spencer rushed by.

Once he was revived enough to speak and realized he would be okay, the young robber babbled all night on the hospital gurney next to Bangs, repeatedly thanking Joey for saving his life.

Eventually, the kid was found guilty of attempted murder of a peace officer and sentenced to more than ten years in prison. Joey didn't give a shit about thanks or commendations—all that mattered to him was that he had just earned himself five days off, with pay. Which meant booze and broads. Having balls and being crazy had its benefits.

Gaming the System

It was during these years that the profitable exam-selling scheme flourished. Capitol police officer Dick Madden continued to allow Jerry Clemente and Tommy Doherty entry into the State House and surrounding municipal buildings, for a small fee. Jerry cleaned up, netting between $2,500 and $3,000 per exam, depending on whether the buyer was friend or foe. In fact, Jerry was so cheap he even made his own brother, Bobby Clemente, pay for his sergeant's exam. And Doherty and Bangs also benefitted in their own ways as temptation got the best of many a good cop and more and more of them flew unthinking into Clemente's tangled web.

There was no doubt that Clemente used the exam scheme not only for profit but also for vengeance. For example, Jerry once informed Joey that he was planning to sabotage a mutual acquaintance, a K-9 cop Bangs referred to as "Wild Bill." Clemente already had Bill's money in hand—a full three grand, plus a surcharge for the answers—and he was debating whether to change Bill's exam grade or withhold the test altogether, out of spite for an offense he refused at first to reveal to Joey.

Bangs advised against the plan for three reasons. First, he liked Wild Bill, mainly because he was a good friend of Bobby Spencer's. Plus, Bangs knew that Bill was a solid cop and might very well drop a dime if he suspected a bigger conspiracy. And finally, Joey insisted that having a K-9 unit in their pocket might come in handy: Bill's German shepherd was one of the force's best dogs, and he had an amazing ability to sniff out the smallest traces of dope, weapons, and other contraband, always making the cops look good. Bangs also took advantage of his acquaintance with Bill and tested the K-9 frequently to learn how to get around drug-sniffing dogs. Jerry reluctantly agreed with Joey's take; Bill and his dog received the promotion without a hitch and were transferred to a cushy job with TOPS at Stoneham Zoo.

Of course, Joey couldn't let Jerry get away with keeping secrets, so he pestered Clemente for the details about Bill. Had Wild Bill ratted on Clemente? Stolen from him? Said something unseemly about his family? Evidently, Clemente had found out through the department's twisted grapevine that Bill had screwed Jerry's longtime girlfriend, Barbara Hickey, years before she and Clemente ever met.

▼ ▼ ▼

Clemente first encountered the unmarried Barbara Hickey in 1976, while she worked as a bail commissioner for the county and Jerry was an MDC lieutenant. Hickey's basic duties were to oversee newly arrested detainees and check their eligibility for bail.

In 1978, Clemente and Hickey began seeing each other romantically while Jerry worked the swing and graveyard shifts at Revere Beach Station, just a few minutes from Barbara's apartment and warm bed.

Hickey was very thin, borderline anorexic, and wore large horn-rimmed glasses, yet she was reasonably attractive. Bangs actually met Hickey the year before Clemente did, in 1975, and attended both Northeastern University and the graduate school at Anna Maria College with her. Joey thought Barbara could be a real pest at times, and she constantly nagged Jerry about giving her money and divorcing his wife. In Joey's eyes, Barbara was looking for a free ride and believed— mistakenly—that Jerry would be her money tree.

Although she didn't at first seem very bright, Bangs knew that Hickey was far from naïve. He knew she was hot for cops and had had numerous affairs with other officers, including a torrid tryst with Wild Bill. Joey often sparred with Barbara by asking her embarrassing personal questions; one time he even asked her if she ever fantasized about being with two men at once and actually got her to admit—with the promise he wouldn't tell Jerry—that she did. But when Jerry learned from other sources that Barbara had a history of gold-digging—and that Joey knew about it—Clemente's paranoia grew and his relationship with his colleagues became strained.

▼ ▼ ▼

It wasn't only Clemente's prickliness that caused him trouble with fellow officers; more than anything, other policemen didn't care for Jerry because he neglected his daily duties. For instance, during work hours at Revere Beach Station and later as watch commander, Clemente often ordered

Bangs and other subordinates not to bother him under any circumstances because he wanted a quiet night.

And Clemente became increasingly bolder when it came to promotional exams. Jerry thought the MDC police department should remain segregated, and he frequently lowered entrance and promotion examination scores of Hispanic and African-American applicants. In fact, in 1979 Clemente told Bangs he had changed the grade of every minority applicant for promotion to sergeant, with the exception of Chris Montgomery, who happened to slip through the cracks. Clemente was beside himself that Montgomery, who he thought was not very bright, actually passed—or more accurately, that he beat Jerry's personal screening process. Clemente used a cardboard overlay to check test results, but on this occasion his tool had somehow failed him.

Bangs never agreed with Clemente's extensive test-tampering and hated the *Schadenfreude* Jerry felt at the failure of minorities. But Clemente had big plans for his exam scheme. Increasingly from the mid-1970s into the mid-1980s, Clemente pressured a few select friends on the MDC, including Bangs, to offer stolen exams and answers to any individual they felt could be trusted.

"I know you're asshole buddies with so-and-so," Clemente would say to Bangs. "Offer him the exam for me."

Bangs used a stolen exam for his own purposes from time to time, especially later on. He was well aware that placing the right candidates in positions of power in various Commonwealth police departments would mean political favors to follow. But Joey also had a bad feeling about the scheme from get-go. In fact, Bangs had his own code of ethics about the exams—he never offered them to any patrolman who had a family because he sensed that Clemente's little venture wouldn't last forever, and he didn't want to see anyone go down because of his deliberate actions.

Bangs also knew that if he offered an exam to a cop with a family and the malfeasance later came to light, the family man would crack in a heartbeat and take immunity in exchange for testimony. Also, if he happened to approach a cop about buying an exam and were turned down, Bangs knew he and that cop would always carry distrust and suspicion of each other, potentially putting himself in jeopardy of disclosure at some later time.

▼ ▼ ▼

In 1979 Clemente was stationed at the MDC's Revere Beach Station as a lieutenant, a rank that in his opinion offered too little opportunity and not enough protection. So he helped himself to a copy of the captain's exam, even though he was brilliant enough he didn't need it to pass. Nevertheless, even after scoring an exceptional grade, Jerry still needed the assistance of his pal Joey to obtain his actual promotion.

Clemente tentatively approached Bangs and asked if he would reach out for John Fox, a person assigned to the governor's office whom Bangs had met while working on the Capitol Police. Fox, a notorious gambler, was also Governor Edward J. King's legal counsel.

Clemente understood that Fox wouldn't be able to give him the promotion outright; he was only looking for assurance that he would be one of three potential candidates for the promotion to captain. Bangs agreed with Jerry, so he reached out for Fox, who in turn asked Governor King to contact MDC Commissioner Guy Carbone, who ultimately saw to Clemente's promotion. To Jerry's delight, all of these conversations transpired within twenty-four hours.

After being promoted to captain, Clemente was transferred to work as watch commander at MDC Police headquarters on Somerset Street, near the State House in Boston—walking distance from the civil service exams.

Left, MDC headquarters on Somerset Street in Boston. Above, Upper Basin station near the Charles River in Brighton.

Selfless Self-Promoters

Promotions among the rogue cops were becoming plentiful. On April, 2, 1979, Bangs and Spencer took the written sergeant's examination and passed with the same score. While both men had sufficient training and experience to merit a promotion, Spencer performed so poorly on the dreaded verbal portion of the test that he didn't qualify for the advancement.

In early 1980, Bangs was still stationed at TOPS in South Boston while awaiting his promotion to sergeant and subsequent transfer to the Upper Basin. Joey had passed the sergeant's promotional examination with a near perfect score—having an advance copy of the test certainly didn't hurt. As close as they were, Clemente had still charged Bangs the usual asking price of $2,500, just like anyone else: business was business.

The written portion of the examination counted for fifty percent of the final grade. The oral exam counted for twenty-five percent, and training and experience counted for the final twenty-five. After the oral exam session, conducted by Boston Police Lt. Bill Bratton—who would soon become executive superintendent of the Boston Police and later serve as superintendent of the MDC, police commissioner in Boston and New York, and chief of police in Los Angeles—Bratton pulled Bangs aside and commented that he was extremely impressed with Joey's responses. Bratton also expressed no surprise at how well Bangs had done on the written exam; of course, he, like so many others who were duped over the years, had no inkling of the extent of Jerry and Joey's testing scam.

Even though Bangs passed his exams with high scores, he faced a larger obstacle in actually securing a promotion. MDC Police Superintendent Lawrence Carpenter ("Larry") had been inundated with anonymous letters about Joey's on- and off-duty antics and consequently refused to slot him in an open sergeant position. Bangs approached Clemente for assistance, knowing that Jerry had previously bagged a DUI case in Medford for Carpenter's son. But Carpenter refused to cooperate.

Left with few options, Clemente picked the lock to Carpenter's office, and he and Bangs made copies of the anonymous complaint letters. They gave the memos to Joey's attorney, Dennis McKenna, who subsequently contacted Carpenter and blindsided him with the threat of a lawsuit against the Metropolitan Police Department if he didn't promote Bangs. Carpenter had the entire office rekeyed and from that day forth stored confidential files in a safe box at his home.

Clemente also leaned on recently promoted MDC Police Captain, Detective Tommy Keough, for assistance in the matter. Keough had always been there for a favor; he had in fact first alerted Jerry that Carpenter planned to pass over Bangs for promotion. Keough went over Carpenter's head—not for Bangs, but for Clemente. With Clemente, McKenna, Keough and MDC Commissioner Guy Carbone, a man Bangs admired, on his side, Joey eventually received his promotion in April 1980. Carpenter himself had the task of pinning the gold sergeant's badge onto Bangs' uniform, a moment that delighted Joey as much as the promotion itself.

But at the end of the day, Bangs' involvement with the sale of stolen civil service examinations was minimal compared to Clemente and Doherty's. Although Joey helped create answer keys and identify potential buyers for Clemente, he never took money in exchange for exams; he merely passed the test on to friends who would later be in positions of power and able to repay the favor. Joey's currency was favors, and his account grew quickly.

The higher ranking the officer, the bigger and better the favor returned, so Clemente and Bangs concentrated on filling the upper echelon of both the MDC police department and forces in the surrounding cities and townships in the greater metropolitan area. Whenever a position opened for a chief, captain or lieutenant, they put their heads together to determine the best candidates for the job—and who would be interested in their assistance. Sergeant slots were more prevalent, since there were usually additional openings for that rank in each department. Although the real money was in the City of Boston, before long the trio believed they could eventually control all the police departments in the State of Massachusetts, within reason. With one more step, Bangs and Clemente believed they could make themselves invincible.

Bangs and Clemente now had the best positions and assignments they could hope for. They had tested the limits of the law and the patience of their peers. Nothing had stopped them thus far, and they could see nothing in the road before them. The beast they had been building—criminal bones dressed in law-enforcement flesh—was groaning to be unleashed.

Bangs received his promotion to sergeant in April 1980, with the badge ceremony presented by MDC Police Superintendent Larry Carpenter.

The MDC Underwater Recovery Team in 1963. Above: Thorpe (3rd from left, standing), Flowers (third from right, standing) and Clemente (second from right, sitting).

COLLEAGUES IN THE METROPOLITAN POLICE

Larry Cleary

Bobby Clemente

Jerry Clemente

Richard Feeney

Dan Gately

Tony LoConte

Robert Mannke

Joe McCoy

Frank McDonald

Dick Nazzaro

Bobby Powers

Frank Thorpe

Thomas Troy

Joseph Vitiello

Anna Maria College

The Trustees of Anna Maria College, Paxton, Massachusetts
on the recommendation of the Faculty of the College have conferred upon

Joseph Paul Bangs

the degree of

Master of Arts in Criminal Justice

together with all the rights and privileges thereunto appertaining in recognition of
the fulfillment of the requirements for this degree.

In Witness Whereof we have hereunto subscribed our names and affixed the
Seal of the College this first day of June nineteen hundred and eighty.

William V. Guerin
Chairman of the Board of Trustees

Bernadette Madore, S.S.A., Ph.D
President of the College

National Automobile Theft Bureau

Certificate of Achievement

Awarded To   SGT. JOSEPH P. BANGS

in recognition of your satisfactory completion of
the course of study in   AUTOMOBILE THEFT INVESTIGATION

in cooperation with   METROPOLITAN POLICE ACADEMY
MEDFORD, MA.

issued this date   FEBRUARY 1981

C. W. Hannert

CHARLES W. HANNERT
Chairman, Governing Board

Paul W. Gilliland

PAUL W. GILLILAND
President

BREAKING THE TRUST

THE RED CARPET LOUNGE WAS A POPULAR WATERING HOLE located in downtown Quincy, Massachusetts, owned and operated by Tommy Delaney ("Red"). Red's brother, Frances Delaney ("Franny"), had married Joey Bangs' aunt Jean, and Joey and Franny spent most Saturday nights drinking beer and shooting the shit at the home of Joey's grandmother, Columbia Salerno. In fact, the entire Salerno–Bangs clan gathered there religiously each weekend to visit the family matriarch and share a traditional Italian dinner.

The Delaney brothers were a scrappy pair, born and raised on the mean streets of Savin Hill. Franny worked full time at the Massachusetts Registry of Motor Vehicles and held down a second job as night manager and barkeep at the Embassy Lounge in Somerville. He was a tough sort who adored beer, abhorred drugs, and tolerated no bullshit from drunken bar patrons.

A wheeler-dealer who could fence anything, Red fit in well with a broad cross-section of improper Bostonians. Apart from business, Red relished fine living. He loved his top-shelf whiskey and brand-new Cadillacs and Lincolns, and he always dressed impeccably—even if his style was casual—in high-end collared shirts and leather jackets. Red was a real player who knew everyone worth knowing in Boston's underworld, even though he himself was not a violent man. Bangs in particular respected his uncle Red's opinion and stopped by The Red Carpet at least once a month to see if Red needed anything done or to run a scheme by him for suggestions before putting it into play.

The Red Carpet was considered neutral turf—with an unwritten rule that anyone who had yank remained anonymous—and criminals of every kind congregated there to enjoy a quiet evening, make a business introduction or close a deal, without harm or foul. The lounge was also a premier spot to unload stolen goods; Red was a master coordinator who could fence anything quickly and quietly, another reason he and his establishment had such a solid reputation and high standing in the minds of so many figures in both the criminal and law enforcement worlds.

Among the frequent patrons of The Red Carpet were Boston's Irish mobsters, including Southie's self-proclaimed ward boss—and FBI mob informant—James Bulger ("Whitey"). Bangs and Bulger had had a few run-ins back in the day and never cared for each other. Bangs had even threatened to kill Bulger on more than one occasion. And despite his own reputation, Whitey wanted no part of Joey and called him a "sick fuck"—among other choice monikers.

Ironically, Bangs had become friendly with Whitey's brother, John Bulger ("Jackie"), who was a court officer and later a magistrate. Bangs was also sociable with a third Bulger brother, former president of the Massachusetts State Senate and president of the University of Massachusetts, William Bulger ("Billy"), whom he had met years prior while working for the Capitol Police at the State House.

In addition to serious business, The Red Carpet offered plenty of entertainment. Under the cloak of its discretion policy, Bangs often showed up with his groupies. Joey knew he could womanize at the lounge without fear of reprisal, even by Uncle Red or Aunt Gloria, and adultery became a vice in Bangs' life that would eventually deal a fatal blow to his marriage.

Bangs partied hard—and with impunity. One late evening in the fall of 1979, Bangs strolled into the Red Carpet with his stripper girlfriend, "Kathy," a smoking-hot sexpot in her early twenties who worked at the Attic Lounge, a popular Combat Zone strip joint owned and operated by Joe Malink.

Knowing Joey's girlfriend was an exotic dancer, Red pulled Joey aside. He explained that a dear friend had just been released from prison and wanted to know if Kathy would give him a dance. Bangs didn't give a shit, so he told Red to clear the bar. Red removed the glasses and bottles, locked the front door, and cranked up the jukebox. Ever the gentleman,

Bangs gave Kathy a boost onto the oak bar where she did her thing for the delighted parolee, a man Bangs had never met before nor saw after.

After the free half-hour striptease, which netted Kathy hefty tips from various patrons, the establishment emptied out, and Red once again pulled his nephew aside. This time, he wanted to speak in private, so they excused themselves from Kathy and found a secluded booth at the rear of the bar.

Red didn't waste a moment. Another friend of his, recently released from a Rhode Island federal penitentiary after serving time for conspiracy to distribute stolen goods, was flat broke and desperately needed a quick score. Joey asked how far the man could be trusted. Uncle Red simply nodded once: one hundred percent. Red knew the man and vouched that he was as solid as they come.

"What's his specialty?" queried Joey. "I don't need any more stick-up or B&E guys."

"Alarms," Red answered, smiling broadly.

"Is he capable?" Joey followed.

"Best in the country."

Joey returned the smile. Red insinuated that Joey and this guy also had a few mutual acquaintances, but he didn't say who. Red never mentioned names, and he made personal introductions only when he could vouch for all parties without reservation. Even then, he usually recommended that they use fictitious names while doing the job together, for protection in the event one got pinched and the other did not. *No honor among thieves*, as the saying goes.

Bangs had encountered many self-proclaimed alarm experts over the years, but he had never had the pleasure of making the acquaintance of a professional like the one he was about to meet. But since Joey didn't know the man's name, he couldn't do his homework. Nevertheless, Red's word was golden, and Joey told him to set up a rendezvous.

▾ ▾ ▾

Shortly thereafter Bangs and Brother O'Leary held a pivotal powwow with Clemente at Jerry's home in Medford to inform him they might have an experienced alarm guy at their disposal. Clemente was more than pleased; he was genius with a lock or safe but much less proficient with alarms. He could Mickey Mouse a bell alarm, for instance, but not much more than that.

Clemente prodded Bangs for details about the alarm guy's capability and credentials, but Joey told Jerry only what Red had related, verbatim, how this guy was supposedly the best in the country. Bangs could barely contain his excitement and rambled about the possibilities a real pro might bring them.

As the conversation unfolded, Bangs mentioned he had his eye on an electronics store just a stone's throw away on Mystic Avenue in Medford. His idea was to rip down an entire wall in the rear of the building, back a tractor-trailer up to the opening, and clean out the joint. Bangs had secured a place to house the stolen merchandise, and with Red's assistance, he had already lined up a number of fences who were eager to get in on the hot market for big-screen projection televisions.

"How much are we talking?" Jerry wondered aloud.

"Maybe two hundred grand a piece, give or take," Joey replied calmly.

A decent take, for sure, but Clemente's wheels were spinning faster.

"Fuck televisions," Jerry interjected. "If this alarm guy is really that good, I've got a bank!"

Joey thought Jerry was pulling his prick. "And which bank might we be talking about?"

"Depositors Trust," Jerry blurted, his giddiness building. O'Leary snorted with excitement. Bangs was skeptical, but Clemente claimed he had blueprints to the bank—which, by the way, he never produced—and that he and Medford police sergeant Tommy Doherty had already discussed the possibility of robbing it, since Tommy had observed that security in the building was lax.

Immediately after the meeting, Clemente called Doherty to fill him in on the developments, and the crew was off and running. All that remained was to meet the mysterious alarm expert.

∨ ∨ ∨

On an overcast Sunday afternoon less than a week after their initial conversation, Bangs received a call from Red Delaney. Joey rarely got calls concerning thievery at home, especially on a Sunday; Sunday was a sacred family day, even for those without family or religion.

Always discrete, Red made small talk, asking whether Joey had seen Franny and Grandmother Columbia the previous evening, and then suggested they grab a drink later that afternoon in Somerville. Although Bangs had planned to remain at home all day in Tewksbury, thirty minutes away, he told Red he was headed to Columbia's house in Somerville, and, sure, he'd love to meet for a drink whenever Red wanted.

Bangs was never late for a meeting, and if it was a serious sit-down like this one, he always showed up a little early and never failed to bring two locked-and-loaded weapons. On occasion, he also brought along Brother O'Leary for luck, and Joey definitely wanted this meeting to go well.

Bangs and O'Leary arrived at their usual Somerville gin mill, the Ten Hills Cafe, and ordered a couple beers to get warmed up. A few minutes later, Red Delaney strolled in as if he owned the joint, accompanied by a diminutive, unassuming gentleman named Arthur Barrett ("Bucky")—the alarm-breaker Joey hoped would provide the heart of his future illicit endeavors.

Bangs sized up Barrett. Bucky was short and a bit soft around the middle, but not overweight; average-looking with a receding hairline; and attired casually, even though he could dress the part when needed. He was low-key and soft-spoken and talked with an odd South Shore dialect and ever-so-slight lisp. Joey would soon discover that Bucky appreciated a good time, especially when lubricated with a Crown Royal whiskey on the rocks. And even though Bucky had influential friends in all walks of life, he despised violence of any kind.

Red wasted little time with introductions, and Joey waited to see what the modest man would have to say for himself. As soon as Barrett spoke, Bangs knew he had been around the block a few times; Bucky was both educated and street smart, and he would in time teach Joey a thing or two about living large. When the conversation drifted to those damn Red Sox, Bangs excused himself to go to the restroom. Red followed.

"He talks the talk but looks a little meek," Joey remarked when Red arrived at the adjacent urinal. "Sure we can trust him?"

"He's already checked you out. Says you're vouched for."

Bangs looked at Red quizzically, zipped up, and headed to the sink.

"Your mutual friend is Jimmy Martorano," Red informed Joey.

Jimmy Martorano

It was news that Bangs never expected, and it put him at ease. Bangs and Martorano had known each other since the late 1960s, well before Joey's appointment to the Capitol Police. They met while Martorano was out of prison on a work-release program, selling supplies to local restaurants, including Uncle Nick Salerno's Villanova Lounge.

Nick was Bangs' favorite Uncle and a class act. Nick also owned a dry-cleaning business in Union Square that fronted a lucrative bookmaking operation—where Bangs learned the fine art of organized crime. Like Uncle Red, Nick had strong ties with both the Irish and Italian syndicates, and Bangs took advantage of his uncle's laundry list of contacts to make many underworld acquaintances, including Martorano.

Joey had facilitated accounts for Martorano with various club and restaurant owners, and Jimmy introduced Joey to the movers and shakers of New England's underworld, especially the influential Italians in Boston's North End. Bangs also had the pleasure of befriending Jimmy's father, Andy, a nightclub owner himself, whom Joey admired and thoroughly enjoyed playing cards with at the Villanova. By the time of the introduction to Barrett, Jimmy Martorano had become a powerful captain in the New England underworld.

"Does Barrett know I'm a cop?" Joey asked Red.

"He's known from the get-go." Red was enjoying dropping bombshells today.

Even though Delaney was family and Martorano a very dear friend, Bangs never trusted anyone completely, and Barrett would still have to win his favor. Joey and Red returned to find Bucky and Brother sitting silently at the table, waiting. Bangs got down to business.

"I understand you know a friend of mine," Joey said.

"That's right."

"What's his name?"

"Jimmy," came the simple reply.

"Answer me this," Joey probed. "Who's his father?"

"Andy."

"Does he have a brother?"

"Johnny," answered Bucky, referring to Jimmy's mob assassin brother.[*]

Bangs continued to grill: "What'd Jimmy say about me?"

"He said you were solid. Period."

"Fair enough. What can you do?"

"What do you need done?"

"Can you bypass an alarm?"

Barrett was short and to the quick: "Any alarm in the country," he nodded.

Joey was sold. Despite his appearance, Bucky was confident and cocky, and that's exactly what Joey needed.

"We've got our heart set on a bank," Bangs offered tentatively.

"Which one?" asked Bucky. "I'll need to check it out."

The name of the bank somehow slipped Joey's mind—he couldn't recall it to save his life. Barrett grew suspicious.

"How the fuck do you forget the name of the bank you want to rob?"

Bangs stammered that he had spoken only once about the job, just a few days prior, and hadn't expected to meet Barrett so soon. Besides, Bangs added, the name of the bank wasn't important, whereas he still needed to vet Bucky.

Barrett remained uneasy, and he looked to Red for an answer. Red tried to reassure him with a faint nod.

Joey stood quickly. "I'm gonna make a call," he told Bucky. "If anything doesn't check out, you and I will have a big problem."

Bangs instructed O'Leary to keep an eye on Barrett, gave a nod to Red, and entered the phone booth. The first call was to Jimmy Martorano, who vouched for Barrett without hesitation. Then, aware that Barrett wasn't eyeing him, Bangs dialed another number.

"Jerry, what's the name of that place we discussed the other day?"

Always overly careful when talking business by phone, Clemente simply described the place: "across the street from Brigham's Ice Cream." Relieved, Bangs nodded—*Got it!*—and returned to the table.

---

[*] Johnny Martorano confessed on national television to killing at least twenty souls, before he cut a deal for himself in exchange for informing for the FBI. Martorano has since been released from prison, after serving twelve years. For the record, Joey and Johnny had what Bangs described as a "personality clash," although out of respect for brother Jimmy, if the men happened to bump into one another, they remained cordial.

Joey played it serious as he approached the men. "Come on, let's take a ride."

Without a word, all four men exited the bar, piled into Bangs' Cadillac, and sped off.

Still suspicious of the unassuming Barrett, Bangs glared into his rearview mirror and questioned him about his name. Barrett explained he picked up the nickname "Bucky" from an insightful childhood friend who recognized early on that his pal had the love of a "buck"—or three, for that matter—and like it or not, it stuck.

∨ ∨ ∨

Bucky Barrett

Born on March 8, 1938, Bucky was abandoned young, along with his three siblings, by their merchant marine father. The children grew up in Maynard, under the less-than-watchful eye of a single mother, who never minded much whether the kids went to school or what they did as long as they stayed out of her way. When Bucky was eight, the state stepped in and placed him and his brother in Middlesex Academy in Tewksbury, a disciplinary residential school that housed truants and other problem students.

A naturally happy sort, Bucky rose above his family's dysfunction and misery and married his childhood sweetheart, eventually having four children of his own before divorcing. A few years later, he wed his second wife, Elaine, the plainly attractive brunette that Bangs would get to know well. Bucky and Elaine had two sons together.

As a young father, Barrett was always in a scramble for work, moving from a supermarket to a meat-packing plant to a heating company, where he finally found enough security to take night classes in steam engineering and receive his fireman's license.

On the side, Barrett picked up tips from his coworkers and classmates about servicing alarm systems and cracking safes, tips which grew into skills that brought him into contact with Benjamin Tilley, the renowned New England bank robber with close ties to Mafia *capo* Raymond L. S. Patriarca.

Under Tilley's tutelage, Bucky honed his skills with alarms and explosives, taking on ever-bigger gigs until he was convicted in the early 1970s for the theft, committed years earlier, of $400,000 in rare stamps from the Cardinal Spellman Philatelic Museum at Regis College in Weston. The senior partner on the job was none other than Joseph Maurice McDonald— "Uncle Joe," in most circles—the co-founder of the infamous Boston-Irish Winter Hill gang, the largest organized crime group in the country at that time. Because of this caper, Uncle Joe found his way onto the FBI's Most Wanted List—as he had twice before—while Barrett found himself on a musty cot in a federal correctional facility.

Bucky was pinched a second time for burglary of safe deposit boxes at the Parker House Hotel in Boston, and later for the larceny of a Dedham bank in 1977. Even though his sentences on both state and federal charges accumulated, Barrett eventually obtained a release from Plymouth Forestry Camp; he knew, however, that he would probably never escape parole.

▼ ▼ ▼

Bangs curbed the sedan at the intersection of Governors Avenue and High Street in Medford, and the men sat silently for a few moments, scanning Medford Square. A scrum of adolescent boys stood outside Brigham's Ice Cream on the corner, counting out coins to make sure they could buy enough dessert to spoil their dinner. The next shop to the right on High Street—Burns Optical & Hearing Aid Center—appeared to be closed already. And to the right of Burns, a man in an ill-fitting suit politely shooed the last customers from the white brick building before ducking back inside to lock the series of deadbolts that lined the door.

"Depositors Trust Bank, huh?" Bucky muttered. "Where's the box?"

Once again Joey peeked at Bucky and Red in the rearview mirror, then flashed a look at Brother, who responded with a wink and grin.

"Walk down the stairs on the side. At the bottom," Joey instructed. "Take a good look and don't worry if any cops roll up—I'll handle them."

Barrett and Delaney slipped out of the car, found the alarm box, and stacked a couple of H.P. Hood milk crates to boost Bucky high enough to examine the system. Upon opening the rubber-encased box, Barrett broke into a broad grin as he surveyed the dense, rainbow-colored arc of wires inside. He poked at the system, then pulled a nine-volt battery from his pocket and used it to mimic the signal sent to the police station, in order to isolate the alarm's current.

Barrett and Delaney returned a few minutes later, just after Bangs had located a parking space, and slid back into the vehicle—"Piece of cake!" Bucky blurted giddily.

As they drove back to the Ten Hills Cafe, Barrett explained that the alarm was outdated and might not even work. Joey and Brother lit up like newly adopted orphans at Christmas. Unable to contain his enthusiasm, Bangs stopped at the first payphone he found to call Clemente at MDC headquarters: *Piece of cake!*

The foursome finished the day with another cocktail before parting ways, and Bangs made sure Uncle Red knew he had earned a small cut for making the proper introductions, even though he would not participate in the actual robbery. Red was a heavy drinker at the time, and if he could have stayed sober, Joey would have definitely included him in the robbery for an equal share. But true to form, after the meeting with Bucky, Red went on a bender, and he and Joey didn't see one another for months.

❤ ❤ ❤

With all pistons firing, Clemente finally decided to introduce Bangs to Medford police sergeant Tommy Doherty. Bangs was already aware of Doherty and had heard about many of his criminal exploits through Clemente, but up to this point, he had never had the pleasure of actually meeting the gentleman.

The trio gathered at Doherty's home on Pleasant Street in Medford in December and soon discovered they had loads in common. Like Clemente, Doherty disliked "real" cops, with the exception of old-timers, as much if not more than Bangs did. Joey often boasted that during his fourteen-year tenure as an officer, he fought more headhunter cops behind police stations than he wrote citations. All three men detested making arrests: whether it was the sense of hypocrisy or an aversion to paperwork, the thought of busting a criminal made them ill at ease. But if someone had to be arrested, they would do it, if for nothing more than to maintain appearances and take home a paycheck, and Joey made hundreds of arrests during his storied career.

Doherty's distaste for honest police work manifested itself in other ways as well: he often dispatched Medford's working cops on wild goose chases throughout the city, sometimes for fun, other times so he could break into an establishment on the opposite side of town without fear of fellow officers rolling up on him. Clemente was more diplomatic with fellow patrolmen and always found a way to justify his actions by some twisted interpretation of department regulations. Clemente was also under the delusion that everyone on the force liked him, but most of the Mets didn't, because he—like Bangs and Doherty—was such a lazy prick when it came to actual law enforcement.

As charismatic as Doherty was, Bangs remained vigilant—no matter how much honor exists among thieves, it's still a group of thieves. Both of these guys were as crooked as a dog's hind leg, and Joey would never be the one sucking hind tit. In Bangs' mind, the electronics store was a sure bet for a solid payoff—and a more reasonable first outing—and he remained hell-bent on pulling it off, regardless of what they decided to do with Depositors Trust. Besides, Joey argued, if they pulled off the store, they'd be that much better prepared for the bank.

❤ ❤ ❤

A week later, Bangs set up a meeting with all the principals—himself, Clemente, Doherty, Barrett, and O'Leary. They congregated at the bank of payphones in the Howard Johnson parking lot at Medford's Wellington Circle, directly across the street from the MDC's Fellsway Division—the same spot they used for all the meetings leading up to the heist. The five men hopped into Doherty's Medford police cruiser and drove to another nearby parking lot to discuss their plans.

Clemente and Doherty were at last formally introduced to Barrett, whom Joey had previously referred to only as "Bucky." Barrett had taken a shine to Bangs but barely tolerated O'Leary's joking, for reasons that Joey never fully understood. Doherty had never met O'Leary, and he too remained unimpressed with Brother's distorted sense of humor.

After introductions and a bit of chitchat, Bangs broached the possibility of robbing the electronics store. Everyone listened politely to Joey's pitch, before Doherty finally piped up.

"Why take the risk for a couple hundred grand? We can do ten times that number at the bank."

Doherty was the most familiar with the bank, and he boasted about the amount of loot he had seen there during routine police inspections and details. He claimed there was so much cash at this branch that cashiers had to stack bags on the floor outside the vault door during the workday, because the main vault was bursting at the seams with currency. Doherty estimated conservatively that there was more than two million dollars in the bank on any given day, not including anything held in the twelve hundred safe deposit boxes. The men weren't interested in securities of any kind, but taking into account jewels and other valuables they could steal from safe boxes, they calculated they would easily walk away with half a million dollars apiece. *Fuck televisions*, Jerry repeated giddily. They discussed the broad plan and each one's duties in the run-up to the job, piled back in the cruiser, and returned to the Howard Johnson.

Once or twice a week after the initial meeting, Bangs, Clemente and Doherty—in full police regalia—accompanied Bucky to the Depositors Trust Bank after it closed so that Barrett could test the voltage of the hundreds of wires in the outdated alarm box. Week after week the men worked on the system. Doherty parked his Medford cruiser directly in front of the bank to provide the cover of a police presence, and Bangs parked in back where he—with Brother, if he came along—kept an eye out for passers-by or employees who might stumble upon them. Jerry held a flashlight for Bucky, who carefully inventoried the wires, pulling, separating and testing them in various combinations thousands of times and making notes about the alarm's inner workings in a small moleskin notebook.

At one point, the crew grew weary of the long hours of tedious work and began wondering whether they could bypass the alarm more easily at the Medford police station. In a ballsy move, Doherty and Bangs walked Barrett into the station one afternoon so he could check out the possibility.

While Medford cops walked in and out of the station, Bucky examined the city's alarm system thoroughly, before informing his partners there was no way to bypass the alarm from the station without alerting ADT Security Systems. The only way to pull it off was to continue the excruciatingly detailed work on the bank's alarm box.

Barrett was obviously more concerned about ADT than his partners were: Doherty had the inside connections to handle anything that came up at the Medford police station while Barrett was breaking the alarm. And if people approached the bank while Bucky was outside, Doherty likewise intercepted them and, as an officer on duty, directed them away from the building. Since Joey and Jerry were both quite a distance from their respective duty areas, they usually remained behind the scenes. Once Barrett had finished each day's prep work, the men hid in the back of Doherty's squad car until he had driven them a safe distance from the bank.

Most evenings during this time, Joey and Bucky went out for cocktails and discussed friends, family, and business. In fact, Barrett was quite open with his misgivings about working alongside rogue cops, and it was Joey's friendship alone that smoothed over Bucky's distrust of Doherty and Clemente and held the operation together.

On nights when they weren't at the bank, the crew met to flesh out the rest of their game plan, deciding that a long holiday weekend would work best. Easter was too soon and family commitments too difficult to escape, so they set their sights on Memorial Day—Saturday night through Monday night to work in the bank, plus the bustle of the town festival to distract from their comings and goings. And Bangs, Clemente and Doherty would bolster their alibis by volunteering to work when most other cops wanted the weekend off.

❤ ❤ ❤

Once Barrett had finished analyzing the bank's alarm system, he still needed a couple weeks to build an intricate bypass device to supplement the voltage from the original box when the crew killed the alarm. However, the bypass box required unique wire clips and other materials that were difficult to find, so Doherty and Bangs decided to do some "shopping" at the Time Warner Cable warehouse.

A few days later, Bangs and Doherty sneaked away during their police assignments and met at the company's building on Locust Street in Medford. Doherty picked the lock, and the two began scouring the storage areas for alligator clips, nuts, bolts, tapping equipment, and other hardware Barrett needed.

While Bangs and Doherty were preoccupied snooping around the warehouse, a shift supervisor for the company strolled in. Doherty remained icy cool: he informed the supervisor that while he and Bangs were patrolling the area, they noted that the side door was ajar and entered to investigate. Doherty ordered the supervisor to vacate the building until he and Bangs could sweep the premises to make sure there was no one else inside.

Doherty assured the supervisor that he would secure the building when he and Bangs left and informed the man that he was welcome to visit the police station to file a report, if he were so inclined. Doherty knew, of course, that the supervisor didn't give a shit and wouldn't be bothered to go to the station. The supervisor thanked Doherty for his help and left him and Bangs alone with the run of the premises.

The duo quickly gathered the items on Barrett's list, along with other materials they thought might be useful, and returned to the station where Doherty wrote an official report about the building's "open door" to cover his ass in the event the shift supervisor changed his mind about filing an account of his own.

Bangs was extremely impressed by the way Doherty worked over the supervisor, and his estimation of the sergeant grew. If it had been up to him, Joey later remarked, he probably would have just shot the supervisor and claimed he mistook him for a burglary suspect. But fortunately for all involved, Doherty's smooth approach prevailed.

❤ ❤ ❤

In March, Doherty had acquired a safe deposit box at Depositors Trust Bank so he could pace off the vault's dimensions for a rough diagram that Bangs had begun creating, on a paper napkin, of all things. Doherty also used the safe box as his alibi, knowing he would empty it on the big day. In fact, Doherty purchased an insurance policy for the contents of his box with the intention of making an additional score for himself.

By mid-April, the bandits began meeting at Joey's home in Tewksbury, where the real pro, Bucky, took charge and made final assignments for the actual heist. In the meantime, on April 20, 1980, upon accepting his sergeant's promotion, Bangs transferred from TOPS at Old Colony to the Upper Basin in Brighton.*

In the weeks before Memorial Day, Doherty worked his regular schedule every night and arranged to be patrol supervisor during the upcoming holiday weekend. All involved also agreed to chip in on a payment of twenty thousand dollars that Doherty claimed he needed to give to officer Arthur Burns, the "walking man" scheduled to work Medford Square on Memorial Day. In exchange, Burns would keep away from the bank and shepherd the crowds attending the holiday carnival to the opposite end of the square, which would be open nearly round the clock on Saturday, Sunday and Monday, May 24–26. To this day, however, Bangs is convinced that Burns knew nothing about the robbery and that Doherty himself pocketed the twenty grand.

On the second Tuesday before Memorial Day weekend, the crew began dry runs of their master plan: the first step was to note how long it took for security and police to respond to a breach. Doherty was on duty and already positioned in front of the bank, and when Bucky tripped the alarm, Bangs and O'Leary excitedly ran around the corner to watch the action. Medford police officers arrived within minutes, and Doherty waved them away, informing them that it was a false alarm. ADT Security never responded.

The following Tuesday, less than a week before the robbery, the men tripped the alarm once again, only this time with Barrett's bypass box attached. No police, no security. Barrett had built a masterpiece in a case the size of a cigar box.

With his work on the alarm complete, Barrett turned his attention to the tasks the others had been assigned. He asked Bangs about plans for transportation. Joey said he had considered borrowing partner Bobby Spencer's box truck—which he had used for innumerable other jobs—but knew Spencer would pry to know why he needed it and then want to be involved. Besides, the box truck was much larger than necessary and too conspicuous to park near the bank. Barrett was peeved that this detail hadn't been locked down.

---

* Bangs remained at the Upper Basin just a little more than six months prior to returning to the Lower Basin for the remainder of his law enforcement career.

"Why the hell have I been busting my back for three months if we can't get our tools to the bank or haul away the loot?" Bucky railed.

"Listen, Bucky," Joey snapped, "I'm a cop—I can get my hands on anything. Hell, Brother and I stole a New England Telephone Company truck in order to tap the line of someone we wanted to rob. Don't sweat it—we'll have a vehicle in plenty of time. And if I have to, I'll steal Doherty's Plymouth wagon."

Bucky found Bangs' answer amusing and backed off. The following day Bangs discussed the vehicle with Clemente, who then phoned Doherty at the Medford police station. Tommy agreed, and the crew had their wagon, current plates and all.

▾ ▾ ▾

Kenneth Holmes, aka "Charlie"

Barrett had been jumpier than usual the last couple of weeks, and even though everyone thought they were good to go, Bucky announced he wanted to bring in an experienced safecracker with whom he had previously worked, a guy he referred to only as "Charlie."

Bangs knew that Barrett liked him, but he was well aware that Bucky didn't appreciate his temper or the fact that he always carried two guns and a pair of hand grenades. Bangs had done his share of collecting for the underworld, and Bucky had likely caught wind of Joey's propensity for violence in any given situation. Furthermore, despite his friendship with Joey, Bucky knew he was the odd man out: Clemente and Doherty were a duo, as were Bangs and O'Leary. Bucky obviously wanted someone to watch his back as well.

Barrett's intuition was dead on. There had been much discussion among the others about killing Bucky after gaining entry to the vault. After all, Barrett was expendable at that point, and his half million dollars would certainly sweeten the pot for the others. However, if Bucky had a partner, eliminating two men instead of one—especially inside a cramped bank vault—would present a near-impossible proposition for the others.

Bangs himself led the barrage of protests over bringing in a sixth man. Although they came from very different backgrounds, one thing all these men shared was love of a dollar—pure, unadulterated avarice. As far as Bangs was concerned, bringing Charlie into the mix meant only one thing: another mouth to feed.

But Barrett laid out his case. There were two vault doors that needed to be opened, he explained, and he wasn't certain that he alone could crack them fast enough. Another expert like Charlie would give them enough time to sweep the vault and clear out before the weekend ended. Bangs countered that the two large freestanding safes inside the vault would be easier to crack than a fucking piggy bank. If it came to it, Joey offered, they could take a torch to the doors and simply peel them back, real easy like. But at the end of the day, the crew wanted their pivotal alarm expert and safecracker to be a happy camper, so they reluctantly agreed to take on the sixth and final partner.

A few days before the heist, the crew gathered to meet Charlie over sandwiches and coffee at the Denny's restaurant in Woburn, Massachusetts. When the others arrived, Charlie had already finished his meal and was starting into a slice of apple pie à la mode.

In his mid-twenties, Charlie was by far the youngest of the bunch, an average-looking guy who kept his body in shape and his thoughts to himself. Charlie told the group that although he lived in the Watertown housing project and had grown up in humble surroundings, he, like Barrett, adored fine living.

Charlie picked through his pie, careful to measure out equal amounts of pastry, fruit and ice cream, as he spun tales about his criminal endeavors. The crew saw clearly that he was an accomplished burglar and expert safecracker whose skills made even Clemente and Doherty envious. In fact, Bangs later learned that Charlie had been formally educated in the construction of safes and knew all the ins and outs of fortified armor.

Charlie also informed the men that he had been arrested only once, in 1977, for the theft of more than a million dollars in gold and silver from a precious metals refinery in Rhode Island. As much as they hated the thought of parting with another cut, in the end Bangs, Clemente, Doherty and O'Leary all conceded that bringing in Charlie was their best guarantee of having a pie to slice.

The final piece of the puzzle involved the equipment needed to break through the bank's ceilings and walls. Several days before the robbery, Bucky and Charlie met in the backyard of Bangs' house in Tewksbury for final tests with the high-powered drills and other equipment that Doherty had collected for the job. Bangs and Barrett had also traveled all the way to Harlem, New York, to purchase the special carbide-tipped core bits needed to drill through the vault's reinforced steel and concrete. After spending an entire day testing the drill on a concrete slab they had dragged into Bangs' yard, the men decided that they were as ready as they'd ever be. They wiped down the equipment and hauled it to their initial staging location—the basement of Brother's house on Trull Street—before moving it again to Doherty's garage, just a couple of miles from the bank.

Game Day

During the crew's final rendezvous over dinner on Friday, May 23, 1980, Barrett made it clear that he was not a violent man and would abandon the job if he found anyone, including Joey, carrying a weapon during the heist. For his part, Bangs was still concerned about his new acquaintance, Tommy Doherty, who was definitely capable, and there was no way Joey was going into the bank without hardware. Based on what he had seen, he wouldn't put it past Doherty to wait until his squad car was loaded with cash and jewelry, then kill everyone in the bank and drive off. Joey wasn't paranoid—he was careful.

Late on Saturday afternoon, Bangs was the first to pull up to Brother O'Leary's ramshackle dwelling. He had a plan to screw with Bucky, to test the nervy fellow before the gig. So he laid out a vast array of weaponry on Brother's kitchen table, picked up a revolver to clean, kicked up his heels, and waited.

Bucky and Charlie arrived a short time later, chattering excitedly about the gig as they entered the front door. But Barrett's face reddened when he saw Bangs' arsenal, and he demanded that Joey pack up the weapons, or he and Charlie were leaving. Bangs tossed one of the Mac-10 machine guns toward Barrett, but Bucky stepped out of the way, allowing the weapon to clank to the floor and slide across the linoleum; he would not even touch a gun. Deep down, Bangs admired that Barrett was not a violent creature—and he told him so. And Barrett, despite being extremely guarded, still had full conviction in Bangs.

That evening, Joey, Brother, Bucky and Charlie had dinner at Twigs Restaurant in Boston's Italian North End and then returned to O'Leary's home to wait for Jerry to arrive.

As the MDC's top cop, Clemente was permanent watch commander for six MDC police stations. He had worked midnight to 8 a.m. on Friday night and was back at work from 4 p.m. to midnight Saturday evening and off on Sunday, though technically he was on call throughout the holiday weekend.

Midnight passed, and by 12:35 Clemente still had not arrived. The men grew anxious—they had estimated the time for each step of the heist, and not knowing what unforeseen problems lay ahead, they feared losing a single minute. Then Brother started throwing out other worries.

"Maybe his car broke down," he offered.

"Not likely," Joey replied.

"You think he got cold feet?"

"Doubtful."

"What if he got in a wreck?"

"Will you shut the fuck up, goddammit?" Joey roared. "He'll show— and if he doesn't, you can rest assured he'll have hell to pay."

Exhausted yet amped on adrenaline, Clemente finally pulled into O'Leary's driveway around 12:45. Jerry had responded earlier that evening to an overturned peanut truck on Commercial Street in Cambridge, a fucked-up mess that took all night to clear. However, the late shift and the accident provided substance for Jerry's alibi, he told the guys, or so he believed at the time.

"No time for stories," Bangs scolded. "We're only an hour in and already dealing with bullshit. Let's get moving."

Bangs hustled into Brother's kitchen, and the crew stood silent while he radioed Doherty, who was on duty and had been staking out the bank the entire evening. Doherty radioed back and instructed the men to make their move, meaning to meet him at the garage behind his home so they could caravan to the bank together. The men downed one last toast for good luck and headed out.

Joey, Brother, Charlie, and Bucky loaded into Charlie's Ford Pinto. They met Clemente at Doherty's garage where the acetylene torches and their heavy tanks, high-powered water drills, twelve-pound sledgehammers, crowbars, sandbags, dynamite, large Army duffel bags, and screwdrivers, chisels, hammers, and smaller sledgehammers bundled up in leather work bags, were neatly packed into Doherty's station wagon. More stuff than they had initially calculated.

Driving a Medford police squad car, Doherty gave the crew an official escort to the Depositors Trust Bank, minus the flashing lights. Clemente drove the wagon, with Bangs riding shotgun and O'Leary in the back. Barrett and Charlie followed in the Pinto.

When they arrived at Medford Square, Jerry backed the station wagon up to the rear door of Brigham's Ice Cream Parlor, and Barrett parked around the corner from the bank on Governors Avenue.

Still wearing his police uniform, Clemente strolled to the front door of Burns Optical & Hearing Aid and picked the lock in seconds, not even bothering to look over his shoulder for any potential witnesses. Once inside, he bounded down the back stairs to the basement shared with Brigham's Ice Cream Parlor and opened the rear door for the crew to enter the dessert shop.

Outside the bank, Barrett fiddled with some alarm wires and set up his ingenious bypass box. Armed with alligator clips, a voltage regulator and probe, Bucky dismantled the antiquated alarm system without a hitch. Meanwhile, Clemente picked the lock on another door in the optical shop that adjoined the bank lobby. And because of potential smoke and dust from the drilling, Barrett then deactivated the smoke alarms and sprinkler system for the entire building.

The rest of the crew entered the building's common basement, tools and all, and Clemente secured the door behind them. Jerry would be the "point man" during the weekend, remaining behind in the basement beneath Brigham's Ice Cream Parlor and staying in constant communication with Doherty, who parked his squad car directly in the front of or behind the bank each night. Doherty and Clemente signaled via VHF police radios, which Bucky had rigged with their own crystals. They used regular police codes, in case a civilian happened to overhear, and set the radios to both Medford Police and MDC Police frequencies, to cover their bases. The "Number 1" radio was inside the bank, and "Number 2" outside; and only Clemente, Doherty, or Bangs—cops who knew the lingo—ever touched them. Doherty kept Clemente apprised of every movement around the square and any sound that emanated from inside the bank building.

All the robbers were dressed in dark clothing—work boots, dungarees, sweatshirt, scally cap and leather gloves. Once inside the building, Joey huddled the men and pulled a small sack from his khaki-green duffel bag.

"Put these on," he said, as he untangled a wad of nylon stockings and passed them around the circle.

"Not really my style, Joe," Brother quipped.

"Put it on your head, dipshit."

"Is it clean?" O'Leary protested.

"Why didn't we just shave our heads?" Bucky offered.

"None of that Kojak bullshit for me," the vain Joey cracked.

Bangs explained that after his recent promotion to sergeant, he had taken a mandatory two-week FBI class on the latest investigation technologies, including DNA testing. Bangs reasoned that since detectives could now analyze strands of hair, they needed to do everything possible to avoid leaving any such clues.

Joey further assured his partners that he had concocted another plan to skew any potential DNA evidence. A couple of months earlier, Bangs had met at a Dorchester bowling alley with members of the Kingston Gang, the famous quintet of violent, takeover-style bank robbers from Montreal. Barrett had refused to launder money for them, and they were in Boston, intent on killing him. So Bangs sat down to try to smooth out the situation. Even though the Kingston Gang relented and allowed Barrett to walk, they were so difficult to deal with that Bangs decided to kill two birds with one stone: he collected the saliva-doused cigarette butts the gang left behind so he could scatter them about the bank. Protection for him and his partners, comeuppance for the Kingston Gang.

Fully dressed and armed with gear, the men made their way up a set of stairs from the basement into the optical shop, and then proceeded to scale a folding ladder into a loft space above the store, which was separated from the space above the vault by a cinder block-and-concrete firewall. The men breached the barrier in less than fifteen minutes: they jackhammered six holes to weaken the wall, knocked out the center with sledgehammers, and cleared the debris to create a large entrance to the top of the vault's ceiling.

Before drilling into the vault, Charlie laid down a heavy burlap covering to minimize airborne dust and debris. Barrett next placed a cardboard template over the burlap sack and used spray paint to mark the spots where Charlie and Brother were to drill.

Luckily, the robbers discovered that Burns Optical & Hearing Aid had just recently remodeled their location, and their loft now housed heavy-duty electrical outlets used for their new high-voltage machinery, so the men tapped the outlets to power their own tools: high-speed, water-cooled core drills to grind through three feet of concrete and acetylene torches to slice through the steel bars embedded within the ceiling. Barrett plugged in the drill, and the men covered their faces with dampened bandannas to filter the air. They were in business—there was no looking back.

Charlie plowed through the first layer of concrete in a matter of minutes and began cutting the rebar with a torch while O'Leary cleared the debris. Bangs and Barrett stood aside, acting the part of supervisors, goading and teasing the grunts. The crawl space quickly became as hot and humid as a steam room, and as Charlie drove deeper, the drill squealed incessantly as it bogged down in the steel and concrete. Even with his experience in construction and extensive research on vaults, Joey was surprised to see how many layers of steel protected this particular bank branch.

After a half hour, the men were getting nowhere fast. There was so much dust and debris, they realized they had to modify their plans to deal with it. Clemente radioed Doherty and asked if he knew where they could get a commercial shop vacuum. The always resourceful Doherty radioed back that he'd have one there in no time, and within fifteen minutes, one was waiting at the back door to Brigham's. Clemente lugged the machine up the stairs to the crawl space, and Barrett cleaned out the channels. However, the drill continued to bind and lock up, so left with no alternative, Barrett decided to use dynamite.

At about 2:20 a.m., Bangs heard unusual noises. He shushed the men to get a better listen—a woman's chattering and a high-pitched whine pierced the silence. Bangs alerted Clemente, who radioed to Doherty outside.

"One to Two: What the fuck? We're hearing something here!"

Doherty scampered from the cruiser to investigate the area, finally peeking through the window of the adjacent Brigham's Ice Cream Parlor. Inside were the owners, John Bonaparte and his wife, who babbled incessantly while helping her husband inventory supplies. Then Doherty noticed the source of the whining: the Bonapartes' German shepherd, who was pacing in a panic around the store, irritated by the squeal of the drill in the loft space above, his cries toward the ceiling unheeded by the preoccupied owners.

Doherty banged on the front door, startling the Bonapartes and aggravating the dog. He asked Bonaparte why he and his wife were working in the middle of the night on a Saturday during a holiday weekend. Bonaparte explained that they had recently purchased the place and that the rush of Memorial Day festivities had depleted their stock.

Doherty began to spin a tale to hurry the couple along: there had been a rash of lootings, burglaries and vandalism that evening, he explained, in part because of all the celebration and in part because the cops were short-handed due to the "blue flu" that struck the police force each and every holiday. For good measure, he added a little lecture on the dangers of operating a cash business such as Brigham's—from both thieves wanting loot and officials wanting bribes—and he encouraged the Bonapartes to wrap up their work as soon as possible. The law-abiding couple was out within minutes.

The coast clear, Doherty radioed: "Two to One: you may resume."

Bucky got back to prepping the blast. Bangs insisted that Bucky go easy at first and use only the minimum amount of nitro needed to evaluate the strength of the ceiling and the sound of the blast. Barrett decided to try a quarter stick. With surgical precision, Barrett sliced the stick with a plastic knife, but the dynamite was so old, the nitro had liquefied and began oozing out. Bangs and the others got jumpy, but Barrett was as calm as if he were slicing a ham sandwich; he finished the cut, ran a fuse down the folding stairs and attached it to an electrical charge.

Because the bank was located in a dense residential area only a hundred feet from an apartment complex, the men had brought dozens of sandbags to place on top of the TNT to muffle the explosion and direct the concussion downward.

Bangs radioed Doherty for clearance and fired the charge—BOOM!

The initial blast was minimal: Doherty didn't hear a fucking thing, and the concrete didn't budge a fucking inch. "Go for a half stick," Bangs instructed Barrett.

Before they detonated the second charge, Bangs ordered O'Leary, Barrett and Charlie to move close to the back door so that they could hide in Doherty's cruiser if something should go awry and the police arrive. For their part, Bangs and Clemente knew all the Medford cops and could talk their way out of any situation.

Barrett carefully incised the sweating dynamite, ran the fuse, set the electrical charge, and awaited Doherty's signal. **BOOM!**

"Getting kind of loud!" Doherty radioed to Clemente.

Clemente asked Doherty if any lights had come on in the adjacent apartment building, and to everyone's surprise, the answer was no.

After the dust settled, the men returned to the loft and found that not only had the explosion opened a workable hole in the concrete and steel below, but it had also blown a two-foot vent through the roof above. Rainwater from the day before dripped from the edges of the opening, and a column of humid, fresh air dropped into the space. The men gazed at the stars glistening in the sky, then peered through a four-inch opening in the floor, surrounded only by flimsy reinforcement rods, into the bank vault.

Barrett sliced through the rods with a blowtorch, and Charlie and O'Leary again set to work on the concrete with drills and jackhammers. Within a half hour, the men had cleared a two-foot aperture, and they were in.

"Popcorn!" Clemente radioed Doherty, signaling that they had breached the vault. Bangs lay on the floor and dropped his head into the hole, peering about the room with a flashlight. He noted that the hole was actually a few feet from their intended mark, but it worked better than planned because it put them directly above a bank of safe deposit boxes that they could use as a platform to step down into the vault.

Bangs secured a rope ladder to a support beam, and one by one, the men disappeared into the hole, except for Clemente, who remained in the loft with the radio to supervise and check in regularly with Doherty on the street.

The thieves were ecstatic, but nobody dared celebrate yet—there was too much work ahead and too many things that could go wrong. They still had to break through the double doors to the main vault. Clemente began passing blowtorches and other equipment through the hole, but within a short time Brother O'Leary began having trouble breathing in the dusty room and was compelled to trade places with Clemente.

With renewed focus and energy, Barrett and Charlie fired up the torches and lit into the corners of the metal doors leading to the main vault, which piggybacked the safe deposit room. They stripped the panels from the doors with crowbars as if they were fruit peels and squeezed their way through the opening.

Meanwhile, Bangs had begun working on the safe deposit boxes, attempting to break the two locks in the center of each door with a hammer and screwdriver. His first strikes had little effect, and in frustration he swung again hard and broke his screwdriver.

"Goddamn screwdriver!" Bangs screamed.

"Goddamn cops!" Charlie yelled from inside the main vault. Bucky joined in the shouting, both of them going berserk, kicking the walls and thrashing about.

"I knew I never should've trusted you fucking cops!" Bucky exclaimed. "Doherty said two million in cash—easy! There's not more than a hundred grand here!"

"You gotta be shitting me!" Bangs murmured.

Charlie burst through the door: "I'm going to find Doherty!"

Bangs shoved Charlie against the wall and pinned him with a forearm across the chest: "Your ass'll stay right here."

Charlie struggled against Joey's grip, cursing him and his cop cronies, while Clemente rushed into the vault to see for himself, ranting as he went. Hearing the commotion, Brother peeked down from the hole in the ceiling and yelled at Joey to find out what was happening.

"You candy-asses shut the fuck up so I can think, goddammit!" Joey yelled. "I'd kill Doherty myself if he were here," he added without blinking.

And he would have: despite Barrett's protests, Bangs had sneaked in his .38 Special, in the event something like this happened. Joey made eye contact with each of the men.

"It's fucking four o'clock in the morning and I didn't get all dressed up for nothing," Joey continued. "So here's what happens next: there's twelve hundred safe boxes in this room . . . let's air 'em out."

"Fuck that!" Barrett retorted. "The boxes were supposed to be a bonus. I ain't risking ten years in the joint for a few grand and some trinkets. I'm out."

Barrett moved to leave, and Bangs pushed Charlie aside, grabbed a three-pound sledgehammer and swung wildly at a box near Bucky's head. Barrett stopped dead in his tracks as Joey wound up and took another swing, smashing the door on the safe box and completely breaking it off the hinges. The door clanked to the ground in a pile of dust and concrete.

"You're a crazy motherfucker, Bangs," Bucky exclaimed. "I'm taking my cut now." Barrett ran into the vault, followed by Charlie, and they and Clemente set about gathering and counting the cash.

Bangs flailed at the rack of boxes with the sledgehammer, cracking doors and shattering hinges on a dozen random cubbies. He pulled open the door on one box after another and then stopped abruptly and studied the boxes. *Fuck me*, he whispered to himself.

"What is it, Joey?" Brother asked tentatively.

Joey reached into a box, grabbed a roll of bills and tossed it to Brother. "A little lunch money for ya," he winked.

O'Leary perked up, shimmied down into the room and joined Bangs in stuffing his pockets with cash, diamonds and strands of pearls. In fact, Brother's wife Margie had sewn additional oversized pockets inside their baggy clothing for just such an opportunity.[*]

The other thieves were still busying themselves in the vault, pissing and moaning about the paltry take, arguing over the count, one-upping each other with threats against Doherty. Joey picked up the hammer and banged and yelled some more to keep his cohorts thinking that he and Brother were hard at work, when in reality they were filling their secret pouches with loot. Only when they had filled their pockets to the brim did they begin dropping the boxes' contents into the duffel bags. Joey busted open a few more doors, flashed Brother a grin and yelled into the vault: "Hey, boys, the real bounty's in here!"

The men in the other room were too absorbed with counting the cash to respond, except for Barrett, who came to the door and watched for a moment as Bangs hammered away at hinges.

"The doors open from left to right," he observed. "It'll go faster if you break them in the opposite direction." Bangs thanked him, and Bucky disappeared again into the vault.

Armed with Barrett's advice, Joey quickly opened thirty more boxes before Doherty radioed that it was almost sunrise and time to stop. But Bangs was on a roll and had no intention of slowing down. Clemente, Barrett and Charlie reemerged from the vault and looked on silently, in greedy anticipation.

By 5:30 a.m., it was light outside, and Doherty radioed a second time. The robbers finally got the message, gathered their tools and hustled back

---

[*] Brother and his beloved wife Margie (née Long) were married for 42 years before she passed away on March 14, 2006.

to Brother O'Leary's Trull Street basement while Doherty returned to the Medford police station to sign out.

∨ ∨ ∨

Originally, the men had planned to remain at O'Leary's home in Somerville to divvy up the loot, but Bangs convinced them it would be safer to gather in the serene surroundings of the suburbs. When Doherty arrived, he and Clemente followed Bangs and O'Leary to Joey's Oxford Road home in Tewksbury, with Barrett and Charlie bringing up the rear in their Pinto. The men made the thirty-minute drive in less than twenty, never losing sight of one another and the three duffels they had divvied up, one per car.

When they arrived at the house around 7:00, Bangs entered the front door and let the dust- and debris-covered robbers into the basement through the rear bulkhead entry. Joey went upstairs to tell his wife, Judy, that he had something brewing and needed her, her mother, and the kids to go out for breakfast for a few hours. Oblivious of Joey's moonlighting, Judy didn't ask many questions in those days, so she gathered the family and left quickly.

Bangs returned to the basement a few minutes later with ice-filled glasses and a variety of sodas for his thirsty cohorts, who were by now both physically and mentally exhausted but still buzzing on adrenaline. Doherty stood out from the others: he sat to the side, still dressed in a clean police uniform, and something in his demeanor belied the fact that he hadn't participated with the others in the gritty work of breaking into the bank.

Barrett and Charlie—who were staying at a motel whose location they refused to reveal—went upstairs to shower, since they would certainly draw attention to themselves if they returned to the motel covered in cement dust. Clemente and Doherty relaxed as Jerry regaled Tommy with the details of the break-in. Sensing their distraction, Joey began puttering around the basement until he could find a moment to slip Brother a cloth bag containing an additional $100,000, more or less, in $100 bills.

Once Barrett and Charlie had returned to the basement, Bangs whacked up the vault money—about ten grand apiece. Barrett and Charlie ranted about the empty vault, and Doherty wilted under their tirade. Bangs began rummaging through a duffel bag, sorting the contents into piles, when all of a sudden his expression changed.

"What the fuck do we have here, boys?" he exclaimed.

The complaints stopped as all the men turned to see Joey drop a heaping handful of jewels on the table and pull out bundle after bundle of cash—about a hundred grand in all. Joey flashed a wink at Brother.

The others grabbed a second bag and dumped its contents on the floor, mesmerized at the sight of the cash and jewelry—black pearls, uncut diamonds, emeralds, sapphires, rubies. Bangs had their undivided attention now, and he explained that it took him only an hour to fill the bags while they had spent the time burning their fingernails for a lousy sixty grand.

A self-proclaimed jewel expert, Charlie whipped a loupe from his pocket with a flourish, grabbed some loose diamonds and bejeweled rings and started examining. Everyone watched in quiet anticipation. He finished studying the first batch, glanced up at Bangs, and then snatched several more stones from the pile. A few moments later, Charlie sat back in his chair, handed the loupe to Bucky, and eyed Joey.

Barrett scrutinized the stones for what seemed to be an eternity, then peered at Joey incredulously.

"This is what you took from the safe deposit boxes?" he quizzed. Joey nodded. His heart stuttered a beat—maybe this cache really was nothing more than worthless trinkets.

"And this was how many boxes?" Bucky continued.

"Forty or fifty, give or take," Bangs answered.

"Holy shit!" Bucky brightened. "Gentlemen," Barrett began, checking his thought with Charlie, who nodded in agreement, "I think we're in for quite a ride, 'cause this shit is worth *millions*. These pink ones alone'll net us each a million—conservatively." Bucky broke into a wide grin and flicked a gem in each man's direction.

The others sat silent; the calculations played across their faces as they recalled the room full of untouched safe deposit boxes. Of course, the stash in front of them didn't even include the cash, pearls, and gems that Joey and Brother had squirreled away. *Second thief, best thief*, went Joey's mantra. In for a ride, indeed.

The crew agreed to return that night for the rest of the boxes—*all* of them, Bucky now insisted—but they would take only cash and jewels, because stocks and bonds could be easily traced. And speaking from experience, Barrett informed the men that it was imperative that they not clutter the vault with documents that could easily pile up and impede their movement.

Barrett also expressed his concern that the optician next door might drop in, but Bangs reminded him that it was Sunday and highly unlikely the man would show up at work, especially on Memorial Day weekend.

"Fuck 'im," Bangs added. "If he shows up, I'll kill the motherfucker."

Barrett nearly passed out at the suggestion and protested that everyone had agreed—no violence.

"All right then, if he stops by, I'll hogtie the cocksucker instead," Joey offered. "And when I get finished with him, he'll look like a fucking mummy!"

The statement broke the tension, and everyone laughed—except Barrett, who knew that Bangs was dead serious. In the end, they all convinced Bucky that if the optician did pop in, he would be bound and gagged with duct tape until the job was over.

As the realization sunk in that they were looking at millions of dollars on the table in front of them—and God knows how much more in the vault—the conversation heated up when it turned to what they would do with the jewelry. Originally, they had agreed that Clemente would fence it through a contact in Florida, but once Bucky realized how extraordinary the pink diamonds were, he feared that Jerry's buyer wouldn't be able to handle the load. Barrett knew, however, that he had contacts who could sell the gems without a hitch. Clemente, of course, wanted to hold the jewels because he didn't trust anyone else.

The bickering continued until Brother, who had kept his mouth shut to this point, took the floor and declared, "If you boys can't agree, then I'll hold the swag!" The men stared at Brother in stone-cold silence and then burst into raucous laughter.

"That's the joke of the century, you asshole!" Bangs jeered.

In the end, Clemente took the bulk of the jewels, as originally agreed, and Bucky took the rare pink and yellow diamonds, along with an array of other precious stones. Charlie asked if he could have a dainty gold Movado watch for his young wife, and even though the others had nothing similar for their kick, nobody objected, and Charlie pocketed the piece. As careful as the men had been not to take checks or other negotiable bonds that first night, a few had accidentally found their way into the duffel bags, and Joey burned the potentially incriminating evidence in his fireplace.

The crew finished sorting the swag, cleared the basement and parted ways, but no one slept a wink all day. Doherty and Clemente returned to their homes, Barrett and Charlie to their secret motel, and Brother hung behind at Joey's to sift through their private stash.

The Mother Lode

Shortly after dark, at around 8:30, all the men met in the North End for a meal at Joey's favorite haunt, Twigs Restaurant, where Barrett again demanded that no one drink alcohol until the job had concluded. Just as they had done the previous night, the robbers regrouped at O'Leary's home to await Doherty's signal that he was on duty and the streets were clear.

Promptly at midnight, Doherty clocked in, drove to the bank, and sent the signal. The crew was there moments later, outfitted the same— including nylons over their heads—but toting extra duffel bags instead of heavy equipment and dynamite.

Once inside the vault, each man picked a column of safe deposit boxes and began banging away with small sledgehammers. Knowing from the night before how noisy it would be, Joey was the only one who had brought earplugs to damp the high-pitched concussion of steel on steel, and he laid into the boxes with gusto.

The men tore open the boxes like kids drunk with the frenzy of Christmas morning, but the excitement quickly morphed to greed. Their agreement to keep the vault tidy went out the window, and deeds, stocks, bonds, wills and other papers quickly piled up around the room as each man scrambled to open more boxes than his partners did. And no matter how careful the men were, hundreds of documents inadvertently made it into the duffels with the cash.

The thieves worked frenetically, but serious crime devolved into free-for-all silliness as the men giddily adorned themselves in necklaces and rings and brooches and earrings. Bangs and O'Leary of course filled their secret pockets with some of the more interesting pieces they discovered, always careful to be seen stuffing their duffel bags at the same time.

As the men grew tired, they sorted the contents of the boxes less and less, eventually just sweeping them into their bags. Bangs, however, occasionally glanced at whatever paperwork he found to see if he knew the box's owner. If he did, unbeknownst to the others, he tossed the contents onto the floor so that the belongings could later be recovered by the authorities and returned to the rightful possessor.

The second night at Depositors Trust yielded a mother lode of hard cash and priceless gems. When Doherty gave his signal at dawn, the exhausted crew reluctantly packed up and lugged their duffel bags— stuffed even tighter than the night before—up through the hole, across the loft, down the ladder and stairs, and out into the coolness of the disappearing night.

Instead of returning to Bangs' home in Tewksbury, the men retreated to O'Leary's in Somerville, where they didn't waste a moment before settling down to separate the cash and sort the gems, gold, silver, coins, stamps, and antiques. By 8:00 a.m., they were back at their homes to sleep through the day.

▾ ▾ ▾

On Monday, the third and final night of the heist, everyone gathered again at O'Leary's home, except for Doherty, who was back on duty, telling his supervisor he needed the overtime.

As senior sergeant, Bangs was assigned desk duty at Brighton's Upper Basin that night. He didn't want to call in sick on the heist's final outing, in case something went amiss: being accounted for at work on the police force was a priceless, airtight alibi. However, he needed to be mobile, and the night's charge had him chained to the desk.

So he and Jerry concocted a scheme to free him up for the gig, a little ruse involving Jerry's younger brother, Bobby ("Blackie"), who was also an MDC police sergeant at the Upper Basin working on the street as patrol supervisor.

Blackie was the complete opposite of Jerry: average height, a thick mustache, olive complexion, and a private, introverted sort who minded his own business and never put the finger on anyone. Nor was he the sharpest cop on the force—in fact, he made sergeant only with the help of exam answers provided by Jerry—and his promotion raised suspicions in the minds of some of his colleagues. MDC Lieutenant Danny Gately, for instance, was beside himself when he learned that Blackie had been promoted. He smelled something fishy—a gross mistake, an undeserved favor—and kept the notion filed away in the back of his mind.

Previously, Blackie had worked days at Revere Beach, but after his promotion, he was transferred to the Upper Basin and drew night shifts. And now the seed Jerry had planted selling exams would mature into just the right answer for tonight's dilemma.

At about 11:00 p.m., just before roll call, Jerry phoned Joey at the Upper Basin. Bangs purposely took the call in front of Blackie, who didn't have the slightest fucking clue what was transpiring. Bangs explained to Blackie that Jerry's girlfriend, Barbara Hickey, had a busted pipe in her house, and Jerry needed his help to fix it.* Bangs told Blackie he needed to save his sick days and asked Blackie to hold down the fort while he helped Jerry. Blackie bought the story and readily agreed to swap assignments for the night—patrol supervisor for desk sergeant—and sent Joey on his way, adding that he'd radio if anything significant happened.

Upon arriving at the bank, Bangs remained outside and acted as radioman. He parked Clemente's Cadillac sedan around the corner on High Street, overlooking not only the bank but also the entire neighborhood.

Doherty, also in uniform, worked as the inside radioman. Although Clemente had done little on the first night of the heist, he was hands-on the second and third nights; after seeing the loot Joey had amassed, Jerry was hell-bent on busting as many boxes as possible—and making sure he got his fair share.

However, on this night, the robbers were operating without the expertise of Barrett, who was traveling to Florida to establish his alibi. On Friday, Bucky had flown to Orlando with his wife, Elaine, under the guise of spending a holiday weekend with relatives and visiting Disney World. Bucky was on parole at the time for another heist but had convinced his parole officer to grant special permission for him to leave the state to visit extended family. On Saturday afternoon, Barrett returned to Boston on a

---

* Coincidentally, Jerry would also use Barbara Hickey as his alibi, for better or worse.

different ticket under an alias, arriving just in time for the break-in that evening. Monday morning he flew back to Florida under the alias to check out of the hotel, before returning to Massachusetts under his real name. Of course, Bucky paid for everything with his credit card—except the airline tickets under his alias—leaving an extensive paper trail that further bolstered his alibi.

Moreover, Barrett most likely figured that if he were going to get whacked during the job, it would be on the final night of the heist, when his work was complete, so the trip to Florida not only established his alibi but also removed him from harm's way, at least for the time being.

With everyone present except Barrett, the robbers entered the bank and looted another raft of safe deposit boxes. The evening passed without incident, and as daybreak approached, Bangs radioed the signal to Doherty, who passed the word to the men in the vault. By sunrise, they had broken into nearly eight hundred boxes and again stuffed five large duffel bags to overflowing.

While the others headed to O'Leary's home as before, Bangs made his way back to the Upper Basin to clock out, and then stopped by the Big Dipper Doughnut and Coffee Shop in Cambridge to pick up a celebratory breakfast for the fellows.

Assembled in Brother's basement, the crew split the cash equally, Charlie taking Barrett's share, which he delivered when Bucky returned from Florida. The men entrusted the diamonds and other jewelry to Clemente for fencing in Florida, and the "hard stuff"—pearls, vintage stamps, gold bullion, silver bars and coins—to Bangs for safekeeping at his home in Tewksbury.

Their business done, the men bade each other a hasty farewell. As the others exited, O'Leary motioned for Bangs to stick around: Brother had managed to fill his secret pockets again that final night and wanted to split the loot with his pal. By Joey's rough reckoning, he and Brother made off with an additional half million dollars, although he suspected the others had probably also pocketed loot surreptitiously.

After the heist, Charlie disappeared from everyone's radar, with the exception of a few encounters with Bangs and Barrett—one later that week, one in Atlantic City, and a couple of times at Bucky's South Shore home. On such occasions, Bangs or Barrett threw Holmes some additional cash for good measure. Because of Barrett and Bangs' relationship, Charlie decided to tell Joey his real name: Kenny Holmes. Holmes and Barrett were cousins in fact, and they trusted each other with their lives. They expected the same loyalty from Bangs. The other robbers melted back into their normal activities, waiting to see what the coming days would bring.

▼ ▼ ▼

On Tuesday morning after Memorial Day, bank manager Steven Nigro arrived at work to discover the break-in and nearly had a stroke, according to Tommy Doherty, who was the first responding officer on scene. The safe deposit room and vault were piled with debris—costume jewelry, documents, concrete, dry wall, and mud from rain and water-cooled drills. Though bank personnel and police could barely move around to assess the situation, Doherty worked the official police detail inside the bank—and did so diligently and with a straight face—until the cops had secured the perimeter and a cohort of FBI agents took over. By the end of the day, the bank's management estimated they had lost between twenty-five and thirty million dollars, the largest bank theft in history to that time.

The press quickly picked up the story, and Doherty himself gave an interview for *Boston Magazine*'s June 1980 issue. Word blazed through the streets, and the robbers soon heard that roughly a million dollars of the stolen currency belonged to members of the Winter Hill gang, and another substantial sum to New England's Italian syndicate, *La Cosa Nostra*.

▼ ▼ ▼

Bangs turned off the evening news, grabbed a bottle of vodka, and walked down into the cellar, where he retrieved a dirty duffel from a storage cabinet. He heaved the bag over his shoulder, trudged out to the backyard, and rolled an empty steel drum to the back of the lot. He pulled all the robbers' dark clothes and gloves and boots and nylons from the bag, drop them onto the ground, and dumped the rest of the duffel's contents, including reams of stock certificates and other traceable documents, into the can. A match, a breeze, and the papers crackled ablaze. Joey let the fire catch for a moment, enjoying the whirlwind of flames that withered the names and numbers on the pages, before he stuffed the clothing into the barrel. He dowsed the pile with vodka, sunk into a lawn chair and downed the rest of the bottle in one long swig, as a plume of smoke billowed up into the red sunset. Joey laid his head back and passed out from exhaustion. The real fun was about to begin.

The Depositors Trust Bank building has been converted into a restaurant, maintaining the bank's vault door as a dining room entrance and leaving the hole in the ceiling used by the robbers.

Above left, the hole the robbers made to access the vault area.
Above right, blocked off for the restaurant restoration.

CAUSE AND EFFECT

WITH NO TIME TO CELEBRATE, Joey Bangs showed up for his regular shifts on Tuesday from midnight to eight and Wednesday from four to midnight, commuting to work in his new Ford T-Bird, which now had a trunk full of gold and silver bullion, jewelry and rare coins, neatly packed into seven olive-drab duffel bags. Joey reasoned that the swag was safer with him at the Upper Basin police station than anywhere else on earth.

After work on Wednesday, Bangs met Kenny Holmes at the Howard Johnson on Montvale Avenue on the Stoneham/Woburn line. Holmes had agreed to deliver the bags to Barrett, who was just returning from Florida—one little twist to throw off anyone who may have been watching either Bangs or Barrett. It was a perfunctory exchange that lasted just a minute—no handshake, no chit-chat, no drinks: Bangs pulled the bags from his trunk and handed them to Holmes, who tossed them into his trunk and drove off without saying a word.

In the following days, Bangs worked overtime details along the Boston Harbor, where the tall ships graced the waterfront for the first time since the bicentennial celebrations of 1976. In his off hours, Joey had been toiling to destroy remaining evidence from the heist, given the flurry of activity from investigators who were now canvassing the Commonwealth for leads. By Sunday, he had completely cleared his home of illegal weaponry—sawed-off shotguns, machine guns, grenades, and silencers, which he relocated or disposed of—and other hardware and heavy tools, which he tossed into the harbor or into the Charles River behind the Lower Basin police station's boathouse. Bangs even got rid of a shotgun that Clemente had given him as a gift by duct-taping it to a cinder block and tossing it into the river from an overpass near the Upper Basin.

Joey also attempted to dispose of the leftover dynamite in the river, but the sticks wouldn't sink and remained visible as they floated downstream. Bangs ordered O'Leary, who was riding along on the errand, to jump into the murky water to retrieve the explosives, and Brother eventually sank them with a broken hockey stick, which Joey had used to crack some heads a few weeks prior.

Even though Bangs had tried to burn the stolen documents in his trash barrel, many fragments remained intact, so he decided to pack the ash-covered papers into a duffel, along with empty jewel boxes, and dump the lot into the Boston harbor. The following evening while on duty, Bangs picked up O'Leary in his police cruiser and drove to South Boston's waterfront, where he and Brother carried the bag out onto a floating wooden pier that, unfortunately, was still busy with commuter boats coming and going. When the coast cleared somewhat, Bangs dropped the duffel from the pier, but to his dismay, the canvas bag didn't sink and began drifting away from shore in the rapid current.

Worried that the bag might wash up on nearby Carson Beach, Bangs ordered O'Leary into the frigid water—again—but Brother balked because it was getting dark. Bangs scanned the area, then dashed into the adjacent yacht club and, hoping to commandeer a vessel, grabbed the first person he saw wearing a skipper's hat.

"What can I do for you, officer?" the tipsy yachtsman queried. Music to Bangs' ears.

"My Navy buddy," Joey explained, "was out on the pier having a smoke when his duffel bag fell into the ocean and floated out of reach. Would you be inclined to assist a fellow seaman recover his only belongings?"

The skipper agreed—anything for the Mets and a fellow sailor—so long as he could take a leak first. Joey rushed outside to school Brother about the plan and how to act.

"Listen, Brother, you're a sailor home on shore leave, and the skipper's going to take you out on his boat to retrieve the only possessions you have in this world. When you reach that goddamn bag, slice a hole in the side and sink the fucking thing. But whatever you do, don't let him see you."

"Relax," Brother laughed, always ready for a gag. "I know what I'm doing."

Famous last words, Bangs thought. "Don't fuck around, Brother," Joey warned.

When the skipper arrived at the pier, Bangs used the spotlight from his cruiser to illuminate the duffel bag, which had by now drifted far from the shore. Joey introduced Brother as the "Navy man" in question, and after the usual niceties, the skipper piped up that he himself was a former Navy man.

Bangs' heart sank: O'Leary didn't know the first thing about the seas. In fact, Brother hated anything water-related, even seafood.

Aware that the skipper was no doubt Irish, Bangs tried to change the subject by poking fun and telling him that O'Leary was Irish as well.

Brother ignored the ribbing and decided to break Bangs' balls.

"What was your rank, sailor?" he asked the skipper.

"Honorably discharged as a chief petty officer," the skipper replied.

"Impressive," O'Leary nodded. "I myself am a rear admiral."

Bangs nearly lost it, but the skipper was too drunk to register the comment, and Joey let it play, watching helplessly from the dock as the two men motored through the harbor toward the bag of incriminating evidence. Bangs soon lost sight of the boat in the gloomy night air and tossed out a prayer to the sea gods that Brother wouldn't fuck this up.

When O'Leary and the skipper returned about fifteen minutes later, Bangs pounced on Brother: "Did you get your duffel bag, young fellow?"

Brother played along smoothly: "You're not going to believe it, officer, but I got my fingers on the darn thing and at the very last second, it sank."

"A shame," Bangs offered. "Anything valuable in the bag?"

Brother flashed a grin: "Nothing I'd want anyone else to find. To be truthful, it was just some dirty laundry."

Joey continued the Good Samaritan shtick and asked Brother if he needed a ride anywhere, but O'Leary was quick to reply that he was all set: he was going to the yacht club to have a couple drinks with his new friend, the skipper, to thank him for his kindness.

Bangs was livid and pressed O'Leary: "I'm going right by the Navy yard, young fellow—I'd be happy to drop you off."

"Not to worry, my good man," Brother insisted, as he started into the club with the skipper. "I'll find my way home."

Bangs yanked him aside: "Never mind the bullshit, you prick!" he hissed. "There's no way you're going drinking with this clown, and that's final!"

The evidence was gone; the charade was over. To the consternation of the perplexed yachtsman, Joey expressed his gratitude, dragged O'Leary to the cruiser and shoved him inside, gave a last nod of acknowledgment, and sped away.

O Captain! My Captain!

Despite their efforts to avoid scrutiny following the heist, the Depositors Trust robbers found themselves under the microscope from day one. Even before the job, the crew assumed that law enforcement would first examine evidence that the theft had involved insiders. Clemente and Doherty reasoned that they would take the most heat because they resided in Medford and had something of a reputation for burglary. Plus, Doherty had been working his assigned route around the bank over the holiday weekend. Barrett, of course, took heat anytime there was a substantial score in the greater Boston area from a crime that involved a sophisticated alarm system. And it didn't help that Bucky's adversaries in the underworld were always feeding authorities all manner of stories that implicated him.

Fortunately, Doherty had the inside track on the investigations conducted by state police and the FBI—in fact, he was working inside the vault while the agencies completed their initial examination of the crime scene. As the FBI agents attempted to reconstruct the timeline of the heist, Doherty watched from the wings, amused by the miscalculations he heard. But despite their incompetence and errors, the FBI soon found their way to Jerry Clemente.

On June 5, just a week and a half after the robbery, FBI agent Gerald Montanari and his partner knocked on Clemente's door and asked if they could question him. During the routine interview, the agents showed Jerry various photos of Barrett, Doherty, and Doherty's brother-in-law, Jackie Gillen.

Clemente was caught completely off guard, but believing he was sharper than the feds, he reasoned that he could outsmart them and talk his way out of the mess. He asked the agents if he could speak off the record, and they agreed, although Jerry knew nothing was ever confidential with law enforcement, especially the compromised Boston office of the FBI.

Nonetheless, Clemente explained that he was a married man, yet a weak one when it came to women, and that he had spent a lot of time with his girlfriend, Barbara Hickey, during the weekend of the robbery. Jerry pretended to confide in the agents and offered to assist in any way he could, so long as his wife didn't find out about his dalliance. The agents listened respectfully, but Clemente couldn't be sure his story had convinced them. Hoping they would take his cooperative attitude as evidence of innocence, he offered to go somewhere else with them—away from his home and family—to answer anything they wanted.

Montanari lobbed a few follow-up queries and asked Clemente if he could search the residence. Again caught off guard, Jerry initially agreed, but abruptly changed his mind, claiming he didn't want to upset his wife. In reality, Jerry was worried not only about the bank swag, but also about another stash in his basement: a stolen television set, still in the box. As a compromise, Clemente offered to take a polygraph test—an agreement he later reneged on.

Bangs exploded when he heard about Clemente's alibi. In his opinion, it was a gross mistake that only gave the agents fodder for further investigation and undercut the trust and reliability of everything else Jerry would ever say about the weekend. The FBI now knew Jerry was a hypocrite and a liar, and he would never be able to chase away that cloud of suspicion. For Bangs, a woman was good for quick sex or a good meal or maybe a quiet evening in front of the TV, but never for something as vital as a solid alibi. If Joey had been in Jerry's place, he would have stated that he was home sleeping. Period.

After the agents left Clemente, they drove straight to Tommy Doherty's Pleasant Street home to conduct a similar interview. However, Doherty was wise and kept the conversation short: *Go fuck your mother.* The answer certainly didn't win Tommy any good will, but it put the agents on notice that they would get absolutely nothing from him. The next stop on the feds' itinerary was Bucky Barrett, who, like Doherty and Clemente, held his tongue and denied any knowledge of the Depositors Trust larceny. Bangs in turn expected a visit from the feds, but for reasons he never understood, his name never arose during questioning, and the knock at his door never arrived.

▾ ▾ ▾

In the run-up to the bank robbery, Bangs and Clemente developed a code for communicating by phone to arrange meetings where they could speak without fear of surveillance. *Come over to Jake the plumber's house for a card game* meant to meet at Twigs Restaurant in the North End, while *Meet me and Jake for coffee* meant they were to rendezvous at the Howard Johnson parking lot in Stoneham. They also met occasionally at a bowling alley in Dorchester, but they eventually stopped referring to "Jake" because Joey had made the acquaintance of Jake Rooney, a friend of Bucky Barrett's, and their using the name had brought Rooney some unwelcome attention.

Clemente also feared that his personal vehicle was bugged, and he never spoke a word about the robbery while inside the car. Instead, he and Bangs took long walks to discuss business whenever they met. They were also careful to avoid being followed, sometimes taking a circuitous route that tripled their drive, or using the time-tested trick of making three consecutive right turns, then pulling over to see if anyone had followed.

Shortly after the FBI visited Clemente, Jerry called Joey from a payphone at the Upper Basin station and suggested they "meet for coffee." They parked at the Howard Johnson and walked about a quarter mile down the street before Clemente told Bangs about the FBI's questioning. The news didn't surprise Bangs at all: even though Clemente and Doherty were both respected police officers, they were also known as renegades and thieves. Jerry asked if Joey would take the jewelry for safekeeping: he had temporarily stashed the diamonds at his father's home next door, and although there would be no way the feds could obtain a search warrant for Gerald Sr.'s house, Jerry didn't want to take any chances.

Bangs had warned Clemente early on about a potentially dangerous situation like this and berated Jerry mercilessly for being distrusting and greedy and dead set on holding the stones. The FBI were camped in front of Clemente's house twenty-four hours a day by now, Bangs added, and Jerry couldn't blow his nose without their knowing about it.

Clemente wasn't in the mood for a lecture. "Knock off the bullshit and help me figure this out," he chided.

"Tell me again exactly where you stashed the swag," Joey asked, both to see if Jerry was telling the truth and to buy himself another minute to think.

"Next door, in a crate tucked in the corner of my father's garage."

Bangs agreed with Clemente that the jewels were definitely safer there than at Jerry's house but still needed to be moved. Besides, Joey never passed up an opportunity to take control of a bad situation or perfectly good merchandise.

"I can't fence it now, you know," Jerry reasoned. "Who can we get to do it?"

"I haven't got that far yet," Joey retorted. "Nobody's fencing nothing if we can't get it out of that house."

So Bangs and Clemente brainstormed a plan. Jerry had consolidated the two bags of jewels into one duffel—bursting at the seams, but manageable. They knew the feds were on the watch around the clock, especially at night, although they hadn't always been able to identify the vehicles or pedestrians who were surveilling the house. Fortunately, the layout of the homes prevented anyone from seeing into the backyards from most angles, so they determined that Jerry could crawl from his house to his father's across the back and likely avoid notice.

The problem, of course, was getting the duffel out of the house and into a car and making a clean getaway. Anyone—Jerry, his wife, his father, Joey—coming out with a large bag would be suspect. Divvying things into smaller bags—and thus requiring more trips—presented more occasion for error or moments that might attract unwarranted attention. Bangs shushed Jerry and sat on the curb to think.

"Fuck it," he began. "Synchronize your watch. At three o'clock tomorrow, I'll drive down the street. If I don't see anything suspicious, I'll back into your father's driveway and release the trunk latch. You run out, throw the bag in, then get your ass back inside. And whatever you do, don't forget to close the goddamn trunk. They won't expect anything during the day. If we're really lucky, they'll be off getting coffee or dozing.

If we're less lucky, I drive like hell. And if they catch me, those no-good cocksuckers will have to fuck, fight, or run."

Bangs also instructed Clemente to place a cardboard silhouette of a man in the front window of his dwelling and to blast the radio to make it appear as if he were home.

"And you better make damn sure there's nothing else incriminating in your house," Joey admonished, "just in case the feds pull a rabbit out of their fucking brown derby and score an actual search warrant."

▾ ▾ ▾

At three p.m. the following day, the plan went off without a hitch. Bangs never determined whether anyone saw him make the pick-up, but within the hour he met Barrett at one of their prearranged locations and delivered the jewels into his keeping, but not before he filled a couple pockets with diamonds for his trouble, an additional bonus of about two hundred thousand dollars that he shared with Brother O'Leary.

By this time, Bangs and Barrett had come to trust each other deeply, and they met almost daily to travel to Braintree, where they buried a king's ransom of swag in a wooded area along a winding dirt road, making a crude map to help them find their treasure when they returned. Unbeknownst to his fellow robbers, including Barrett, Bangs also moved many of the items in his possession—mostly the gold and silver—to Cape Cod, where he buried them in the backyard of his Aunt Josephine's summer cottage.* The remainder he buried behind the fence of his own backyard in Tewksbury, just on the neighbor's side of the property line. Of course, Joey kept close tabs on the loot, especially during inclement weather, checking each stash at least weekly. And as the weeks passed, Bangs and Barrett became emboldened enough to retrieve bits of the loot to sell for a little extra jingle in their pocket, while Clemente and Doherty remained embroiled in an intense federal investigation.

---

* When I was a kid, my family spent many summer days at Josephine's cottage with the families of my father's cop friends. I remember well playing in this very backyard where Joey buried his treasure. Of course, Josephine had no idea that Joey was stashing anything—especially ill-gotten gains—on her property.

❤ ❤ ❤

When the crew first got word of the FBI's increased presence in the area, they all supposed that one of their fellow robbers was a weak link—and thus a link to be eliminated—but no one could figure out who it was. The fact that the feds picked up their trail so quickly after the crime was no coincidence, but the attention from the FBI would prove to be the least of their hassles.

Just after the feds came knocking, Bangs and Barrett were summoned to the North End to meet the formidable *La Cosa Nostra* captain Donato Angiulo ("Danny") at a restaurant on Hanover Street. Angiulo shared with Bangs and Barrett what he knew about the FBI's activity, including how the feds were using rental cars from East Boston. Little did Angiulo know that the FBI had come to Boston not to investigate the bank robbery, as everyone assumed, but to investigate and arrest him and his brothers, Gennaro ("Jerry") and Francesco ("Frank"), whose office was located on nearby Prince Street. The fact that there were a large number of agents on hand to investigate the heist was the true coincidence. As Bangs learned more, he began to suspect that someone outside his crew was feeding information to the FBI.

The criminal investigation came back around to Bucky Barrett. On June 21, the FBI and state police photographed Barrett in conversation with James "Whitey" Bulger, the self-proclaimed leader of the Irish mob, and his henchman, Steve "The Rifleman" Flemmi, outside Bulger's Lancaster Street garage in the North End, near the Boston Garden. It was obvious to investigators that Bulger and Flemmi were attempting to shake down Barrett, but they did nothing to intervene and simply continued to observe. Later that afternoon, Bulger and Flemmi met with Vernon Gusmini ("Gus"), who appeared to the investigators to have an established relationship with the gangsters.

❤ ❤ ❤

Gusmini was born and raised in Medford and attended Catholic elementary school with the Clemente brothers, becoming closer to Blackie than Jerry. Gus had a slight build and dark complexion and dressed appropriately for a nightclub owner, an occupation that no doubt contributed to his heavy drinking. Gusmini owned and operated the club Yesterdays on Route 1 in Saugus, next to the Kowloon Chinese Restaurant, and held a majority interest in a few shady strip lounges, including the Cabaret in Saugus and King Arthur's in Chelsea.

Bangs met Gusmini at a Back Bay lounge in the early 1970s, around the time he joined the MDC. Even though Uncle Nick made the introduction, Bangs never took to Gusmini, who more often than not talked out of school, dropping names—including Clemente's—and blathering on that if Joey worked the police job like Jerry, he'd earn a "barrel full" of supplemental income in payoffs and bribes. Bangs warned Clemente repeatedly to have a discussion with the loudmouth about his inappropriate behavior, but Clemente never seemed inclined to put Gusmini in his place.

Bangs later learned that the relationship between Jerry and Gus ran deep—Clemente had previously done "odd jobs" for Gusmini and had even attempted to sandbag a criminal case involving two of Gusmini's Mafia associates, Ricardo Oulette and Billy Oldham. The duo had been arrested by undercover MDC narcotics detective, Billy Thompson, for possession of one hundred thousand dollars' worth of drugs and another four hundred grand in ill-gotten cash. Despite Clemente's meddling, Thompson made the charges stick. And Jerry now had one more enemy on the force.

▾ ▾ ▾

A few weeks after the heist, Gusmini tracked down Clemente to deliver a message from the South Boston heavies. Bulger and Flemmi, Gus recounted, had kidnapped him at gunpoint, placed a hood over his head, taken him for a ride, and tortured him for two days, at times stabbing him with an ice pick. Bulger wanted his end of the bank loot, Gus continued, and he meant business. Even though Clemente could see no evidence of physical harm, his trust in the friend he had known "since the playpen" silenced his usual suspicion, and he bought the story.

When Clemente related the incident to Bangs, Joey surmised that Gusmini must have been the one to drop the dime to the FBI, and he offered to kill him. And Whitey, too, for that matter. The Irish hoodlums never bothered a person like Bangs—in fact, Joey was the player who took care of the serious players, and as far as he was concerned, Bulger, Flemmi, and Gusmini were all expendable. Clemente calmed Bangs and assured him he'd at last handle Gusmini, but Joey had his doubts.

Clemente denied to Gusmini that he had any knowledge of the Depositors Trust robbery, and he promised to let both law enforcement and the Mafia know about some of Gus's questionable dealings if he brought it up again. Gusmini's attempted shakedown of Jerry crumbled instantly.

But Gusmini knew his hunch was right—and he wanted a payday. He calculated a way he could not only get back at Clemente but also score some cash in the process, so he asked a Medford police lieutenant to act as an intermediary with the FBI. Gusmini figured the feds would pay handsomely for prime information about the bank theft, and he proposed a $500,000 payout. And he let the rumor run that he had a deal, even though the terms of his cooperation were never revealed. The only fact everyone agreed on was that U.S. Attorney William Weld later refused to turn over any information about the discussions to the state courts. Bangs always assumed Gus was full of shit.

But Gusmini pressed on. He wore a wire to a meeting in which he asked Clemente for $25,000 in order to settle the score with the mob once and for all. Willie Davis, the attorney who later represented Gusmini, also alleged that he possessed other taped conversations of his client warning Clemente to return the stolen money to the Mafia or suffer the consequences. Clemente didn't take well to being implicated in the robbery in this manner. As he wised up to Gusmini's machinations, he went on the offensive himself, recording conversations and collecting incriminating evidence against Gus that he provided to his superior officers in an attempt to clear himself of suspicion. Over time, Gusmini's strategy failed and his price tag dropped. Clemente eventually told him to fuck off.

Unbeknownst to Clemente and other MDC leadership, Gusmini's allies in the FBI tipped him off that charges against him were developing, and Gus left town in a hurry. The MDC had Clemente swear out a warrant in Cambridge District Court for Gusmini's arrest on attempted blackmail charges, but Gus couldn't be located for nearly two years after his last conversation with Jerry.

After Gusmini's disappearance, Clemente played the victim, contending that he and his family were in imminent danger. Despite

Bangs' advice to ride it out and stop drawing attention to himself, Jerry persuaded the MDC to place his family under round-the-clock protection until Gusmini was apprehended. Massachusetts state troopers accompanied the Clementes from the compromised sanctity of their Medford home to the Holiday Inn in Somerville, and following protocol, later shuffled the family to a safe house on Moon Island, deep in the crest of Boston Harbor.

While in protection, Clemente remained under the scrutiny not only of the FBI but also of plainclothes state police detectives—an arrangement that frustrated Jerry's mischief, especially his trysts with Barbara Hickey. So whenever Jerry needed to go somewhere unescorted, he phoned Joey and asked him to distract the agents until he could slip away. Clemente even had the gumption at times to call Bangs in the middle of the night to ask for a ride to Hickey's home. Clemente knew the feds had visited Barbara and were keeping an eye on her, and he wanted to see how she was holding up—or so he said. More often than not, Bangs reluctantly agreed to play chauffeur to Jerry's playboy.

State Police Lieutenant Detective Tommy Spartichino* finally arrested Gusmini in Florida on September 25, 1982. However, the MDC Police had jurisdiction in the case and sent detectives John Bacardi and Joe McCain† to Florida to drive Gusmini back to New England. At the time of his arrest, Gusmini was in the hands of Florida State Corrections for unrelated felony drug charges, and he waived an extradition hearing and returned to the Commonwealth without a hitch. Undoubtedly, the heist crew wanted to eliminate Gusmini, especially Bangs and Doherty, who were convinced he had provided the tip that put the federal investigation in motion. But now that Gus was in custody, revenge would have to wait.

As if it weren't enough to have Bulger and Gusmini looking for a piece of the take, the robbers soon discovered a long line of goodfellas

---

* Bangs and Spartichino had the utmost respect for one another. Spartichino (1929-2001) was one of my father's closest friends and like an uncle to me. Tommy was a Marine and MDC police sergeant before entering the state police, where he became a lieutenant detective and later a colonel. He worked as a robbery–homicide detective and solved more than 500 cases—a record in Massachusetts—where he retained "Top Cop" status. Our families spent many summers together in York Beach, Maine, where Tommy and his wife, Ann, owned a cottage close to ours, which was across the street from the home of former MDC Police Commissioner John Snedeker ("Jack"). I have fond memories of competitive games of bocce on the beach with these men—Spartichino, above all, always played to win.

† My father and I knew McCain well. Both McCain and his son, a police sergeant in Somerville, survived gunshot wounds received in the line of duty.

circling like seagulls, including a local Mafia associate who had been fired from the Medford police force.

At the time of the Depositors Trust heist, Medford was infested with Mafia captains and soldiers, and for years to come the community continued to pay tribute to a who's who of reputed gangsters.* Reportedly, many of the gangsters—capos and soldiers alike—kept money and other valuables in the safe deposit boxes that Bangs and his crew had pillaged during the bank heist. The Mafia associate told Clemente and Doherty that he too had tucked away a tidy sum in Depositors Trust and now wanted it returned with interest. The shakedown routine was growing tiresome, and according to Bangs, Jerry and Tommy denied having anything to do with the robbery and told the Mafia associate to go pound sand up his ass.

Once Bangs discovered that *La Cosa Nostra* was attempting to shake down the robbers, he came to believe that it was this Mafia associate, rather than Gusmini, who had tipped the FBI. So Joey had Brother disguise his voice and make an anonymous call to the FBI to inform them that the Mafia associate was actually the man they were looking for. The call worked like magic, reducing the heat on the crew and putting the Mafia on the defensive. Apparently, the feds tapped the associate's phone, learned exactly who he was and what he was up to, and focused their investigation on him for a time.

In addition to the Mafia, Doherty had to deal with another member of his department who was trying to extort him, claiming that Winter Hill gang leader Howie Winter wanted $50,000 cash to keep things copacetic. As Gusmini had done with Clemente, the Medford cop claimed the money would cover Winter's losses from a safe deposit box he held at the bank. Doherty handled the situation as Clemente had and took the problem to his superiors, who launched an internal investigation that resulted in suspension for the blackmailing cop.

With the taint of these allegations and the FBI still breathing down Doherty's neck, Tommy's superiors at the Medford Police Department ordered him to undergo a lie-detector test. Left with no alternative, Tommy

---

* In 1989, the FBI allegedly wiretapped the home of a reputed *La Cosa Nostra* member who resided in Medford and succeeded in obtaining the now famous recording of the traditional induction ceremony and blood oath that set aspiring thugs on the path to becoming "made men." For the first time, the feds claimed to have tangible proof that *La Cosa Nostra* actually existed.

did what anyone else would have done in his predicament: he checked himself into Lawrence Memorial Hospital for severe chest pains. The ruse worked to avoid the polygraph, but Doherty nevertheless remained under the scrutiny of state and federal authorities after his release from the hospital.

John Connolly

In time, the bank robbers discovered that it was none other than Whitey Bulger himself who tipped off Angiulo about the FBI's presence and put the finger on the thieves in the days following the heist. Bulger and Flemmi had been FBI informants since the mid-1960s, so the tip to Angiulo helped maintain their cover with the Mafia, while the information about the robbery gave Whitey's FBI handler and childhood friend, John Connolly ("Zip"), additional juice in the bureau. Bulger learned of the robbery through the underworld's extensive network when word got around that Bucky had bypassed the alarm and was looking to fence some diamonds. A quick call to Zip brought the agents to the doorsteps of Barrett, Clemente, and Doherty.

Barbara Hickey

Bangs had expected all the heat from law enforcement and grief from the underworld that he and the other robbers received in the aftermath of the heist. What he hadn't planned on was the time he would waste dealing with Clemente's private life.

The relationship with Barbara Hickey had been wearing on Jerry since the bank heist, to the point that he had the gall to approach Joey about killing her. Barbara had chosen Jerry over all the other cops at Revere Beach station when she worked there as bail commissioner. Although Joey didn't care for her flakiness and dumb-blonde act—in his opinion, she was intelligent but lazy and unscrupulous—his opinion did little to sway Clemente, who could always be found in Barbara's home if he weren't at the station during shift hours.

Joey had had cocktails and dinner with Jerry at Barbara's residence many times over the years, and he had watched the relationship devolve

US DEPARTMENT OF JUSTICE PHOTO

Whitey Bulger (right) at his gang's garage on
Lancaster Street near Boston Garden in 1980
with mobster Donato "Danny" Angiulo.

The context

The inside story of the FBI's two-decade entanglement with James "Whitey" Bulger and Stephen "The Rifleman" Flemmi can now be told as a result of extraordinary court hearings to determine whether or not the 1995 indictments against the pair should be dismissed.

DAVID, BUCKY & I MET WITH
DANNY SEVERAL TIMES, WHEREAS,
HE WARNED US THAT THERE WAS
A LOT OF FBI IN THE BOSTON
AREA & TO BE AWARE THAT THEY
WERE USING RENTED CARS, FROM E. BOSTON.
LITTLE DID HE KNOW ALL THE F.B.I. AGENTS
THAT WERE SENT TO BOSTON WERE THERE
REGARDING HIM, NOT US.

Joe

predictably to its current disastrous state. Despite his intellect, savvy and charisma, Clemente was blind to the dynamics of all interpersonal affairs: Jerry considered himself a wizard on the job and a god in the sack, while to his colleagues, he was a lazy prick, and to Barbara, a lazy prick with money.

Clemente confided to Bangs his concerns about Hickey's loyalty. Jerry had promised Barbara for years that he would divorce his wife, yet he always stalled the process and reneged on his word. Barbara also knew about the bank heist and Jerry's using her as an alibi. Clemente feared that if the FBI forced her to take a polygraph test to determine his whereabouts the weekend of the robbery, she would fail miserably, or worse, that his dilly-dallying with the divorce might cause her to turn on him.

So Jerry asked his lawyers to draw up the divorce paperwork, gave Barbara a copy to pacify her, and made her sign a deposition under oath concerning the holiday weekend. Now, if Hickey attempted to recant her story, she could be found guilty of perjury. If she played her part, she had the enticement of the pending divorce.

In all likelihood, Jerry would have paid Barbara a tidy sum just to leave, since she was already bleeding him dry with living and house expenses and everything else that went along with sustaining a mistress. Under the current circumstance, Bangs believed Hickey would turn on Clemente and the rest of them without batting an eye if she felt threatened: Barbara stood to lose Jerry's financial support and would certainly cave to the FBI's questioning and take their reward if she couldn't salvage things with her lover.

Bangs wanted no part of Clemente's personal life: *If you wanna play, you gotta pay*, he always chided Jerry. And right now, Joey's blood boiled that he was even engaged in a conversation about how to solve a problem like Barbara Hickey.

Clemente tried to assuage Bangs' anger by claiming he could paint Barbara as a jilted lover if she changed her story, but he knew there were too many other allegations and suspicions to overcome. Deep down, Jerry had no idea how to handle Barbara, and so Bangs claimed that Clemente asked him to whack her. Of course, it may have been the other way around.

In any event, Joey told Jerry to ask Doherty to do it—Tommy had never liked Barbara and wanted her gone from the onset. Ironically, at one point Doherty had talked to Bangs about killing Clemente, again because he was concerned that Barbara would crack and Jerry would follow. Bangs found Doherty's suggestion amusing because Clemente had talked about having Tommy killed, since Tommy had begun using cocaine and was now a bit of a loose cannon.

Once Clemente realized that he couldn't convince Bangs to eliminate Barbara, he asked him, at the very least, to burn down her house to send her a message. Some gasoline and a hair dryer would make it appear to be a household accident, he suggested. Bangs informed Clemente that he didn't hurt women or children—the answer was still *no*, knowing that if something happened to Barbara, the hateful bitch would in turn cause them endless grief.

Clemente finally relented and asked Bangs if he would just keep an eye on Hickey. Joey agreed, and while on duty, he and partner Bobby Spencer kept a close watch on Barbara's every move, even going so far as to follow her and anybody else that went in or out of her home.

On one occasion, Bangs ran the registration on a car parked outside Hickey's residence. The report came back "Not In File," which most likely meant that the vehicle was law enforcement of some kind. Obsessed with Barbara's behavior, Clemente placed a listening device on her house and tapped her phone line, once catching a limited conversation with a few unidentified men that he supposed were FBI agents. But Jerry was never able to manipulate Hickey to get a clear response one way or the other.

Dereliction of Duty

Each week brought some new hassle for the crew to contend with. One evening not long after the heist, Jerry was lazing around at Barbara's home during his shift, watching the national evening news, when his Medford house appeared on screen. The reporter broadcasting live from the property stated that a suspect in the Depositors Trust Bank heist lived at the location. While the newsman didn't mention Jerry by name, everyone knew it was his house. Horrified, Clemente phoned Doherty looking for solace and advice.

"You're the captain. I'm just a sergeant," Doherty offered in exasperation. "What do you want from me?"

In the days that followed the newscast, vandals hurled rocks through the Clementes' windows, and Jerry's son, Barry, was taunted at school and nearly run down by a street thug on a motorcycle. Pressure mounted on Jerry from both good guys and bad guys—as if anyone could tell the difference.

When the MDC's brass got word of the newscast, Clemente's immediate superior, Deputy Superintendent John McDonough, advised him to take the forty days of vacation time he had accumulated until the situation settled a bit. Moreover, because the FBI reported that Clemente admitted to committing adultery with Hickey while on duty, the department would have to investigate those allegations, since adultery was considered conduct unbecoming an officer and cause for dismissal. MDC Captain Tony LoConte, Lieutenant Daniel Gately, and Sergeant Jack O'Brien immediately began surveillance of Hickey's Revere Beach home to gather evidence concerning this charge against Clemente.

Bangs was surprised that Clemente's superiors were just now catching on to his dalliances, because in all the years he had known Jerry, Jerry had spent little time doing police work and could usually be found parked on Barbara's couch—his police cruiser parked on the street out front— morning, noon, and night, almost always during his duty hours.

With the departmental charges pending, Clemente asked Bangs to break into the Lower Basin police station's administrative storage room in order to steal five years of logbooks, which Jerry intended to doctor with backdated reports. Clemente didn't want the brass to discover that on top of everything else he was lazy. So one night, Joey broke into the station by crawling through a window that had been left open purposely and swiped the books for his pal. Clemente doctored the logs daily until Bangs got word that Internal Affairs officials planned to retrieve them from the Lower Basin. Again, Bangs slipped in under cover of night and replaced the volumes cleanly.

Following a thorough internal investigation and unyielding pressure from the feds, MDC Superintendent Larry Carpenter ordered Clemente to take a polygraph test and provide a detailed account of his whereabouts during the Memorial Day weekend. The FBI had gathered sufficient hearsay evidence to compel Clemente to take the test, but they ran the lie-detector order through the MDC so as not to step on toes, as they so often did.

Clemente hired an attorney and worked out an agreement that the test questions would pertain only to his movements and actions during the holiday weekend. But Clemente knew he was in for a double-cross when he learned that former FBI Special Agent Edward McGrath would conduct the test at Scientific Securities in Boston. In fact, McGrath pounded Clemente with a battery of unrelated and incriminating questions. When Clemente ultimately failed the test, he protested vehemently that many of the questions had breached their agreement.

▾ ▾ ▾

The situation spun rapidly out of control for Clemente at this point, and over the next three years, he would take a precipitous fall from commander to commoner.

In August 1980, Clemente received an additional three-page questionnaire from Superintendent Carpenter—an attempt to elicit different answers and trip him up. Then, in October Clemente was transferred to the Old Colony station as captain-in-charge and station commander, a move intended to disrupt his life further and apply pressure that might cause him to crack. All the while, Bangs watched the sparring carefully, advising Clemente on parries and counterpunches, although Jerry generally remained too proud—or punch-drunk—to acknowledge the insight of his corner man.

In March 1981, Carpenter retired and Deputy Superintendent John McDonough became acting superintendent. Despite his so-called friendship with Clemente, McDonough continually prodded Jerry with more questions regarding the bank heist and the Vernon Gusmini incident. On June 4, MDC police attorney Lawrence Ball also grilled Clemente about his activities during the Memorial Day weekend, generating a 120-page deposition. As the attention on Clemente increased and he became a prime suspect in the robbery investigation, other friends distanced themselves from him, including George McGarrity, a by-the-book state police lieutenant detective who had been involved initially in the case. Moreover, the FBI had been taping conversations between Bangs and Clemente all along and playing them for Barbara Hickey to curry her favor and turn her against the men.

Hickey had first appeared before a Middlesex County grand jury less than three months after the bank robbery. She knew her way around a courtroom: besides working for the court, she had studied criminal law at Bunker Hill Community College and later received a master's degree in the subject from Anna Maria College, finishing her degree in the same class as Joey. Barbara knew that the matter wouldn't die with this hearing, and she wasn't about to make any mistakes—thirty-three times she invoked her Fifth Amendment protection against self-incrimination, leaving the grand jury with scant usable testimony.

By October 1981, the jilted Hickey feared for her life and felt she had no alternative but to testify against Clemente. Hickey told the grand jury that Clemente said there were "other people" who could get very rough with her if she didn't do what he said. According to Hickey, Clemente also told her "these people" were capable of "burning down her home" and "blowing up cars." Although her hearsay testimony was compelling, authorities still did not have enough to warrant an arrest, and for the time being, the rogue cops continued to game the system. Clemente and Hickey's affair finally ended for good just before Christmas.

Following another six months of inquiry, on July 19, 1982, Lieutenant Gately filed departmental charges against Clemente for dereliction of duty. At the commission hearing, Bangs was asked, among other things, if he had ever seen Clemente's watch commander cruiser parked near Porter Avenue in Revere—at Barbara Hickey's house—during Jerry's shift hours. Joey backed his friend and fellow robber completely, answering "no" to every accusation, and was quickly excused from further inquiry.

Gately was obsessed with the investigation and practically stalked Clemente, accumulating a detailed logbook of his work and whereabouts dating back to the 1970s. By the end of the lopsided hearing, Gately had hung his enemy out to dry, and the commission voted to demote Jerry two ranks, from captain to sergeant. Clemente later exhausted his appeals to the Civil Service.

Clemente was subsequently transferred back to MDC police headquarters on Somerset Street in Boston, confined to a desk so the brass could keep an eye on him and try to curtail his mischief. However, Clemente had the last laugh when he went out on a work-related disability after a file cabinet allegedly toppled over on him. Bangs believed the incident was a crock of shit, but Clemente's superiors were legally compelled to grant the leave. While out on disability, Clemente leaned on his buddy, Superintendent Tommy Keough, for assistance, but Keough could do nothing. MDC Commissioner Terrence Geoghegan made Jerry's demotion official on April 9, 1983, and Clemente returned to work as a sergeant in August.

During these tumultuous months, the hypocrisy of the police job almost became too much for Clemente to handle; the years of conduct unbecoming had ground him down to the point that he could no longer pretend to wear the badge as anything more than a disguise while he broke the law. Jerry tried to escape by spending more time on his boat, away from the claustrophobia and accusing eyes of the station. He simply wanted to live however the fuck he pleased, knowing it could all come crashing down at any moment.

▼ ▼ ▼

As time passed, Bangs and Barrett were finally able to fence the diamonds with ease in metropolitan areas such as Miami, New York, Pittsburgh, and especially Philadelphia, where they disposed of about half the merchandise, mainly to associates of their friends in *La Cosa Nostra.*

Bangs and Barrett also succeeded in moving most of the gold and silver in Boston itself with the assistance of their mutual acquaintance, Vinny D,* owner and operator of a jewelry store in Downtown Crossing near the Jewelers Building. Bangs and Barrett had so much gold they had to make a dozen trips to deliver the swag, and Vinny then melted the precious metal into bars before selling it, netting Joey and Bucky nearly four million dollars from the sale of the bullion.

Bangs, Barrett and Vinny later invested a million dollars each in a working gold mine located in the Durango region of Mexico, which Bangs brazenly named "Depositors Trust"; but after running afoul of Mexican authorities in a substantial marijuana investigation, Bangs and Barrett were forced to sell their shares, albeit for a hefty profit.

Joey and Bucky also sold a small portion of the loot through a jewelry store that Barrett set up in Lynn, Massachusetts, but Bucky closed the operation after about six months when it began to draw too much interest from law enforcement.

---

* Vinny also later became one of Barrett's most profitable marijuana customers.

With Bangs and Barrett controlling the disposition of the stolen goods, the other members of the crew saw little of the additional profits they rightfully deserved. Bangs justified his lopsided accounting by rationalizing that Clemente had certainly held back a portion for his own kick while he was in possession of the jewels.

Bangs made sure, of course, that the right people got a taste and stayed happy. Red Delaney received twenty grand for introducing Joey and Bucky. Doherty received the twenty grand for Arthur Burns, the beat cop he claimed had turned a blind eye during the weekend of the robbery. Kenny Holmes received his end, and so on and so forth. But at the end of the day, it was pocket change to the new millionaires.

Bucky's Bedfellows

And then there was the mob. For a number of years, Bucky had close ties to *La Cosa Nostra* captain Francis Salemme ("Cadillac Frank"). Salemme was fresh out of prison on a work furlough and at the time a captain under Raymond Patriarca, who ran the New England underworld from the cozy confines of his vending machine company office in Providence, Rhode Island.

Before the bank theft, Salemme smelled something in the air and pressed Barrett for information until it became obvious to the robbers that their best move was to strike a deal: if the heist came to fruition, they'd pay $200,000 to the Italians—well-deserved, after all, since a vast portion of the bank spoils belonged to various heavy hitters in the Mafia. Finally, in July 1980, Barrett introduced Bangs to Salemme, further distancing everyone involved in the heist from Bulger and the Irish mob, to whom they never paid any tribute.*

Enraged at being cut out of the tribute payment, Bulger and his crew put the screws to Barrett by kidnapping him and taking him for a ride, as they had allegedly done with Gusmini. When Bangs caught wind of it, he threatened Bulger in person that if anything similar should happen again, he would toss a few hand grenades down his chimney. Bangs had never liked Bulger, going back years to a time he was having a drink in a South Boston

---

* In 1989, Jerry Clemente gave a telephone interview to the *Boston Globe* from federal prison in Terre Haute, Indiana, where he was serving a sentence for racketeering. Jerry told the reporter that Barrett had split the $200,000 between Salemme and Bulger, when in fact Bulger had received nothing.

gin mill and Whitey made sexual innuendos toward him. Bangs had heard that Bulger had a reputation for being a bit perverted, with an interest in underage companions of both sexes, and Joey flatly rejected the solicitation, with the caveat that he would kill Bulger if he ever tried it again.

As soon as Bucky informed Salemme about his encounter with Bulger, Cadillac Frank instructed Whitey to knock off the bullshit and gave him a severe dressing down, forbidding him to go within a hundred yards of Barrett or his partners—a mob restraining order of sorts. Even though he had Salemme's protection, Barrett took it upon himself to steer clear of Bulger, but the whole situation did not sit well with Whitey, who, despite his impulsive nature, decided to bide his time.

Later that month, Joey and Judy Bangs and Bucky and Elaine Barrett met Salemme and his charming wife for an elegant seafood dinner on Cape Cod. Bangs picked up the $700 tab, a gesture that Salemme noted and appreciated, and the couples eventually became close friends. Salemme also began calling on Joey for "odd jobs" now and then. Bangs admired the honor and integrity of Salemme and his associates, in contrast to the hypocrisy he noted throughout the ranks of the police force.

Seeing the Italians' keen interest in Bangs and Barrett, the Winter Hill gang left the pair in peace. Besides, the gang had too many issues of its own to spend time on Bangs and Barrett: their bookkeeper, Salvatore Sperlinga, had been murdered in January of that year, and Uncle Joe McDonald, Howie Winter, and Jimmy Simms were now in prison for attempting to extort the owner of Melo-Tone Vending company, officed on Broadway in Somerville, and fixing horse races at Suffolk Downs in Revere.* Winter Hill was a fucking mess and no one had any clue what to do next, so Whitey Bulger decided, wisely, to deploy his resources to consolidate his power on The Hill.

Brother's Keeper

Of course, Bangs also had to monitor O'Leary's shenanigans. In the months following the heist, Brother was what Joey referred to as "street rich": he

---

* Sal Sperlinga's son, Ricky, was one of my closest friends growing up in Somerville, and he was one hell of an athlete. Shortly after completing the 2010 Boston Marathon, Ricky passed away. I will always remember him with tremendous respect, admiration and love.

wanted everyone to know he had a few bucks in his pocket, and he regularly bought rounds of drinks at his favorite watering hole as if he had hit the lottery. And within a few months, Brother had purchased a fancy home on Beach Street in Tewksbury, just around the corner from Joey.

Even though Bangs feared that O'Leary's sudden spending might raise suspicions, he and Brother undertook the purchase of a saloon in an upscale Brighton neighborhood. The Fallon brothers were the proprietors of the gin joint, and one of them also owned and operated an auto body shop nearby. Bangs had taken his girlfriend Cheryl Fisher's car in for repairs after an accident and become friendly with the brother, who sold him a shit-box metallic-green Chevrolet Impala for four hundred dollars. The conversation about the barroom arose naturally from there.

Just before closing the deal, Bangs and O'Leary stopped by the bar on occasion to put an eye on the regular patrons. Bangs had plans to build his own scofflaw hierarchy around the locale—like *La Cosa Nostra's* associates in the North End—and some of the people they encountered needed to go, including a local bookmaker who had set up shop at a corner table. Joey and Brother harassed the undesirables and left no question about who was in charge. The bookie soon disappeared, the best patrons got the best tables, and Joey's domain began to take shape.

Brother liked what he saw and declared that he intended to work full-time at the bar, as part of his deal. Joey was willing to be fair, even generous, with Brother in this venture, but he refused to have O'Leary hanging around the cash enterprise full-time.

On the day Joey and Brother were to finalize the deal and take legal ownership, Bangs was redeployed from the Upper Basin to work Revere Beach. Brother called first thing that morning to inform Joey that the establishment had burned to the ground during the night. The fire department ruled the blaze arson, and O'Leary suggested it must have been the disgruntled bookmaker they had strong-armed. But Bangs knew better: he blamed O'Leary, who of course denied the accusation and acted insulted, before Joey's fierce probing eventually ground him down. Brother took full responsibility, reluctantly, albeit defiantly; however, he never gave Joey a clue as to why he put a match to the barroom in the first place.

Bangs saw O'Leary less frequently in the following months, but when they did cross paths, their criminal relationship flourished. To keep his *La*

Cosa Nostra associates in check, Bangs did some "back-scratching" from time to time. On one occasion, Joey agreed to collect money from a Chinese man who resided in Chinatown and was seriously past due on a tidy sum owed to a heating oil company proprietor associated with the Mafia.

Joey took sidekick O'Leary along on the gig as backup. When they arrived at the debtor's weathered building, they agreed that Brother would attempt to "talk some sense" into the aging foreigner, while Joey played lookout from the police cruiser. However, their *La Cosa Nostra* clients had ordered that if the Chinaman didn't produce a payment, Bangs was to burn his fucking building to the ground. Joey had plenty of experience and no scruples about doing it, so he brought along a five-gallon container of gasoline and an assortment of throw-away weaponry, just in case. Bangs waited for what seemed an eternity before O'Leary reemerged from the building, stumbling drunkenly and looking silly, wearing a paper party hat. When O'Leary finally flopped into the cruiser, Bangs laid into him for taking so long.

Brother slurred out an explanation: he burst through the man's front door to find his family throwing the old-timer a surprise birthday party. The clan nearly startled him to death when they all yelled *"Surprise!"* in Chinese. Then the partiers welcomed Brother in for cake and cocktails, and when the Chinaman finally arrived, O'Leary even helped him blow out his candles. The old man took a shine to Brother and agreed to make weekly installments until the debt was settled. Bangs was livid but knew he couldn't now torch the building, and luckily the man held true to his word and paid off the debt.

Shortly thereafter, Brother found himself in a pickle after he lost a hefty sum to a bookie, but he decided to stall on paying until he could figure out another gaff to run with Joey. Plus, he didn't want Joey to find out about the huge loss and lecture him on his foolish bets. Fortunately for Brother, Joey soon lost four hundred dollars on a horse race and attempted to make it up by betting a thousand on the Boston Bruins, who lost badly to those goddamn Montreal Canadiens.

Bangs could have easily covered the losses with his police salary, the money he made from his booming collection business, or the millions from the bank heist, but for pride, ego or sheer greed, Bangs never paid bookies with his own money. So when Joey approached Brother about working a gaff, Brother was already in.

When they met for drinks a few days later, O'Leary told Bangs that he too had a debt with a bookie, a guy who always kept at least ten grand in a home safe. It would be an easy theft: the only catch was that Bangs would have to do the home invasion on his own, since the bookie knew Brother personally. The men reasoned that this was the perfect victimless crime, because the bookie himself was engaged in criminal activity and would never approach the police about his loss. Besides, added Brother, the bookie was "an effeminate, purse-carrying sissy" who had no weapons and would provide no resistance to Bangs' alpha-dog presence.

Brother described in excruciating detail the bookie's extravagantly decorated apartment. O'Leary's intimate knowledge of the place piqued Bangs' curiosity.

"Why did you even go to this guy's pad in the first place?" Joey queried.

"You know, the usual," Brother explained. "I met him through one of those personal ads, so every now and then I go over and let him suck my dick. Then I rob the son of a bitch blind."

Joey's jaw dropped. Brother looked at him earnestly.

"What?" Brother asked quietly.

Joey studied Brother's face incredulously. Brother exploded with laughter.

"You should see your face, Joe! You really think I'd let some queer blow me?"

Joey eventually joined in the laughter, more or less convinced that Brother was telling the truth. But Joey was never completely sure after that and often used the story to gibe Brother over the years.

After a few cocktails, Brother finally convinced Joey to pull off the home invasion that same night. Upon arriving at the bookie's apartment building in the exclusive Back Bay area of Boston, O'Leary again explained how the robbery was to go down and gave Bangs a password to use at the call box to get buzzed in. He'd be in and out in a couple minutes max, Brother assured. Bangs grabbed a ski mask and his .38 Special, checked that the gun was loaded, and headed off across the snow-covered sidewalk.

O'Leary played lookout as Bangs rang the buzzer and slipped into the brownstone. He pulled the ski mask down as he approached the first-floor apartment and then knocked.

As soon as the bookie cracked the door, Bangs forced it open and wedged his way inside. The man began screaming hysterically with ear-piercing wails that sent shivers down Joey's spine. The bookie dropped to his knees and wrapped himself around Joey's leg, hanging on for all he was worth. Joey stopped dead in his tracks—despite everything he had ever experienced, this moment completely befuddled him. Bangs pointed the gun at the man's head and ordered him to shut the fuck up, but the man's screams only grew more panicked.

Joey heard doors open and concerned voices chatter in the hallway and knew he had to act quickly. He asked where the safe was, where the money was, where anything valuable was, but the man would not stop his high-pitched yowls or release his vise-like grip on Bangs' leg.

When Joey heard a distant siren, he pistol-whipped the bookie until he had bloodied his head and face, but the beating only amplified the man's hysterics. Unable to escape the man's grasp, Bangs dragged him from the apartment, through the hallway, and out of the building, slamming him against the walls and door as he went. Brother saw the commotion and dropped down out of sight—if he did anything to help Joey, the bookie would undoubtedly recognize him.

When Joey hit the icy sidewalk, he nearly toppled over, but the crazed bookie attached to his thigh steadied him, and Joey found he could actually slide the man easier on the slippery concrete.

Joey heard the siren closing in as he struggled with the car door, but he still couldn't shake the bookie. Seeing the police lights from the next street over flash against the dense winter sky, Bangs let loose on the man, knocking him unconscious and flinging him into the blood-spattered snow.

Joey and Brother sped away, passing the Boston police who were en route to the apartment building. O'Leary peppered Bangs with questions about what had gone wrong, how much money he had stolen, whether the bookie were dead. Joey drove silently, unsure himself exactly what had just happened. Bangs and O'Leary made their way back to the safe haven of Cambridge and stopped at a local watering hole.

The traumatized men sidled up to the bar and sat silent, in a state of disbelief.

"I know another guy," O'Leary informed Bangs.

"You gotta be shitting me, you cocksucker!"

But Brother wasn't joking, and he explained that he knew of a liquor store owner who lived in Arlington and took the store's cash home every night to deposit it the next morning on his way to work. The guy was ripe for the picking, Brother continued. He had broken into the store once before—avoiding capture by hiding in an elevator shaft—and had heard the man explain everything to the cops. The man was a little older, overweight, and out of shape, and as far as Brother could tell, not too handy with a weapon.

Bangs downed his drink and sat in deep thought.

"Fuck it. Let's go," he muttered.

Bangs agreed to have a look and informed Brother that this time he was going in, too. Joey and Brother downed a final cocktail, stumbled back out to the car, and headed to Arlington.

When they arrived at the house, O'Leary once again finagled his way out of the dirty work by telling Bangs he was a regular customer at the liquor store and the proprietor would certainly know his face. This job would be easier than the last, Brother assured him, because all Joey needed to do was say he was a friend of the man's son and he'd be welcomed into the house—no craziness, no neighbors. Joey scrutinized Brother's face— maybe he was being sincere. Bangs walked to the front door and knocked.

"Who's there?" the man called from inside.

"A friend of your son."

Silence. Joey waited a long moment, glanced back at Brother, and started to leave, when he heard the chain rattle at the door. The man opened and peered outside just as the masked Bangs bounded back onto the porch, gun in hand, and forced his way into the house.

Bangs ordered the mark into the closet. The man offered feeble protests as Joey shoved him in, and then began clutching his chest and pleading for his heart pills. Joey slammed the door and pushed a side table against it.

"Fuck your heart pills—where's the money?"

The victim panicked and pushed back at the door—Joey shoved his revolver into the crack until the man backed down so he could close the closet.

"Tell me where your money's at or I'll shoot you through the door!"

The petrified man insisted he had just made a deposit, but Bangs didn't buy his story. Joey fired a shot at the top of the door.

"There's five grand under the bed, goddammit!" the man wheezed.

Bangs scrambled down the hall to the bedroom and found the cash, along with some pricey jewelry; but Brother would see none of that. In fact, because he did all the dirty work, Bangs later told O'Leary he had confiscated only three grand.

Bangs stuffed the loot into his jacket and made his way from room to room ripping phone cords from the wall to buy himself a little time. He finally disappeared into the kitchen for a moment and then stalked down the dark hallway toward the closet. He flung the door open and handed the man a pill bottle and glass of water.

"Lose some weight, you fat bastard," Joey deadpanned. He slammed the closet and slipped out of the house.

Bangs slid into the front seat, and O'Leary peeled away from the curb. When they had safely cleared the neighborhood, Brother ventured a question: "Just like I said, right?"

Without saying a word, Joey unleashed a barrage of punches on Brother, stopping only when O'Leary purposely lost control of the wheel and sideswiped a delivery truck.

"Just like you said, my ass. Take me home, you motherfucker."

Brother later ascertained from a conversation with the victim's son that his father had made a twenty thousand dollar deposit earlier that afternoon. The news was a kick in the balls to Joey that pained him for years.

Second Commendation

Although he would have preferred to enjoy his millions in solitude, Bangs knew he had to play out the alibi of being a cop until the feds' fairy dust swirling around Clemente and Doherty had settled. So he showed up for police work every day, without fail, like it or not. As much as he felt jailed in the police station, Bangs swore he'd never do time in prison for the heist or any other crime—including the robberies, mob collections, home invasions and shakedowns he still pursued in his off-hours.

Bangs was not only a sergeant at this time but also a patrol supervisor, which entailed additional responsibility that he neglected as much as possible. However, the perks of the gig included having a cruiser to himself and no one to answer to, even if he missed working with his partner in mischief, Bobby Spencer.

On a bitter cold afternoon in early February 1981, Bangs caught reports over his portable police radio about a gunfight and car chase that was unfolding. The suspect had eluded the Arlington and Somerville police, so the charge now passed to the Mets to engage in the pursuit. Bangs monitored the developments as two other officers in the area, Joe Vitiello and Larry Cleary, picked up the fleeing vehicle on the Fellsway.* Vitiello was a first cousin of Joey's wife, Judy, and a man Bangs admired, so he was particularly concerned about the potentially fatal events.

At the moment, however, Bangs was actually shirking his duties to "get a haircut," as he euphemistically referred to his romantic encounters with girlfriend Cheryl Fisher at her condo in Saugus, about twenty minutes north of Boston. Why he didn't turn off the radio, he never knew.

As the chase drew on, Bangs grew uncharacteristically distracted from his present engagement, until in exasperation he jumped out of bed, threw on his clothes, and sped to the vicinity of the pursuit, which by this time was nearing a Somerville/East Cambridge auto salvage yard, after a chase through multiple jurisdictions and additional shots fired at the police cruisers. Following police protocol—again, uncharacteristically—Bangs swung by the Lower Basin station and picked up a shotgun, extra ammo, and his "paddy-wagon guy," Howie Williams, for backup.

Within minutes, Bangs and Williams arrived at the junkyard, where they heard an intense barrage of gunfire bursting from the piles of scrap metal as bullets ricocheted around the auto carcasses. Being the senior officer, Bangs ordered Vitiello and Cleary to cease fire; Joey needed to

---

* Vitiello was one of my father's dearest friends, a friend of mine, and one of the most respected cops on the force. "Joe Vit" is an avid weightlifter, and we trained together for a time at Universe Gym in Somerville.

figure out where the shots were coming from and how many suspects and weapons they were dealing with.

Silence dropped over the cluttered yard. Joey felt like he was back in Vietnam, waiting and watching for he-didn't-know-what. He caught movement in his peripheral vision, and in a blink he and his team were pinned down by the suspects' desperate fusillade—they were indeed alive and well armed.

The other officers covered Bangs as he crept through the stacked cars and behind a barrier, where he apprehended one of the assailants who had been shot up badly. The second suspect was determined to remain free and managed to shoot his way out of the junkyard. But Bangs knew the surrounding area like the back of his hand and set off with Williams to track down the criminal, while Vitiello and Cleary secured the scene and waited for an ambulance and backup.

As Bangs and Williams scoured the neighborhood, Joey rode shotgun, navigating Williams through side streets and alleyways and down a dead-end drive where railroad tracks led to an adjacent rail yard. As soon as the cruiser turned the corner, Bangs spotted the suspect's feet protruding from beneath a parked automobile. Williams rolled to a stop and moved to exit the cruiser, but Bangs held him back.

"Sit tight, Howie," Joey ordered. "You got two small kids at home, and I don't wanna see you get shot. I'm already a sergeant, and you're still a patrolman. I'm gonna do this motherfucker, but the collar is yours."*

Bangs stepped from the cruiser and peeked under the parked vehicle with his flashlight. He noted that the wounded suspect still had a firm grip on his weapon, but because of his awkward position, lying face down, there was no way he could shoot backwards. Bangs took a position at the man's feet and announced himself.

"Okay, son, this is Sergeant Bangs of the Metropolitan Police. I don't want to kill you, but if you shoot at me, I will. Now, come out, but do not come out with the gun in your hand, because if you do, I'm gonna blow your fucking head off."

The suspect muttered that he'd cooperate and slid from his hiding place. Bangs noticed that the man had been shot through the right arm,

---

* Of course, Bangs also had two small children at home.

and he asked the suspect how many times he had been hit. Just once, the man replied, by Joey himself, no less.

Bangs transported the man to Massachusetts General Hospital in the police cruiser and scolded him en route: "I guess it just wasn't your day, pal. I was fifteen miles away spending quality time with my girl when I received the call to arms. Never fuck with a dog who's eating or a cop who's getting a haircut."

The suspect offered his own sob story. He and his wounded partner were career criminals who had both been recently paroled from the state prison in Walpole (now called MCI-Cedar Junction). During his incarceration, the suspect's girlfriend had met a Latin dance instructor and fallen madly in love during a passionate tango. Upon release from prison, the jilted convict and his accomplice paid a visit to the interloper and discovered him in bed with the woman—a heated confrontation ensued, and the suspects tried to kill the lovers.

By the time they arrived at the hospital, Bangs was nearly tempted to allow the wounded man to walk, but, *fuck it*, his wave of generosity quickly passed. The felons eventually received twenty years each for attempted murder of a peace officer, and Bangs received his second Certificate of Commendation for his leadership and bravery in apprehending the suspects. The crook had once again proved himself a hero of the people.

THE COMMONWEALTH OF MASSACHUSETTS
METROPOLITAN DISTRICT POLICE
20 SOMERSET STREET. BOSTON 02108
TEL. 617-727-5220

JOHN D. McDONOUGH
SUPERINTENDENT

CERTIFICATE OF COMMENDATION

OFFICIAL RECOGNITION IS HEREBY ACCORDED TO THE FOLLOWING OFFICERS FOR THEIR PERFORMANCE OF DUTY IN AN OUTSTANDING MANNER WHICH EXEMPLIFIES THEIR COURAGE AND DEVOTION TO DUTY IN ACCORDANCE WITH THE HIGHEST TRADITION OF THE METROPOLITAN POLICE SERVICE.

On February 10, 1981, Sergeant Joseph P. Bangs, Officers Howard F. Williams, Joseph T. Vitiello, and Lawrence T. Cleary, while assigned to the Charles River Lower Basin Division, were alerted by Headquarters that a motor vehicle chase was in progress involving one of our officers and shots were being exchanged. The above-mentioned officers immediately responded to the area where the suspects had fled on foot.

These officers followed the suspects on foot into a junk yard in Somerville and after an exchange of gun fire, they apprehended and took into custody two armed and dangerous felons.

Per order,

John D. McDonough
Superintendent of Police

JDM/FLM:cj
cc: Sgt. Bangs

The Commonwealth of Massachusetts

Metropolitan District Commission

Certificate of Commendation

Awarded to

Sgt. Joseph P. Bangs

For Outstanding Performance of Duty

While assigned to the Charles River Lower Basin Division, was alerted by Headquarters that a motor vehicle chase was in progress involving one of our officers & shots were being exchanged. He immediately responded to the area where the suspects had fled on foot and followed the suspects into a junk yard in Somerville where with the help of other officers he was able to apprehend the suspects.

Issued at Boston, Massachusetts   February 1982

Superintendent   Commissioner

Treasury

In December 1981, after a year and a half with no grand jury indictments and noise about the bank heist fading, Joey decided to celebrate as only he could—with another bank job. After all, the only problem with being Joey Bangs was having cojones.

Bangs had met a professional hustler and friend of Bucky Barrett's whom he knew only by the name of "Ben" (LNU, or "Last Name Unknown," as federal officers noted in their reports). Ben was a tall, handsome, flashy, Irish-Canadian kid who dressed impeccably, wore lots of jewelry, drove fancy cars and lived lavishly in a beautiful South Shore estate, spending every penny he stole as soon as he stole it. Ben had developed a reputation for delivering what others couldn't, especially after he played an important role for the notorious Kingston Gang in securing .30-caliber machine guns from the Winter Hill crew, following the bloody McLean–McLaughlin feud. Ben had no reservations about his pitch to Bangs.

The plan was simple: rob the night deposit box and basement vault of the Saugus Bank during the Christmas holidays. Ben estimated that between deposits from busy merchants and cash on hand for customer withdrawals, the bank would have about a million dollars in currency.

Ben had initially approached Bucky Barrett about the heist, but after thoroughly casing the bank and making his own calculation of the potential take, Barrett ultimately turned down the job, as he had recently done with similar propositions. Barrett took a pass on this robbery because he never did a job unless he was certain there would be at least a quarter million dollars for his kick. After all, with his millions from the Depositors Trust heist, Barrett was contemplating retirement and felt no compulsion to take unnecessary chances, unlike his adrenaline-junkie cohort Bangs. So Bucky cut Joey into the mix in his place and made the introduction to Ben, after which Bangs persuaded Clemente to go along for the ride.

According to plan, Clemente was assigned to pick all the locks and then remain in the parking lot as lookout. Being a police captain was extremely useful in a situation such as this: Clemente knew quite a few of the local cops, and MDC police often ate at restaurants along Route 1 in Saugus, so it wasn't unusual for them to patrol the surrounding area as well.

Bangs, Clemente, and Ben had been in the basement of the Saugus bank several times and were in the process of constructing an alarm bypass box when Ben began getting heat from a prior bank robbery. Bangs' instinct told him something wasn't right, and he decided to postpone the job. Besides, Joey had been concocting his next scheme, which promised a much larger score for the same amount of work.

❯ ❯ ❯

With law enforcement losing steam on the Depositors Trust investigation, Bangs was emboldened to meet in public with the entire posse—Barrett, Clemente, Doherty, O'Leary, Ben, and Barrett's friend Jake Rooney. They gathered for drinks to discuss a new target—the State Treasury Department.

Bangs laid out the plan for his partners until four in the morning, after which the men agreed that this was "the one" they'd be remembered for, although at thirty million dollars, the Depositors Trust job was then the largest-ever heist in the world.

While serving in the Army, Bangs had dreamed about robbing the military payroll, and now that vision resurfaced in a more accessible guise. The idea of robbing the treasury first materialized while Bangs was working as a Capitol police officer in the early 1970s. When he was bored on duty, Joey filled his head with schemes for taking back a bit of his taxes, as he figured it—brainstorms that ranged from stealing gas and cars from the motor pool to stripping the gold from the State House's dome. But taking the treasury soon became his favorite dream.

During those years on the Capitol Police, Bangs took detailed notes on the regular Brinks deliveries and eventually finagled the assignment of escorting the armored-delivery personnel while they wheeled sacks of cash into one of two Treasury Department vaults.

The first vault was located on the ground floor of the State Office Building, and the sister vault was in the State House itself. Brinks delivered money every week, but on the second Wednesday of the month, they brought in larger amounts to cover the massive monthly payroll. The guards hauled cash into the building in large, four-wheeled carts that remained under the scrutiny of at least two Capitol police officers, one of whom was usually Bangs. Once construction of the McCormack Building in downtown Boston was complete, the Treasury Department was consolidated there, and all state currency was delivered to an enormous safe on the twelfth floor.

A pair of Joey's Capitol police officer friends were scheduled to be on duty the night of the planned robbery and agreed to allow Bangs and his partners into the McCormack Building, even though Bangs, Clemente and Doherty each still possessed a master key to all state office buildings, including the State House itself.

Members of the crew had actually been in the same room as the Treasury vault at least a half dozen times while they searched for soft spots in the steel to drill funnel holes. Although Bangs did the drilling, funnel holes were Ben's expertise, given his previous experience in burning through confined safes and creating makeshift ventilation systems. The holes allowed smolder to make its way from the building without setting off smoke detectors or triggering the sprinkler system. And even if the robbers disconnected the alarm system, smoke from drilling could create breathing and vision problems for them, in spite of their using oxygen tanks with masks and goggles. In the months leading up to the heist, Joey made a dozen or more holes and concealed them behind air vents about five inches from the floor.

When *La Cosa Nostra* caught wind of Bangs' latest machinations, capo Frank Salemme wanted in on the action, so Joey suggested he drive the getaway vehicle in exchange for a cut. Even with another mouth to feed, the men agreed it would be prudent to bring in Salemme to keep the Mafia satisfied concerning any potential issues with tribute.

The thieves had included Brother O'Leary from the start, but he began missing pivotal meetings and stakeouts, and Barrett soon lost patience. When Brother failed to show for a final strategy meeting on Christmas night, he was finished as far as this gaff was concerned. *Fuck Brother! Even Santa Claus works on Christmas*, Bucky scolded. Bangs knew where Brother was: he had a pocket full of cash and a new extramarital squeeze and was more interested in his usual vices than in blueprints and practice runs.

In addition to the payroll for all state employees, the Treasury housed millions of dollars of unclaimed money, jewelry and other valuables, including assets from unresolved estates. The crew estimated conservatively that each thief would net between two and four million dollars from the job, and they agreed to kick the Capitol police officers involved $200,000 each. Bucky decided to trade his entire cut of the Treasury score for Jerry's share of the Depositors Trust swag, if Clemente would quit his constant pestering and complaining about not receiving his end on the Depositors Trust heist. At Bangs' behest, Barrett continued to profess to the others that the goods were too hot to fence and urged them to bide their time. But the robbers were losing patience, especially Jerry.

During the early stages of prepping the Treasury job, Bangs again surveilled the incoming and outgoing Brinks trucks while he was on duty with the MDC. He was also able to gain access to the building after hours and discovered paperwork in a cashier's drawer that confirmed the Brinks delivery schedule and included the combination to the vault. The job was shaping up to be the easiest to date, but conflicts were brewing among the men that ultimately led them to call off the venture just weeks before the robbery.

▼ ▼ ▼

Bangs' days were growing hectic, and he had begun to spread himself paper-thin. His lifestyle had transformed dramatically over the previous year from a decidedly working-class existence colored by uncertainty and violence to a position that, although modest in appearance, allowed him to live like a king. Joey had installed an in-ground pool behind his Tewksbury home the summer after the Depositors Trust robbery and allegedly used some of the heist money to purchase a luxury condo for Cheryl Fisher, the new love interest who had become the focus of his after-hours life.

Moreover, Bangs and Barrett had finally landed on the right contacts and methods for piecing out the Depositors Trust swag, and their working relationship had developed into a strong personal bond—"brothers from another mother," they liked to say. They enjoyed spending money together, sometimes up to fifty thousand dollars a week. In fact, Bangs often neglected to cash his measly $4,000-a-month MDC paycheck, which was a rounding error compared to the amounts he and Barrett netted from pawning the bank loot.

Bangs and Barrett spent considerable time vacationing in Miami, Atlantic City and Las Vegas, traveling under phony identities, usually as "doctors." Bangs was known at the Riviera Hotel and Casino in Las Vegas as "the world-renowned gynecologist Dr. Robert Taylor," and he loved to play the part. Bangs and Barrett also used chips from Las Vegas and Atlantic City casinos to launder their money, purchasing hundreds of thousands of dollars in casino currency, gambling lightly, and then cashing in the chips, always careful to obtain a receipt for tax purposes.

Bangs not only gambled big in those days, he was also becoming a drinker without peer, downing anything in sight—Goldschläger, Courvoisier or Stingers in Las Vegas, piña coladas one after the other in sunny Florida, or his lifelong standby, Miller Lite with ice, wherever he happened to be. But Joey was never out of control, and he had no respect for anyone who couldn't hold his liquor.

Bangs threw money around with abandon and never let a friend reach into his own pocket. He always had a woman on each arm, custom-made jewelry—including a diamond-faced Rolex Presidential—a flashy new champagne-colored Cadillac Seville, thousand-dollar suits by Blass,

Armani and Boss, and yachts, condos, and swimming pools. Joey also missed work often as he and girlfriend Cheryl Fisher traveled frequently to the Bahamas, Aruba, Puerto Rico and other exotic locations.

Joey and Bucky traveled the world, and the $2,000-a-night escorts were lush and plentiful. They made so many trips to Vegas that they began winning or dropping a hundred grand a night playing blackjack or craps, and the kicker was that they thought nothing of it either way.

While Clemente and Doherty were under scrutiny by various state and federal law enforcement sources, they still hounded Bangs and Barrett about the disposition of the jewelry and their split of the earnings. Bangs simply told them Barrett had buried it for safekeeping until things cooled off or the statute of limitations expired. Joey played Mickey the Dunce and never gave the others a penny from the goods he and Bucky were fencing. Jerry and Tommy believed Bucky was the one taking them for a ride, and they often told Bangs to let Barrett know he'd be a dead man if he tried to swindle them.

So Joey called a sit-down with the Depositors Trust principals—minus Kenny Holmes, who had long-since disappeared—to try to silence the squabbling once and for all. As far as Bangs was concerned, this would be a one-time deal. And in fact, it would be the last time Clemente, Doherty and O'Leary ever saw Barrett again—Joey would see to that.

Bangs corralled the men at Cheryl Fisher's condo in Saugus one evening while she was at work and incited Clemente, Doherty and O'Leary to lay into Barrett, demanding to know where the loot was and when he would sell it. The men threatened Bucky wildly and aggressively, especially when he persisted in claiming the swag was still too hot to move. Barrett advised his fellow robbers to be patient for a few more months, but tempers flared. Joey jumped into the attack and aimed a sawed-off, pump-action, 16-gauge shotgun at Bucky's head.

"What do you think of this, Bucky?" Joey demanded. "Interesting piece, isn't it?"

Barrett panicked and nearly shit himself. He and Bangs had orchestrated the meeting to convince the others it was still too dangerous to fence the loot—even though the two of them had already made millions—but Joey's improvisation with the shotgun threw Barrett completely off script.

Barrett sat speechless while Bangs spewed insults and threats, warning Bucky that he needed to work out a solution on the double. Bangs then ordered Barrett to leave so he and the others could discuss the situation.

Once Barrett had gone, Bangs continued to manipulate the irate crew, convincing them Bucky's wife knew everything and if anything happened to her husband, she would go straight to the authorities. Bangs promised to monitor Barrett on their behalf and get things sorted out. Joey was convincing; the men acquiesced.

Barrett didn't appreciate playing the patsy in Bangs' charade, but he was drowning and knew he had little choice in the matter. As the group's muscle, Bangs would never allow any harm to come to Barrett, and Bucky reasoned that Joey was not about to bite the hand that was feeding him, so he tamped down his fears.

But Bucky made it clear to Joey that he should never again point a loaded weapon in his direction ever again, especially if he were going to improvise with such gusto. Bangs half-heartedly apologized, but he knew the stunt would keep Bucky honest and remind him who was boss.

None of the others communicated with Barrett after the meeting, and Bangs and Barrett thus established the ideal scenario to hoard the swag. Clemente whined incessantly about getting some scratch from the heist, so Joey pretended to find a way to liquidate a few pieces of jewelry. In reality, Barrett gave Bangs twenty grand for each man from the money they had already received for the gold and silver bullion, and Joey in turn gave each man ten grand, keeping the other half, he reasoned, as payment for putting up with such pains in the ass.

Clemente wasn't satisfied, however, so Bangs and Barrett agreed to give Jerry a special gift: the gray diamond satchel, filled not with the pink and yellow diamonds—they were too valuable and definitely too hot to move—but stuffed with a variety of lesser stones and jewelry that Joey and Bucky had already picked through. Jerry couldn't tell a genuine piece of jewelry from a genital wart, so he was thrilled to receive the bag and promised to keep this exchange a secret from the others and allow Joey to work in peace. Until, that is, he attempted to pawn the goods off to a fence in Florida who examined the pieces and informed him that, yes indeed, he had gotten fucked.

Clemente had believed he would garner about $200,000 from the sale, but he managed to pull in only $15,000; Jerry returned from the Sunshine State raising a ruckus and looking for blood. Bangs instructed Barrett to lie low and allow him take the heat from Jerry, as well as from Tommy and Brother, who were incensed not only that the jewels were nearly worthless, but also that Jerry had received special consideration over them.

Bangs knew that no matter how angry the other men became, none of them had the balls to kill him or Barrett, so he alerted Bucky that he too would feign indignation over the low valuation of the jewels to divert the others' anger—a little good thief, bad thief, so to speak.

Bangs let the idle threats and chatter run in one ear and out the other, for the time being. He was playing with found money, and after the shitty hand he felt he had been dealt for so many years, he now basked in his charmed life. He thought often of his heinous Vietnam experience and promised to squeeze life for every ounce of pleasure it had, for the young comrades who would never have the chance.

VIVA SIN CITY

WITH THEIR BUSINESS PARTNERSHIP FIRING ON ALL CYLINDERS, Barrett introduced Bangs to a number of influential players who were also living the good life. They "vacationed" (that is, laundered money) frequently in Beverly Hills, California, where Barrett initiated Bangs into the finer points of living large on a level Joey had never dreamed of, indulging in the finest food, shopping and women—usually actresses—that La La Land had to offer. Bucky was in fact maintaining a relationship with a shapely actress from the hit TV show "M.A.S.H." They had met at the Beverly Wilshire Hotel and clicked instantly—actresses seemed to have a thing for the company of real-life wise guys rather than the glossy Hollywood types they were accustomed to.

Bangs and Barrett also took extended vacations to Las Vegas. Bangs himself—or rather, his alter ego, Dr. Robert Taylor—was recognized everywhere as a high roller, and he soon had a designated suite at the Riviera, which was also a favorite spot for many of the day's most popular entertainers. The suite included two spacious bedrooms, a pair of steam baths and hot tubs, a fully stocked bar with top-shelf booze—with plenty of Goldschläger, per Joey's request—and a baby grand piano that Bangs often used as an extra bed when the crush of hookers he entertained spilled out of the bedrooms. After a particularly raucous affair in the suite, the hotel management replaced the baby grand with an upright piano, which weathered the frequent parties much better.

Initially, Bangs hired a chauffeur when he arrived in Vegas, but on one occasion he spotted a champagne-colored Cadillac while passing a dealership and ordered his driver to pull in. Joey tracked down the sales manager, told

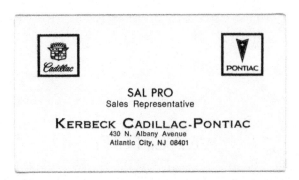

him he wanted the car immediately, and listened impatiently as the man explained that it wasn't for sale—it belonged to his girlfriend, who would kill him if he sold it. "Everything's for sale," Joey retorted. He made an unrefusable offer and within the hour drove away in his new Cadillac.

Bangs stored the car in Las Vegas, and the Riviera staff kept it polished and ready for whenever "Dr. Taylor" rolled into town. On a whim, Bangs purchased an identical car in Atlantic City, New Jersey—again from a sales manager whose wife had had her eye on it—and drove it back to Boston to use as his daily vehicle. Bangs adored his Cadillacs.

Between 1981 and 1983, Joey and Bucky went on dozens of "safaris," as they also referred to them, gambling and binging sometimes for weeks at a time, always hunting for the next big quarry. On one jaunt, Barrett introduced Bangs to another Arthur, an old-school Jewish wise guy named Arthur Strahl ("Artie")—sixty-two years old, diminutive but intense, always impeccably dressed in suit and tie, and adorned with an abundance of gold chains, rings and bracelets. Strahl was a world-renowned jewelry smuggler, money launderer and all-purpose hustler, and Bangs surmised that he and Barrett had served time together in a federal penitentiary, even though Strahl worked mainly in Europe. In fact, Strahl had been convicted in Italy of bank embezzlement and served five years in an Italian prison before being deported under a lifetime ban against returning. Strahl often quipped that he went to Italy for a month, wound up staying for five years, and could never again get his fill of authentic pizza and pasta. Bangs and Strahl hit it off immediately.

After months of legal wrangling and incessant appeals to a who's who of high-profile string-pullers, Strahl was deemed a "rehabilitated ex-offender" by the state of Nevada. He soon obtained a gaming license and began running legitimate junkets for the New England mob from Boston to Las Vegas and Atlantic City. Strahl was also a big lover of marijuana who smoked every chance he got. Artie adored the lavish life of his "twilight years," as he often called them, and everyone from the service staff at the Riviera to the very young women he groped admired him for his quick-talking charm and free-flowing cash.

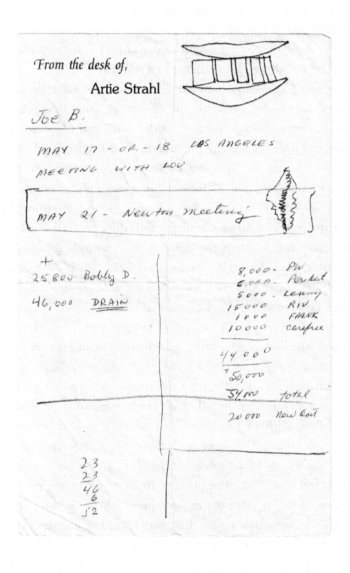

When Bangs and Strahl eventually came around to talking business, Bangs learned that Strahl was stuck with some serious cash-flow issues and needed an infusion of currency. Having fallen into financial straits with the Riviera and a few "influential" individuals from Chicago, Strahl had gone for assistance to Cambridge's Irish godfather Paul Walker, whom he had met through Bangs during a gambling junket. On the strength of that connection, Walker lent Artie $18,000. But Strahl fell into further difficulties, and by the time he sat down with Joey, he was more than $200,000 in the red, and the mob was growing impatient. Worse, Joey realized that Artie's creditors would look to him to clean up the situation, given that Artie had used Joey's name as a reference.

Bangs and Strahl hammered out a deal: Joey would collect on Artie's many unpaid debts—for a sizeable cut, of course. Bangs calculated he could complete the work quickly, pocket a tidy sum, and, most important, do damage control with Walker and the mob in New England and Chicago.

Artie jumped at the deal and provided Joey with all the names and pertinent details. Yet after all the "bumping and grinding"— Joey's euphemism for debt collecting—he had managed to collect only $150,000, despite many games of Russian roulette and other common techniques for extracting payment. Most of the debts were ultimately uncollectible; that is, the debtors could not be located to satisfy their obligations. And because of his friendship with Bucky, Joey never pocketed any of the collections; he gave everything he gathered to Artie.

In the end, Joey helped to straighten out each of Artie's debts, fronting him additional money as necessary. In exchange, Strahl gave Bangs fifty-one percent ownership in his lucrative Cape Cod-based company, Travel Brokers of America, Ltd., which ran the nationwide gambling junkets. The operation also illegally transferred credit card payments from Strahl's escort company, Show Girls of Las Vegas—of which Joey also became a proud part-owner—a thinly veiled front for a prostitution ring operated under the purview of the Rhode Island syndicate.

Bangs and Strahl ran the junkets and escort service professionally, observing an FCC regulation that required junketeers to pay for their chartered plane sixty days before departure from Logan Airport in Boston. Bangs and Strahl required big gamblers—aka "whales"—to pay half of the hefty price tag for their seats upon reservation and the balance at least thirty days in advance. If there were vacant seats on a flight, Bangs wholesaled them to a junketeer named "Captain Bill," who operated out of New Orleans, or gifted them to family, friends or business associates on both sides of the law.

Bangs received a minimum upfront payment from the Riviera of $400 cash per high roller, plus a fair percentage of any money the gamblers lost at the hotel's casino. After a period of bringing the establishment increased income, the hotel gave Joey business cards imprinted with the alias "Joe Banks."

Bangs also took responsibility for collecting unpaid markers or cash advances the casino offered to the junket gamblers. Bangs or Strahl approved every advance beforehand and were on the hook if a whale tried to avoid settling. One way or another, every debt was paid. In addition, if a high roller exceeded his marker limit, Bangs offered a subsidiary package in the form of a short-term loan, which carried a hefty markup. Many unlucky gamblers attempted to settle their accounts by offering Bangs gems, jewelry or other personal items well below market value, but Joey had already had his share of fencing such items and was interested in nothing but cold cash, small bills only.

Bangs averaged ten to twenty thousand dollars per junket, not including kickbacks or favors. He also earned a percentage from blocks of rooms he rented for the Riviera and from the Eastern Airlines flights he chartered and filled with 252 passengers per flight, using Strahl's established mailing list. Soon, the business was growing so fast that Bangs and Strahl brought in Artie's son, Butchie, to run the junkets from Boston to Atlantic City, where Artie had been unable to obtain a gaming license. Because of Strahl's criminal record, New Jersey was not as forgiving as Nevada.

The cherry on Joey's cake was the cash he skimmed from accompanying expensive, high-class escorts to the rooms of any "lucky" whales. And Bangs himself entertained women—sometimes five at a time—in his own luxury suite at the Riviera. An ambitious young bell captain dubbed "Joe the Bellboy" shuffled women to and from Bangs' room, filling Joey's orders for hair color, complexion and breast size and earning tips of $100 to $500 for his efforts.

Bangs' suite quickly became a favorite gathering spot for the Las Vegas glitterati that counted, among others, the celebrated middleweight boxing champ Marvelous Marvin Hagler and his entourage, including Hagler's mother, Ida Mae, who adored Bangs, and Hagler's half-brother, the middleweight contender Robbie Sims.

Bangs was introduced to Hagler by Strahl, who had met the fighter's trainer-managers, the brothers Goody and Patrick Petronelli, while living in Brockton, Massachusetts, and he and Hagler soon became fast friends. In fact, Bangs was partly responsible for the back-scratching deal that brought Hagler from Caesar's Palace to the Riviera, where Bangs and Strahl received cash kickbacks every time the champ fought at the casino. Whatever name he used—Joey Bangs, Dr. Taylor, Joe Banks, Joe Fisher, or even, on occasion, Mickey Mouse—Joey had his way in Vegas.

The junkets provided the most fun the men had ever experienced. For one trip to Atlantic City led by Butchie, Bangs accompanied an old-time Met cop from the Fellsway Division to the airport, where he introduced him to Artie, Bucky, and Bucky's wife, Elaine. Artie informed Joey that there was a vacant seat on the flight and insisted that he come along. Bangs declined; he had come from work still dressed in his police uniform—his holstered revolver slung low on his hip—and, unfortunately, didn't have a change of civilian clothes in the cruiser, which he had left in front of the terminal.

Bucky flashed him a look. *Fuck it,* Joey mused, *carpe diem.* Bangs called the Lower Basin Station from a payphone and told them to send two officers to pick up his cruiser, along with his service revolver, which he secured in the trunk. And away he went.

Upon arriving at the Resorts Hotel in Atlantic City, Bangs discovered that the distinguished hotel's foremost apparel shop was closed on Sunday, so he ventured into the only open store he could find—a country-western themed outlet, of all things. He purchased a pair of pearl-white cowboy boots, white pants, and a white shirt covered in shiny rhinestones and silver buttons, with tassels running the length of the sleeves, and, of course, a matching ten-gallon hat to complete the ensemble. He sized himself up in the mirror—*Buffalo Bill on crack*, he thought—and swaggered out of the store and into the laughter of his traveling companions.

Fun times turned serious, however, when Bangs and Barrett quickly lost thousands of dollars and found themselves nearly out of cash. Bangs phoned his girlfriend, Cheryl Fisher, and asked her to bring him a briefcase he needed for "work," or more accurately, for the fifty thousand dollars locked inside. Reluctantly, Fisher hopped a shuttle to Philadelphia, where Bangs had a stretch limousine waiting to drive her to the resort. When she arrived at the casino, she found Joey hunkered over a table trying to squeeze a few last plays from the cash he had.

Bangs was still sporting the cowboy get-up when Fisher tried to drag him from the table to catch the latest flight to Boston. After a few minutes of cajoling, she left him there and took their hired car by herself. Joey finally snapped out of his trance, realized what was happening, and grabbed a taxi, arriving barely in time to slide in next to Cheryl, who refused to speak for the entire trip. He was down about twenty grand for the weekend, and it ate at him so badly that by the time they landed in Beantown, he had pulled all the tassels from his sleeves. Bobby Spencer met Bangs and Fisher at the airport to give them a ride home but lost himself in Bang's outfit and had to let Cheryl drive because he was laughing so hard.

On another junket, Barrett brought along his oldest son, who had just turned eighteen, and prodded Joey to help the kid get laid. Bangs summoned to the suite at the Riviera one of his favorite escorts, a beautiful twenty-something who loved to play, and Bucky's son had a blast, as did Joey.

Despite brisk business and riotous living, Bangs and Strahl were not immune to tragedy. During this time, Butchie Strahl perished in a crash when his chartered dual-prop plane caught fire and went down, killing everyone on board. Strahl was devastated by grief and guilt and never recovered from the blow, declining thereafter into self-destruction.

▼ ▼ ▼

During the course of Bangs and Strahl's two-year stint as partners in Travel Brokers of America, the men ran hundreds of gaming junkets and shook down dozens of other New England-based travel agencies that had the gall even to consider running junkets of their own, eventually putting most of the competition out of business.

On one trip to Las Vegas, Strahl introduced Bangs to a couple of travel agents from Orange County, California—slick, well-groomed Hollywood types—who ran five-star golf junkets that catered to avid golfers who were fanatical about playing the nation's top PGA courses. Over a few too many drinks at the Riviera, the men revealed that they were actually interested in running gaming trips to Vegas from California.

A few weeks later, Bangs and Strahl flew west. A stretch limousine picked them up at John Wayne International Airport near Anaheim and chauffeured them to a five-star hotel on the coast. The following day, they joined the other junketeers on an eighty-foot yacht to talk business, while a crew of topless, buxom blondes catered to their every whim as the yacht made its way to picturesque Catalina Island.

The California-based agents proposed a collaboration and insisted that the new venture move from leasing planes to purchasing their own, to take advantage of tax breaks. In fact, the agents had already found two Boeing 707s at a good price. After additional research, Bangs discovered that if they named the new service "American Indian Airlines" (AIA) and hired a minimum number of Native Americans, they could reap even greater financial incentives from the federal government.

Bangs' mind raced in the following weeks as he continued his due diligence—his gut told him this deal was huge; he just had to play it right. Orange County didn't yet have a gambling junket or charter service to Las Vegas, and Joey knew that southern California had plenty of potential clients, including wealthy entrepreneurs, professional athletes and entertainers. He summoned an astute businessman from Atlantic City named "Ricky" to evaluate his research. Ricky had a wealth of experience in the aviation industry, and he confirmed Joey's calculations and examined the 707s. They were pristine, he told Joey, and priced unbelievably well.

Bangs negotiated hard for four months to put the deal together, all the while working as an MDC sergeant in Boston and traveling frequently to Las Vegas. During the tedious bargaining process, Joey spent more than $50,000 of his own money on various expenses, including pricey gifts for his west-coast partners. On several occasions, he overnighted live Maine lobsters to Orange County and hired top California chefs to prepare sumptuous meals for the travel agents.

As part of their negotiations, Bangs and the agents determined that the business start-up costs would total $14 million—$7 million from Bangs and Strahl's partnership and the other end from the California agents. Joey and Artie managed to scrape together about half of their share, before they approached various reputed New England gangsters, who agreed to provide the remainder. Joey's numbers were good, and he and Artie knew this was an industry in which they could easily skim from the top and launder money.

As the AIA launch date approached, Bangs hired Giles Robb, the marketing director for the Riviera, to design and print advertising and business stationery and handle all other set-up for the venture. A retired Air Force officer, Robb nailed every detail, down to the vanity toll-free telephone number. American Indian Airlines was ready to fly.

But Joey's suspicions grew when the California agents began pressuring Bangs and Strahl for their half of the money. Bangs noted that mechanics seemed to be working on the planes more than necessary, even though Ricky had given them a passing grade. And then, just hours before Bangs and Strahl were to sign the paperwork to close the deal, they received notice from the plane charter company scheduled to fly them to Orange County the next day that the check from the California agents had bounced. *Bullshit!*

Naturally, Bangs put the deal on hold—a move that made the agents livid—and began investigating deeper. Joey had wondered all along how the golf junketeers would raise their end. Junkets such as theirs were legitimately lucrative, but crunching the numbers based on his best guess of what they made, he couldn't see $7 million dollars in profit. But they said all the right things to convince Bangs that they could deliver; they must have other businesses or investors, Joey reasoned, but he hadn't been able to put the pieces together. Obviously, the agents didn't have their half of the cash ready and likely didn't even have the ability to raise the funds. Bangs had no doubt they were attempting to scam him, but as a businessman, he remained professional, cool, and collected.

After much deliberation, Bangs flew an "acquaintance" from Boston to Las Vegas and set off by car with his mob associate to Venice, California, where they picked up another player, a one-time Providence, Rhode Island, resident who was on the lam out west. Well-armed, the trio headed down the coast to Orange County, stopping off at Dana Point to take in the ocean view and enjoy a fine seafood lunch.

When the gun-toting Bangs and his armed associates arrived at the agents' office, the Californians were terrorized. Joey warned them to get out of "the wise guy business" and find another line of work, and he demanded they reimburse his $50,000 in out-of-pocket expense money. In actuality, Bangs was tempted to commandeer the golf junket agency, but ultimately he realized the business wasn't worth the time or hassle; he was making so much money from his other ventures that he wanted to avoid unnecessary entanglements with anything less profitable or potentially troublesome. Bangs and his cohorts dished out a brutal beating on the agents, and Joey never heard from them again.

After the deal for the 707s fell through, Bangs purchased a Lear jet under the name of a shell company and used the plane for business trips between the east coast and Las Vegas, as well as increasingly frequent flights between Florida and South America, for his other ventures.

Shortly thereafter, Strahl lost his Nevada gaming license and was later barred from the city altogether. Apparently, Artie had developed a reputation among the Riviera's waitresses for his incessant groping and harassment, and after he tried to offer several women illegal drugs as tips, Robb confronted Strahl and saw to it that he was promptly removed from the casino. Robb also warned Bangs never to try the same shenanigans.

Bangs tried to help Strahl find a soft landing. They reasoned that they could use Joey's contacts, including a former Maryland state delegate who was taking bribes to help support his high-maintenance wife. The scheme was to install illegal slot machines in a Caesar's Palace resort located in Pennsylvania's Pocono Mountains and let Artie keep the earnings for managing the machines. But the plan went awry. The politician and his wife were subsequently convicted of mail fraud and sentenced to probation, while Strahl's conviction carried a four-year sentence in the federal penitentiary in Lewisburg, Pennsylvania. Strahl's criminal woes continued when he was later convicted of money laundering and mail fraud in excess of $500,000 and sentenced to serve a concurrent one-year term. Nevertheless, by the conclusion of the lengthy trial, Artie had already served the time.

The AIA affair and the slot machine debacle took a toll on Joey, but, ever the sly one, he managed to keep himself off the radar of law enforcement and was never charged with any wrongdoing. Though difficulties such as these might have knocked out lesser men, Bangs pulled himself up by the bootstraps and was soon back in Boston, business as usual.

Times got even better and faster after Spencer and Barrett introduced Bangs to "chirping powder"—cocaine. And it didn't take a self-starter like Joey long before he drew comparisons around town to Tony Montana, Al Pacino's character in *Scarface*. With coke now in the mix, the bars and banks and police departments of Boston offered much too small a canvas for Bangs' brush.

A LITTLE DAB'LL DO YA: THE DRUG YEARS

IN THE LATE 1970S, BANGS' LONGTIME PARTNER BOBBY SPENCER decided he wanted in on the blazing-hot disco craze. Bobby borrowed twenty grand from Bangs to buy a majority share in a popular Boston discothèque, Club Max, and after that tranche ran out, he convinced Joey to invest another pretty penny to keep the joint afloat. Bangs didn't give the request a second thought—he trusted Spencer with his life and knew he was good for it.

Located just outside historic Faneuil Hall Marketplace, Spencer's nightspot provided a hub for the booming cocaine scene and a haven for Bobby's promiscuity. Bangs frequented the club regularly, becoming acquainted with the scene's players, and Spencer regaled him with tales of banging two or three coke whores at a time and discovering the world of BDSM. Although Spencer was accustomed to the effects of cocaine, Bangs had never sampled hard drugs. In fact, Joey detested narcotics, and like the old-time cops who were his preferred drinking buddies, he didn't even smoke pot, as so many of the younger officers did. The older cops remembered all too well the confrontations with anti-war protesters in the 1960s and early 1970s. The violent clashes left many hard-working policemen seriously injured by bricks, bottles, and Molotov cocktails, and the police attributed the conflicts to the irrational behavior of drug-fueled young adults.

Spencer pestered Bangs to give cocaine a try until Joey finally agreed to snort a pinch. The experience only confirmed Joey's anti-drug stance— he hated the euphoria and vomited violently. Spencer persisted until he got Bangs to smoke it, but Joey had a similar reaction. Nothing, it seemed, would ever hook Bangs on drugs—until Spencer told him how much money he could make from the shit.

Of course, Spencer's true motive lay in finding a long-term cash supply for himself: the nightclub was running through the typical highs and lows of an alcohol-based business, and Bobby's drug use was burning up any potential profits. Later, after the Depositors Trust bank heist, Spencer grilled Bangs for well over a year: Bobby knew that Clemente and Doherty were involved somehow, and he suspected that Bangs had participated as well. Now Bobby wanted to figure out how to tap into Joey's deep pockets.

▼ ▼ ▼

It was about this time in 1981 that Bucky Barrett introduced Bangs to the man who would soon become Joey's most profitable acquaintance: Joseph "Irish Joe" Murray. Irish Joe was the most powerful man in Charlestown— the armored-car robbery capital of the world—and an independent operator who ran the city with an iron fist and was known to have jacked a number of armored cars and banks himself.

But by now Murray spent most of his days tending to the more urgent affairs of controlling the town and managing the Celtic Tavern in Charlestown's Sullivan Square, which he had purchased and restored to its original glory. Murray took on the tavern's bartender as a partner because he reasoned that the man would be less likely to steal from himself. Of course, the common joke was that the way a Charlestown gangster split his loot was short and to the quick: he killed his partner. But nobody in his right mind fucked with Irish Joe.*

Murray served honorably in the Navy during the Vietnam War and was a well-known supporter of the Irish Republican Army. He backed his play in the Boston underworld with an intimidating personality and an imposing physical presence—handsome, chiseled, six-foot-two, light brown hair, piercing eyes and a quiet manner that belied the violence beneath the surface. Murray had battled alcoholism, but by the time he

---

* There's certainly no love lost between Winter Hill/Somerville, where I grew up, and Charlestown. I played semi-pro football for the Charlestown Townies under the tutelage of John Houlihan, who was a hell of a head coach and a one-time friend—as well as a convicted felon. Go Townies!

met Bangs, he didn't drink, smoke, or use drugs of any kind. Nevertheless, he had parlayed his take from the scores he and Barrett had pulled off into millions by investing in the drug trade, mainly cocaine and marijuana.

The mutual respect and admiration between Barrett and Murray persuaded Bangs to test the murky waters of drug trafficking, but he told Murray he needed to consult with his partner Spencer before diving in. So Bangs purchased an ounce of cocaine from Murray, worth two thousand dollars on the street, and took it to Club Max, where Spencer had a setup for measuring the drug's quality. Spencer had learned to judge cocaine's purity by examining it under a microscope: if the layers of sparkling powder looked like grains of salt, he knew the drug had been cut, or diluted. If the powder looked like shiny snowflakes, they had a winner.

Spencer was dazzled by the consistency of Murray's cocaine—in fact, he told Bangs it was unequivocally better than anything he had ever seen in Boston. Spencer's mind raced when Bangs said he could get as much product as Spencer could move; Bobby assured Joey he could move it by the truckload.

Bangs purchased a sizeable amount of cocaine from Murray, and Spencer taught him how to cut it with either powdered procaine or inositol, and schooled him in the finer points of weighing, packaging and selling the product. In the early 1980s, a kilo of cocaine cost Bangs about sixty thousand dollars, and even without cutting it, Joey could easily make five grand in profit per kilo. His customer base of fellow cops and civilians alike expanded rapidly, and Bangs was soon moving ten kilos and netting fifty grand a week without breaking a sweat.

The transactions couldn't have been easier. Even while in uniform, Bangs dropped into Murray's Liquor Store in Day Square, a predominantly Italian neighborhood in East Boston, and gathered a few grocery items. At the checkout, Michael Murray, Joe's younger brother, slipped the drugs into the brown paper bags and topped it off with bread, milk and eggs. Bangs already had orders in place and made his deliveries—and his fifty grand in profit—in less than an hour.

For his part, Joe Murray was delighted; he was picking up the ninety-seven percent pure cocaine for thirty grand a kilo and doubling his money. As Bangs became a top earner and his friendship with Murray tightened, Irish Joe eventually dropped his price from sixty grand to fifty. Before long, Bangs and Bucky Barrett ruled a growing cocaine empire, with Bucky handling the South Shore and Joey managing greater Boston's inner-city area and all of the North Shore.

When demand for cocaine began to outstrip supply, Bangs and Barrett searched out additional suppliers in case Murray's sources fell short. And the pursuit of powder led them into some of their finest adventures yet.

❧ ❧ ❧

One of Barrett's *La Cosa Nostra* contacts, known around town as "Jake Bag-o'-Doughnuts" for his insatiable love of the confections, offered to let the pair in on a home invasion, which, he assured them, included a sizable stash of cocaine.

Jake was an old-school criminal fifteen years Bangs' senior who had done hard time with the Winter Hill gang's Howie Winter. He now resided in Cumberland, Rhode Island, and had found his niche among the Raymond Patriarca Mafia clan. Jake was short and quite stout, a casual dresser who always drove a newer Cadillac or Lincoln and never failed to bring an offering of doughnuts whenever he visited a friend or business associate. Jake and Bucky were big friends; in fact, Jake stopped by Barrett's South Shore home at least once a week, doughnuts in hand, come hell or high water.

Jake met with Barrett and Bangs and explained that the proposed robbery was an inside job: an acquaintance of his was angry that his drug-dealer uncle had screwed him on a deal, and the man wanted to steal back his money. Jake and the others could have any other cash or drugs they found. Ever the non-violent type, Barrett decided to pass on the job and offered his end to Ben, the safecracker he had recruited to plan the abandoned Saugus Bank and state treasury heists. Ben would have no problem cracking a home safe like the one in question, and for Bangs, this seemed like the perfect job to hone his own creative criminal talents and investigate a potential new way to acquire drugs.

The robbery started auspiciously: Bangs and Ben waited outside the house in a stolen vehicle, plundering the box of doughnuts Jake had supplied, while Jake and another Rhode Island acquaintance forced their way inside the residence and tied up the occupants. Once the husband and wife were bound and gagged, Jake signaled Bangs via police radio that he and Ben could enter.

Bangs began a sweep of the premises and quickly discovered an assortment of weaponry, mainly hunting rifles and handguns, from which he helped himself to a revolver and a sawed-off .410 shotgun. Ben set to work on cracking the safe and within minutes summoned Joey to the room. Bangs bounded up the stairs and into the master bedroom, anticipating a booty of ten kilos and a pile of cash. Instead, he found Ben kneeling in front of an empty safe. Bangs went ballistic and stormed from the house. Jake and his man scrounged up a few pieces of jewelry and some cash, but when everything was accounted for, Bangs' take totaled a lousy twelve hundred dollars, which he gave to Ben, who was strapped for cash at the time.

Jake's big mistake, however, was selecting the wrong target. The Italian couple he robbed was also in good standing with associates of the Rhode Island *La Cosa Nostra*, and they identified Jake—the only one of the crew they recognized. Shortly thereafter, Bag-o'-Doughnuts was discovered dead, shot in the face, along with his beloved German shepherd, who had apparently fought ferociously before meeting his demise.

While investigating the murder and animal cruelty case, the FBI tracked down Bangs for questioning—the first time they had approached him concerning any crime. They showed him an extensive collection of surveillance photos they had accumulated of him with various underworld characters, including Jake, but in every case, Bangs had a plausible reason for being seen with the suspected criminals.

One of the individuals was a Cuban named Glenn Castro, whom Jake had befriended in prison and introduced to Bangs just a few days before he was killed. Jake knew that Castro had a broad network of drug connections along the eastern seaboard, especially in Florida. And since Castro had just been released and was in dire need of work, Jake reasoned that Bangs might be able to use the kid's services.

Bangs knew Castro's type well: clean-cut, well dressed, with a finely measured mix of charm and hustle. Bangs eased into the relationship with Castro by testing him with a simple gig. The New England Telephone Company was having union trouble, and the company's attorney approached Bangs about working as a bodyguard for another company executive. The job was too small for Bangs, so he referred the lawyer to Castro. Castro acquitted himself well and made a few grand for some easy work.

Meanwhile, Bangs checked out Castro and confirmed that he had strong connections in Miami and could source quality cocaine for thirty thousand dollars a kilo instead of Boston's price of fifty to sixty. The hassle for Bangs was that he frequently had to travel out of state, or even to the Bahamas or South America on occasion, to close deals and retrieve the goods. And on top of that, he now had to deal with the treacherous Colombians, whom he detested. Ever cautious, Bangs developed a protocol for drug buys that limited his contact with foreigners and provided ample protection.

Most of Bangs' deals involved at least five kilos—worth approximately $500,000 on the street—and Bangs did not trust anyone, including Castro, regardless of how much he liked the kid. So Joey hired a pair of hustlers to assist in the transactions. One was Big Jake Rooney, a cool-headed operator Bangs had known for years, and the other, a well-known and respected truck hijacker from the Savin Hill area who went only by the name "Cavanaugh."

Rooney and Cavanaugh would drive to Miami with a trunk full of "heavy equipment"—guns, grenades, bulletproof vests—and a suitcase of cash. The money, of course, was never Bangs' personal wad—it belonged to Clemente, Doherty and O'Leary—and Joey was just "investing" it for them, he always joked.

Three days later, Bangs and Spencer would fly to the Sunshine State to meet Rooney and Cavanaugh at a predetermined location, usually a flea-ridden motel on the outskirts of town. Joey detested Miami, which he dubbed "the devil's shithole," and each and every drug deal that took place there was a tense standoff. Bangs would rather have dealt with the Colombians in their own country, where he thought they would be more at ease and thus more trusting.

Bangs' cash always remained secured in the trunk of the vehicle driven by the heavily armed Rooney and Cavanaugh. The skeptical Colombians were offended that Joey didn't trust them enough to bring the money into the motel room, and they resented the fact that Spencer always had to set up his portable microscope to test the product; the Colombians had never seen anything like it, and they suspected it was all for show. Nevertheless, Spencer never closed a transaction without consulting his prized equipment.

Under the strained circumstances, Bangs demanded that there never be more than two Colombians in the meeting, and Castro stood to the side, hands in his pockets, serving as a neutral interpreter and playing peacemaker if the transaction got sticky. The only advantage Bangs and Spencer had in dealing with Castro's contacts was that Castro had painted them as "Americanos locos." Joey and Bobby maintained the appearance by strolling into the meetings brandishing M-16s and hand grenades strapped to their chests.

As Bangs and Spencer entered the motel for one particular exchange, Joey spotted a half dozen Colombians in an adjacent parking lot trying to conceal machine guns beneath their oversized Hawaiian beach shirts. When Bangs and Spencer entered the room, the Colombians making the deal tried to throw them off guard and began snorting the product, chasing it with spiced rum and inviting the Americans to join in. Spencer fell to and sniffed everything he could, but Bangs stayed on the bright.

In fact, Bangs and Spencer were playing the Colombians. Bangs started to rant about receiving at least eighty percent of each kilo in rock form, with the rest in shake, which he knew was most likely mixed with cut. The Colombians protested, as usual, that their powder was pure, but Bangs argued that in Boston everyone wanted rock—period.

While the others were distracted by the confrontation, Spencer retrieved a plastic baggy filled with an inositol cut and swapped it with cocaine as he tested—and rejected—individual kilos of product. Bangs and Spencer were risking their lives for a measly few grand, but Spencer played the part perfectly and made the switch unnoticed.

Because of the tense atmosphere—everyone snorting coke, the crazy Americans covered in pineapple hand grenades, Bangs yammering without pause while Spencer clattered about with his testing equipment—as the meeting drew on, the Colombians wanted nothing more than to get their cash and get out. When Rooney and Cavanaugh finally delivered the money, the Colombians didn't bother to count it, and Bangs, of course, promised that if there were a problem, he'd make it up to them "next time," knowing full well he had shorted them several thousand dollars.

The same routine played out regularly for years—Rooney and Cavanaugh driving money and drugs to and fro, Bangs and Spencer zipping in on first-class flights to hold chaotic meetings with their Colombian counterparts—interactions and relationships that walked the razor's edge between trust and treachery.

In the early 1980s, the Colombian invasion was in full swing, the coca was plentiful, and Castro had extended his network of suppliers to New York and other major metropolitan areas along the east coast. He introduced Bangs and Spencer to a new group of Miami-based dealers who were hungry to cut a deal and prove themselves, and Bangs figured he could easily work over the newbies for a sweet profit. The initial deal was one of Bangs' best, but as he and Spencer left the motel room, they walked into an ambush by their former suppliers, who had caught wind of the transaction.

Heavily armed with machine-gun pistols, the jilted Colombians shot up everything in sight, yet failed to hit their intended targets, Bangs and Spencer. Joey and Bobby returned machine-gun fire, tossed a hand grenade in their general direction for good measure, and made their escape with Rooney and Cavanaugh. They never saw the Colombians again.

▾ ▾ ▾

After this near miss, Spencer became increasingly paranoid from all the cocaine he was ingesting, and on one occasion, he lost control when Rooney left him and Bangs stranded in a shady Florida motel with five kilos of coke, a suitcase of money, and a couple of twitchy Venezuelans. Bangs and Spencer concluded the deal, but as they waited for Rooney to arrive to take possession of the drugs and courier it home, their anxieties mounted.

Rooney, it seems, was a devoted family man, and he had arranged to return to Boston for a son's Pop Warner football game before heading back to Florida to finish the job. But he didn't show in time. Bangs was beside himself, and Spencer was losing his mind. Frustrated, bored and anxious, Spencer embarked on a two-day bender of coke and booze, until Joey decided they had no choice but to fly back to Boston with the cocaine in their possession so he and Bobby could report at work. They were still cops, after all.

Spencer hadn't slept in days and was becoming delirious. Bangs wrangled him to Miami-Dade airport and thought the situation was under control, until Bobby disappeared just minutes before the flight was scheduled to leave, sending Joey on a frantic search for him. Spencer had ducked into a restroom and locked himself in the back stall, where he began taping packets of cocaine beneath his clothing, accidentally dropping his police badge and ID into the toilet in the process. Spencer was also toting a carry-on bag stuffed with ten thousand Quaaludes he had purchased on the side.

Spencer exited the restroom and headed toward the gate, trying his best to conceal his frenzied mental state. An announcement over the PA called out his flight; Bobby froze, his mind raced. He thought he heard that all passengers would be searched before boarding. Spencer took off running through the crowded terminal, ripping the packets of coke from under his shirt and dropping them on the floor, emptying his pockets in a panic and stashing the carry-on under a bench. Bangs noticed the commotion and made a beeline toward Spencer, scooping up the packets and stuffing them into his jacket, cool as a cucumber. Bangs finally sidled up to Spencer, grabbed him hard around the shoulders, and calmed him long enough to get on the airplane. No agents, no police, no suspicions, and to Joey's relief, all packets accounted for.

Shortly after his return to Boston, in November 1982, Bangs was offered a piece of a bank robbery in New Hampshire, but his gut told him to pass. Castro took the slot, and the crew was busted. Facing lengthy federal prison time, Castro broke with code and started telling stories about Bangs' illicit activities to FBI Special Agent Brendan Cleary.

The following year, Cleary testified to a federal grand jury that Castro claimed he was with Bangs when a fifteen-ton shipment of marijuana arrived in Boston—a cache that Bangs sold in the course of two hours, via telephone. Castro also gave up the other participants in the deal, including Jake Rooney, Bobby Spencer, and Bucky Barrett, but the grand jury never subpoenaed Bangs or his cohorts. Joey's luck seemed infinite.

❧ ❧ ❧

Following the close call in Miami and the bust in New Hampshire, Bucky Barrett hounded Bangs to wean himself from the dangerous cocaine business in order to move more marijuana instead. Although Barrett's advice to Bangs usually went in one ear and out the other, he could be convincing when he had a strong opinion. Bucky reasoned that cocaine was becoming a hot political topic and drawing far too much attention, whereas pot was generally regarded as harmless and not worth prosecuting. In fact, many of Bangs' cocaine buyers were already purchasing bales of marijuana from him. Even so, Bangs never completely abandoned cocaine sales, but he did double down on his trade with Murray and began moving marijuana by the boatload.

Murray was ballsy and fearless, distributing an entire cargo ship of pot in a single evening with the assistance of Bangs and other rogue Met cops who packed bale upon bale into police paddy wagons and scurried into the night on their assigned delivery routes.

Murray was careful to change up his operation routines regularly, never telling anyone when shipments were due in port and sometimes forgoing the paddy wagons for rented U-Haul trucks and hired loaders. In such cases, Murray called Bangs from a payphone—he hated using phones at all—and arranged to meet him at a local coffee shop or diner. There, he doled out detailed information on where to find the preloaded trucks, whether keys would be delivered or hidden, and what the timetable was for making deliveries and returning the trucks.

Moreover, Murray advanced bales of marijuana to Bangs and Barrett "on the sleeve," after which they had two weeks to pay for the shipment. Because he liked and respected Joey, Murray sold him the choicest grass for a quarter of its street value of a thousand dollars a pound. Bangs never worried about being cheated by Murray—he knew Irish Joe was a man of integrity and had always treated him fairly—and in turn Bangs never attempted to take advantage of Murray's good nature. If a bale was light or wet, as so often happened, Murray made it right on the next shipment.

Although he was always respectful of those above him in the pecking order, Bangs was not so congenial when it came to the average Joe. He and Spencer conjured up one particularly profitable gaff while distributing drugs. Bangs would meet a potential customer at a lounge or restaurant, and after the transaction was complete, invite the buyer for a drink. Almost everyone accepted the offer, so Bangs and his mark would lock the goods in the target's trunk and return for a drink. Meanwhile,

Spencer—who was usually on duty—would break into the vehicle, steal the contraband, and have the vehicle towed or stolen.

Eventually, they figured out how to simplify the maneuver even further. Spencer waited in his cruiser until the mark left the parking lot and then pulled him over on some fabricated infraction, performed a search of the vehicle, seized the contraband, and gave the dupe the option of being arrested or just driving away. Nothing could be easier.

Although they were making money hand over fist, Bangs and Spencer continually butted heads over the method of distribution. Bangs sold cocaine only in large portions and wanted all the cops beneath him to do the same. However, Spencer contended they could make higher profits selling the narcotic in small packages from his nightclub. Bangs advised Spencer, who was by this time smoking as much as he sold, that unloading the shit from the nightclub—in essence, opening a public retail location instead of selling wholesale—was far too risky and that they needed to keep the businesses separate. But Spencer had lost all sense of danger—he was brazen enough to sell eight-balls of cocaine from the saddlebag of his police motorcycle while on official duty, in broad daylight.

Of all the people Bangs dealt with, his longtime friend Spencer was the only one he would front ounces or kilos to, and without fail, he ended up chasing down the payment. Spencer's disco drove his life, and Bobby flaunted his drug use and promiscuity. As their friendship waned, Spencer asked Bangs not to come into the club in his police uniform, because it frightened off the more skittish clientele, and Bobby kept a plaid, double-breasted sports jacket in the coat check room for the times Joey did drop in. And Bangs stopped by frequently, usually to collect payment for cocaine, and was never surprised by whatever he saw: full-scale, after-hours orgies in the middle of the dance floor, illuminated by numerous mirror balls; Spencer ingratiating himself with the richer clientele by serving Moët champagne as if it were tap water or chatting up the sluttiest women in the house in hopes of scoring a threesome in the back office. Peeved that Joey refused to join the debauchery, Spencer demanded that he at least drink his beer from a champagne glass.

One Saturday evening about ten o'clock, Bangs tracked down Spencer in the stockroom of the club. Bobby had been dodging Joey all week, knowing that a $2,000 coke tab was due. The partners squared off.

"I'm not in the mood," Bangs warned. "Your wise-guy valet just threatened to tow my Cadillac. I want my money."

"Where's your car?"

"On the sidewalk, right out front!"

The men burst into laughter, and the mood lightened for just a moment.

"Enough bullshit. Where's my money?" Bangs picked up again.

"I told you I'd pay you 'Saturday night' and Saturday night's not over yet," Bobby tap-danced.

"This place is mobbed," retorted Bangs, "and you're telling me you don't have two grand? What do you do with all the club's money?"

Spencer smiled and shuffled Bangs back out to the dance floor, grabbing him a cold beer and a champagne glass of ice on the way. Spencer gestured toward the pulsating throng of sweaty bodies.

"Pick any girl you like."

Bangs perked up—maybe he'd score some trim while he waited for Bobby to cough up the cash. Bangs played along and pointed out a smoking-hot young blonde in a skintight yellow dress: "That one—with the tits!"

"You see," Spencer explained philosophically, "that's the difference between you and me: you want one, I want them *all*."

Bobby's smart-ass attitude infuriated Bangs, who was in no mood for dilly-dallying.

"Tonight, Bobby," Joey remarked coldly, before wandering into the crowd in search of the yellow dress.

At the stroke of midnight, Spencer waved Bangs to a booth and handed him an envelope. Joey pocketed the cash, nodded and slipped out the door to his Cadillac, still parked on the sidewalk. Before driving away, Bangs gave the wise-guy valet an unexpected tip—an open-handed slap that nearly knocked him out.

▾ ▾ ▾

Unfortunately, Bangs ignored the wisdom, *Never mix drugs and friends,* and Spencer was not the only longtime pal Joey had to deal with. In the beginning, Bangs had tried to include Brother O'Leary in the profitable drug gaff, but it never took. He once fronted O'Leary an ounce of cocaine, but Brother didn't really associate with the kind of people who used the narcotic, so he managed to sell only a small portion and returned the rest to Joey, before dropping out of sight for more than nine months. Brother was an old-school drinker who socialized with other drinkers, and in reality, Brother was fine—he had a fat wad of cash from the Depositors Trust job, a new love interest, and an old habit of getting lost in a partying binge for days at a time.

Bangs was relieved, in fact, that O'Leary had drifted out of his life. Because of the potentially dangerous consequences of his insane capers, Brother was not a welcome sight at most of the nightspots Joey frequented, and Spencer, Barrett, Cheryl Fisher and Paul Walker all strongly advised Bangs to stay away from O'Leary.

Then there was Jerry Clemente, who caught wind of Bangs' new enterprise and desperately wanted to get involved in the drug game. Just as greedy as Bangs, Clemente envied the action that Joey had found, but like Brother, he was not friendly with the type of people who indulged in narcotics, and he had no knowledge of the drug world except for the standard notions taught at the police academy. Bangs had no inclination to teach an old dog like Jerry new tricks—he was far too busy and wealthy for that—but he did once front Clemente a single ounce of pure cocaine to see what he could do with it. Somehow, Jerry managed to sell it to a girl who worked at MDC police headquarters, but it took him nearly two weeks to do so—and that was that.

❧ ❧ ❧

By 1982, cocaine was devouring the City of Boston. Doctors, lawyers, politicians, police, "Indian chiefs" and everyone else who could beg, borrow or steal was using the drug in those days, and Boston's elite knew that Bangs and his renegade cops always had the best shit in town. Bangs and his police foot soldiers covered the entire metropolitan area, with contacts in the MDC, Capitol Police and Registry of Motor Vehicles, as well as police departments in Boston, Revere, Medford, Somerville, Cambridge, Chelsea, Everett and Malden. Strangers regularly approached Bangs looking to make a purchase, but if Joey didn't trust the person, he simply told them, "Don't ask me—I'm a cop!"

Jerry and Brother soon faded from the picture, and Spencer became a heavy cocaine user more obsessed with ruling his disco than working his police job or making money. But Bangs and Barrett picked up their pace and eventually involved Depositors Trust partner Tommy Doherty to help them move even faster—or so they thought.

Doherty had never tried cocaine before Bangs approached him, but he easily got a number of Medford cops hooked on the stuff—including himself. Tommy started by snorting a line or two at a time, but once he began freebasing, he smoked day in and day out. He became increasingly paranoid from sleep deprivation and lost all sense of reality and responsibility. Once, for instance, Doherty promised to remodel his mother Mary's house on Pleasant Street while she was vacationing in Florida, but instead he wasted the weeks in anything-goes parties with a handful of Medford cops and a menagerie of friends and coke whores.

Doherty's Medford police department fell hard to cocaine. Many officers smoked and snorted in the police station itself, even the officer-in-charge. Sometimes, Doherty and the OIC would get high and make their way to the firing range in the basement of the station, where they'd vent their anxiety by shooting illegal Mac-10 machine-gun pistols wildly at the targets.

Bangs never knew what would happen next when he entered the Medford station. Most of the officers were in bad shape, stumbling through work like zombies, and the effects of their drug use spilled out of the station and into their personal lives: they floundered in the muck of divorce, domestic violence, and petty crime such as shoplifting. When Doherty managed to get himself on the department's disabled list, many believed he was looking for a way to avoid a polygraph test and stay off the department's radar, but others figured he just wanted an excuse to stay home and make merry.

It was about this time that Bangs met two of Doherty's closest cronies—Tommy's brother-in-law Jackie Gillen and former Medford police officer Al Roberts. Most days, Doherty, Gillen and Roberts holed up in Tommy's garage to smoke coke, as they would do for months to come. Jackie egged on Tommy, and Joey suspected there was an ulterior motive at play. Maybe it was Jackie's wee stature or his slovenly dress or the way he spit his sloppy speech, but Bangs never had any use for Gillen, whom he considered "a wannabe wise guy." For years Gillen skulked around Tommy's garage, mooching food and drugs, hoping to glom onto the spoils of some scam or another concocted, financed and executed by somebody with the sack to actually do the work.

On the other hand, Roberts, a former tenant of Medford firefighter Jimmy McGaffigan, lived in Doherty's garage and worked odd jobs to earn his room and board. Roberts was a lanky, balding man—an affable, non-assuming type that some referred to as Doherty's gofer, since he had served alongside Doherty as a Medford police officer for eight years before resigning due to his failing mental health. A self-taught mechanic, Roberts more often than not wore the same tattered, grease-stained shirt and jeans every day.

The story was that a mental stress disorder had put Roberts out of commission sometime in the early 1980s, but Bangs realized that Roberts had become so addicted to cocaine he had a nervous breakdown and was forced to resign. Nevertheless, Doherty believed in second chances and wanted to help Roberts get back on his feet so he could some day return to the police force. But Roberts' addiction was too much; Bangs often found Al on his hands and knees searching for crumbs of cocaine on the floor of Doherty's garage office.

Despite his troubles, Roberts was mechanically inclined and had become an exceptional carpenter and master at making glass bubble pipes for smoking rock cocaine. He also loved to take things apart, but usually failed to stay focused long enough to put them back together. Once, during an all-night coke-smoking binge while vacationing in Florida, Roberts took apart Bangs' brand-new telescope. When Joey awoke the following morning, he found Roberts sitting stone-silent on the kitchen floor, staring at the dozens of parts strewn in a circle around him. Bangs warned Roberts that he had better take another hit off the cocaine pipe and put the telescope back together or there'd be hell to pay. Roberts reassembled the unit in record time.

Even though he pitied Roberts' state, Bangs had fun playing on Al's paranoia, screwing with him every chance he got, especially when Roberts was high. Sometimes, it was as simple as moving his lips without making a sound, a sight which freaked out Roberts and made him believe he had gone deaf.

Bangs himself only hit the pipe when there were women around—as an aphrodisiac, he rationalized—and on those occasions, he would summon Roberts to his apartment to give him a little "something." When Al arrived, Joey would slip a rock of cocaine between the breasts of one of his call girls and offer, "Hey, Al! Put that in your pipe and smoke it." Bangs' adventures and free-for-all, fuck-it attitude became legendary among friends and foes alike.

▾ ▾ ▾

Once the heat from the Depositors Trust heist had subsided a bit, Doherty purchased a business—Do-It-Yourself Tool Rental, located on Middlesex Avenue in Medford—buying up used items, most of which were stolen, for pennies on the dollar and renting them at premium prices.

Bangs began making cocaine drop-offs to Doherty in the store's back room, taking every precaution possible during the deliveries: he parked a half mile away from the often-crowded store and climbed over a half dozen fences, scampering from watch dogs while trespassing through backyards to remain unseen as he sneaked into the rear entrance of the establishment. Meanwhile, in through the front door walked familiar Medford cops, high as a kite while on duty, looking to purchase additional packages of cocaine. Bangs berated Doherty for his reckless behavior—selling drugs openly while legitimate customers were shopping—but in the end Bangs was too busy to give Doherty and his rogue crew much thought.

By this time, Bangs had cultivated sources that sold him kilos at less than half of Joe Murray's price, and he began using accumulated vacation days to drive or fly to and from Florida to make sizeable purchases—as well as to have a few days away from Cheryl, who had grown unreasonably jealous of his time and attention.

On one of his Florida excursions, Bangs took along Doherty, who had offered the use of his car. The men enjoyed a week of sun and fun and women, and purchased several kilos, which they packed tightly in coffee grounds, talcum powder and duct tape—to throw off drug-sniffing dogs—and stashed in nondescript luggage in the trunk.

On the long drive north, Bangs fell asleep somewhere in the Carolinas, oblivious of Doherty's own drowsiness. When Tommy began swerving, an enthusiastic state trooper fresh out of the academy pulled them over on a deserted stretch of I-95. Doherty flashed a Medford police captain's badge, even though he was only a lieutenant at the time, but the trooper wasn't deterred. Tommy lost his temper, and now on high alert, the trooper ordered him out of the vehicle and told him to open the trunk.

Just as Tommy was about to comply, Bangs awoke, sized up the situation, and began sweet-talking the officer. Neither his charm nor his MDC credentials won points, however, and the suspicious trooper again asked to see inside the trunk. *Fuck it,* Bangs thought, opening the trunk. To the trooper's amazement, he discovered hundreds of dollars' worth of fireworks that Bangs had purchased for his kids at the last gas stop. The men all shared a good laugh, and the trooper bid them a safe trip and departed.

▾ ▾ ▾

Over time, Bangs enlisted other colleagues to work as mules for his drug trafficking. Joey hadn't seen his Capitol Police pal Dick Madden for three or four years, but Clemente had mentioned once in passing that Dick had fallen on hard times financially and was in Florida with his wife, Shirley, trying to figure out their next move. Coincidentally, Bangs and Doherty were in the process of purchasing several kilos of cocaine from a new Florida supplier named Ed Levine.

Bangs and Doherty met Madden on a Saturday around noon at his beachfront condominium in Dania Beach. Bangs was put off when Shirley greeted him as "the infamous Joe Bangs," so he asked Dick if they could reconvene at the Pirates' Den, a favorite watering hole a couple blocks away.

After discussing business over cocktails, Madden agreed to transport the packages of cocaine to Boston, and Bangs advanced him a meager thousand dollars. The next morning, Joey delivered a suitcase to Dick's condo, and two days later, after an uneventful drive, Madden met Bangs and Doherty back in Beantown at the Howard Johnson on Route 128. They pulled around to the rear of the hotel, checked the suitcase, handed Dick an envelope and parted with a handshake.

Bangs and Doherty next headed to Cheryl Fisher's condo in Saugus, where they unpacked the kilos in Fisher's bathtub to minimize the mess of the coffee grounds and talc. Doherty convinced Bangs he could sell the kilos, and against his better judgment, Joey agreed to front him the coke. That simple deal was the beginning of the end.

▼ ▼ ▼

Doherty was usually good for moving five to six ounces per week, mainly to other Medford cops, but before this time, he had never had more than an ounce or two in his possession at any given moment. The temptation was too much for Tommy: he sold to his usual buyers, but ended up smoking most of the lot—and owing Bangs a serious debt.

Bangs would be damned if he were going to let this situation get away from him. Joey moved into the second-floor unit of a dwelling that Doherty owned, situated directly across the street from Tommy's longtime Medford residence, just to keep an eye on his self-indulgent friend. A quiet, urban neighborhood where Doherty owned a number of other properties, Pleasant Street would never be the same.

Living across the street from Doherty turned out to be a big mistake. One morning just after Bangs had stepped out of the shower and was toweling off, the doorbell rang repeatedly. Bangs covered himself with a towel, grabbed a loaded .38, and answered the door to find Doherty's wife, Carol, who informed Joey that Tommy needed him right away, although she couldn't say why. Bangs was not pleased that Doherty, now a police lieutenant, was too out of control to handle whatever problem there was and had sent his wife over to get help.

Bangs threw on a robe and hustled down the stairs. Carol scrambled along behind Joey, apologizing for the intrusion. Bangs scanned Doherty's property as he approached, trying to suss out the situation, and glimpsed Tommy peeking through the curtains anxiously.

Then Bangs spotted the source of the problem, lurking about the front door: the Murphy brothers. The Murphys were serious players, ex-convicts from the Somerville housing projects—the Brick Jungle—a notorious pair of dangerous men who were apparently looking for Tommy's son, Michael. Michael was a good kid, a younger version of Tommy—hands-on, blue-collar, hard-working, with an electrical background. Unlike his father, Michael was laid-back and preferred marijuana to cocaine, but like Tommy, he was now finding his way into troubles of his own.

Bangs approached the Murphys without regard to his bathrobe, which flapped in the breeze, fully exposing his nudity. Joey knew the brothers well.

"What do you two assholes want?"

The brothers asked if he knew a fellow by the name of "Doherty."

"Yeah, he's a fucking Medford police lieutenant! What's it to ya?"

"You must be mistaken," the younger brother replied. "This is a young guy, and definitely not a cop."

"Are you heavy?" Bangs queried, scanning their clothing for bulges that might indicate a weapon.

The brothers showed Bangs "theirs," and Joey showed them "his," withdrawing a .38 Special from his bathrobe pocket.

Bangs calmly instructed Carol to call the Medford police, and he told the brothers it was in their best interest to hand over their weapons before the *real* law arrived. Knowing Bangs as they did, the brothers reluctantly complied. Once Joey had the weapons in his possession, he asked the brothers to give him the story straight, from the beginning: they explained that they had been offered five hundred dollars to break Michael's legs, apparently after Michael had flipped someone off. Bangs was livid.

"You jokers come into *my* neighborhood packing heat because a kid flipped off your asshole buddy?" The brothers simply shrugged.

"Who sent you?" The brothers knew they were in the shit now.

Bangs removed a package of cocaine from his other bathrobe pocket and placed it into the hand of the older brother.

"Now I'll shoot you both then put your guns back in your cold hands if you don't tell me what moron sent you. And I'll get a letter of commendation for doing it."

The brothers rattled off the name of a young man whose father owned a popular restaurant in Teale Square in Somerville.

A Medford police squad car arrived on the scene, and the officers began their approach. Bangs retrieved his cocaine and told the brothers he was going back inside to smoke it. The Murphys asked if Bangs intended to keep their weapons or give them to the cops.

"Are you clean?" The boys nodded yes. "If you're clean, come back later and get them," Bangs answered.

Unfortunately for the Murphys, when the police ran their driver licenses, the National Crime Information Center listed outstanding felony warrants for both men, and they were apprehended on the spot.

As soon as the Medford squad car disappeared around the corner, Bangs returned to his apartment, got dressed, smoked his shit, and went straight to Teale Square to inform the restaurateur what his son had done and to warn him that it had better not happen again. The restaurateur, a friend of Howie Winter's, got the message and reassured Bangs that he'd handle the situation.

▾ ▾ ▾

Although the drug trade was lucrative, it was extremely difficult collecting money from certain individuals, but Bangs always got paid, one way or another—usually the other, in the form of vicious beatings bestowed on delinquent debtors.

At one point, Bangs became too enamored of such street justice for Barrett's taste, and Bucky worked hard to convince him that other methods would settle the debt faster. Barrett persuaded Bangs to give select customers additional product to sell in order to make up their delinquent accounts, rather than administer brutal beatings, which temporarily satisfied his ego but did little to improve his bottom line. Bangs agreed to try Bucky's method, with a twist: Bangs balanced the accounts—from his side, in any case—by diluting his clients' cocaine with extra cut.

By now, Barrett had all but given up the dangerous coke business to focus on his expanding marijuana trade, and, growing tired of the cocaine grind himself, Bangs continued shifting his efforts to marijuana as well. In turn, because of Doherty's growing financial obligation and personal drug problem, Bangs attempted to wean his friend from cocaine and steer him to marijuana, and over time, Tommy became a superb provider, moving five to ten hundred-pound bales at a time.[*]

Bangs himself moved 150 to 200 bales from each new shipment in the first evening, storing the remainder in a broken-down paddy wagon or a U-Haul truck parked behind the MDC's Fellsway station and police academy. In fact, as he had done for card games years prior, Bangs

---

[*] After subtracting the weight of a bale's waterproof wrapping, each hundred-pound bale contained about 94 pounds of marijuana.

removed the paddy wagon's carburetor and placed an unpickable Medeco lock on it for good measure. Joey even conducted many multi-million-dollar deals behind the station, often in broad daylight.

In addition to commandeering fleet vehicles, Bangs stashed kilos of cocaine and other contraband in the police stations' evidence rooms, especially at the Lower Basin, which had a huge storage space that served as a temporary hold for items being taken to the various courts. However, Old Colony's room was a fortress, complete with an alarm system, surveillance cameras and other security measures, and the average police officer could not penetrate it—Bangs, of course, was not the average officer. The locker at the Upper Basin, on the other hand, was very accessible: it was in the sergeant's office. At every station, a sergeant needed to sign for and seal all evidence before placing it into the locker. Once he made sergeant, Bangs helped himself to whatever he wanted, including weapons, booze and drugs, and, after filling out all the proper "John Doe" paperwork, placed his own contraband in the locker, ensuring it would remain uncompromised.

∨ ∨ ∨

Bangs, Clemente, and Doherty not only stashed their illegal gains in certificates of deposit and lucrative mutual funds, but they also invested heavily in real estate. About this time, Bangs and Doherty each sank $82,000 into a sunny Pompano Beach, Florida, penthouse condominium. Clemente also owned a unit in the complex, and Dick Madden's place was just five miles away. Bangs and Doherty had been leasing a condo for about a year, and they reasoned that buying a place would make a nice investment, given that their business showed no signs of slowing.

They paid cash for a corner unit overlooking the pool and placed the title in the name of Doherty's mother, Mary, as a measure to steer clear of law enforcement and the IRS. Although the new condo was plush and had an exquisite ocean view, Bangs slept there only a handful of times after he purchased it, and the property later became a bone of contention between him and Doherty. As Tommy spiraled faster into the cocaine abyss and his debt to Joey surpassed $100,000, Bangs demanded that Doherty quitclaim his share of the condo to cover the deficit. But Doherty neglected to do so, despite Bangs' furious threats of *You pay or you die!* Finally, Bangs began cutting off Doherty's supply.

In spite of his issues with Tommy, Joey enjoyed Mary Doherty's company and often accompanied her for drinks when she was in Florida. On one occasion, after a few rounds, Mary decided she wanted to dance with a much younger man seated at the end of the bar. Bangs approached the young man and explained how it would make the old woman's day if he would dance with her. However, the fellow was preoccupied with putting the moves on a girl his own age and couldn't be bothered. So Bangs did what any good surrogate son would do: he threatened to break the clown's legs. The young man stood up, walked over to Mary, and politely bowed as he asked if he could have the next dance; Mary was thrilled. On their way out of the bar, Bangs dropped the kid twenty bucks for his trouble and a wink for good measure. Mary talked about the dance for months to come.

▼ ▼ ▼

As time passed with no indictment in sight, Clemente began to feel safe enough to spend his measly portion of the Depositors Trust loot, although he was not as circumspect as Bangs. Despite his characteristic slyness, Clemente couldn't fight the thought that Bangs and Doherty were trying to compete with him by buying the Florida condo. Never to be outdone, Clemente spotted an $81,900 sport boat at Edward Thomas' Needham Boat Dealership, and he dropped a cash deposit of $37,900 and financed the remaining $44,000 on his stated annual salary of $26,000. Clemente took delight in christening the vessel *The Fifth Amendment*, but the transaction was a critical mistake, as he would soon learn.

In actuality, the collective forces of federal and state law enforcement, including the Treasury Department, DEA, FBI, ATF, CIA, Massachusetts State Police—and, as Joey liked to gibe, even the Boy and Girl Scouts of America—were breathing down the cops' necks. Bangs knew the government was watching their every move, but somehow he managed to shake the stalkers at will and get away with all manner of malfeasance. He knew that nothing could be routine: he changed up every single action of every single day. That was, in fact, the key to longevity in the underworld, where enemies on both sides of the law—as well as the Grim Reaper himself—could snare anyone coming or going.

Nadine

Although Bangs occasionally bought cocaine from other sources, he continued to purchase marijuana from Joe Murray and was soon making much greater profits than with coke. In an effort to keep Murray content, he often escorted high-priced call girls to Murray's home when his shrewish wife, Susan, was away. For more than two years, Bangs regularly hired a particularly beautiful twenty-one-year-old woman named Robin Benedict, aka "Nadine," to take care of Murray and other select friends and associates.

Nadine eventually became romantically entangled with one of her other clients, William H. J. Douglas, a Tufts University medical professor who resided in Sharon, Massachusetts. When Douglas wasn't jealously stalking Nadine, he was embezzling from the prestigious university and cashing bogus checks at Bobby Spencer's nightclub.

Before long, Douglas discovered Nadine's trick book and decided to inform Susan Murray about her husband's infidelity. Murray caught wind of the call, and knowing the domestic shitstorm that was sure to ensue, made plans to kill Douglas.* However, on March 5, 1983, before Murray could act on his intention, Douglas beat Nadine to death with a hammer and disposed of her bloody body in a dumpster at University Heights Mall in The Bronx.

Douglas managed to evade capture for a time, until the state police discovered Benedict's car at JFK airport and identified her blood and brain matter on the seats. The police had also obtained Benedict's business calendar from her mother, Shirley, who lived in Methuen, and learned that she was on her way to Murray's home when she disappeared. Murray had sufficiently strong alibis to exonerate him, but the heat cut into his business for a number of months, and his home life remained miserable for much longer.

Represented by Boston's premier defense attorney, Thomas Troy ("Tommy"), Douglas accepted a plea bargain to reduce the charge from first-degree murder to manslaughter, and he subsequently received eighteen to twenty years for killing Benedict. He also pled guilty to embezzlement and received a three- to five-year sentence that ran concurrent to the manslaughter sentence. Douglas was a model prisoner, teaching and

---

* In a sad testament to a violent life, Joe Murray was killed in 1994 by his wife, Susan, who claimed that she shot Joe—with his own .357 Magnum—in self-defense after he attacked her.

advising fellow inmates, and accumulated significant credit for good behavior, earning his release in 1993 after serving about half of his sentence.

Dusted and Delusional

After orchestrating the largest bank heist in history, becoming one of the largest drug distributors in New England, and pulling off a lifetime of other crimes, Joey Bangs was nearly impossible to rattle. But sometimes he just wanted to be left alone, and trouble, it seemed, followed him everywhere.

One stifling summer night, Bangs had just knocked off work and stopped at the Embassy Lounge on Somerville Avenue for a nightcap. Wearing a t-shirt and police pants, he was enjoying a beer with ice at the bar when a grungy stranger approached and asked for a light. Peeved by the intrusion, Bangs replied curtly that he didn't smoke. The brazen man asked if Joey wanted to buy a gun and opened his coat to display a .38 Special revolver. Taken aback, Bangs motioned to the bartender, Uncle Franny Delaney, and flashed him a questioning look. Franny shrugged and shook his head to warn Joey to be careful.

Bangs reasoned that, since it should be obvious he was a cop, the man must be either mentally deficient or an undercover ATF agent trying to snare him. Joey decided to let it play and asked how much.

"A hundred fifty."

"I only got seventy-five on me, but I can make a quick call and get the rest. Meet me at the gas station across the street in about ten minutes."

The man exited the bar and trotted across the street, while Joey watched through the window. Bangs made his way to the bar payphone and dialed MDC headquarters. He described the screwball and instructed the dispatch to send a cruiser to the gas station, warning that the man had a weapon and should be considered armed and dangerous. Within five minutes, the cruiser arrived, and the stranger got pinched for possession of an illegal firearm. Bangs later learned that the screwball was in fact just a simpleton who didn't realize who Joey was.

A few months later, while on duty around five o'clock one Sunday morning, Bangs decided to stop at a convenience store in Magoun Square to grab a newspaper before ending his shift. The streets had been quiet—

even desolate—all night, but as Bangs approached the square, he noted the silhouette of a man lurking on the side of the road. Bangs slowed to peer into the shadows, and all of a sudden the man hurled a metal trashcan into the cruiser's windshield. Bangs screeched to a halt and leaped from the cruiser, drawing his weapon as he approached the still man.

The suspect was a sizable goon in his mid twenties who appeared to be under the influence of drugs. Bangs initially thought he might be able to confiscate some contraband and just release the man with a warning, but he determined that the whack job was embroiled in a raging domestic dispute with his girlfriend, who crouched by the building, sobbing desperately.

Bangs and the suspect exchanged words, and the man stated that his uncle was a Cambridge police detective. Bangs knew the detective well and was friendly with his brother, who owned a gas station, but unfortunately, Joey was unable to calm the man and had no choice but to arrest him for disorderly conduct and damaging the cruiser, which was state property.

Bangs grappled the suspect to the ground and withdrew his handcuffs. In a moment of hesitation, Joey considered letting the crazed youth go; he could say the cruiser was damaged while he was in the convenience store and thus avoid the lengthy paperwork an arrest would require—especially near the end of his shift. Bangs briefly released his grip on the suspect's arms, just long enough for the man to turn and sucker-punch Joey, shattering his nose—for the fifth time in his life. Bangs dropped like a ton of bricks, and the suspect took the boots to him, smashing his head and body during the fray. Joey caught just a glimpse of the man's new cowboy boots.

Badly injured, Bangs finally found his feet and began battling back, exchanging heavy blows that broke his left hand—for a second time. Somehow Bangs managed to get the outraged man in a chokehold with his left arm and held on for dear life while he pummeled the man with his right fist. Joey dragged the thug toward the cruiser to try to radio for assistance, but the hysterical girlfriend noticed her man struggling for air and began to punch, kick, bite, and pull Joey's hair. Bangs drew his revolver and pointed it at the woman.

"You won't shoot me!"

"The fuck I won't!"

For just a moment, the suspect began to fight back in panic, and Joey almost decided to pull the trigger. *Too much hassle*, he thought again. Instead, he spun the revolver and started pistol-whipping the suspect. The girlfriend launched herself at Joey again and managed to wrest the gun from his bloody hand, and then dashed up Broadway in an attempt to distract Bangs from beating her boyfriend. Bangs struggled to the car, found the radio and called in "Signal One"—officer needs assistance.

Within moments, five or six vehicles from various departments arrived on the scene. Officers assisted Bangs in restraining the subject and forcing him into the back of Joey's cruiser until a paddy wagon arrived. The man exploded into a rage and kicked out the windows of the cruiser, shredding his new boots in the process.

Exhausted, Bangs sat on the sidewalk, tending his wounds and instructing the other officers to track down the girlfriend, who still had his service revolver. MDC officers apprehended her a few minutes later, less than a mile from the scene of the original incident.

Bangs was rushed to Lawrence Memorial Hospital in Medford, but the ER doctors were unable to stop his nose from bleeding. Specialists expressed concern that Bangs would continue to choke on his blood and might in fact bleed to death. They eventually succeeded in cauterizing the blood vessels, and Bangs returned home later that afternoon. However, he required a series of operations to repair the shattered nose so he could again breathe properly.

Bangs later learned that the suspect's rage and strength were fueled by the angel dust he and his girlfriend had smoked earlier that evening. When the suspect later appeared for arraignment in Somerville district court, the judge tried to dismiss the case as a favor to the man's uncle, the Cambridge police detective. The judge informed Bangs that he felt justice had already been served, since the suspect needed more than one hundred stitches to close the lacerations on his face and head. But Bangs laid out a gripping tale of fighting for his life against two drug-crazed suspects and persuaded the judge to refer the case to a grand jury. The man was ultimately convicted and sentenced to two years in the Billerica House of Corrections. Bangs ended up on medical leave for three months because of his injuries—which of course meant more free time for his other profitable endeavors.

Little Rascals

As the allure of the drug business began to fade, Bangs and Barrett invested in a nightclub on ritzy Broad Street, near Faneuil Hall, dubbed "Little Rascals." When Clemente and Doherty learned about the transaction, they grilled Bangs about how he had pulled off such a purchase. Bangs told them he had gone in on the venture with Barrett and Barrett's dear friend, Jake Rooney, and claimed they had paid fifty grand each for the cash-strapped establishment. In reality, Bangs, Barrett, and Rooney had put down only $75,000 total against a purchase price of $250,000, and Bangs later figured out a scheme to avoid paying the balance.

The original owner of Little Rascals was a character named "Andy," who also owned a nautical shop on the waterfront that provided food, clothing, rope, bait and other supplies to mariners from around the world. Although Andy was an astute businessman, he was also a heavy gambler. So Bangs obtained all of Andy's gaming action for pennies on the dollar or in trade and advised Andy to use the $75,000 down payment to settle part of the gambling debts and forgo the remainder of the purchase price to cover another portion. In the end, Andy lost thousands of dollars to Bangs, who at one point also considered taking control of the nautical shop, but changed his mind because of his hectic schedule.

Little Rascals ran like clockwork and made money at every turn. The restaurant served food all day, including hearty breakfast options and a popular, deli-style lunch menu. Nonetheless, dinner and alcohol at night— including a booming after-hours business—brought in most of the revenue. In addition, the truck drivers who delivered liquor, wine, beer and other food items always unloaded a few unaccounted-for cases of product, for which Joey dropped them a little extra cash or a package of cocaine. Bangs also used the nightclub as a point place to meet various members of New England's organized crime world, many of whom he met through Barrett.

Bangs floated in and out during the day, and Barrett worked the establishment during the lunchtime rush from noon until 2:00 p.m., when he left to beat traffic on the Southeast Expressway en route to his South Shore home. Rooney ran the day-to-day affairs of the establishment masterfully, arriving early in the morning and staying until closing.

A well-liked "regular guy" with a wife and kids, Rooney stood six-foot-two with a solid physique and salt-and-pepper hair, wore reading glasses, and always dressed like a dockworker in a Navy pea coat, stocking cap, chinos, and boots. Like Jake Bag-o'-Doughnuts, Rooney was Bangs' senior by at least fifteen years and had a world of experience in dealing with the variety of personalities that made their way to Little Rascals. In fact, Rooney was big pals with all the bookmakers, shylocks, and hijackers from the Dorchester/Roxbury area.

Rooney also fit in tight with Southie's Whitey Bulger and his crew of Irish hoodlums who were by this time operating in the Winter Hill/Somerville area. A former state trooper assigned to the State House, Rooney became a driver for Massachusetts Governor Foster Furcolo early in his law enforcement career. Nevertheless, he got pinched on a misdemeanor charge for bookmaking while on duty and was subsequently fired, despite his drag with the state police.

Along with most of the older-generation cops, Rooney didn't use drugs—like his pal Barrett, he was satisfied drinking Crown Royal neat—even though he'd eventually start dealing from his spot behind the bar at Little Rascals. And though Jake had a high tolerance for alcohol, when he did become inebriated, he grew quite belligerent.

Jake's father owned a well-known hoodlum hangout in Dorchester that doubled as a barroom, called "Rooney's Tavern." After Rooney and longtime friend Jimmy Melvin became partners in the establishment, they allegedly torched the place for the insurance money and soon found themselves caught up in a major arson investigation. Rooney later bought yet another dive bar in South Boston before becoming the minor partner and full-time manager of Little Rascals.

Of course, Jake was acquainted with all sorts of questionable characters, including a well-known hijacker from Southie named Knickerbocker. Knickerbocker took his work seriously, leaving home at 8:00 in the morning and returning on time for dinner each day, like clockwork. His mother-in-law lived with him and got up early every day to fix him a lunch for "work" and send him off with a goodbye kiss. Bangs and Rooney could never figure out whether the mother-in-law—or even Knickerbocker's spouse—knew what he did for a living, but they were amused by Knickerbocker's tales of domestic bliss and became tight friends. After Knickerbocker found himself locked up at "Concord Farm," a minimum security correctional facility located across the street from the main prison in Concord, Bangs used his cover as a policeman to sneak a half pound of marijuana to the convict.[*]

As Little Rascals found its groove, Bang's girlfriend, Cheryl Fisher, got into the action by working as a waitress and occasional afternoon bartender. She kept an eye on Bangs' interest in the club, given that it was, after all, a cash business.[†]

Bangs felt like his world was finally falling into place: he had a thriving business with no boss to answer to but himself, two partners he could trust as much as one could expect, a comfy locale where he could relax and conduct his affairs, and a beautiful woman to sweeten the mix all around. As far as Joey could see, he had clear weather and smooth waters ahead.

---

[*] In 1987 my softball team, the Pirates, played a goodwill game against the inmates at Concord Farm, who, despite their best efforts to cheat, still lost badly.

[†] Ironically, Fisher and Bangs met through Barrett in 1980, just after the Depositors Trust heist, while she was working as a cocktail server in the high-end Pier Restaurant, and they remained together until 1984. The entire time, Fisher had no idea what Bangs was up to.

BYE, BYE, BUCKY: BARRETT'S DISAPPEARANCE

SITTING THERE ON IRISH JOE MURRAY'S COUCH, all afternoon on a sunny Tuesday in spring, Joey Bangs knew that something was afoot. Murray, a recovering alcoholic, had been plying Bangs with drink for hours and had just a moment ago stepped into the kitchen to take yet another phone call. Joey strained to hear, but all he could make out were Murray's grunts of *yes* and *no*. Momentarily, Murray returned to the parlor and sat on the edge of the recliner across from Bangs, saying nothing and avoiding eye contact.

Joey was impatient to leave: he had a number of stops to make before picking up Cheryl from her job at The Pier. Bangs was protective of Fisher and never allowed her to work or even be on site when the evening crowd began rolling in, because he knew that as the club's reputation grew and attracted a more diverse clientele, chances increased that something serious would go down. Irish Joe, however, had won this chess match and kept Bangs checked in his house for hours, under one guise or another.

Bangs tried to ask about Joe's kid brother, but Murray was talked out, preoccupied. The phone rang again, and Irish Joe slipped once more into the kitchen.

When Murray returned less than a minute later, he was a-chatter, babbling with uncharacteristic antsiness about the Red Sox's current road trip while he topped off Joey's drink and glanced furtively at the clock.

"What's up, Irish Joe?" Bangs asked respectfully. "You're not fooling anyone here."

At that moment, a non-descript coupe idled in the parking lot of The Pier restaurant across town. Two men sat inside: Michael Donahue, the driver and owner of the car, and Brian Halloran, a friend who was bumming a ride home from the bar. Halloran glanced at his watch and asked Donahue to hang on just a few more minutes: he was awaiting a cocaine delivery—possibly from Bangs or one of his men—and didn't want to miss the drop.

An old sedan pulled alongside Donahue's vehicle and waited until Brian and Michael looked up—two masked men then opened fire with .30-caliber and Mac-10 machine guns. Halloran and Donahue had no chance to fight or flee: Donahue was shot in the head while trying to dodge the fusillade, and Halloran was hit 22 times.

POLICE DEPT.
BOSTON, MASS.
18 2-4 3 3 4-08 7

Brian Halloran

Brian "Balloonhead" Halloran had provided the FBI vital information concerning Whitey Bulger's alleged role in the murders of bookmaker Louis Litif in 1980 and Jai-Alai Executive Roger Wheeler in 1981. Halloran told FBI agents that Litif, who had been suspected of cooperating with authorities, was summoned to Triple O's in Southie, where Bulger shot him dead before stuffing his remains into a green trash bag and tossing him into the trunk of his Lincoln. At Bulger's order, Halloran reported, Wheeler met the same fate at the hands of Bulger associate John Martorano and wheelman Joe McDonald. Oblivious of his stalkers, Wheeler was seated in his luxury vehicle when Martorano approached and shot him in the head. Halloran's fate was sealed when Bulger learned he had been cooperating with authorities.[*]

Bulger had decided to eliminate Halloran after learning from his own FBI handlers—including John Connolly—that Halloran had "talked out of school" to several agents and informed them about Whitey's involvement in the Litif and Wheeler murders. And now, on May 11, 1982, Halloran was silenced. Allegedly, Kevin Weeks, a one-time surrogate of Bulger's, kept an eye on Halloran until the coast was clear and then signaled Bulger by radio—"The balloon is in the air!"—a derogative

---

[*] Halloran was also allegedly the perpetrator of the infamous Black Friar killings. In an ill-planned attempt to steal a large amount of cocaine and cash, the masked Halloran and his co-conspirators stormed the after-hours lounge and executed five upstanding businessmen, including a local television news reporter, who were enjoying a game of cards, after one of the men recognized Halloran's idiosyncratic voice.

reference to Halloran's bulbous head. Bulger and another masked associate pulled the trigger.[*]

Joe Murray had caught wind of the hit and summoned Bangs to his home, fearful that Joey might cross paths with Bulger while Whitey was in South Boston for the job. Murray's motives were selfish, of course: Bangs was one of his best earners, and Murray had fronted him substantial amounts of cocaine and marijuana, payment for which he might never recover if Bangs and Bulger happened to clash.

The phone squealed again, and Murray dashed to the kitchen. He picked up, listened for a moment, replaced the handset without saying a word, and then unceremoniously shooed the bewildered Bangs out the door.

Bangs didn't know about the hit until he arrived at The Pier, saw the crime scene taped off, and heard the chatter among the crowd and reporters. After Joey caught a glimpse of the bullet-riddled car, he rushed Cheryl home, pulled the blinds, and sat down with a drink to plan his next move.

v v v

In the year following the Depositors Trust heist, Bulger and Steve "The Rifleman" Flemmi harassed Bucky Barrett in an attempt to locate any remaining loot, but Barrett invoked the protection of Cadillac Frank Salemme, who was now capo of New England's *La Cosa Nostra* syndicate. Barrett never stopped paying tribute to Salemme and felt comfortable asking for his help. So Bulger opted for a more subtle approach, reasoning that he could bypass Salemme if he could show a legitimate claim to the bank spoils, which included an estimated one million dollars in illegal gambling profits accumulated by the Italian syndicate and the Winter Hill mob. Bulger actually produced a ring of small keys and receipts for security deposits on safe boxes, but Salemme saw through the ruse and ordered Whitey to knock off the bullshit and leave Barrett alone.

On occasion, when Barrett didn't want to bother Salemme, he escaped the greedy Bulger by telling him to talk to Bangs about the matter. Barrett knew how much Bangs and Bulger despised each other and had no doubt that Whitey would never have the balls to challenge Joey. Bangs' threat to

---

[*] The Donahue family later brought a civil lawsuit against the FBI and demanded that federal judge Richard G. Sterns compel Kevin Weeks to name Bulger's accomplice and detail the murder, but the judge refused their request.

toss hand grenades down Bulger's chimney if he didn't lay off Bucky still came up in conversation around town, much to Whitey's chagrin.

However, Bangs and Bulger did have one encounter around this time. Bangs threatened to plant a kilo of cocaine and a handgun in the trunk of Whitey's car, informing him: "I'm not a real cop, pal. I don't play by the rules. I play dirty, and I will get your ass one way or another." Bulger reluctantly left Barrett in peace for the time being, but soon enough he would have the chance to get a piece of both Bucky Barrett and Joe Murray.

The marijuana operation run by Murray, Bangs, and Barrett had expanded to the point that Murray took over an abandoned warehouse in South Boston for receiving shipments and staging deliveries. The setup worked perfectly, more than doubling Murray's capacity, until a DEA sting operation shut down the enterprise, crippled Murray financially, and landed Barrett in hot water with both Bulger and law enforcement.

Whenever Barrett picked up bales, he was usually careful to cover his tracks. However, on one occasion DEA agents conducting intermediate surveillance followed a tip from Bulger and tailed Barrett to the warehouse.

Barrett lived in Squantum, and the feds knew he had to use the island's only road, Quincy Shore Drive, to reach the mainland. They had no problem following Barrett from his house to the warehouse, even when Bucky pulled his usual maneuver of stopping for a coffee and circling the block three times to make sure he didn't have company.

Within minutes, eager DEA agents swarmed the warehouse, arrested Barrett and five other men, and seized fourteen tons of marijuana worth millions of dollars. Murray was beside himself for the enormous financial loss, as well as for Barrett's uncharacteristic carelessness, which ultimately led to dozens of arrests and the disruption of the enterprise. In addition, Bulger was infuriated that Murray had moved operations from Charlestown to South Boston without asking permission or offering to split profits. Now that Murray's activities had brought DEA heat into Bulger's backyard, Bulger drilled Murray and threatened, "You can always make more money, but if you don't pay me now, I'll kill you." Going forward, Irish Joe never failed to pay tribute to Whitey for any activity conducted in and around Southie.[*]

---

[*] FBI reports of Bulger's reaction were released in 1998.

The morning after the bust, Bangs drove straight to the U.S. District Courthouse at One Post Office Square in downtown Boston with a trunk full of money to pay Barrett's $250,000 bail. But *La Cosa Nostra* captain Jimmy Martorano had arrived earlier that morning with Barrett's wife, Elaine, and had already posted bail.

Bucky was running scared. He now owed the Mafia a quarter-million dollars (which, luckily, he was able to pay back), and Bulger tried to shake him down once more, this time not for the Depositors Trust swag but for the marijuana profits. Word on the street was that Bangs was so furious about the raid—and even more about the financial hit—that he was aiming to kill Barrett himself.

▾ ▾ ▾

Only forty-six years old and the father of six children—the youngest just thirteen weeks old—Bucky Barrett had been out on bail for only a couple of weeks when he disappeared on July 26, 1983. Common sense implicated Murray in Barrett's disappearance: Barrett's negligence had, after all, cost Murray millions of dollars in marijuana, jeopardized his entire operation, attracted the attention of federal investigators, and put Murray in the hot seat with Bulger. Plus, Bucky was expendable, a weak link in Boston's criminal world, and Murray worried that Barrett would drop a dime on him if pressed.

Early on the morning he disappeared, Barrett called Jake Rooney at Little Rascals to tell him he was sending a "Chinaman" to pick up $20,000 that was stashed in the business safe. And Murray later told Bangs that Barrett had also made a desperate call to him in search of an additional $1,000,000. Bangs pumped Murray for information about Bucky's final calls, and Murray insisted that Barrett sounded as if he were talking over a speakerphone and reading from a script. But even with the motivation Murray had to eliminate Barrett, most insiders believed that Bulger himself actually did the honors.

Bulger had had a hard-on for everyone allegedly involved with the Depositors Trust score. In fact, Whitey saw Bucky as the most docile of the group and decided to put the screws to him. Though the details aren't clear, someone Barrett apparently trusted led him to a Bulger safe house on East Third Street in Southie, where Kevin Weeks was posing as a street thief with stolen diamonds for Barrett to appraise and possibly purchase. As soon as Bucky entered, Weeks and Flemmi apprehended him at gunpoint and chained him to a chair in the kitchen.*

Bulger went to work ripping out Barrett's teeth with a pair of rusty needle-nose pliers, promising to stop only when Barrett revealed the location of the Depositors Trust swag. Bucky knew he wouldn't survive, and although he did give up some cash and personal belongings to Bulger, he never disclosed anything about the heist or the whereabouts of its spoils. In desperation, Bucky promised to pay Bulger twenty grand a month from the marijuana sales, and as tempting as it was, Bulger knew he could no longer trust Barrett—if Bucky ran to Bangs or Salemme as he had done in the past, Bulger was a dead man.

Now and then, Bulger paused the torture to allow Barrett to make phone calls in search of additional money. As it turned out, the Chinaman was actually a cab driver sent by Bulger and Weeks to make the pick-up at Little Rascals. Later in the day, he forced Bucky to call his wife, Elaine, and tell her to take the kids shopping so he could meet privately at the house to conduct some important business. Bulger and his crew escorted Barrett to his home, where Bucky scraped together whatever he could find in cash and jewelry—probably no more than twenty grand total, although Joe Murray claimed that it could have been as much as $300,000.

Back at the safe house, Barrett was granted a final call to his wife around 11:00 p.m. Bucky asked about his boys and then told his wife, "I won't be home for a while. I love you."

Bulger had grown tired of the situation—he put a gun to the back of Barrett's head and pulled the trigger. CLICK—a misfire. Barrett's hopes rose just as his heart sank. Bulger pulled the trigger again, and Bucky was dead. Flemmi chopped off Bucky's hands and feet and disposed of them, and Weeks buried the remainder of Barrett's torso in the dirt floor of the house's basement until it could be moved safely to another locale at a later date.

At the time of Barrett's disappearance, Bangs was vacationing on Cape Cod, where he had rented a beachfront mansion from a doctor acquaintance for $5,000 a week, money the feds would later claim had been laundered.

---

* After his arrest on federal gun charges stemming from the *Valhalla* incident, Joe Murray allegedly told federal investigators that another known Bulger associate was in fact the culprit who led Barrett to Whitey's lair. Bangs believes it could have been Murray who led Barrett to his demise.

Bangs tried to contact Barrett on the day he was killed, without luck. He eventually called Rooney at Little Rascals and learned about the Chinaman's pickup and Bucky's unusual calls, and Rooney indicated that Barrett was nowhere to be found. It was not uncommon for Bucky to stay away for a day or two if business beckoned, but Bangs' intuition told him Bucky was dead.

The realization shook Joey to the core and tormented him for years. If he had known for sure at the time whether it was Bulger or Murray to blame, he would have avenged Barrett without delay. But as much as he wanted justice, without concrete evidence, Joey waited to act. He decided to lie low for a few weeks and headed to Las Vegas to gamble and sift his thoughts. Bangs determined that when he returned to Boston, he'd arrange a meeting with Salemme's son, Frankie Jr., to request permission from his father to eliminate Bulger once and for all.

| Kevin Weeks | Whitey Bulger | Stephen Flemmi | Frank Salemme |

▼ ▼ ▼

Bangs sensed that things were falling apart rapidly, and, although he trusted capo Frank Salemme and his son, he didn't want to move in public without a weapon. Before Joey left Las Vegas for Boston, he called Tommy Doherty from a payphone and instructed him to get two handguns and meet him at Blinstrum's Restaurant, where he and Frankie Jr. had planned to sit down. Salemme picked up Bangs at Logan Airport, and they headed to the Dorchester dining establishment as planned.

Doherty arrived first and placed the guns in the bottom of the restroom trashcan. The meeting went well, but Frankie Jr. refused to give Bangs permission to kill Bulger and told him to sit tight. He did, however, give Bangs his word that his father would handle the matter in due time, but nothing ever happened as far as Joey could see. In the end, Bangs reasoned that nothing he could do, including killing Whitey, would bring back his pal Barrett, so he had no choice but to let it play, although the situation never ceased to eat at him.

▼ ▼ ▼

Elaine Barrett didn't share Joey's opinion and later said she felt the government, mainly the FBI, was responsible for her husband's death. She reasoned that if the FBI had put away Bulger and Flemmi, rather than use them as informants, Bucky would not have been killed. Attorney Kevin Glynn, who was a close friend of Bucky, represented the family in a civil lawsuit filed against the federal government and stated on the record that "[Barrett] was no choir boy, but he was never violent, and they killed him for power and greed. Bucky was not a part of the treacherous Bulger group, but rather a victim of it."

Barrett's oldest son, who was serving in the Marine Corps at the time of Bucky's death, threatened to kill Bangs, and his mother could do little to persuade him that Joey wasn't involved. An undercover state police officer overheard the young man's threats at the Celtic Tavern, and troopers later grabbed him and warned him not to attempt anything with Joey, who, they assured him, was indeed innocent. Shortly thereafter, heartbroken with the loss of his beloved father and unable to find justice, Bucky's son apparently committed suicide by stepping in front of an MBTA train, as did his younger brother not long after.

Bangs remained suspicious of Murray with regards to Barrett's disappearance, but he knew it would do no good to cross Murray or try to take him out. Ultimately, he had to press on and solidify his alliance with Irish Joe. Murray and Bangs maintained an uneasy peace for the next year, until Bangs decided to show a measure of good will.

In 1984, Murray orchestrated the largest-ever shipment of arms to the Irish Republican Army. He and other staunch followers of the IRA's activity loaded the 77-foot fishing trawler *Valhalla* with weapons they had purchased or collected from local supporters. On October 16, Irish authorities intercepted a vessel—ostensibly the *Valhalla*—off the coast of Kerry, Ireland, but according to Murray and others involved, the captured vessel was a decoy that allowed another boat to skirt past seven navies and find its way to the freedom fighters.

Bangs donated a number of weapons to the effort: a dozen revolvers, a half dozen M-16 machine guns, a crate of hand grenades, an ample supply of C-4 explosive, and a dozen or so bulletproof vests. The gesture scored Joey increased respect and friendship from Murray and his Irish friends, and from that time forth the men got along better than before.

Not long after, however, the feds caught Murray smuggling marijuana into Boston harbor on an Irish freighter and later implicated him in the *Valhalla* gunrunning, along with Robert Anderson and Southie's Pat Nee, who pleaded out. In the end, Murray also took the deal, and in return, the feds dropped the racketeering charges, which carried a minimum twenty-year sentence.

∨ ∨ ∨

The truth about Barrett's disappearance wouldn't come to light for nearly two decades. On January 13, 2000, former Bulger lieutenant Kevin Weeks led state and federal investigators to a gully that ran alongside the Southeast Expressway on Hallet Street, across from Florian Hall in Dorchester, where, he said, they would find Barrett's body, which had been relocated from Bulger's Third Street safe house when the property was sold.

After painstaking excavation, authorities discovered four bodies, two male and two female, including remains that they identified as Barrett's from the few teeth remaining in the skull. The next day, when asked whether he thought the bodies would lead to the capture of Bulger, who had been on the lam since 1995, U.S. Attorney Donald K. Stern replied with exasperation, "Well, we don't believe he was one of the two male bodies discovered. . . ."*

Whitey Bulger had taken Weeks under his wing when Kevin was an eighteen-year-old bouncer at Triple O's barroom and groomed him to play a significant leadership role in Boston's Irish mob. Weeks had become one of Bulger's closest confidants and partners, but once he began serving a life sentence on November 17, 1999, for money laundering, extortion and racketeering, Weeks' only objective was to save his own skin.

---

* Bulger was captured in Santa Monica, California, on June 22, 2011, after sixteen years on the lam.

The feds in Boston were interested in minimizing the fallout from their dealings with the mob, so Weeks' attorney, Dennis Kelley, had no trouble hammering out an immunity deal with U.S. Attorney Stern and Suffolk County District Attorney Ralph C. Martin. Weeks downloaded his vast knowledge of the mob's activities and was eventually released from prison in December 2004.

The male body discovered with Barrett was that of John McIntyre, a 32-year-old fishing trawler captain from Gloucester who was known for smuggling. McIntyre was an IRA sympathizer and operative who had been arrested on the *Valhalla* and was cooperating with Quincy police and U.S. Customs on the subsequent investigation. McIntyre disappeared on November 30, 1984, on his way to meet Pat Nee, who he had told authorities was also aboard the *Valhalla*. FBI agent Connolly intercepted the intelligence and informed Bulger and Flemmi, who took matters into their own hands.

The female victims were former lovers of Stephen Flemmi: Deborah Hussey, Flemmi's own stepdaughter, and Debra Davis, a stunning 26-year-old who had disappeared in 1985 after she broke up with then-live-in boyfriend Flemmi.

On April 7, 2003, Elaine Barrett filed another in a long line of federal lawsuits—the sixteenth against the compromised Boston office of the FBI—this time seeking damages of fifty million dollars. Elaine wanted justice and was looking to implicate eight former FBI agents, whom she considered the real criminals responsible for the death of her husband.

It was later ascertained that shortly after the Depositors Trust heist, Bulger urged FBI Supervisor/Special Agent John Morris to tell Barrett that he and Flemmi knew Bucky was in on the theft and that they were planning to shake him down. Morris laid out the threat in brutal detail and promised to protect Barrett if he gave up his fellow thieves, but Barrett flatly refused to cooperate.

Of course, Morris had no intention—or even ability—to protect Barrett from Bulger. Bulger and Flemmi "loaned" thousands of dollars to Morris, which he never paid back, and Bulger constantly held the obligation over Morris' head, vowing to take him down if anyone else dared cross them.

From the outset, Elaine Barrett was convinced that Bangs had had nothing to do with her husband's disappearance, but others weren't so sure. Friends of Bangs and Barrett knew the two had an appointment at

Vinny D's jewelry store on the day Bucky disappeared. In addition, the other bank robbers knew Bangs had suggested on several occasions that they eliminate Barrett and keep his share of the loot. However, despite any disagreements Joey and Bucky may have had, their friendship and respect had grown far stronger than their misgivings.

For years Bangs remained a prime suspect in Barrett's disappearance even though the FBI knew he was innocent. The feds nevertheless kept the heat on Joey with illegal wiretaps, surveillance, and any other harassment they could devise to trip him up. Bangs tried repeatedly to clear his name by subjecting himself to interviews and polygraph tests—including an intense interrogation the day after Christmas, 1984—which were, alas, inconclusive, skewed in all likelihood by Joey's military service and long history of violent criminal acts and intentions.

Bangs and Barrett spoke for the last time during a christening celebration for Bucky's youngest son at Little Rascals. On this auspicious occasion, the inebriated Jake Rooney confronted Bangs with accusations that Brother O'Leary was making the rounds in South Boston looking for a handgun with a silencer. The thought of Brother with a gun was enough to make anyone nervous, but Rooney believed that Bangs was conspiring with O'Leary. They were either planning to kill Barrett, Rooney babbled, or send Bucky a message to be more careful in his movements and intimidate him into coughing up his portion of the Depositors Trust loot.

If the scene had been anything other than a christening for the Barrett family, Bangs probably would have escalated the conflict with Rooney. As it was, Bucky had to intervene to calm the situation: he proposed a shot of Crown Royal—his favorite drink—to toast his son's well-being, and the men drank out of mutual respect for Barrett.

Although in the months after Barrett's disappearance Bangs continued to make money hand over fist, his criminal empire was beginning to crumble. Bucky was missing and presumed dead, trust among the other bank robbers had disintegrated, and Rooney's troubles with the drug business were bringing heat and chaos into Joey's world. The only upside to Barrett's vanishing was that Bangs could now assert to his Depositors Trust cohorts that Bucky hadn't told him the location of the remaining swag—when in fact, Joey was in possession of it the entire time. Fortunately for Bangs, the robbers bought it and backed off.

But Bulger now knew what was happening around town, and he was determined either to direct or dismantle all the action. Operating with impunity, he fed information to the FBI on everyone who was anyone in the Boston drug trade and underworld, and most of them sooner or later ran into trouble with the law.

Rooney, along with his hijacker crony, Knickerbocker, and another well-known thief named Hobart Willis—who was Bulger's main source of intel on the street—approached Bangs at a bowling alley in Dorchester to see if he wanted in on a "sure thing," but Joey had heard about other stings around the state with similar terms and decided to pass.

Within the week, Rooney and his partners got pinched in a DEA setup for a measly ten thousand pounds of "barny"—moldy marijuana that stunk like a barn—that the DEA had used in previous stings and rewet after each operation to give it the heft of fresh grass. The DEA had by this time infiltrated not only Boston but also all of New England, and its influence was closing in around Joey's heretofore impenetrable fortress.

Portland, Maine

During this chaotic chain of events, Tommy Doherty's brother-in-law Jackie Gillen approached Bangs and Doherty about a drug deal he had set up: twenty-five tons of marijuana—with a street-value of about $50 million—that was scheduled to arrive in Portland, Maine, on a Haitian cargo ship. Bangs was skeptical: Gillen had never successfully pulled off a considerable score, and this deal was out of his league. But Jackie was irrepressible, and he laid out the plan time after time for Joey, answering each objection Bangs raised.

First, they needed several tractor-trailers to transport the cargo from Maine to Massachusetts: the smugglers would load them and have them ready to roll. Then, they needed easily accessible storage: Jerry Clemente said he could arrange to keep the goods at his brother Richard's home west of Boston, a deal that would also get Jerry off Joey's back over the disputed Depositors Trust profits. And finally, Joey wouldn't have to front one red cent. Not to mention, Doherty could pay Bangs his share to supplement any sum he still owed Joey. A win-win-win scenario.

The last disagreement was how to sell the product. Bangs didn't want just a piece of the load—he wanted the entire shipment. Joey was nervous about not controlling the deal from the start, and despite the big numbers, he knew he had just escaped several close calls and couldn't risk getting sucked into Jackie's bad luck. If he couldn't take over the deal completely from the moment the shipment hit Boston, he would pass. Gillen reluctantly conceded.

Gillen wanted to introduce Bangs to his marijuana connection, but Joey had no interest in such a meeting. He had enough money to last a lifetime and enough friends to last two, and at this point, he didn't want any new business associates. This haul would be his last, he thought.

Bangs refused to take part in the actual transaction—there was no way he was going to risk being locked up in some decrepit Maine jail cell—but he gave Gillen his best advice: do it right from the get-go, share a motel room with the smugglers, don't let anyone out of your sight until the transaction is complete, make certain no one touches a telephone of any kind, watch their every move. Bangs and Doherty gave Gillen guns and police radios for the long interstate drive, and they all reviewed the plan for the shipment.

They decided that Bangs, Clemente, and Doherty would wait at Tommy's garage on Pleasant Street, across from Joey's apartment, until Gillen called to say the trucks were on the road, at which point they would time their drive to meet Jackie at the Massachusetts border crossing at Route 128 and Interstate 93, where their police cruisers and credentials would facilitate the trucks' entering the state. Bangs and Clemente would then escort the trucks in their cruisers to Richard Clemente's home in Westford, a town in rural western Massachusetts.* Bangs would later unload the cargo—which he had already pre-sold—and expedite delivery using a fleet of paddy wagons.

The day of reckoning came on a gloomy Sunday afternoon. Bangs, Clemente and Doherty holed up in the garage and watched football while they awaited the call—which never came. As soon as the Haitian ship

---

* Richard Clemente was an upstanding citizen, and as far as Bangs could tell, he never knew about the deal or Jerry's intention to store the product on his property.

dropped anchor in Maine, DEA agents swarmed the dock and arrested Gillen on conspiracy to distribute a controlled substance.

Gillen told Bangs that DEA agents pressed him to find out what connection he had to Boston defense attorney Joe Flak. The feds had recently captured the men together in surveillance photos in Quincy—but only from the waist up—and couldn't tie Flak to any wrongdoing. Gillen told the agents only that Flak was "shucking oysters" and warned them to drop their fishing expedition. Flak represented Jackie in the subsequent trial, ostensibly because he knew his reputation was safe with Gillen.

Doherty scraped together bail money for Gillen by mortgaging one of his houses, which infuriated Bangs, given that Tommy still owed him a hefty sum. And to make matters worse, Doherty explained that when the bank robbers needed a commercial vacuum during the Depositors Trust heist, he had returned to his garage to retrieve the equipment. Gillen happened to be hanging around, saw Doherty load the vacuum into his cruiser, and began asking questions. Doherty shrugged him off, but he surmised that Jackie put two and two together when the news came out about the robbery. Bangs knew the conversation would never pass muster as evidence in a trial, but he couldn't believe Doherty had so lost control of himself as to talk about the heist to anyone, much less to Gillen, who now had the DEA stuck up his ass.

After Gillen's arrest, Bangs continued to hound Doherty for his money, going so far as to threaten Tommy's life, and he never missed an occasion to break Tommy's balls and remind him that he had been right about Gillen all along. Once Gillen was released on bail, Bangs never spoke a word to him, except to call him a "stupid motherfucker" any time they crossed paths.

❧ ❧ ❧

As early as February 1983, Clemente alerted Bangs that he had been mentioned in connection with an internal investigation, and Joey subsequently contemplated retirement. He had had enough of the shenanigans with Tom and Jerry and realized it was probably time to cut his ties completely. Up to this point, Bangs was the only one of the three police officers the feds had not questioned about the bank heist, and Joey wanted to keep it that way.

Before retiring, Bangs acquired from Doherty the promotional examination for an open lieutenant slot and, of course, passed with flying colors, hoping thereby to increase the base salary used to compute his pension. Bangs' pal and respected colleague Nelson Barner ("Sonny") had previously obtained the captain's exam from Clemente and was now the MDC's deputy superintendent; Joey expected to receive his promotion without delay. Unfortunately, because of the ongoing internal investigation, Barner was unable to approve the advancement for Joey.

Bangs was incensed by the news, especially since he originally researched the answers to the captain's test that Barner had purchased. Bangs and Clemente bickered until Jerry convinced Joey about how much scrutiny the state and the feds were directing at Barner. Bangs agreed to be patient but resented that Barner hadn't stepped up when he really needed him. Clemente advised Bangs to submit his retirement papers as a sergeant in order to silence his critics and fly under the radar of the internal investigation. Bangs had his mind set on going out a lieutenant, because of the supplemental income the rank would provide, and he had been going to the doctors religiously for more than a year in anticipation of his long-overdue retirement. If Joey had known he'd be stuck with the rank of sergeant, he would have retired sooner and devoted extra time to his more profitable enterprises.

By early 1984, Bangs was feeling the increased heat from the Treasury Department, U.S. Customs, the Massachusetts State Police, and the FBI, DEA, and ATF. In January, he was legitimately placed on the MDC's permanently disabled list for hypertension, no doubt arising from his erratic lifestyle and occasional drug use. In February, he retired officially with a full disability package after serving the MDC Police—"faithfully"—for eleven years.

Friends and family feted Bangs at a less than memorable retirement party held at the Irish-American Club in Malden. The joint was packed with people who mostly respected or feared Joey more than they understood him or cared to understand him, as much as they may have enjoyed the liveliness he brought to any setting. Bangs received a cheap watch and a handful of other small gifts, and bid a short but heartfelt farewell to his colleagues.

After the festivities, Joey invited a few select cop friends to join him at an after-hours strip club in the Combat Zone, where the indulgence continued into the wee hours. When the joint closed, Bangs and a half dozen other MDC cops stumbled to the parking lot to say their goodbyes.

Without provocation, a group of eight rowdy college football players descended on the men, and one of them smashed a full beer bottle over Bangs' head. Joey retaliated by grabbing a nightstick from his vehicle and viciously beating a few of the men while his buddies and the other players sparked a melee that left everyone cut up badly and in serious need of medical attention.

By the time the Boston police arrived on scene, all eight of the students were bloody and unconscious. The Boston officers checked the IDs of Joey and his colleagues and told them to be on their way. Each injured cop went to a different hospital in order to limit the questions that would inevitably arise and incite the interest of law enforcement.

❥ ❥ ❥

Bangs' personal life also took a hit when he retired from the force. As long as Joey was on the job, he was able to use "overtime" as an excuse for his frequent absences from home. But Bangs' physical and emotional distance had already taken its toll on his family, and once he was out on full disability, with no justification for his excursions, his marriage to Judy fell apart at the seams. In the end, Judy couldn't accept Joey's incessant infidelity, and they separated in 1984, although they didn't divorce until February 1986, after nearly twenty years together. Ironically, Bangs' longtime girlfriend, Cheryl Fisher, had no idea about Joey's wife and children or his extracurricular moneymaking activities.

Bangs remained his family's sole provider, signing over all his payroll checks to Judy, and he spent as much time with his kids as possible—given the demands of running one of the largest criminal enterprises in Commonwealth history.

Bangs obtained a real estate broker's license so he could more easily launder money by investing in property—and, of course, save a few dollars on closing fees.

ACTIVE RETIREMENT

IN JUST A FEW SHORT YEARS, JOEY BANGS HAD EARNED ENOUGH money to make a Rockefeller envious. A couple of months of retirement had shown Bangs how much he despised the bullshit and bizarreness of the life he had been living, so he decided to extricate himself completely from the drug racket.

With no daily job, drug trips or safaris on his schedule, Joey spent too much of his time at home, and by April he and Cheryl Fisher had begun growing apart.

▾ ▾ ▾

Just before Bangs and Fisher split, Cheryl scheduled an appointment to have her wisdom teeth pulled. Cheryl's mother agreed to drop her off, leaving Joey free for a couple of hours to take care of some important business. Cheryl never asked about Bangs' work or enterprises and had no inkling what he did with his time outside the house. But she was quite stern that he had better arrive on time to pick her up at the dentist—or else.

Joey arranged with Tommy to drop by to collect a portion of the money owed him—which now totaled about $180,000—but arrived to find another of Doherty's free-for-all, frenzied parties in full swing, about fifteen people half-naked and puffed out of their minds. Bangs wanted no funny business—he demanded his money. Doherty handed Bangs an envelope containing a thick stack of bills and smirked. Joey shut down the levity with a stare.

"What? You gonna count it?" Doherty quizzed.

"Of course I'm going to count it. What do I look like, some kinda asshole?"

Trying to show off to his guests—a number of Medford cops and a handful of personal friends, including a blonde bombshell named Debbie—Tommy asked if Debbie could count it for him.

"What do I look like," Bangs deadpanned again, "some kinda asshole?"

Bangs took the package of cash into a bedroom and slammed the door. He reappeared a few minutes later and made a beeline for Tommy, who was foisting a drink on a petite brunette he had cornered in the kitchen.

"That's only eighty grand, shithead," Joey bellowed for the room to hear. The conversation noise stopped, except for the giggles of a wasted young woman who was making out on the couch.

"If I don't have the other hundred by the end of the week, you can kiss your ass goodbye."

Bangs spun to head for the exit. In an attempt to pacify Joey and avoid a scene, Tommy grabbed his sleeve and whispered: "Listen, Joe, I'll get you your money. Stay for a drink, and I'll get you laid."

Bangs scanned the room and caught Debbie's eye.

"Who's the blonde honey with the tits?" he asked Tommy.

"Someone you need to meet," Tommy winked.

Bangs said he'd be back in a moment. He ducked outside and locked the cash in the trunk of his brand-new, champagne-colored Cadillac Seville, then bounded back into Tommy's place.

Joey grabbed a drink, did a line of coke and tracked down Tommy to get an introduction to Debbie. Debbie was a bit evasive and disinterested at first, but Tommy finally cornered her and presented his friend.

"Deborah Ann O'Malley, meet Joseph Paul Bangs, a true gentleman."

"So you're the asshole I've been hearing about?"

Tommy froze. Joey laughed—this was his kind of girl, regardless of how little she thought she was interested in him.

"You got a boyfriend?" Bangs asked brusquely.

"Two, in fact," Debbie replied coolly.

Bangs grinned: "Then you'll love me, 'cause I have two girlfriends."

Debbie laughed, and Joey knew he was in. Bangs asked O'Malley on a proper date, but as he expected, she played hard to get and told him she wasn't interested. She had two teenage daughters, she said, and he of all people wouldn't be a good role model.

Joey finished his drink, shook Debbie's hand, and made sure to get her number from Tommy as he left the party. A few nights later, Bangs phoned O'Malley, but she still refused to go out with him. Regardless, Joey's mind was set: he called her several days later, last minute on a Friday.

Debbie could sense that Joey was just horny, but she told him that if her current boyfriend didn't show, she'd meet him for a cocktail. Joey had finally found an opening to exploit. He asked what her boyfriend's name was, and thinking nothing of it, she told him—Jay Mitchelson.

After they hung up, Bangs called Spencer at the station and told him to run a database check on the guy: lo and behold, Mitchelson had an outstanding misdemeanor arrest warrant for failing to pay a traffic citation. So Bangs instructed Spencer to swing by Mitchelson's home and arrest him. With the boyfriend out of the picture for the entire weekend, Bangs called Debbie later that night.

"Is Jay back?" he questioned coyly.

Even though she was agitated at being stood up—and conceding a win to Joey—O'Malley agreed to meet Bangs for a drink, so long as it stayed on the QT, given that she still had a boyfriend, after all.

Bangs and O'Malley rendezvoused at Carroll's Diner, across the street from the Medford police station. To calm her nerves about being seen with him, Joey instructed Debbie to park her car behind the station where Mitchelson would never see it, even though he knew that Spencer was in the process of towing Jay's car and having it compacted, while the sap was sitting in jail eating baloney sandwiches.

The date went swimmingly, and after a few more encounters, a piece or two of fine jewelry, and a "business trip" to Aruba, Mitchelson couldn't compete, and Debbie and Joey were an item.

But upon returning from a trip to Florida, Bangs' commitment was put to the test. When they arrived at Debbie's apartment, her key wouldn't open the door. Irritated, Joey snatched the keys and tried it himself, without luck. He asked who would have pulled such a prank—re-keying the apartment—and Debbie's expression gave away that she knew.

O'Malley's landlord, James McGaffigan ("Jimmy McGaff"), was jealous of her relationship with Bangs and had been giving her a hard time. Joey dragged out a confession that Debbie and McGaff had dated for a short time, and after they split, Jimmy grew increasingly agitated by her dating other men, going so far as to beat up one of her boyfriends. When Debbie later found herself without an apartment, McGaff offered her a deal on a unit in the building—a peace offering, as she saw it, although McGaff obviously had ulterior motives.

Incensed, Bangs stormed downstairs and rang McGaffigan's doorbell, but McGaff was away. The following week, Bangs began to terrorize McGaff, stopping by his apartment several times a day and pounding on the doors and windows, making a ruckus that disturbed the entire neighborhood. At his wit's ends, McGaff eventually reached out to Bangs' cronies, Tommy Doherty and Bobby Spencer, for assistance, but neither could calm Bangs, who simply wanted McGaff to open the apartment so Debbie could retrieve her belongings.

When all else failed, McGaff called Medford police lieutenant Billy Padula, who arranged to meet Joey at Carroll's Diner to discuss the matter. The old colleagues enjoyed laughs over a hearty breakfast, and then Billy got around to the situation with McGaff. Like others who knew Bangs, Padula feared that Joey might in fact kill McGaff if he didn't return O'Malley's belongings. Padula told Bangs that McGaff was losing sleep over the trouble and threatening to press charges. In addition, McGaff blamed O'Malley for a number of problems in the building and claimed she was the one instigating the problem.

Bangs eyed Padula for a moment; there was more to this story. Joey headed to the door, motioning for Billy to follow him to the parking lot for a private discussion. As soon as the men stepped outside, Bangs grabbed Padula by the throat and pinned him against the wall.

"It's none of your fucking business," he told Billy, "and if you ever disrespect Debbie again, I'm going to kill you."

Billy nodded silently, stunned. He knew exactly what Joey was talking about.

❮ ❮ ❮

Debbie lived on the second floor of the three-story dwelling, with McGaff below, and above, former Medford police officer Al Roberts, who would soon after move into Tommy Doherty's garage.

A few months prior, just before Bangs and O'Malley began dating, Roberts was throwing a party that got a little out of hand, and Debbie went upstairs to ask him to quiet things down. Wanting to respect Al's guests, O'Malley entered the apartment from the back door, which led into the kitchen area. She was immediately accosted by Padula, whose drinking had made him a bit aggressive. Billy backed Debbie up against the refrigerator and grabbed her hard by the shoulders.

"You bitches are all the same!" he screamed repeatedly at Debbie, who stood frozen, tears streaming down her face. Another off-duty Medford officer intervened and whisked Debbie out of the apartment.

The next morning, Padula showed up at O'Malley's apartment with a dozen roses, wanting to apologize for the encounter. She didn't answer his knock, but he tried the door, found it open and decided to leave the flowers inside. However, Debbie was in the shower, and in yet another irrational moment, Padula entered the bathroom to present the gift to her, realizing too late that he had just made the matter worse.

In the days to follow, McGaffigan pestered Debbie to turn in Padula to his superiors, but she chose not to make an issue: she had learned that Padula's wife had recently left him, and he was struggling with the ugly separation.

❤ ❤ ❤

Outside Carroll's Diner, Bangs tightened his grip on Padula's throat and told him he had just retired from the Mets and wasn't afraid of any professional repercussions: a brutal beating for Padula, Joey continued, wasn't out of the question. Bangs released his hold, and Padula caught his breath, promising Joey that nothing unseemly would happen again.

❤ ❤ ❤

Despite Bangs' efforts to retrieve Debbie's belongings, O'Malley was the one to track down the elusive McGaff. She demanded that he give her her clothes and threatened to send "her new boyfriend" if there were any more problems. McGaffigan called her a "fucking bitch" and told her to send whomever she pleased—she wasn't getting anything back.

After O'Malley recounted the exchange to Bangs, Joey went straight to McGaffigan's apartment and rang the bell repeatedly, as he had done many times before. As usual, no answer. Bangs phoned McGaff later that afternoon and got him on the line. The orders were simple: McGaff would open the apartment for Debbie at 7:00 the next morning or Joey himself would come over to take care of the matter.

The following day Bangs showed up at McGaff's home in place of O'Malley. McGaffigan answered the door immediately and opened Debbie's apartment without saying a word. Bangs collected some of Debbie's things, packed them into his Cadillac, and took them to his apartment. Joey hadn't planned on Debbie's moving in with him, but now that she was without a place to stay, he welcomed her and her older daughter, Kelly, into his home.

Even though he wouldn't say a thing to Bangs, McGaff felt compelled to have the last word with Debbie. He called her incessantly and claimed she had broken the stove in the apartment. Debbie in turn claimed he had stolen her brand-new microwave. When Bangs caught wind of this petty bullshit, he went through the roof and called McGaff, who played tough and said he too was tired of the bullshit and would meet Bangs anytime, anywhere. Joey called his bluff, and McGaff told him to meet in Magoun Square—a place he thought might intimidate Joey, since it was a known hangout for the remaining members of the Winter Hill gang. But Bangs agreed without hesitation.

On the appointed day, Bangs showed up early—with two guns on his person—and waited for McGaffigan, who never showed. Bangs reasoned that he didn't get all dressed up for nothing, so he entered the tavern they had selected and informed the local wise guys that McGaffigan had stood him up. For good measure, Bangs added that he believed McGaff might be a child molester, since he had caught him trying to take photos of his young niece. The fabricated story infuriated the mobsters, and they promised to deal with McGaffigan when he showed up again.

Bangs left the bar, picked up O'Malley and made a beeline to McGaff's apartment to end the nonsense once and for all. More than anything, Bangs feared he'd be forced to fight McGaff—who had had open-heart surgery a few years before—and might accidentally kill him in the fray.

When Joey and Debbie arrived at McGaffigan's place, they spotted his vehicle hidden at the back of the driveway. Bangs flew from his car and began kicking in McGaff's front door. Still defiant, Jimmy yelled at Joey through the splintered opening but refused to step outside. Bangs finally lured McGaff just outside the doorway with the promise that he wouldn't hurt him in front of O'Malley, and then yelled at Debbie to roll down the car window so she could hear the conversation clearly.

Bangs berated McGaff and warned that if he ever called Debbie again, he'd break his jaw, and if he ever found the balls to lay a hand on her, he'd kill him. The gutsy McGaff told Bangs he was going into the house to retrieve a weapon, but Joey told him not to bother—he had two guns on his person and Jimmy was free to take one. McGaff respectfully declined; he wanted his own.

"Fine," Joey advised. "But if you come out of that house with a gun, I'll put a bullet in your head."

McGaffigan stormed into the house, slammed the remains of the busted door behind him—and didn't return. Bangs waited for a few minutes, ready, listening, unmoved. McGaff got the message. He later unlocked O'Malley's apartment so she could collect the rest of her belongings, but never contacted her again. However, Debbie took him to small claims court when he wouldn't return her microwave. It wasn't an expensive item, but for her the principle of the matter was priceless. On Gillen's recommendation, McGaffigan hired Joe Flak to represent him in the case.

Flak was an average-looking guy who nevertheless made an impression with his snappy dress and stunning Spanish girlfriend, Vera. Although Bangs had never hit the coke pipe with Flak and Vera, Vera invited Debbie to parties with Doherty's cronies Jackie Gillen and Al Roberts—cocaine-smoking marathons that became so frequent Bangs finally told Flak that if Vera gave Debbie any more drugs outside his presence, he'd break his jaw.

Doherty and Gillen also intimated that Vera was open to relations with other partners and even suggested to Joey that she was interested in getting together with him. Despite Vera's drug use, the idea piqued Bangs' interest, but when he asked Debbie a few innocent questions about Vera, she sniffed out his intentions right away and threatened to hack off his balls if he tried anything. Joey let the idea lie: he liked Debbie, she and

Vera were friends, and, besides, he didn't need to spend any more time with Doherty, Roberts or Gillen.

As Bangs expected, Flak botched "the case of the microwave oven," and O'Malley ultimately won her claim with ease. Because of McGaff's obstinacy and greed, Bangs tracked him down some days later and gave him a brutal pistol-whipping. Bangs believed at the time he'd never see McGaff again, but Jimmy would reappear in Joey's life in the most unexpected manner.

JACKSON, MISSISSIPPI

BY THE END OF AUGUST 1984, JOEY BANGS DECIDED he had had enough of both the junket business and the narcotics game, and he began tying up loose ends. Tommy Doherty begged Bangs to let him work off his debt—which was still more than $100,000 and climbing—by acting as a gofer on Joey's business trips. But in those days Bangs wouldn't have taken Doherty out for an ice cream, much less to a business meeting.

Tommy's life was a shambles: he dressed shabbily and spent his days locked away in the barn with Al Roberts, smoking cocaine. Doherty had covered all the windows in his barn to make the office pitch dark, and cocaine and cigarette smoke choked the air. Roberts used a bullet casing container to hold thirty lit cigarettes at once so he could collect enough ashes to keep up with the coke consumption—Al and Tommy used the ash in their glass pipes to help the cocaine burn slowly. Now out on bail, Gillen occasionally dropped by the garage for a hit, but he was spending most of his time prepping his defense for the Maine marijuana bust.

Bangs had done plenty of cocaine, but always in party situations or occasional lost weekends with friends drinking and drugging and carousing with as many women as they could rustle up. For Tommy, things had deteriorated to the point that Joey could barely stand to look at him. And eventually, after yet another argument over Tommy's debt, Joey cut off Tommy's supply of cocaine and marijuana and advised his pal to seek help.

Within a week, Doherty claimed he had located another supplier—Michael Fouchette, a former Registry police officer who later worked with Doherty on the Medford force. A few years earlier, Doherty had singled out Fouchette as a future partner in crime, first enlisting Mike's help to break a display window at Zayre's to pilfer a load of console televisions. But their schemes ended prematurely when Fouchette was convicted of tax crimes for mailing multiple fraudulent returns and sent to a federal penitentiary in Florida. And while in custody, Fouchette met a convict from Nashville who claimed to have access to an endless supply of pure cocaine.

Now that Fouchette had been released, he approached Doherty about a potential cocaine deal and invited Tommy, Al, and Doherty's girlfriend, Nancy, to drive to Tennessee with him to meet the contact.

Doherty asked Bangs to ride along and guide them on the purchase of two kilos, but Bangs refused, reminding Doherty that he never dealt with strangers, especially now, after Gillen's marijuana fiasco. Besides, Joey was ready to be done with the trade—or at least he thought so.

Doherty believed this deal was his break, so he borrowed money from everyone to make it happen, even taking a $10,000 loan from bookie Jimmy McGaffigan. Nevertheless, he still found himself short ten grand. With no other options, he turned to Joey for the final tranche, swearing to Bangs that Gillen had nothing to do with the deal and even plying Joey with drink and his favorite country songs.

Bangs was equally appalled and impressed by Doherty's gumption. Out of friendship, he had carried Tommy's drug tab, plus numerous "favors," far too long already, and out of frustration, he informed Doherty he was only days away from killing him, never mind lending him additional money. Summoning all the charisma his drug-choked soul could muster, Tommy pleaded that if Joey lent him the money, he'd be first in line to be paid back from the profits, with interest. Against his better judgment, Bangs yielded once again.

A few days later, Doherty and Roberts packed their suitcases, money and guns into Tommy's Lincoln and headed for Interstate 95 South. They stopped one last time, around midnight, to call Joey to try to persuade him to go, but Bangs stood firm—he was out.

Three days later, on August 21, 1984, Doherty's son Michael phoned Bangs and asked to meet with him as soon as possible. Joey already knew what he'd hear, but he invited Michael to his apartment that night. As expected, he learned that Tommy needed more cash for the deal. Joey assumed Tommy was no doubt getting fucked up smoking the drugs he had gone to buy. But Michael explained that his father was now in

Meridian, Mississippi, of all places, and that the deal was even better than anticipated. Tommy wanted to make a larger purchase, and to make it work, he needed an additional $14,000—a week ago yesterday.

Joey needed time, he said, and sent Michael away empty-handed. In reality, Bangs hoped that if he stalled, Doherty would locate the money elsewhere, and this nightmare would vanish. Bangs ignored Michael's persistent phone calls for two days before Doherty himself began calling—and reversing the charges, to boot. Bangs remained guarded—his gut told him no. For two more days the phone rang off the hook. Joey never answered.

Then came another knock at Bangs' door, and Joey opened to find Michael, sleep-deprived, beaten down, sheepish, apologetic. Michael pleaded with Joey on his father's behalf, claiming that Tommy was desperate to make the deal happen. Finally worn down himself by the situation, Bangs agreed to front the money.

First thing the next morning, Joey and Debbie drove to the East Cambridge Savings Bank in a car Bangs had borrowed from Jackie Gillen. Not surprisingly, Gillen's car broke down in front of the bank, and, infuriated, Bangs simply abandoned the shit-box. Joey withdrew several thousand dollars and then hailed a cab to the State Employees Credit Union, where he closed his account after withdrawing the rest of the cash Tommy needed, thus clearing up some personal business at the same time, since these were the last accounts with his wife Judy's name on them.

Bangs arranged to meet Michael at Carroll's Diner, across the street from the Medford Police Station, where he and Debbie planned to grab a blue-plate special, but by the time the taxi dropped them off, Michael had already arrived and sat waiting for them in his truck.

Bangs didn't waste a moment: he hopped from the taxi and dropped a small paper bag through Michael's window. "Fourteen grand," he told him, "Don't bother counting it." In fact, the bag contained only $13,000—Joey reckoned his trouble was worth at least a grand. Doherty would have to figure out how to handle the shortage on his end of the transaction.

Bangs watched as Michael dashed across the street and handed the package to Mike Fouchette, who was idling in his black Datsun 280Z. Fouchette sped away, and Michael returned to the diner to offer Joey and Debbie a ride back to Pleasant Street. Bangs peppered Michael with questions and learned that Fouchette was responsible for wiring the money to Tommy.

Bangs was suspicious of the scenario—*Why wouldn't Michael himself wire the money?* he wondered. Bangs surmised that Fouchette was planning to drive the money down south so he could be in on the deal. Or else there was some other scam afoot. In any case, there was little Joey could do about it at this point, and he already had Tommy on the hook.

Two days had passed when Joey noticed Tommy's Lincoln Continental parked outside his barn across the street. Bangs hurried over to find Doherty and Roberts tearing around the garage, gathering an arsenal of guns and ammunition. Joey learned that Doherty and Roberts had holed up in a dumpy motel to wait for the drugs to be delivered anonymously by cab, and the cash to be dropped off by Fouchette—as Bangs had guessed—once the deal was in motion. Doherty was planning to fly back to Boston while Roberts drove the product home. However, Fouchette claimed he passed the money—more than $50,000—to his intermediary contact, who then absconded, leaving Doherty and Roberts alone in a cheesy motel with no cash and no product, pricks in hand, as the saying goes. Doherty and Roberts were now headed back to Mississippi—this time without Nancy—to kill the no-good hillbilly cocksucker who had fleeced them.

Bangs was beside himself at first, and he warned Doherty not to return to Boston without the money or the product or both. But as Tommy and Al squealed out of the driveway, Joey couldn't help but find the incident somewhat amusing. After all, he had warned Doherty not once but twice never to deliver money without first having the product in hand, and here Tommy had been taken by a backwater chucklehead.

Upon arriving in Mississippi, Doherty and Roberts put out the word that they would hunt down the thief if the drugs or the money or both weren't produced immediately. Fouchette reached out to his contact to attempt a reconciliation. The hillbilly returned the favor by dropping a dime to local narcotics detectives and explaining everything that had transpired. The narcotics team moved quickly, arranging a meeting between Doherty and Roberts and another "dealer," who would deliver not only the two kilos of cocaine previously promised, but also an additional half kilo for Doherty's trouble.

On August 29, 1984, the world began to unravel for Doherty and Roberts. Too angry to think clearly, Doherty agreed to meet with the new players at another motel in Meridian. However, when Tommy and Al arrived at the appointed time and place—sawed-off shotguns in hand—there was a message at the desk that they needed to meet Fouchette at the Holiday Inn in Jackson, Mississippi. From there, Fouchette drove them to the parking lot of a Red Lobster, where they met the alleged drug dealers and Fouchette's contact—who had been a confidential informant for years. After making introductions, Fouchette excused himself and drove off, not to be heard from again, leaving a cloud of suspicion about his involvement in the sting.

One of the undercover detectives approached Doherty's car, carrying a paper grocery bag. Tommy tossed the keys to Roberts and nodded for him to open the trunk. Al promptly popped the trunk, and the detective dropped in two and a half kilos of product—100% pure, all-purpose flour.

Police swarmed the parking lot and arrested Doherty, Roberts, and the informant—to maintain the CI's cover. Doherty protested that he was vacationing, on his way to Nashville's Grand Ole Opry. When this alibi failed, Lt. Doherty produced a Medford police captain's badge and claimed he was posing as a drug dealer in order to apprehend a suspected narcotics distributor who was operating in his Massachusetts hometown. But the circumstances, as well as the lock-picking and burglary tools found in Doherty's trunk, told a truer tale.

The detectives confiscated Doherty's brand-new Signature Series Lincoln Continental, since it was used in the commission of a crime. Tommy had just paid nearly $30,000 in cash for the car, after arranging a special price with the dealer, a personal friend, for three identical vehicles. Clemente bought one, and Bangs had agreed to buy the third. But when Joey learned they were all the same color, he backed out of the purchase—three partners in a bank heist driving identical luxury cars was flouting the law more than even Bangs was willing to risk.

Doherty continued to push his luck. Once he was out on bail, he asked his car dealer friend to change and backdate the paperwork to reflect a finance contract rather than a cash transaction and refund him the money he had already paid. The dealer's hands were tied, however—the police had already been to the dealership to seize the paperwork pertaining to the vehicle.

▾ ▾ ▾

Bangs learned about the arrest while he was enjoying a typical weekend on Cape Cod. He and his crew of rogue Met cops had rented rooms in a cozy motel in Dennis, Massachusetts, where they could kick up their heels, drink and smoke a little cocaine. Bangs glanced at a newscast on TV and spotted Doherty's and Roberts' mug shots plastered across the screen. But unlike Jerry Clemente's media debut, Bangs was not at all surprised to hear that Doherty and Roberts had been arrested on a narcotics offense.

Tommy Doherty was charged with possession of a sawed-off shotgun and conspiracy to purchase narcotics with the intent to distribute; Al Roberts, only with a single count of conspiracy. Doherty summoned the expertise of Eugene Patrick McCann,* a partner in the prestigious Boston law firm of Troy, McCann & Bolton—a firm founded by former Metropolitan patrolman Thomas Troy and well known among renegade cops.†

McCann hustled to the log cabin in Jackson that doubled as a police station and was escorted to Doherty's cell. Tommy had by this time worked his magic and charmed the other inmates, many of whom were African-American and referred to him as "Snowflake." Being well versed in law, Doherty offered legal advice to his newfound friends, who for the most part were penniless and underprivileged. McCann took a shine to Doherty because of his quick wit and generosity and promptly posted bail for Tommy and Al. Doherty and Roberts scrounged up a "Rent-a-Wreck" and slogged their way home, 1,500 miles with no radio and no air-conditioning in the stifling, humid heat of August in the south.

Bangs suspected that Fouchette had set up Doherty and Roberts, but he was never able to piece together enough details to make the story stick.

---

* The entire McCann clan was devoted to law and law enforcement. Pat's father was a Lowell police captain, and his wife of 45 years, Michaelene O'Neill McCann, a lawyer. His oldest son is a sergeant on the Lowell Police Department, and his youngest boy was a Lowell police officer before becoming a Navy SEAL. Sadly, McCann passed away on March 23, 2009, at the age of 68, during the research and writing of this book.

† When I was a child, my dad took me to purchase ice skates at the Hyde factory outlet in Cambridge. Afterwards, Dad wanted to stop to see a colleague who lived nearby in the Cambridge housing projects—Tommy Troy. Evidently, Troy was flat broke while putting himself through law school on a cop's salary, and the subsidized living situation was all he could afford. Troy was a respectable and honorable man.

When the drug deal went awry, Bangs realized that Doherty would probably never be able to pay his debt, especially with the $24,000 amount added to the already hefty total. Tommy's borrowing was out of control, he had exhausted all of his sources, and he no longer possessed the mental faculties to find his way out of the labyrinth. He was now more of a liability than a friend, and he was becoming more unreliable with each passing day. He had to go, reasoned Bangs.

Doherty sensed that the end was near, and in a desperate attempt at reconciliation, he again approached Bangs about doing "odd jobs" to pay off a portion of his debt while he was still out on bail. Out of patience, Bangs gave Doherty two weeks to pay, publicly threatened his life, and refused even to speak with him until the debt was settled. In his own way, Doherty was left with limited options.

∨ ∨ ∨

In the first week of October 1984, Brother O'Leary showed up on Joey's doorstep at eight in the morning, looking for work, after a year of no contact. Not surprisingly, Brother had pissed through most of his Depositors Trust earnings. But Bangs had nothing to offer his childhood pal: he had no interest whatsoever in the one-off gaffs they had once perpetrated, and he was getting out of the drug trade and into a legitimate business. In fact, a Cape Cod-based company looked to be Bangs' next venture, and he had already acquired his broker's license.

After two hours of O'Leary's cajoling, Bangs caved—if Brother wanted to, he could collect Joey's outstanding cocaine and marijuana debts for a small percentage. Brother was thrilled.

Before Brother left, Joey broke out a cocaine pipe—a peace offering, as it were. O'Leary indulged readily, but once he was feeling good, he refused to leave. Joey tried to shoo him off with a small package for the road, but Brother returned a few hours later, looking for more, and pounded on the door for more than fifteen minutes. When Joey didn't answer, Brother strolled across the street to Doherty's garage to say hello and look for a hit.

Doherty had also not heard from O'Leary in over a year, and seeing him in an altered mental state shook him up, especially after Brother informed Tommy that he was going to be collecting Joey's outstanding drug debts. Doherty quickly stuffed a cocaine package into Brother's pocket and shuffled him out the door—he felt he was in imminent danger, and he now had to do what he had to do in order to survive.

Later that day, Doherty summoned Bangs to his garage and told him he had serious concerns about Jackie Gillen's integrity. He reminded Joey that Gillen, who was still out on bail, knew about the Depositors Trust robbery and said he suspected Jackie might be cooperating with federal authorities. In fact, Doherty suggested that the feds had offered Gillen a deal if he would give up the bank robbers. Bangs listened intently and scrutinized Doherty's face; he needed to know where Tommy's loyalty lay—with him or with Gillen.

Doherty knew that there was no love lost between Bangs and Gillen and that Joey would jump through flaming hoops to get a piece of Jackie. Bangs made it clear that taking out Gillen was not a problem and that he'd be more than happy to do so. Doherty in turn suggested that Bangs whack Gillen while Jackie was at his girlfriend's South Shore home. Tommy even offered to drive, but Joey informed him that if he were to commit murder, of all things, he would certainly not bring along a witness, especially someone as unreliable as Tommy.

Bangs and Doherty discussed the idea several times over the coming weeks. On one occasion, Bangs told Doherty he was apt to walk next door to Gillen's home while his wife was at work, give Gillen a hit off the cocaine pipe, and put a bullet into the back of his head, leaving his cold cadaver on the floor for his wife to discover.

Don't shit where you eat, Doherty warned. As gratifying as it sounded, killing Gillen that close to their own homes would only bring additional heat, especially since Jackie's trial for the Maine marijuana bust was about to begin.

Doherty then tempted Bangs by saying there was money to be had by whacking Gillen the right way: Jackie had no children, but he had recently purchased a million-dollar life insurance policy and named Doherty's teenage daughter the beneficiary. Bangs could help himself to a sizeable cut if he did the dastardly deed. Joey despised Gillen so much that he would have done it for free. Hell, he would have paid for the privilege, but this approach—too blatant in its stupidity—alerted Bangs to the fact that Doherty may indeed be trying to set him up.

When he couldn't incite Bangs to murder, Doherty found other ways to direct Joey's attention away from himself. As his own trial in Mississippi approached, Tommy asked Joey to accompany him to Billy Padula's vacation property in the country so they could have some quiet time to discuss strategy for his upcoming defense. Suspicious, Joey asked who else would be there. Doherty replied that he had also invited Tommy Troy. Troy, Doherty said, had agreed to assist in an illegal game plan that included subornation of perjury. Bangs didn't buy it. He now had little doubt that Doherty and Gillen were conspiring to kill him and that if he were alone with one or both of them, they wouldn't hesitate to strike.

Bangs told Doherty he wasn't inclined to drive to a secluded cottage when they could rent a suite at the Royal Sonesta Hotel in Cambridge and get all the quiet time needed to discuss the case. Bangs even offered to call Troy himself and set up the meeting, since he personally knew the attorney, who was a former Met cop, and could reach him easily at the Banister Lounge, a local watering hole located directly across Cambridge Street from the Middlesex County Superior Courthouse. Doherty graciously declined the offer and said he'd take care of it.

A short time later, Doherty told Bangs he had seen a couple of local "heavies" driving by his home at odd hours, one man positioned in the backseat as a shooter. Tommy made sure that Joey's girlfriend, Debbie, overheard the conversation: if anything were to happen to Bangs, Doherty wanted her to have a preconceived notion of who may be involved.

The only problem with Doherty's assertion was that Bangs personally knew the heavies in question—a couple of brothers—so he and Bobby Spencer approached the players and put the screws to them. After a tense sit-down, it became obvious that Doherty was lying. The heavies were offended and wanted to pay Doherty a visit, but Bangs deflected their anger, promising that he'd take care of Tommy. Joey now realized that the showdown was set: either he or Tommy would soon be dead.

SMOKING BARREL

ON THE MORNING OF OCTOBER 16, 1984, Jerry Clemente had coffee with longtime pal Tommy Doherty. According to Clemente, Doherty was talking out of school, prattling on about how Bangs had threatened to kill him. He detailed how word on the street was that Bangs had a problem with "the people from Rhode Island," that is, *La Cosa Nostra*, and how everyone on Pleasant Street agreed that Bangs was an out-of-control menace.

Later that day, however, Tommy crossed paths with Joey and greeted him warmly. Doherty thought he would have some money later in the evening, he said, and he wanted to buy some cocaine. Bangs rolled his eyes—he had heard this song before—and told Tommy to call if he struck it rich.

Just before six o'clock that evening, Joey took a hit from his glass cocaine pipe—an expertly crafted, handmade gift from Al Roberts—and drove to the Memory Lane Lounge in Somerville in his pale-green Chevy Impala, which he used mainly to transport drugs. Bangs met an old friend from the MDC, Sergeant William McKay ("Billy"), to shoot the shit over drinks before Debbie O'Malley and her teenage daughter Kelly Ann met them for dinner.

After a final drink and toast to good health, the group made their way to the parking lot. Debbie had driven Joey's new champagne-colored Cadillac Seville, and while she and Billy McKay said their goodbyes, Bangs discretely transferred several items from the Impala to the trunk of the Cadillac, including a briefcase and a gym bag containing various guns and jewelry—among them a few select items from the Depositors Trust robbery—and a kilo of cocaine. Before closing the trunk, Bangs removed a .357 Magnum from the spare tire well and tucked it under his jacket, just in case he met with any trouble in South Boston, where he and the girls were headed for dinner at Kelly's Restaurant, a notorious mob hangout.

The evening passed uneventfully. A few better known underworld figures greeted Joey as he entered the restaurant, and others stopped by his table to pay their respects and meet his new love interest, Debbie, since most of them knew only his former girlfriend, Cheryl Fisher. On a few occasions, Joey excused himself and disappeared to a booth in the back, remaining to speak with shadowy figures for what seemed an eternity to Debbie and Kelly Ann.

As Joey had promised, Debbie and Kelly Ann were delighted with the meal, which had been prepared by a "Chinaman" that Joey had known for years. The chef also practiced eastern medicine and acupuncture out of a small room in the basement kitchen, and he had in fact treated Bucky Barrett to help him stop smoking. To Joey's surprise, the Chinese chef's magic needles worked remarkably well.

Between 9:30 and 10:00 p.m., Joey, Debbie and Kelly Ann arrived back at their Pleasant Street apartment. As Kelly Ann got ready for bed, Debbie told her she and Joey were stepping out for a couple of hours and warned her not to open the door if anyone should stop by. If there were a problem, she could call Al Roberts, who was living in Doherty's garage across the street while he was out on bail for the Mississippi mishap. Even though Al barely got along by running errands and cleaning up for Tommy in exchange for room, board and drugs, he was an agreeable sort who bore no malice.

Debbie ducked into the bathroom to touch up her hair and makeup, while Joey changed his shirt. The telephone rang—odd for this hour. Joey hesitated, then picked up. It was Tommy Doherty—he had Joey's money and wanted him to come over. Bangs said he and Debbie were on their way back out for a night on the town and asked Tommy to tell Roberts to keep an eye on the apartment for him. To Joey's delight, Doherty informed Bangs that he had enough money for a kilo and wanted it as soon as possible. Naturally, Bangs perked up and agreed to stop by on his way out, so long as Doherty showed good faith and gave him $50,000 toward his debt. That was the way Bucky did it, he added—let a man work off his debt—but Tommy's time was running out. Sensing that he had

Doherty in a vulnerable moment, Bangs told him that if he didn't come up with the balance within two days, he was still as good as dead.

Around 11:00 p.m., Bangs smoked a quarter gram of cocaine, slipped on his favorite leather jacket, told Debbie he'd be right back, and walked across the street, with another quarter-gram package in his pocket as a teaser for Tommy, in the event he didn't actually have the money.

Bangs usually carried two guns, but tonight, uncharacteristically, he wasn't wearing either of them because he didn't want Kelly Ann to see him walking around armed. Although Kelly Ann and her younger sister, Shauna, lived primarily with Debbie's parents on Rodgers Avenue in Somerville, from time to time she would spend a weekend with Debbie at Bangs' apartment, and Debbie always asked Joey to hide his guns while Kelly Ann was present.

As Joey exited the apartment, he scanned the neighborhood's dark streets and quick-stepped across the driveway toward Doherty's garage, careful not to scuff his expensive Italian shoes with the chic Cuban heels. He looked for lights in the house and garage and listened carefully for voices. All quiet. Too quiet.

Oddly, the entrance on the north side of the barn was locked. "What the fuck!" He bellowed as he banged on the steel door. "Let me in, goddammit!"

It took only a moment for Al Roberts to open the door, and Bangs pushed past him, demanding to know where Tommy was hiding. "Upstairs," Roberts grunted, as he pointed a massive, grimy monkey wrench toward the metal spiral staircase. Bangs charged across the garage, pausing slightly when he heard Roberts deadbolt the door behind him. He noticed that Roberts had been working on an unfamiliar vehicle inside the garage bay, a maroon Pontiac Monte Carlo, and his instinct kicked in— this was not right.

Fuck it! he thought. *I'm done with this cocksucker.* He flew up the stairs and through the open door at the top of the staircase, stormed down the hall, and yanked hard on the door to Doherty's office—locked. Joey pounded on the door, yelling for Tommy to open. The lock engaged, and the door opened slightly.

"Come on in," a voice beckoned.

As Joey reached for the handle, the door flew outward, and Joey found himself staring down the double barrels of a sawed-off 12-gauge shotgun, which Jackie Gillen held tight to his hip. Gillen clenched his jaw and squeezed the trigger—BOOM! The double-ought pellets—nine of them, each roughly equivalent to a .33-caliber bullet—sprayed across Joey's right chest and shoulder, spinning him around with the impact. He grasped his chest with his left hand and felt the warm, sticky blood gush from his wounds.

Bangs looked back at Gillen, incredulous. "You shot me, you motherfucker!"

Time froze, Joey's mind raced. Then the adrenaline kicked in. Joey darted toward the exit but got only a few steps down the hall before another blast seared the upper left area of his back with more buckshot. Somehow he remained on his feet. Oddly, he wasn't in pain, but he fought for his breath as he tried to clear his head. *Why the fuck did I leave without a gun?!* He staggered down the winding staircase, never looking back, intent on avoiding an ambush by Roberts or another unseen accomplice in the garage ahead of him.

Joey's head swirled, the blood seemed to gush faster, and he began to panic: he had seen this kind of wound in combat, and the result was never good. He couldn't believe he was going down like this—in an ambush perpetrated by two coked-out ex-cops and a two-bit criminal.

With his right arm rendered useless, Bangs momentarily released the pressure on his chest wounds and reached for the sliding deadbolt with his left hand. Blood pooled around his pricey Italian loafers as he fumbled with the doorknob and lock, a heavy, commercial bolt mechanism that the paranoid Doherty had installed to buy time in the event of a drug raid.

Instinctively, Joey peered over his shoulder to see if his assassins were pursuing. Standing silently near the bottom of the spiral staircase was Doherty, stone-faced, his right arm fully extended, a chrome-plated .38-caliber revolver trained on Joey's head. Bangs didn't hear the shots, but state police later removed two slugs from the doorjamb, just above the height of Joey's shoulders.

When Bangs finally opened the door, moonlight flooded the entryway, illuminating the figure of Al Roberts, who cowered in the corner, monkey wrench still in hand. Joey flashed him a glare, stumbled outside and dragged himself across the street to his Cadillac, where he attempted to retrieve a pair of handguns secured in the trunk—a .357 revolver and a 9mm automatic. He was going back to kill the cocksuckers.

Joey rummaged frantically through his pockets for his keys, unwittingly dropping the teaser package of cocaine. Weak and delirious from blood loss, he couldn't manage to open the trunk and dropped the keys beneath the car and beyond his reach.

He shuffled across the street to his building and crawled up a set of stairs to the side entrance of his second-floor apartment, where he pounded on the door and rang the bell and yelled for Debbie. He glanced across the street—no one had followed him outside.

When Debbie opened the door a moment later, Joey flopped across the threshold, blood spewing from his chest, nose, ears and back. He coughed up coagulated blood and tried to instruct Debbie, but faded in and out of coherence. Debbie dragged Joey's blood-drenched body into the living room where she could surround him with furniture and keep lookout from the windows over the street.

Bangs mustered enough strength to prop himself against the sofa and asked Debbie how bad he had been hit. Debbie paused for a moment, then began to bawl. Not realizing he had been hit from both sides, she said it looked as if the blast had gone into his chest and out his back. Kelly Ann ran into the room to see what the commotion was and also burst into tears. Joey made eye contact with them both and assured them everything would be okay—they just needed to follow his directions closely.

Debbie frantically searched for the Smith and Wesson .38 snub-nose revolver hidden in the bedroom, in case Gillen or Doherty ventured across the street to finish the job, while Kelly Ann grabbed towels to stanch the bleeding. The white cotton turned crimson instantly, so Kelly Ann pressed a sofa cushion against the wounds on Joey's back and used her knee to keep pressure on it. Debbie helped load the revolver and cleared Joey's sightline to all the doors before propping his arm across a coffee table, the gun pointed at the front entrance.

Joey told Debbie to call the Medford Fire Department, but in her frenzy, she instead called the Medford Police Department, home to many of Doherty's corrupt cronies. Police officers arrived within minutes, and Debbie ushered them through the front door, hysterically jabbering about the gore. Bangs had become extremely pale and continued to cough up clotted blood.

Joey heard the officers stalking through the apartment, calling out as they approached, until they entered the living room with guns drawn and found Bangs, his weapon trained on them. The officers yelled at him to drop the gun, but Joey only tightened his grip and shook his head to clear the shouts and smells and shrieks around him that were crushing his thoughts. He didn't recognize the first officer in and couldn't see the second one standing in the hall, and he wasn't about to trust any Medford cop in this moment.

"Fuck you!" he screamed. "I'm not releasing my gun until some civilians get here!"

Debbie pleaded with him to give her the weapon, but the police isolated her in one corner and Kelly Ann in another. Joey again strained to steady his shaky hand, then dropped the revolver. The second officer—whom Joey now recognized as Buster Longo—stepped to his side, kicked the gun out of reach, pressed a clean white towel into his wounds and pinched a severed artery in his chest, an action which saved Bangs' life.

However, the tension broke only when medical personnel arrived and assured Joey they would help him. Unable to stop his bleeding and stabilize his condition, the EMTs loaded Bangs onto a stretcher board and hustled him to the ambulance below. Local residents had lined the streets, and a television news crew arrived as the ambulance was leaving. The cat was out of the bag.

The female EMT spoke calmly and labored to stabilize Joey on the way to nearby Lawrence Memorial Hospital, less than a mile away. Nevertheless, Joey's heartbeat and breathing stopped before they arrived at the hospital.

❤ ❤ ❤

Back at the apartment, the police officers kept Kelly Ann separated from Debbie and took the teen to the police station to interview her without adult supervision or representation, a major violation of protocol. Another squad car escorted Debbie to the hospital.

By the time the Bay State ambulance arrived at the hospital, Bangs had regained a faint pulse and strengthening vital signs. Once the ER doctors stabilized him enough that he could respond to his surroundings, Joey looked at the lead physician as if to ask how badly he was hurt.

"You're a cop," remarked the doctor, "you know how bad you're hurt."

As the doctor cut away what remained of Joey's tattered jacket, a handful of shotgun pellets tumbled from his shoulder to the gurney. The policemen attending Joey quickly scooped them into evidence bags.

Once he could speak, Bangs continually requested that Metropolitan and state police be notified—he knew the Medford cops would attempt to sandbag the case, especially if he were to die. In fact, the Medford officers in the room were already peppering Joey with leading questions, which he ignored, stating firmly that he would speak only with Metro or state police and that they could go fuck their mothers if they didn't like it. The physician asked Bangs about his religion—"Catholic," he replied—and whether he wished to receive last rights. "What difference does it make?" Joey queried sincerely. He knew what awaited him on the other side.

Bangs heard Debbie's voice in the hallway just outside the ER door and asked the physician for a moment with her before surgery. Covered in Joey's blood, the doctor said there wasn't time—Bangs was still losing blood rapidly and in no condition to be stirred up. Besides, the doctor reasoned, she'd be traumatized to see him in this state.

Joey begged—he had to speak with her one last time. The doctor conceded and covered Joey with a thin white sheet, while a nurse ushered Debbie into the room. Joey beckoned her close and whispered in her ear for a few moments before being sedated and wheeled into the operating room.

Debbie rushed from the ER and asked an officer to accompany her home. Joey had made his final request, and she had promised to fulfill it: get the two grand in cash taped behind that painting of the naked woman in the living room, and drive the Cadillac—with the contents of the trunk—away from the house and stash it in a safe place. What should have been a tender moment was in fact criminal collusion.

By the time Debbie arrived home, state police Lt. Detective Tommy Spartichino—who worked directly with Middlesex County District Attorney Scott Harshbarger on murder investigations—had taken charge of the scene. With the assistance of state troopers Billy Flynn, Billy Lisano, and Greg Foley, Spartichino tightened security to protect any evidence.

When Debbie tried to sneak past, the troopers denied her access to both the car and the apartment. She eventually prevailed on them to let her retrieve a sweater, a move she hoped would allow her to clear any drug paraphernalia from the home and sneak the car away, but they sent along an officer to watch her every move.

All three troopers were ballsy, no-nonsense professionals who took their job seriously. Flynn and Lisano were large and physical—six-foot-three and six-foot-four, respectively, Lisano a little beefier than Flynn. Foley was prematurely gray but still fit from his years as a semi-pro baseball pitcher; and if anyone ever doubted his grit, his weapon of choice—a sawed-off shotgun—let everyone know he took no shit.[*]

The troopers had been briefed by the Medford officers and shown Bangs' apartment. Despite the tremendous amount of blood throughout, it looked like little had been disturbed since the time Joey was taken to the hospital. But Doherty's garage was an altogether different story.

Once inside, Spartichino saw that someone had sprinkled Speedi-Dry, an absorbent powder, not only on grease spots around the area where Al Roberts had been working but also over crucial blood evidence on both the first and second floors. The crime scene had been badly compromised, and Spartichino knew he'd have a hell of a time sorting things out, especially if Bangs didn't recover.

$$\vee \quad \vee \quad \vee$$

Joey had received life-threatening wounds from a total of eighteen pellets, plus the force of the discharge from the close-range blasts. Miraculously, the shots missed his face and vital organs, even though they tore a palm-sized chunk of flesh from his shoulder and back and severed an artery in his chest. Bangs' heart stopped a second time during the surgery as a result of receiving too large a blood transfusion too quickly, but the medical team resuscitated him immediately.

---

[*] Flynn was married, with no children, and known as a tough trooper whose wife was even tougher. Hailing from East Boston, Lisano was a stand-up cop and superb influence on the younger troopers, who respected him immensely. Lisano retired from the state police and received a lifetime appointment to Lowell Superior Court by the Governor of Massachusetts, per order of George W. Bush, whom he had guarded during election primaries in Boston. Foley—a match to Flynn and Lisano in every way—was reared in Medford.

In an ironic twist of fate, Joey Bangs recovered quickly, and though he knew he had always lived a charmed life, he now felt invincible. He relished telling people he had come back to life to haunt Tommy Doherty. And he knew that death wouldn't be so bad either, if it were anything like the bright, white lights and shitload of beautiful angels with big tits he saw when he checked out on the operating table.

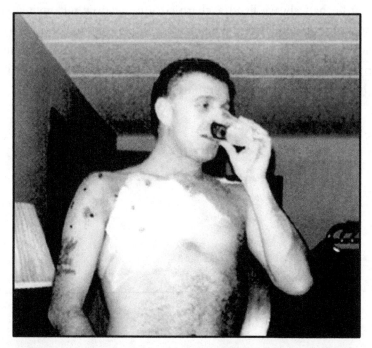

With wounds from eighteen bullet-sized pellets in his chest and back,
Bangs had difficulty for months removing his shirt, even for therapy.

THE INVESTIGATION

LT. DETECTIVE TOMMY SPARTICHINO ARRIVED at the Medford station around 3:00 a.m. He had spent the previous hour studying the crime scene, and now he commandeered an office and barked out a list of everyone he wanted to interview. John C. Kirwan was Medford's Chief of Police at the time, but age-related illness had taken its toll on him, so big Jake Keating—who was considered an upstanding individual—was serving as acting chief. Nonetheless, everyone stepped aside for the state's top detective.

Spartichino wanted to talk first to Debbie O'Malley, who had been pacing the halls, waiting for someone to interview her since 12:45. A police escort had ushered her away from Joey's apartment and dropped her at the station, where she was reunited with Kelly Ann and questioned briefly by Medford police captain Paul Murphy, an old-school Irish cop who was well liked and respected throughout the Medford community. Short, graying, and soft-spoken, Murphy was as good a policeman as Joey was a bad one.

Debbie was a chain smoker, and especially under circumstances this stressful, she couldn't inhale cigarettes fast enough, despite the repeated demands of the officers for her to stop. She would extinguish her smoke for a moment, then shuttle back and forth across the room nervously, rubbing her hands to try to stop them from shaking, only to light up again as soon as the police walked out. Finally, around 3:30 a.m., Spartichino summoned Debbie into the office.

Spartichino knew Joey and his wife, Judy, personally, but he had never met Debbie. Little he had heard or seen that evening made sense, so he started by speaking with Debbie off the record, trying to win her confidence in such sensitive circumstances.

"How do you know Joey?" Spartichino asked respectfully.

Debbie knew she didn't want to get caught up in Joey's mess, especially since she thought he might very well die.

"Just good friends," she claimed. "Met him about five months ago."

"Five months?" probed Spartichino.

"Yeah, give or take," replied Debbie, her hands still trembling.

"Why are you shaking?" he asked, feigning concern. Debbie wasn't taking the bait.

"'Cause it's the middle of the night, a man almost died in my arms, my kid's terrified, the cops who brought me here were assholes, and I need a goddamn smoke. Shame on you for asking such a stupid fucking question."

O'Malley's fire focused Spartichino's attention.

"How long have *you* known Joe?" she blasted back.

"Me? I've been tailing Bangs for better than ten years now," Spartichino offered.

"Ever arrested him for anything?"

"Not yet."

"Shame on you again."

O'Malley's retort stung Spartichino, as much because he saw that he couldn't bully her as that he knew she was right.

Debbie brought the conversation back to the shooting and laid out the night's timeline. She and Kelly Ann had returned with Joey from dinner in South Boston sometime between 9:30 and 10:00 so Kelly Ann could go to bed before Debbie and Joey headed out again for a nightcap. Around 10:30, Doherty called and demanded that Joey come over to the garage. Joey reluctantly agreed, and after changing his clothes and smoking a little cocaine with her, he went to the garage around 11:15. Then all hell broke loose. She heard what sounded like a car backfiring, and moments later someone started pounding on the side door. She opened to find the half-dead Joey drenched in blood and dragged him into the living room, where the police found him.

That was enough for Spartichino.

Medford police sergeant Patrick Carr interviewed Kelly Ann—with Debbie in the room this time—and, without prompting, Kelly Ann corroborated her mother's story. The testimony was also consistent with what she had told Captain Murphy earlier.

Spartichino thanked Debbie, confirmed her contact information, arranged for an escort home, and made sure she knew how to contact him for anything she needed. Spartichino then reviewed the list of officers he had encountered at the crime scene. He would later learn that many of them were wrapped around Doherty's billfold—whether through trafficking drugs or dealing out civil service exams. But for now, he needed to piece together what had actually happened that evening—and why. He began with the two young officers who had arrived first on the scene.

Spartichino was one of the state's best detectives.
Above, as an MDC sergeant. Inset, as a young MDC patrolman.

Officers Eddie Lee and Cesar Delatorre stated that on that crisp October night they were the first officers to respond at #59 Pleasant Street, where they saw Debbie O'Malley standing outside, frantically waving them into Bangs' second-floor apartment, which was actually #2 Pleasant Street Court.

Sergeant Buster Longo arrived a moment later and ordered Delatorre to guard the rear door while he and Lee entered. Lee moved cautiously into the apartment, with Longo directly behind him. Lee confirmed that there had been a brief standoff with Bangs, but that Joey calmed once he saw Longo, who administered first aid until the EMTs arrived.

Longo and Bangs knew each other well—Longo sold bales of marijuana for Bangs, through mutual friend Bobby Spencer. However, Longo was also big pals with Tommy Doherty. In fact, Doherty had sold Longo a stolen civil service exam that had helped him make sergeant, just before the shooting. Longo didn't want to get caught up in any bad blood between Bangs and Doherty, and mysteriously, his written report on this incident never came to light.* But everything Lee and Delatorre said confirmed Debbie's account of the circumstances inside Bangs' apartment. Still, Spartichino didn't have a clear picture of what had happened earlier that night.

▼ ▼ ▼

Spartichino next summoned Sergeant Allen Stone ("Stoney"), who had been the first officer to enter Doherty's garage after the shooting. A close friend of Tommy's, Stone was a fifteen-year veteran of the Medford force who had made sergeant just the previous November. From eight o'clock to midnight that evening, Stone had worked a detail at the Willis Avenue Housing Project. He then returned to the station for his next assignment and was dispatched to Joey's apartment.

When Sergeant Stone arrived at Pleasant Street, the officer directing police activity was Lieutenant Billy Padula—the longtime pal of Tommy's who had always been a thorn in Joey's side. Padula directed Stone to secure Doherty's garage and search the premises for weapons. As Stone left the Pleasant Street Court apartment and crossed the street to the shooting scene, he noted blood splattered on the driveway and in various spots leading to the garage. He shone his flashlight on the barn's side door and saw bloody handprints smeared around the handle.

The barn appeared empty, but Stone entered cautiously, concerned that anyone inside might be under the influence of drugs, adrenaline, and fear. His flashlight reflected off the black pool of blood just inside the door and glinted on the drops and puddles that trailed across the floor and

---

* Later in his career, Buster Longo was accused of rape, and Assistant District Attorney Tom Reilly prosecuted the case, which resulted in Longo's termination from the Medford Police Department and a lengthy prison term.

up the spiral staircase.* Stone stooped to examine the blood stains closely and found that the floor had been hastily dusted with an absorbent powder. Footprints in the powder crisscrossed the pavement and tracked up the steps. Stone flashed his light around the room and yelled Tommy's name. A faint reply echoed from the upstairs office: *Up here!*

As he pushed into the dark garage, Stone smelled gasoline but no gunpowder. He assumed the fumes wafted from the disabled motor in the center of the high-ceilinged space, where Roberts had been working on the maroon Monte Carlo.

Stone tiptoed up the staircase, careful to avoid the blood, and called out again to Tommy, this time identifying himself in a calm voice. As Stone made his way down the hall, he peered into a storage room—nothing but a dismantled motorcycle. Near the office at the end of the hall, the blood splatters grew larger, covering swaths of both floor and wall. Stone finally arrived at the office door—voices on the other side conversed softly.

Stone eased the door open—there sat Doherty, Gillen, Roberts, and the attorney, Tommy Troy, drinking coffee and talking calmly. Doherty had his legs propped up on his desk, not a care in the world. Stone took in the scene for a moment and then asked the men to leave so he could secure the premises. Without speaking, all four men stood, gathered their belongings, and filed past Stone, down the stairs, and out into the night air, never mentioning the commotion or questioning why Stone was there.

Stone followed them out and watched as they crossed the property to Doherty's house. A few moments later, Roberts took his leave of the others and returned to the barn. He had forgotten to feed the cats, he told Stone, and wondered if he could go in for a moment to take care of them. The request was so unexpected that Stone unthinkingly glanced around the property and waved Roberts in. He peered through the door and watched as Roberts popped open a can of food, dumped it into a dish, and put away some tools while he waited for the cats to appear. When Roberts exited a few moments later, he asked if Stone needed anything from the store, since he was running out for cigarettes. Again, Stone blithely responded that he was fine, and Roberts slipped into the maroon Monte Carlo and sped off.

---

* When the Twin Drive-In Theatre in Medford was remodeled, Doherty used a cherry-picker crane to steal the spiral staircase.

According to Stone, it was now around 12:30 a.m., more than an hour after the shooting. Doherty re-emerged from his home and ambled toward Stone, striking up a conversation about being indicted earlier that day for his trouble in Mississippi. Officer Mark Rudolph, who was guarding Bangs' apartment with Officer Alfred Lanzillo, saw Doherty and walked over to join in the chat. Rudolph tried to make small talk by asking Tommy if he had lost weight—about fifteen pounds, Doherty said—but eventually he decided he didn't want to hear about the indictments and other heavy business Tommy seemed intent on discussing. Rudolph then excused himself to return to his post. Doherty left a few minutes later, and Stone remained at the garage until about 1:30 a.m., when Captain Murphy arrived with Officers Fargo and Murray to take charge of the scene until the state police arrived.

Stone's observations matched what Spartichino himself had seen at the garage. It was clear that Joey had been shot upstairs and then made his way back to his apartment, but there were still too many pieces missing for Spartichino to puzzle out the confrontation—What caused it? Who fired first? Where were the weapons? How was the crime scene compromised in the hour after the shooting? He next called in the two officers who were guarding the area on the other side of the street from Stone.

❧ ❧ ❧

Alfred Lanzillo, a ten-year Medford veteran, and Mark Rudolph, a third-year cop, had worked Sector One—the Wellington Circle area—from four to midnight in the 341 cruiser. Just after they turned in their Officer Progress Report to Sergeant Longo at end of their shift, two calls came in—the first concerning a seriously injured person at #59 Pleasant Street, and the second reporting a shooting. Lieutenant Carmine Merullo heard the dispatches and left with Longo, Lee, and Delatorre, making it to Joey's apartment just before the ambulance arrived. Lanzillo and Rudolph arrived a few minutes later, as EMTs were carrying Bangs from the apartment on a stretcher board to the awaiting ambulance.

Lanzillo and Rudolph spotted Mrs. Natale, who also resided at #59 Pleasant Street, standing beside her husband on the front porch. The couple claimed they had heard a vociferous argument upstairs in the back, where Bangs' apartment was located, and added that every night of the week they would hear some kind of disturbance, mainly yelling, coming from the same unit.

Lanzillo also noted three people standing in front of Tommy Doherty's residence, but he neglected to investigate, instead returning to the station with Rudolph for roll call after the ambulance departed with Bangs.

Following roll call, Rudolph and Lanzillo were dispatched back to the crime scene along with Sergeant Stone, arriving there at approximately 12:15 a.m. Rudolph claimed that he saw Doherty make three or four trips between his garage and home, located directly across the street from Bangs' apartment. Rudolph shared some small talk with Doherty, but he never bothered to ask what had occurred, nor did Tommy volunteer any information.

According to Rudolph, Sergeant Stone was safeguarding Doherty's garage the entire time. Rudolph and Lanzillo were positioned at Joey's apartment, Lanzillo on the Pleasant Street Court side, Rudolph on Pleasant Street, parked across the road. At around 1:45 a.m., Rudolph observed Al Roberts driving a maroon Monte Carlo, headed east on Pleasant Street. Roberts pulled alongside Rudolph's police cruiser and told him he'd like to get his car back into the driveway—indicating the entry to Tommy's house—where a detective unit was parked at the time. When Rudolph exited his squad car to move the vehicle in question, Medford Police Detective Brady approached and began conversing with Roberts, but Rudolph wasn't able to hear what was said.

While crossing the street, Rudolph noticed the blood-soaked packet of cocaine that Bangs had dropped in the driveway—a two-by-two-inch glassine baggy containing a white powder. When the state police arrived, Rudolph turned over the baggy to Trooper Billy Flynn. He also briefed the troopers on the evening's events and gave them a tour of the immediate area, including all the homes in question, as well as the bloodstains in the driveway, which he had tried to preserve by covering them with a tire iron and jack.

Spartichino's frustration mounted as he listened to Rudolph—the mistakes made in handling the crime scene would complicate the investigation and potentially jeopardize the prosecution. First, Spartichino wondered whether Lieutenant Billy Padula—who was present at roll call when the initial dispatch came in—had delayed taking action to cover the scene adequately, raising suspicion about whether he had prior knowledge of the incident. And why had Rudolph and Lanzillo returned to the station for roll call, leaving the garage completely unattended? Doherty and his crew would have had free rein to tamper with the evidence for more than a half hour.

Spartichino was also still trying to understand why Sergeant Stone had allowed Al Roberts back into the garage—certainly the cats could have survived for a few hours. And had Roberts been tasked with disposing of the weapons and succeeded in taking them right from under Stone's nose? Rudolph's efforts to protect the blood splatters with a tire iron, though well intentioned, would unfortunately taint the evidence further. And finally, why—out of the slew of Medford cops who encountered Doherty that evening—had no one posed a single question to Tommy about the shooting?

▼ ▼ ▼

Following Rudolph and Lanzillo, Paul O'Riordan, the commanding officer of the Patrol Division and an eighteen-year veteran, took the hot seat in front of Spartichino. O'Riordan was a tall fellow with light hair and a medium build who rarely appeared in public without mirrored sunglasses, especially while on duty. At the time, O'Riordan was one of Doherty's best friends and closest allies on the force.

O'Riordan said he was called to Doherty's home at 11:35 p.m. and arrived at Lawrence Memorial Hospital in Medford at 12:05 a.m., at which time he instructed Sergeant Stone to notify Captain Murphy and Acting Chief Keating about the incident. At the hospital, O'Riordan saw Longo outside the treatment room and asked him for the scoop, before trying to interview Bangs, who was unable to speak clearly through his bloody oxygen mask. But O'Riordan told Spartichino he eventually got Bangs to make a statement: Bangs told him that Doherty and Gillen had jumped over him as they left the barn after the shooting.

O'Riordan then left an officer on duty at the hospital and returned to the Medford station with Longo to file paperwork. But according to Spartichino, of all the reports, O'Riordan's appeared blatantly fabricated, and Spartichino suspected he had never actually spoken with Bangs in the hospital and was merely trying to protect Doherty.

▼ ▼ ▼

Sergeant Carmine Merullo told his story to Spartichino next. Merullo had been on the Medford force for thirteen years and was the Night Command Officer on duty that evening. The first call about the incident came just minutes after he began work, and Merullo left immediately with Longo. They had planned to take the 346 squad car, but when they got into the cruiser, there were no keys, so they hopped into the back seat of Lee and Delatorre's 344 squad car. Longo then realized he had left the station without his service revolver, so Merullo gave his own weapon to Longo—knowing he wouldn't have to enter the scene first, since he was unarmed.

When the foursome arrived at Pleasant Street, they noted that Officers Colorusso and Coholan had pulled over a vehicle and were talking to a white male, who, it turned out, had nothing to do with the incident. They continued to #59, arriving just before the ambulance and another Medford squad car coming from Park Street. Merullo was the first to spot the blonde female—Debbie O'Malley—who was beckoning them to come up to the side door.

Lee and Longo entered the premises first, Merullo confirmed, and overcame Bangs' initial antagonism. As Merullo followed, he noticed a lot of blood smeared on the storm door and along the hall floor. Once inside the living room, he saw what he thought was another revolver in front of the television set, in addition to the one Joey dropped, but Longo still had Merullo's weapon in hand. Longo then grabbed the .38 revolver on the floor, while Bangs repeatedly yelled, "Get me to a fucking hospital! Get me to a fucking hospital! I don't want to die now!"

According to Merullo, Bangs was pale and appeared to be dying. Merullo tried to calm O'Malley and ask her questions to make sense of the situation. But Debbie was shaken and incoherent, and she insisted on riding to the hospital in the ambulance with Bangs. However, Merullo refused to allow her to ride along, asserting that the EMTs needed space to work and that her hysterics would only make matters worse for Joey. He insisted that she ride with him and Longo in Coholan's cruiser or else get there on her own. Debbie glared at Merullo, then slid into the patrol car and slammed the door, swearing at him through her tears.

As Bangs was being loaded into the ambulance, he looked Merullo in the eyes and muttered, "The barn. Doherty and Gillen in the barn. Roberts downstairs."

Everyone knew what "the barn" meant, yet Merullo instead walked to the home of Doherty's brother and police colleague, Brian, knocked on the front door, and asked if he had seen Tommy anywhere. Brian stated that he hadn't. Brian's wife, Jane, walked out of the kitchen and asked if her sister, Nancy Ward, who also resided at #59 Pleasant Street, was okay—Merullo reassured her that Nancy was safe. Merullo then asked if he could use the phone to contact the Medford station, and Brian nodded, excusing himself to speak with Jane in the living room. Merullo called in and learned that Acting Chief Keating, Captain Murphy, and Lieutenant O'Riordan had already been notified of the incident and were mobilizing the forces.

Spartichino asked why the Medford police officers had left the bloody crime scene unattended and unsecured, even if events were somewhat chaotic. Merullo said he assumed Rudolph was guarding the crime scene at the time, but when he later saw Rudolph seated at roll call, he dispatched him back to the scene along with Lanzillo and Stone, ordering them to lock down both Joey's apartment and the garage. And once state police took control of the investigation at Pleasant Street, Merullo was relieved of his duties and set about making sure that all the officers filed proper paperwork.

▾ ▾ ▾

Finally, around 6:30 a.m., Spartichino brought in for questioning the last two officers who had been at the crime scene—Patrolmen Ronald Coholan and James Colorusso. The partners were near the end of their shift working Main Street (Route 16) in Sector 343 when they received a dispatch that shots had been fired and a person severely injured. Turning onto Pleasant Street a few minutes later, they spotted a green Ford approaching and pulled the cruiser in front of it to block its progress. The vehicle was registered in Maine. Colorusso jumped from the cruiser and approached the car's driver—it turned out to be the Reverend Ralph Knight. Knight was driving another pastor friend home, and obviously neither man had been involved in the shooting, so Colorusso allowed them to leave.

When Colorusso and Coholan arrived at Joey's apartment, they noted the blood stains across the driveway and on the rear storm door. They made their way into the building and spotted Longo, who ordered them to secure the perimeter. After the ambulance left for the hospital, Coholan and Colorusso returned to the station for roll call, like their colleagues, leaving the scene completely unattended.

▼ ▼ ▼

It was clear to Spartichino that the Medford cops had been either negligent in their handling of the crime scene or complicit in giving Doherty and his accomplices time to clean up, clear out, and concoct their alibis.

What Spartichino didn't know—and probably couldn't have discovered at the time—were the Medford cops' behind-the-scenes machinations to cover their asses: paperwork filed, reports omitted, confabs held in secret, conversations delayed or avoided. With Bangs headed into surgery, Doherty's colleagues wanted to buy time to see what story would materialize—in particular, how their pal Tommy would spin the circumstances and whether Bangs would survive the night.

At one point in the night, for instance, word filtered back to the station that the state police wanted to know what had happened to Bangs' .38 snub-nose revolver after the paramedics cleared him out of the house. Merullo slipped out of sight—he had pocketed the gun and now slipped into an isolated workstation to run the weapon's serial number. The report came back negative—the gun was not stolen, nor had it been used in the commission of a crime. He handed over the revolver to Captain Murphy, who logged and sealed it. But by this time, so much evidence had been compromised that the disposition of this weapon would have little meaning.

If Bangs had been in any condition to talk, he would have certainly put the pieces together for Spartichino—as he did once he had recovered from surgery. Bangs believed Merullo may have been the person to phone Tommy Troy, who had successfully represented Carmine a few years earlier, when he was arrested for breaking and entering a convenience store located at Medford's Wellington Circle to steal cigarettes. And Bangs supposed that Merullo most likely called Doherty at his home, instructing him to stay put, since Keating and others were on their way to the scene.

▼ ▼ ▼

After Spartichino had interviewed the Medford police's first responders and the EMTs, Doherty, Gillen, and Roberts were arrested for attempted murder. The responsibility of booking them fell to Captain Murphy. Doherty's attorney, Tommy Troy, arrived at the station within minutes to counsel his client and continue shaping the story.

Murphy advised Doherty that he was arresting him for armed assault with intent to murder and assault and battery with a dangerous weapon. He Mirandized Doherty and asked him to sign the rights card.

"If you'd like to say anything," Murphy offered, "I'll listen."

"I'd love to," Doherty nodded, "but on the advice of my attorney, I can't."

"Point me in a direction, Tommy," Murphy urged.

Doherty hesitated. "Check the neighborhood and see how this guy has been acting lately, and look in the trunk of his car. I can't say more than that."

Doherty knew only too well that Bangs had a kilo hidden in the Caddy, as well as a few pieces of jewelry from a recent armed robbery, but he had no inkling that the trunk also hid a small stash of swag from the Depositors Trust heist.

Murphy advised Doherty that he would have to take his clothing for further examination and perform a "C" acid test on his hands to determine if he had fired a firearm.

"They'll be negative," Doherty retorted confidently.

When the state police finally conducted the search of Bangs' Cadillac, they found an assortment of items that pointed to activities far beyond the scope of what anyone had imagined. The official catalog included the following items:

- $10,000 in Canadian currency, in twenty-dollar bills
- Bangs' birth certificate from the City of Cambridge, dated May 5, 1943
- an 1880 ten-dollar gold piece and a 1928 two-dollar-and-fifty-cent gold piece
- a bag of jewelry, including herringbone and tri-colored chains, a gold Piaget watch, a gold-and-diamond Rolex, another gold watch with a diamond face, diamond studs, various loose diamonds, a woman's gold ring with the letter "C" in diamonds (ex-girlfriend

Cheryl's), and a man's gold ring with the initial "J" in diamonds (Joey's)

- a plastic container of loose diamond chips, various gold bracelets, a gold-and-onyx chip watch, a gold lion's head charm, various men's and women's gold-and-diamond rings and a dressy woman's gold-leaf watch
- an Eastern Airlines ticket from Boston to New York to Miami to Barbados to San Juan to Boston
- a brown vinyl travel bag containing a pair of deep-sea diving goggles
- savings account passbooks from East Cambridge Savings Bank and Baybank Middlesex
- business cards for attorneys Anthony M. Traini and Martin S. Leppo
- an Eastern Airlines ticket from Boston to Ft. Lauderdale to Boston, for Debbie O'Malley, scheduled for September 2-6, 1984
- two State of Florida traffic citation slips in Joey's name
- USAir tickets for A. Fisher and J. Fisher
- a Delta Airlines ticket in the name of Dr. R. Taylor (Joey's favorite alias)
- a purchase order and owner's manual for the Cadillac Seville
- a firearms transfer card
- personal mail
- sixty-one snapshots of people in various stages of undress— including one of Joey playfully donning Debbie's undergarments
- a gym bag containing two weapons—a .357 long-barrel magnum and a .380/9mm
- and several items which the state police refused to return to Bangs, even after a heated discussion on illegal search and seizure, including a brown briefcase containing 800 grams of pure cocaine and a glass vial containing white residue, which also proved to be cocaine.

Later that morning, the state investigators also retrieved $2,000 from Joey's house, before moving on to search Doherty's property. There, they dug two .38-caliber slugs from the jamb around the door where Bangs had escaped the garage and confiscated four revolvers, a .25-caliber semi-automatic Beretta and two shotguns, none of which, however, were used in the Bangs shooting.

To their surprise, the troopers also discovered numerous stolen home and office items, including fifteen kitchen cabinets still in their original cartons, a kitchen range with matching hood, two portable heaters, three pneumatic hammers, and an array of other tools. Then they hit the jackpot: a police lieutenant's promotional exam, protruding from a set of law books on a bookcase.*

Doherty would later testify that the exam was in a sealed manila envelope, and Tommy's brother-in-law, Richard Graham, a former Boston cop who witnessed the entire search, confirmed his story. According to Doherty and Graham, Spartichino could scarcely contain himself when he shouted, *We got one! We finally got one! We got 'em now!*

---

* The stolen civil service examination discovered in Doherty's garage was the first and only one ever seized by authorities in the United States. Doherty told Bangs that he had given police entrance and promotional examinations to many Medford police officers.

EYE FOR AN EYE: BENT ON REVENGE

AT 3:30 A.M. ON OCTOBER 17, 1984, Medford Police Lieutenant Carmine Merullo called Jerry Clemente to inform him that Bangs was in emergency surgery for gunshot wounds, but he failed to mention that Tommy Doherty had been involved in the shooting.

Bangs had been shot at such close range that most of the slugs passed through his torso; however, a fair amount of red plastic wadding and residue from the shotgun casings had embedded itself in Joey's flesh, so surgeons had to open his chest cavity to remove as many of the minuscule particles as possible in order to reduce the risk of infection.

Bangs awoke later that morning to discover his old friend, State Police Lieutenant Detective Tommy Spartichino and Assistant District Attorney Thomas Reilly* hovering over his bed in the intensive care unit. When Bangs spotted Spartichino, he shut his eyes and pretended to sleep in order to avoid questioning.

But Spartichino knew Bangs was playing possum. He leaned over the bed and whispered: "Good to see you again, Joe."

Spartichino knew Bangs wouldn't be able to speak because of the tubes in his throat, so he handed Joey a small chalkboard he had brought, along with a fresh piece of chalk. Determined, Spartichino asked Bangs if he knew what had happened to him. Groggy, but still shrewd, Joey scratched out an answer: *Heart attack?*

---

* Reilly served as First Assistant District Attorney under Middlesex County DA Scott Harshbarger from 1983 to 1989. Reilly was later elected to replace Harshbarger for two terms (1991-1999), before serving as Attorney General of Massachusetts for two terms (1999-2007). Bangs was impressed with Reilly, who struck him as a fair-dealing man always in control of his affairs. Medium-framed, fit and well-tailored, Reilly was an avid runner until he suffered a knee injury.

"Then where did all this blood come from?" Spartichino countered quickly. Joey noted the thick crust of dried blood still covering his arms and hands and caked around his jewelry.

Amazingly, Joey had never before been questioned officially about his involvement with any crime, except for the murder of Jake Bag-o'-Doughnuts and the disappearance of Bucky Barrett. Spartichino persisted, explaining that he had discovered weapons, almost a kilo of cocaine, a large sum of Canadian currency, phony identification, airline tickets, and jewelry in the trunk of Joey's Cadillac.

"Cut the bullshit, Joe. Who shot you?"

Joey feigned fading in and out of consciousness—Spartichino was wise to the game.

"Good enough, pal. Get some sleep," he admonished as he wrapped up his visit. "We'll have a nice long talk later." Before departing, Spartichino had a final word: "You're in a world of shit, my friend. Sweet dreams."

Spartichino and Reilly turned to leave, and Bangs peeked to make sure he was safely alone. He glimpsed Spartichino's profile—a twisted, southern Italian nose that appeared to have been broken, distorted even further in Joey's eyes by the effects of his pain medication.

On October 18, Bangs was finally stable enough that Clemente was permitted to visit. Despite his extensive wounds, medicinally altered mental state, and an array of tubes and monitors strapped to his body, Joey ranted breathlessly to Jerry about the wrath he would soon unleash, launching death threats at Doherty and Gillen, and finally Clemente himself—after Jerry let it slip that he had loaned Doherty money for bail. Joey was astounded that Jerry had helped Tommy: Doherty had often talked about killing Clemente and his lover, Barbara Hickey, simply because he didn't trust them to hold their tongues if the bank heist shit hit the fan.

Later that afternoon, Spartichino, Reilly, and a female stenographer, Deborah Christerson, returned to the ICU to interview Bangs in depth, but even at death's door, Bangs refused to comment about the events of October 16. When Spartichino persisted, Bangs again drifted in and out of coherence, giving Spartichino and Reilly little to work with.

For two weeks, Bangs remained in critical condition. Two armed state troopers stood guard outside Joey's private room at all times, and state police had him moved to a new room every couple of days, since they had no idea who might actually be out to silence him. In addition to Tommy Doherty, Jackie Gillen and Al Roberts, scores of others now feared that Bangs might sing to the state police, including cops who had obtained entrance and promotional exams and both Italian and Irish underworld associates whose crimes Joey knew intimately. It wouldn't be a stretch to say that, at that moment, Joseph Paul Bangs was the most sought-after man in New England.

During his subsequent outpatient recovery, Bangs returned to his doctor's office in Medford every third day to have his wounds drained of fluid and infection. While convalescing, Bangs also got word that Doherty had been joking to associates that he intended to be a pallbearer at Joey's funeral. But Joey knew that the last laugh would be his, once he was free of the pestilence called Tommy Doherty.

Several days after his discharge from the hospital, Bangs was ordered to meet with Assistant DA Reilly. Reilly laid his cards on the table: he told Bangs what charges he potentially faced for the cocaine possession and informed him that Doherty, Gillen, and Roberts had already been charged and were out on bail. Reilly wanted Bangs to testify before a grand jury about the night of the shooting only—nothing else. Bangs agreed.

Thomas Reilly,
c. 2006

Before the hearings, Bangs discussed the situation with Clemente, who promised to make things right by helping Joey recoup a portion of the money Doherty owed him in return for his not testifying about the shooting. Doherty's floating tab was now over $150,000— twenty-four thousand in cash, eighty-two for the condo in Pompano Beach, and more than fifty thousand in cocaine Bangs had advanced him. Again, Bangs agreed—though he believed Jerry was on a fool's errand.

Bangs knew what he wanted to do: recoup as much money as possible from Doherty, nail Gillen for the shooting, keep the bank robbery under wraps, squirrel away any remaining swag for himself, and then kill the unsuspecting Doherty. Joey had an ax to grind, and the sharpening stone was spinning fast.

Despite his earlier promise to Reilly, when Bangs later appeared before a Middlesex County grand jury, he invoked the Fifth Amendment and refused to answer any questions. Nevertheless, on November 7, 1984—just three weeks after the shooting—the grand jury returned indictments against Doherty, Gillen, and Roberts for armed assault with intent to murder and assault by means of a dangerous weapon, for the shotgun and handgun blasts, respectively.

The grand jury's findings laid the groundwork for one of the most sensational trials in New England history. Reilly conducted the grand jury probes and ran the show from behind the scenes, although Assistant District Attorney Carol Ball would take center stage during the trial the following year.

At this point, Bangs didn't fear for his own life one whit—*Let 'em come*, he often intoned, *I don't give a fiddler's fuck!* But the Commonwealth still hoped to turn him to their side, so they did everything possible to keep him safe and on the bright.

▾ ▾ ▾

Unable to travel any distance, Bangs spent the next seven months rehabilitating at various suburban Boston motels, mainly adjacent to the North Shore on the New Hampshire border. He always used an assumed name and was never without round-the-clock monitoring by two of the state police officers who had investigated the shooting, Billy Flynn and Billy Lisano—seasoned pros who knew every danger lurking about Joey and who came loaded for bear with shotguns, M-16 machine guns, and multiple handguns.

Safeguarding Bangs proved to be one of the most difficult assignments Flynn and Lisano would ever work. They moved Joey from hotel to hotel every few nights, and if Bangs happened to spot someone he recognized on the elevator or in the restaurant—which happened frequently, given the reach of Joey's network—they packed up and moved again. Furthermore, one of the men had to stay awake at all times, since Bangs often attempted to sneak away for a drink or a night out with Debbie, who was with him twenty-four hours a day.

The troopers were also concerned for their own safety, given they didn't really know the full extent of Bangs' involvement with New England's criminal underworld or, even more dangerous, corrupt cops scattered throughout the Commonwealth. The good, the bad, and the ugly were all gunning for Bangs, who had become the most wanted man in the country.

Keeping Bangs in line was no easy task. He no longer gave a fuck about the force or his associates, and he grew more withdrawn and callous than ever. As much as he respected and appreciated his state police escort, Joey constantly tried to lose them, often returning to his old haunts in downtown Boston, Cambridge or Somerville for a nightcap. If he could have eluded them long enough, he no doubt would have driven directly to Doherty's home for a shootout. In fact, more than once he offered a duel through his go-between Clemente, but naturally, Doherty declined every time.

A few months after the shooting, Bangs summoned Clemente to the Embassy Lounge in Somerville, where he cornered Jerry in a back booth, with Brother O'Leary on the other side of the table to wedge Jerry in. Bangs growled at Clemente that he wanted the money Doherty owed him paid back immediately. In return, he promised not to testify against Doherty and agreed to pin the entire attempted murder rap on Gillen, who was the actual shooter anyway. This maneuver would also allow the men to conceal their involvement in the Depositors Trust robbery until the state statute of limitations expired later that year and they were all home free.

Sensing that Clemente was still trying to play good guy with Doherty, Joey lit into Jerry: "If Doherty shot you, I'd have gone to his house and broke his jaw, bare-ass minimum!" Humbled, Jerry replied, "You're right, Joe. You're right."

Unknown to Bangs, seated at the table behind him was a friend of Doherty's, who had been eavesdropping and heard the threat. Though inebriated, the stranger interjected himself into the conversation. Bangs glared at the man—who continued to yap—and then excused himself, strolled calmly to the man's table, and decked the old timer. As a bouncer dragged the man from the lounge, the loudmouth threatened to return with a gun to finish the conversation. Without hesitating, Bangs offered the man one of his own guns to settle things right there, but the man wisely declined.

In the following weeks, Clemente worked ceaselessly to mediate between the incensed Bangs and the oblivious Doherty. Clemente somehow persuaded Doherty to quitclaim his interest in the Pompano Beach condo to Bangs to settle a portion of the debt, but in the end, Tommy neglected to complete the paperwork, further infuriating Joey. Bangs ordered Clemente either to buy Doherty out or else to burn the condo to the ground for the insurance money—whatever it took to get his cash in hand.

When all else failed, in January and February of 1985, Bangs' attorney, Ralph Champa, and Doherty's counsel, Tommy Troy, attempted to negotiate terms for the conditional sale of the property, but they never finalized the deal. Instead, knowing that he would soon incur significant legal expenses, Doherty agreed to place a lien on the condo in favor of his attorney. The move pushed Bangs over the edge—he would have told the authorities he had shot himself, if Doherty would have agreed to meet him like a man and fight it out old-school, but Tommy wanted no part of Joey, injured or not.

As the relationships among the bank robbers unraveled, they all at one time or another conspired to kill each other. In the beginning, Bangs and O'Leary discussed the prospects of killing Barrett. Then Bangs told Barrett he was considering knocking off O'Leary, and later, Clemente, especially if they tried to move against Bucky. O'Leary, Clemente and Doherty had conspired against Barrett, and Bangs in turn planned to kill Doherty, on more than one occasion. But no one had dared make a move on Joey—until now, and Doherty had failed.

❥ ❥ ❥

Being threatened didn't sit well with Bangs, whose pride got the best of him. He hounded Clemente to set up a "wild west" shootout with Doherty and Gillen, but not surprisingly, both Tommy and Jackie again declined the challenge. Bangs suggested an old-fashioned, man-to-man, stand-up style brawl behind the Medford police station, so all of Doherty's cronies could watch him get his ass kicked by a man who had come back from the dead. Again, no takers. Joey wanted satisfaction—his money, Doherty's blood or both—and one way or another, he planned to have it soon.

Day after day Bangs tormented Clemente, who at this point was stuck in the middle and just trying to hold things together until the state's six-year statute of limitations on the bank heist expired. The five-year federal deadline had passed, and there were only six months left on the state's clock. Although Clemente got Doherty to cough up some cash and a half kilo of cocaine to pay part of his debt to Bangs, it wasn't enough—and now Joey was ready to do whatever it took to put Doherty in his place. Doherty knew his days were numbered, and he smoked more cocaine than ever to escape the reality of his predicament.

Clemente finally concocted a deal whereby Tommy agreed to give Joey an additional $24,000 in cash and another half kilo of cocaine, worth about $23,000, and then pay the remainder of the debt in installments over the following months. At Jerry's urging, Bangs reluctantly agreed.

When Clemente arrived at Doherty's garage to pick up the first payment, he found Tommy smoked out and incoherent—and short on both cash and cocaine. Clemente scrounged up about $14,000 and 100 grams of cocaine, hoping he could persuade Joey to take something rather than nothing.

Clemente had agreed to meet Bangs at the United Airlines terminal at Logan International Airport for the exchange, since he was afraid to leave the items in an airport locker. Jerry brought along Brother O'Leary, believing his presence would calm the potentially volatile encounter and protect him from any sort of set-up or double-cross Joey might orchestrate.* Clemente had always been terrified of narcotics, and now, under the strained circumstances, he was even more paranoid.

Clemente and O'Leary met Bangs at a designated lounge and handed over an envelope of cash and a cigar box full of cocaine, trying their best to smooth over the sticky situation, but Joey was livid that Doherty had shorted him yet again. Bangs was a man of integrity and principle, he explained to them. If he borrowed money, he paid it back. If he said he'd take care of something, he did. If he told you he'd be somewhere, he was there on time, if not early.

Doherty, he continued, was not an honorable man. They had bought a condo together, and now Doherty refused to sell the property and give Joey the proceeds to resolve his debt. Instead, he was planning to use the funds to pay the attorney fees he incurred after he tried to kill Bangs. And to boot, he had instructed authorities to search Joey's trunk, knowing full well that it contained evidence to incriminate Bangs. The loss of the items

---

* Whenever Bangs flew into Boston, he arrived at the Eastern Airlines terminal and then took a cab to the United terminal, where Brother usually picked him up. He reversed the order for outbound flights. He could never be too safe, he reasoned, even with Brother.

confiscated from his trunk stuck in Joey's craw as much as the shooting itself. Joey was done with Tommy's bullshit.

After the encounter at the airport, O'Leary insisted that he take Bangs for a drink. Bangs and O'Leary had limited contact during this time, but Brother told Joey he had a profitable gaff brewing in Pelham, New Hampshire. O'Leary plied Bangs for information on where he was staying, but Bangs knew Brother had more to gain if he were dead than alive, so he told O'Leary he was staying at the Holiday Inn in East Boston. He was actually staying at the Logan Airport Hilton under Debbie O'Malley's maiden name, "Hill."

O'Leary convinced the restless hustler in Bangs that this score would work, but Joey didn't want any more attention from the state police, so he suggested that Brother call him later with a place to meet. Brother did as instructed, and they reconvened that evening at the Howard Johnson in Stoneham for a late-night supper, during which they hatched a plan.

But then Bangs put Brother's potential score on ice—he had another scheme brewing. He had received a call from a reliable *La Cosa Nostra* associate in Medford who asked if he were interested in a briefcase full of precious gems and jewelry. Bangs got the dupe: the mobster and his accomplices had lured a New York jeweler to Boston, kidnapped him at gunpoint at the airport, and taken him for a ride in the country. Even though Bangs was under close scrutiny, the local wise guy knew Joey could fence this kind of loot and was looking to make a quick score.

Bangs could smell the money, so he picked up Bobby Spencer, met the mobster at the Town Line Motor Lodge on the Malden–Saugus line, and examined the merchandise. After a few calls, Bangs and Spencer took the swag to another associate, who offered them $200,000 for the lot. Bangs returned to the Town Line and told the mobster that even though the goods were worth much more, he could get him only $150,000. If he'd take it, Joey could deliver within a half hour. The Mafioso balked at the amount but needed the cash quick, so he agreed. Bangs gave Spencer ten grand for his support and pocketed the other forty for a few hours' work. And of course, unbeknownst to the other parties, Bangs also pocketed a few pricey gems on the side—*Second thief, best thief:* Joey Bangs.

▼ ▼ ▼

Clemente had his hands full managing Joey's prideful anger and Tommy's addiction. He counted the days until the statute of limitations lapsed and brainstormed ways to delay Tommy's shooting trial. At one point, Clemente and Doherty decided that Tommy should fake a heart attack to prolong the trial, but Doherty's high-priced lawyers convinced him that Bangs' lack of credibility would ensure a speedy trial and Tommy's ultimate exoneration, and thus there was no need for such a charade.

In addition, Doherty attempted to turn Clemente against Bangs by showing him receipts for wire transfers he had made to Joey in Las Vegas and Atlantic City during a few of Joey's legendary benders. But Doherty miscalculated: he had, of course, wired Joey his own money, a fact that Tommy had either forgotten or reckoned Bangs wouldn't remember after the trauma of the shooting. But Joey never lost track of a dollar he earned, and Tommy's ill-conceived deception only riled Bangs more and showed Clemente that Doherty was slipping fast.

Just before Doherty was scheduled to stand trial, Bangs called him and Roberts frequently, challenging them to a duel and threatening them in various ways. On one occasion, Bangs informed Doherty and Roberts that he was on his way to the barn, but when he arrived with his Uncle Eddie Bangs in tow, Doherty's home and garage were pitch dark, and Tommy and Al were nowhere to be found.

Jackie Gillen had by this time pleaded out in the Maine marijuana sting and was serving an eight- to twelve-year term in a decrepit federal penitentiary, where Bangs knew he couldn't get to him, at least not any time soon.

▼ ▼ ▼

A few days after the jewelry gig with Spencer, Bangs went to see Paul Walker at Walker's Shamrock Lounge in Cambridge to enlist his assistance in fencing some other stolen merchandise from a hijacked truck. Bangs and Walker settled into a private booth in the rear of the lounge.

Although Walker was thrilled to see Bangs, especially with news about a hijacking, he was less than pleased that Joey hadn't come by earlier. They had agreed that whenever Joey returned to the city, his first stop would be to meet Walker for an update on the current situation in

Beantown and the status of the case. In this particular instance, Joey had simply neglected to do so. Bangs lied and said he had just returned to Boston a few hours earlier, but Walker asserted that he knew exactly when Joey had blown into town—never mind *how* he knew—and that he better never leave him hanging again.

Walker told Bangs he had heard both good and bad about his grand jury appearances. Bangs gave Walker a detailed account of his testimony and assured Paul that he would never do anything to hurt him or any other former underworld employer, whom Joey held in higher regard than many of his corrupt police associates.

"Where do things stand with Doherty and Gillen?" Walker queried.

"Jackie's already incarcerated—if I could get to him, I'd snap his neck. I'll handle Doherty before I leave for Florida."

"Absolutely not! If you try to kill these cocksuckers, the law will let you, then take you down. That way they can clean up everything, nice and neat. If you feel the need to take care of business, you shouldn't do it yourself, and it should be done when they're old and gray, or else you're as good as gone."

As much as Bangs hated it, he knew Walker was right. Even the state troopers protecting him had advised the same thing: don't throw away the rest of your life for lowlifes like Doherty, Gillen, or Roberts.

Walker asked Bangs if he planned to go to New Hampshire any time soon. Joey hesitated—"Yeah."

"Pelham?" Walker continued.

"Now how the fuck did you know that?"

"As soon as you walk through the front door of the house you're supposed to rob," Walker explained, "you'll be shot dead by the owner."

Then came the biggest surprise for Joey: Brother O'Leary—his oldest childhood friend—had also tried to order a hit on him. Walker explained that O'Leary had sent a messenger to discuss putting a contract out on Bangs and that he himself had agreed to do it if Brother could scrape together $50,000. The realization stung like nothing before in his life, even though Bangs believed the contract was little more than Brother's half-assed attempt to intimidate him, given that O'Leary had never killed anyone.

Bangs was thankful for the information but puzzled that Walker had agreed to accept the hit from Brother. Joey wondered whether he had crossed Walker in some way. Why would Walker put his name out there on this deal? Had Walker actually taken money from O'Leary? If so, where did Brother get that kind of cash? Bangs knew O'Leary was flat broke and had no sources for loans. Was Brother in cahoots with Doherty and Clemente, and were they funding the hit?

Walker sensed Bangs' agitation and assured Joey that if he hadn't accepted the contract, someone else would have—and most likely would have succeeded in eliminating Bangs. The way Walker figured it, by taking the contract, he could control the situation and make sure he alerted Joey before any attempt on his life went down. When Bangs was a no-show earlier that day, Walker grew concerned and put out the word for Bangs to get to the Shamrock on the double.

"Steer clear of Brother, Joe," Walker warned. After a beat of tense silence, Walker queried: "So what do you want to do?"

Joey scanned Paul's face—yes, Walker would let it be his call.

"Did he give you any money?" Joey asked.

"The messenger promised to return, but the money never arrived."

"Brother can be foolish at times," Joey replied. Walker nodded knowingly. "But there's no good reason to kill him. Let it play."

Even after the misstep with Walker, O'Leary continued his blunders. Bangs learned later that Brother had approached a mutual friend and offered $25,000 just for Joey's address.

"What are you going to do with it?" the acquaintance quizzed O'Leary. "You know Joey will be waiting for you. Besides, you don't want his address, because he already has yours."

Brother reflected for a moment, nodded, and walked away.

And a month or so later, when Bangs' grandmother passed away, Joey received word from Walker that Brother intended to shoot him with a high-powered rifle as he exited the wake. Bangs knew Brother was handy with a bat but not a rifle—in fact, he didn't even own one—so Joey attended the service without fear. Brother failed to show, as Joey had expected. For safety, however, state police had positioned sharpshooters on adjacent rooftops, lying in wait—just in case. Although circumstances had changed, many cops were still jumping through flaming hoops for Bangs.

▼ ▼ ▼

With no one to trust except Walker, Joey knew it was time to make tracks—and fast. There were too many people walking around Boston who wanted a piece of him, and all the bullshit was a bit much to manage, given the holes in his body, the noise in his thoughts, and the treacherous road that lay ahead.

Shortly thereafter, Joey and Debbie eluded the state trooper detail by parking in the lot at Lechmere Sales and slipping out the back of the store, where Bobby Spencer was waiting with another vehicle. They blew town with pockets full of loot and landed in North Carolina, taking up residence in a rented seaside condo in Carolina Beach. But the culture clash between the Yankees and the Southern folk caused friction from day one, so Joey and Debbie hit the road again and soon found themselves in Miami.

One day while drinking in a local tavern, Bangs looked up and saw a couple familiar faces: two Massachusetts state troopers who obviously didn't appreciate his disappearing act. Bangs asked if they were lost or on vacation—they enjoyed his comedy routine even less.

Following protocol, the officers identified themselves and informed Bangs that his joyride was over—one way or another, he was returning to Boston. They explained he could either willingly return to testify, or else they could arrest him on the spot and compel him to turn state's evidence.

Bangs convinced the troopers to have a drink, which turned into a few too many for Joey. Meanwhile, Assistant District Attorney and newly appointed lead prosecutor, Carol Ball, was at a nearby hotel awaiting the troopers' call. When the police finally notified her that they had located Bangs, she instructed them to move the party to the hotel lounge.

Bangs loved Ball's moxie from the outset: she was an energetic, witty, aggressive, no-nonsense prosecutor with a keen legal mind and the charisma to win favor with all sides. Bangs was sure she would eventually become either a judge or a politician.*

Ball laid it out for Joey: *To put it delicately*, she said, *you're fucked*. Go along or go down in flames; either way, she'd get paid and sleep well at night. Bangs was persuaded—he returned to Boston without incident.

---

* In fact, Carol Ball was later appointed to a superior court judgeship.

Like Walker, Ball was able to talk sense into Bangs whenever he flew into one of his tirades and threatened to kill Doherty. She could see from the start that he was bent on revenge, but as the case developed, she helped him see a better way to give Doherty and crew their comeuppance. And most important of all, Ball schooled Joey in the legalities of the case and warned him about perjuring himself.

▾ ▾ ▾

Although Clemente had yet to turn against Bangs, he taped every phone call between them and saved all the threatening messages. And after all negotiations with Doherty broke down, Bangs' frequent calls to Clemente grew more abusive. Following one conversation in particular, Jerry stopped answering altogether. When Bangs again phoned the Clemente home, Jerry's son, Barry, answered, stating that his father was away. Joey threatened the boy: "If you don't get in touch with your father, he'll be going to jail with me for the rest of his life."

After that, Bangs never got an answer at Jerry's house, so he left vile messages promising he'd testify against Clemente. Joey had never fully trusted Jerry, and now that the façade around the bank heist was crumbling, he suspected that Clemente would soon roll over in exchange for immunity. At the end of the day, Joey didn't give a shit—he was looking to save his own ass, and his own ass was all he would need to save.

▾ ▾ ▾

Jury selection for the trial of Tommy Doherty, Jackie Gillen, and Al Roberts began in mid-July 1985 and was completed by early August. Since the federal statute of limitations for the bank robbery had already expired, Doherty once again agreed to try to fake a heart attack in order to prolong the shooting trial until the state statute of limitations for the heist expired in May 1986. However, Doherty's myocardial infarct never came to pass, and the trial proceeded apace.

Knowing that Bangs would be a reluctant witness, after experiencing it firsthand during Joey's grand jury appearances, ADA Thomas Reilly persuaded Middlesex County Supreme Judicial Court Justice Paul J. Liacos to issue Bangs a grant of transactional immunity regarding only the night of the shooting. Liacos made it clear that Bangs' immunity applied only to the Commonwealth of Massachusetts, not to any other federal, state or foreign jurisdiction. From the outset, it was evident that the district attorney's office wanted Medford Police Lieutenant Tommy Doherty more than Al Roberts or the previously convicted Jackie Gillen or even Joey himself.

Bangs was concerned that some of the items seized from his Cadillac may have already been identified as loot from the Depositors Trust heist or another of his many robberies. Nonetheless, he accepted the immunity deal and started preparing for the showdown with Doherty. And though he knew the coming legal struggles would be an uphill battle, not even he could have guessed what would happen next.

METRO/REGION

EX-POLICEMAN GUNNED DOWN IN AMBUSH

The Boston Herald, Thursday, October 18, 1984

...oherty (center), a Medford police officer, are arraigned in Somerville District Court in
........ant, and Albert Roberts, a former Medford connection with Tuesday's shooting.   POOL PHOTOS VIA UPI

Officer, 2 others arraigned in shooting

A Medford Police lieutenant and a former Medford patrolman were among three men arraigned yesterday, charged in the Tuesday night shooting of a retired Metropolitan Police sergeant.

Lt. Thomas K. Doherty, 42, and John Gillen, 49, a civilian, pleaded innocent ...rday in Somerville District Court to ...ges of armed assault with intent to ...der and assault and battery with a ...rous wea...

... ...ed ... ...iss...pp...
... ...rently for... ... sho... ...ng ...o ...
ph... ... at his home, which is ac...ss the street from Doherty's ho... a..d the caller asked him ... go to Doherty's house.

Investigators said Bangs was ... ... with a shotgun. ... ... to run across the ... ...ouse and called Med... ... an ambulance, po-
...ce said.

Bangs underwent emergenc... surgery at Lawrence Memoria... Ho...al in Medford yesterday, w... his condition was listed a... ...ab...a ho... ...lice sa...un at ...ed t...

trooman, Albert Roberts, 41, pleaded innocent to charges of being an accessory before and after the shooting of retired Metropolitan Police Sgt. Joseph Bangs. All are Medford residents.

Judge Henry Tampone set bail of $5000 each for Doherty and Roberts. Bail for Gillen, a defendant in a drugs ca... in U...District Court in Maine, was se... at $20,000 double surety.

leged attempt to buy cocaine from an undercover police officer in Jackson in August, police said. Doherty was free on $30,000 bail and Roberts on $15,000 bail after pleading innocent to charges in that case.

Medford Police said Tuesday's shooting ...occurred about 11:15 p.m... in the sec-ond...loor of a refurbished ... in the rear of Doherty's house at 50 ...asant st. Gillen, who was identified by ...osecutors as ... ...other-in-law... ... c... ...
the ...rt of Plea... ...
ME...... ...e 24
Co...ted ... Atty. ....li...
ba... ...cced se... ...
and searched for the ...
the homes of the three ...
They would not say w...
search was a success.

Doherty, a 20-year ...
the Medford Police D...
was suspended from th...
night by Acting Police ...
Keating. Keating said ...
been on sick leave sinc...
jured while on duty ...
year.

Doherty and Robert ...
rese...ed at yesterday ...
Thomas Troy ...
They told the ...
...ere schedulec ...
raigned Monday in Mis...
the indictments issued t...
week

...angs, cited twice...
...tling police w...k du ...
...ars as a Metr...olis
r. retired in ...eb... ...
ing a heart a... ...g the Metropolitan ...
served with the ...iptol ...
two years.

... ...an Irish government
source said yesterday.

In addition, Irish authorities believe one of five men they arrested Sept. 29 crossed the Atlantic on the arms-laden Valhalla, according to a report in today's editions of the Cork Examiner, an Irish newspaper.

In Boston yesterday US Customs officials searched the Valhalla, which they seized Tuesday at Pier 7, for other evidence linking it to the gun-running.

Customs spokesman Edward Callanan would not comment on evidence that may arrive from Ireland or on what, if anything, was found on the boat, except to say that nautical charts onboard indicated the Valhalla "could have been in Irish waters." On Tuesday authorities on the boat.

Last mon... a confiscation of weapons ... ...o...at ... ...l...rest ... ...e ...loc...d bap... ...dec-

3 arraigned in shooting

Trooper tells of scene after alleged slay attempt

CAMBRIDGE – A State Police detective testified yesterday that when he arrived at the scene of an alleged attempted murder in Medford last Oct. 17, he found attor-
...y Thomas Troy and two of the

Account of shooting challenged

CAMBRIDGE – The initial story told to police by the victim of a shooting in which a former Medford police lieutenant and his brother-in-law are charged with attempted murder differed from what he later told a grand jury, according to a defense witness who testified yesterday.

Capt. Paul J. O'Reardon of the Medford Police Department was the first defense witness called by attorney Thomas Troy, who represents former Lt. Thomas K. Doherty, 43. Doherty's codefendant in the Middlesex Superior Court trial is John Gillen Jr., 49.

O'Reardon said that retired

■ MEDFORD

Gillen when he was about to enter Doherty's upstairs office in a converted barn and that as he slumped to the stairs, Doherty

State troopers Billy Flynn and Greg Foley guarded—and had fun with—Bangs during the trial.

The ever-affable "Big Billy" Lisano rounded out the bodyguard detail.

34   THE BOSTON SUNDAY GLOBE   AUGUST 4, 1985

3 face trial in shooting of ex-policeman

Ex-policeman charged in murder attempt testifies that shooting victim had shotgun

Ex-MDC officer testifies about rift with suspect

Girlfriend testifies on shooting

CAMBRIDGE – The girlfriend of a former Metropolitan Police officer who was shot in an alleged murder attempt testified yesterday that he had come home bleeding from shotgun wounds to the chest and back, and that he had placed himself atop the stairs aiming his revolver at the door.

Deborah O'Malley, 35, testified in Middlesex Superior Court that

Ex-policeman says he rehearsed, taped testimony

CAMBRIDGE – Former Medford Police Lt. Thomas K. Doherty, accused in the shooting of former Metropolitan Police Sgt. Joseph Bangs, testified yesterday that he and his lawyers had rehearsed his testimony last Sunday, videotaped it and critiqued it.

Doherty, testifying for the second day in Middlesex Superior Court, said that Thomas C. Troy, one of his two attorneys, had played the role of prosecutor and

with your lawyers, was it videotaped?

A. Yes.

Q. And you reviewed the tape, didn't you?

A. Yes.

Q. You had a recording this past Sunday afternoon?

A. Yes, that's right.

Q. One of your attorneys, Mr. McCann, acted as your lawyer?

Whether from his own reflexes or

beca
him,
arou
onto

Retired officer says he dealt drugs with neighbor accused in shooting

CAMBRIDGE – A retired Metropolitan Police officer testified in Middlesex Superior Court yesterday that he and one of three men accused of trying to kill him had

Bangs will then say that he fumbled with the keys to the barn's side door, finally unlocking it as Roberts stood there, and that he saw Doherty on the third step from the top aiming a silver-col

SHOOTING FROM THE HIP

Joey Bangs' Opening Statements

TUESDAY, AUGUST 6, 1985

JUST MINUTES BEFORE ENTERING THE PACKED COURTROOM, Bangs was lounging in the office of the state police at the Middlesex County Courthouse, shooting the breeze with his trooper detail, Flynn and Lisano—"The Two Billys," as Bangs referred to them—when he received a phone call from his ex-girlfriend, Cheryl Fisher, who was in a panic.

Fisher explained that she had just received a call from Brother O'Leary, who told her, "You better get in touch with Joey and tell him to be careful on the witness stand, or else I will take any action necessary."

Bangs calmed Cheryl and assured her that he would take care of business as soon as he was done testifying in court. Joey figured he'd be on the stand for a short time and planned to set Brother straight as soon as he was dismissed.

Lisano and Flynn subsequently escorted Bangs to the witness stand, and he was sworn to tell the truth, the whole truth and nothing but the truth—which he had no intention of doing, at least not at the moment.

Assistant District Attorney Carol Ball began her quizzing:

"Mr. Bangs, do you know Thomas Doherty, a defendant in this case?"

"Yes, I do," Joey responded flatly.

"Do you know Al Roberts and Jackie Gillen?"

"Yes, I do."

"Do you intend to answer any further questions?"

Defiant as expected, Bangs leaned forward, adjusted the microphone, and fixed his gaze on Ball: "No, I do not."

"On what grounds do you refuse to answer, sir?"

"On the grounds it may incriminate me."

Ball demanded a sidebar and pressed the court to act on a motion she had filed earlier that morning with Superior Court Judge Hiller Zobel. Zobel granted transactional immunity to Bangs, pursuant to the original order by Justice Liacos, and ordered him to testify.*

The transactional immunity protected Joey against civil or criminal legal action for allegations arising from his testimony, except in the case of perjury or contempt of court. Further, Bangs faced jail if he refused to cooperate. Champing at the bit to tear Joey apart, defense attorney Tommy Troy tried to intimidate Bangs by reminding him about the limits of his immunity and the risk of concurrent indictments in other jurisdictions.

Judge Zobel confirmed with Bangs' attorney, Somerville's Ralph Champa,† a highly regarded criminal attorney in his own right, that Joey understood the legal landscape—especially that the transactional immunity applied only to the laws of Massachusetts—and again ordered Bangs to answer all questions and produce all evidence regarding the subject of the indictments before the jury. Joey ran the calculations quickly in his mind—*Fuck it*, he realized, *If you're in for a penny, you're in for a pound. I guess I'm telling the truth.*

Champa had tried to negotiate the broadest possible pass for Joey, and in the end, the deal covered the years 1978 to 1985. Fortunately, the statute of limitations had expired on many of Joey's earlier misdeeds. The only exception was a charge for unlawful possession of a controlled substance—the kilo of cocaine found in the trunk of Joey's Cadillac. Despite Champa's urging to cooperate and testify, Bangs was bent about losing the car and the cocaine—which he said was some of the best shit he'd ever had. Because of what he considered an illegal search and seizure of the vehicle, which was not used in the commission of a crime, Bangs believed the Commonwealth should return the Caddy and all of its

---

* Bangs' transactional immunity was agreed upon on August 6 and officially signed on August 8, 1985.

† Champa was a dear friend of my father's and later a friend of mine, and he was one of the best attorneys I've ever met.

contents, legal or otherwise. Bangs engaged First Assistant U.S. Attorney Robert Mueller in a heated debate over the issue, and in the end, the state returned the car. After exhausting every argument he could muster, Bangs gave up chasing the coke.[*]

Champa also succeeded in convincing the district attorney to limit questions to the night of the shooting, although both he and Reilly knew that Doherty and Gillen's defense team would likely interrogate Bangs about many other indiscretions. Joey wasn't concerned, however—he knew that whatever jeopardized him would also jeopardize Doherty and Gillen.

Of course, Bangs had made it clear to Doherty on many occasions that he was willing to testify that Gillen had acted alone in the shooting, as long as Tommy did the right thing and paid back the money he owed. For his part, Doherty figured that that cocksucker Bangs wouldn't keep his word, even if he got his money, so fuck it—let the games begin.

▼ ▼ ▼

As the proceedings continued, Judge Zobel prohibited the press from taking photos of the jury and alternates—nine men and seven women—or of bench conferences or counsel conferring with clients. He also ordered them not to move from their initial position during testimony.

Defense attorney Troy requested a sidebar and informed Judge Zobel that he had received a disturbing phone call from Carol Ball, who said she feared for her life and wanted the courtroom "swept" everyday. According to Troy, Ball was afraid "outside forces" might bring a bomb into the courtroom or incite other violence. Troy argued that such allegations would plant enough fear and suspicion in the jury's mind to prejudice them against the defendants, especially if they saw the judge himself taking protective measures.

Judge Zobel tried to make light of the situation:

"In terms of 'sweeping' the courtroom," he asked Troy, "I take it you mean an electronic sweep of the courtroom?"

"I don't know what she meant by it, Your Honor."

---

[*] Mueller was from a long line of old Yankee blood and had served as a First Lieutenant in a Marine Corps rifle company, where he was highly decorated for his service in Vietnam. Although Bangs didn't care for Mueller's interrogation tactics, he admired his gutsiness and managed to find some common ground in discussing their shared combat experiences.

"If it's going to be with a broom or a vacuum cleaner," Zobel quipped, "I'm all in favor of it."

Zobel subsequently ordered that any visual, mechanical or electronic checking of the courtroom be finished before the jurors arrived each morning. Troy continued to protest the increased presence of armed guards using walkie-talkies and metal detectors, but to no avail.

When prodded about the alleged threats on her life, Ball told Zobel she wasn't concerned about her life only, but based on confidential information, she feared for Bangs' life as well. When Zobel pressed, Ball explained:

"Joey Bangs is somebody with a great deal of knowledge about substantial other criminal activity, and we are concerned that there are people out there, not these defendants per se, who are very worried about what might come out during his cross-examination. We have had numerous reports and information from informants that 'other people' are out to get Bangs, again, not these defendants necessarily. And I personally do not believe these defendants are going to do anything during the trial, but I do have some worry about these other people."

Troy of course wanted to put on record the names of these "other people," but Ball refused to disclose her confidential sources.

At this point, Troy requested a mistrial because of Ball's refusal to identify her sources and because of the negative publicity the trial had already received: the influential Boston *Globe* alone, he argued, would unfairly prejudice the jurors. Zobel denied Troy's request but agreed to bring the jurors into the courtroom from the back stairwell, so they wouldn't see the heightened security at the main entrance.

Troy didn't back down—if Ball and Bangs could register threats, he could too.

"Consistently, so far in this case," Troy explained, "there have been threats made against my client, Mr. Doherty. There was also a threat made against me personally, and I believe it to have been Mr. Bangs. I may just as well put it on the record now that I received a phone call some months ago. I have told Ms. Ball, and I told everyone connected in this case about it. I received a call from a person suggesting he was Mr. Bangs and that I had better not fool around during my cross-examination, and I had better watch my step, and so forth and so on. He knew that I was in my office every night, you know, if he were coming to see me. I think at this point in time, since we're raising threats, maybe I should put that on record as well."

Zobel concluded, "It is awful early and an awful warm day to get heated up. Let's push on."

Troy's fears were not exaggerated: Bangs had in fact threatened him and warned him not to "fuck around" during cross-examination, in particular, not to ask about the jewelry found in the trunk of the Cadillac. That was a cat not even Doherty would want out of the bag. Bangs also warned Troy not to bring up his alleged drug use or chaotic personal life or anything else that might embarrass him or make him look like an asshole. And of course, if Troy tried to probe Joey's activities with any of Boston's underworld figures, he'd have to deal with a whole different world of unhappy observers.

Troy was unfazed by Bangs' threats. As a former pugilist, Marine, and MDC patrolman turned defense attorney, he had seen it all before. He knew the law cold and was a master at manipulating the bench and jury box, as well as the press and public opinion. And even though he had suffered a mild heart attack on July 17, just three weeks before the trial began, he was still on top of his game. In addition, Troy had an ace in the hole: an intense and talented co-counsel, Eugene McCann, who had flown to Mississippi to bail out Doherty and Roberts after the drug deal gone bad.

Doherty's co-defendant Jackie Gillen was represented by Joe Flak, the same attorney who had unsuccessfully defended Gillen in the Maine marijuana case and Jimmy McGaffigan in the suit by Debbie O'Malley, who represented herself, over the microwave oven that McGaff had taken from her rental unit. Even though Flak knew Bangs and O'Malley had dirt on him, he saw this as his one chance to get back at Joey, and he would go after him with a vengeance. Bangs and O'Malley wanted to fight fire with fire, but Ball reminded them that Flak was not on trial and extraneous issues would only hurt their own case.

Al Roberts' attorney of record was Anthony Baccari, a sharp-dressed, skillful orator. The Commonwealth's case against Roberts was weak, but Ball contended that all three defendants conspired to murder Bangs and thus to exonerate Roberts at the outset would have ultimately weakened the rock-solid case against Doherty and Gillen.

After the formalities and opening statements had concluded—including thirty minutes of initial testimony from Joey—Bangs dashed across the street to Smitty's Barroom to call Brother O'Leary, informing troopers Flynn and Lisano exactly what he was doing as he passed them at the door. O'Leary's wife, Margie, answered and passed the receiver to Brother. Bangs was short and to the quick: *Fuck with me and you know what I can do to you.* Thinking that Bangs was trying to record a confession, Brother at first denied threatening Fisher. But after Bangs continued his own threats, Brother realized Joey was serious. O'Leary tried to explain that he only wanted to warn Joey to be careful what he testified about, but Bangs resented the attempted intimidation. *Fuck it*, Joey thought, *that straw just busted this camel's hump.* It was now Joey against the world.

Bangs returned to the witness stand the following morning, where his crooked ass would remain firmly planted for three more grueling days.

Joey Bangs' Testimony – Day 1

WEDNESDAY, AUGUST 7, 1985

The Commonwealth's infuriated star witness began the day by standing up in the witness box, and with unfettered anger and threatening gestures, shouting obscenities at the stone-faced Doherty: *If you get exonerated, you better fuck, fight or run, you motherfucker!*

Zobel blasted Bangs for his outburst and warned him—not for the last time—that his immunity didn't cover contempt of court.

Bangs calmed and fell into strikingly candid testimony that quieted even his fiercest critics. He admitted to all the shortcomings and indiscretions brought up against him. At this point, he didn't give a shit what anyone thought of him and just wanted to get on with the proceedings and put the matter to bed. He would take care of personal business later.

Under direct examination by Ball, Bangs testified that his relationship with Jackie Gillen was a casual one, while he knew Al Roberts much better and often asked him to babysit Debbie's daughter Kelly Ann when Joey and Debbie would step out for the night. The questioning veered off into a tangent when Ball asked how often he ate out, and Joey explained that he was so obsessive about cleanliness that he never ate at home, for fear of the mess, and kept nothing in his fridge except Velveeta cheese, Ritz crackers, and pimiento olives.

Ball then launched into a series of detailed questions that prompted Joey to lay out the events of October 16, 1984. Bangs testified that Doherty had phoned and asked him to stop by to pick up some money and drop off some cocaine.

Troy punctuated every statement with an objection, to the point that Judge Zobel ordered the counselors to approach the bench. Ball was merely attempting to establish that Doherty was involved in a conspiracy to murder Bangs, given that he called Bangs over to the garage where Gillen shot him.

Ball also attempted to establish the notion that her witness brought along a packet of cocaine, but Zobel didn't see the relevancy.

"Please tell me what difference it makes legally," he quizzed, "whether he was asked to bring a bag of cocaine, a cup of sugar, or a model airplane kit."

Ball explained that she assumed the bloody package of cocaine would be introduced later as evidence and that Bangs would admit to dropping it. Besides, with the exception of collecting an outstanding debt, this was in fact Bangs' sole purpose for going to the garage in the first place. When Zobel ordered Ball to refer to the "cocaine" as a "package," Troy again objected, and after a bit of wrangling, the parties agreed to refer to the cocaine simply as "something." Ball still argued that the package of cocaine was the heart of the motive in the case, whereas the relationship between Doherty and Bangs was based mainly on drug dealing—but the judge had ruled.

Ball resumed the questioning, and Joey continued with the night's timeline: returning home from dinner, Doherty's call, changing clothes, smoking some cocaine, heading across the street.

"Were you armed?" Ball asked.

"No," Bangs stated.

"Did you bring anything worth mentioning to the garage?"

"Yes, I brought *something*."

"What was the size and shape of this *something*?"

Judge Zobel quickly intervened. "I assume, Ms. Ball, that we're not going to get into whether it was bigger than a bread box, or something like that." Ball took her cue and pushed on.

But Troy tossed so many objections into the ensuing exchange and both attorneys requested so many sidebars that Judge Zobel finally declared, "There are to be no more sidebars unless it's an emergency! Or else write it down on a piece of paper, hand it to the clerk, and I will have a look at it. If it needs attention, then I will give it attention."

In fact, objections became so prevalent during the testimony and Troy's tone so belligerent that Zobel felt it necessary to give the jury a lesson in courtroom procedure.

"A judge is like an umpire calling balls and strikes," he explained. "In this case, an objection is noted, then sustained or overruled. A pitcher pitches the ball trying to get it over the plate. Sometimes it goes over the plate and sometimes it's a little wide—that's what's happening here."

When they returned to questioning, Bangs stated that he went to Doherty's garage armed only with a set of keys and "something else." Bangs went on to detail each moment of the night, from the time he arrived at the locked garage door to charging past Al Roberts and up the stairs, to the shotgun blasts and his struggle to escape the garage. At crucial moments in the narrative, Ball painted the scene for jurors, handing them photos of the barn or having Bangs diagram the garage's layout on a chalkboard or act out Gillen's stance and expression as he fired the shotgun. Although this exchange seemed surreal, Joey's focus never waivered—he was on a mission to tell the greatest tale he had ever told, and he occasionally flashed Doherty a glare to make sure he knew that the game was on.

"Were you ever afraid?" Ball asked Bangs at one point.

"Yes."

"Of what?"

"Of dying. For the first time in my life, I was afraid of dying. Never in Vietnam, never on the police force. Only on that night. That's why I wanted the gun from my car."

Joey could tell he had the jury's attention. Judge Zobel continued to ignore Troy's sidebar requests and overruled objection after objection.

Bangs described how he dragged himself up to his apartment and banged on the door until Debbie came to his aid and helped him into the living room. He chronicled how he armed himself and waited for his assailants to come after him, then feared that the Medford cops would do the dirty work themselves. How he was too weak to defend himself, how he flatlined in the ambulance and again at the hospital, how much he had suffered during his recovery.

At this point, Ball displayed pieces of the tattered, bloodstained shirt Bangs was wearing the night he was shot.

"Is this your shirt?" she asked Joey.

"Yes, it is."

"And did it look like this before you went to Doherty's garage that night?"

Joey snickered. "It was in one piece then—and nicely starched."

As Ball displayed the tattered shirt, Bangs couldn't tell the front from the back, and for that matter, neither could anyone else, including the jurors. She then presented the bloodstained leather jacket Bangs wore that evening and pointed out the two sizeable holes. The jurors were impressed.

Ball next asked Bangs about his blood type (A+) and his handedness (right-handed) and had him write his name on the chalkboard with each hand to prove it. She queried him about the visible scars on his chest, right arm, and back that resulted from the shooting injuries and asked him to remove his shirt to display the scars to the jury. However, Troy gamely objected that there were exhibit photographs published for the jurors to examine. Zobel took a moment to review the pictures, then asked Bangs to examine them and attest to their validity, before giving them to the fascinated jury members. Ball finished by asking Joey a few carefully crafted questions about the things found in the trunk of his Cadillac before ceding the witness to Troy.

Troy swaggered to the witness stand and launched into his cross-examination by badgering Bangs about his deal for transactional immunity, attempting to cast it in a negative light. Then, hoping to trip him up, he asked Joey to go back to the beginning and recount every moment of the night of October 16, 1984. Bangs went back further than he had with Ball:

three beers with Billy McKay—a good, clean cop—at Memory Lane; driving the shit-box, green Chevrolet, which was registered to ex-girlfriend Cheryl Fisher, with whom he had broken up just a few months before the shooting; moving the items from one car to another; a couple more cocktails at dinner; then home to Pleasant Street Court.

Troy pounced on the drinks—five in a short time. Ball objected—sustained.

Troy pressed to discover whether Debbie knew about the cocaine and other items in the trunk. No, Bangs explained, and, until the night of the shooting, she was never in the car while the items were in the trunk. Bangs added that neither she nor Kelly Ann had seen him transfer the cocaine from the Chevrolet.

Then the question of the jewelry. Bangs detailed how he had given some of it to Fisher, and she later returned it when they broke up. The rest was his.

And the Canadian currency? Won from a Canadian pilot and smuggler, John Clarke, in a card game.

What about the Cadillac itself? How did he get it back from the state? Since it was never used in the commission of a crime, state trooper Billy Flynn had returned it. Bangs testified that Tommy Doherty had a spare key to both the Cadillac and the green Chevrolet, and he had driven both vehicles on occasion, with cocaine in the trunk.

Drug use on that particular evening? Emboldened by this new honesty shtick, Bangs answered without hesitation that he did in fact smoke a quarter gram of cocaine prior to going over to Doherty's garage and that, yes, he had possessed the pure cocaine discovered in the trunk for somewhere between ten and fourteen days.

Troy asked Bangs to explain the various weights of street cocaine. Twenty-eight grams per ounce, Bangs explained, 16 ounces to a pound, and 2.2 pounds to a kilo, approximately 35 ounces total. Bangs admitted to freebasing cocaine on a regular basis over the past six months to a year—it calmed him, he claimed—and he swore that he had not consumed any other illegal drug. At this point Troy entered as evidence photographs of drug paraphernalia seized from the trunk of Bangs' vehicle as well as from his apartment.

Troy paused and scanned his notes, then studied Bangs for a moment, pacing the room with determination. Next came the question heard around the world—a question Troy never should have asked. But he wanted to know more about the jewelry found in the trunk of Joey's Cadillac: Whose was it? How had Joey obtained it? What did he plan to do with it?

Bangs felt the dark cloud of perjury hovering over him, knowing that if he lied, he would lose his immunity and be arrested and tried for any crimes he admitted to while on the witness stand. But it was surprisingly easy to tell the truth, he thought, especially after Brother's threats to Cheryl and Clemente's refusal to answer phone calls and Troy's loaded questions. Bangs had ample motivation to say *fuck it all*.

Troy had now painted them both into a corner: "Where did you get that jewelry, Mr. Bangs?"

Joey cleared his throat and locked Troy's gaze. "Some of the jewelry was taken from a robbery," he began, the syllables slipping from his lips of their own volition. "Labor Day Weekend. Correction: Memorial Day Weekend . . . Depositors Trust in Medford."

None of the insane moments of Joey's life compared with the surreal feeling of those words falling from his mouth. Years of hiding, covering, cajoling his cohorts, threatening, scheming, worrying—all gone in a breath. Joey's head spun with giddiness.

The air in the courtroom froze. A duet of objections rang out from Troy and Flak. Dozens of reporters and state police scrambled from the room and latched onto payphones in the lobby. Troy realized his blunder and shouted for a sidebar—Judge Zobel beckoned the attorneys. Troy demanded a mistrial: the look on the jurors' faces showed that they believed Bangs, even if the story was hearsay.

"The district attorney set me up, Your Honor! She set me up!" Troy hyperventilated. "Ball told me that all of the jewelry was owned by Cheryl Fisher and Bangs' estranged wife, Judith."

"Then what possessed you to ask that question?" retorted Judge Zobel.

Flustered, Troy blurted out his uncharacteristically half-baked reasoning: he thought the jury would believe that everything in the trunk belonged to Doherty, so he wanted to catch Bangs in a lie. Plus, he wanted to show that the items were not a motive for the shooting and that Bangs was an extremely violent and unstable person who had recently gone through a bad break-up with his girlfriend, Cheryl Fisher, whom he believed the jewelry belonged to. In addition, if he could show that Bangs acted erratically and that he had enough money to lavish gifts on both a wife and a girlfriend, he felt he could persuade the jury that Bangs was a drug dealer and thus prejudice them against him. Troy again pointed the finger at Ball.

"Your honor, ADA Ball assured us this morning that the state police had verified that none of the items in Bangs' trunk were reported stolen," Troy pleaded. "You must declare a mistrial!"

"Calm down, counselor," Zobel threatened.

Troy spiraled faster. "The only reason I got trapped is that I trusted a DA in a skirt. I never trust men!"

"Mr. Troy, as a man who's married to a judge who wears a skirt," the judge fired back, "I find your remark—"

"I find this conversation absurd, your honor. This must be cause for a mistrial!"

"Denied!" Zobel gaveled. "Congratulations, counselor, you have now established that some of the jewelry came from a hold-up that had absolutely nothing to do with this case. As far as I can see, Ms. Ball had no knowledge that the witness would answer as he did. Every time the witness was given the opportunity, he denied that the items belonged to the defendants. So tell me again why you asked that question?" The fact is, Troy had broken Attorney Rule One: Never ask a question to which you don't know the answer.

Flak chimed in to ask whether Bangs would receive immunity for the Depositors Trust Bank robbery, which, he reminded the judge, had been called the largest heist in the world up to this point.

"The witness only receives immunity for what he testifies to," Zobel informed them.

"Well, he's trying to get it right now!" Troy snapped.

"So be it!" Zobel shrugged. "Remember, this particular problem arose from *your* excursion into the irrelevant."

Tommy Doherty hung his head in disbelief. Al Roberts' attorney, Anthony Baccari, who had been silent up to this point, now insisted that both the question and answer be stricken from the record, given that the comment was a bombshell and the insinuation of involvement in the heist would be insuperably prejudicial to his client. He echoed Troy's call for a mistrial.

Zobel had had enough. As Troy continued to fall apart and protest, Zobel admonished him to contain himself or risk being found in contempt. But Troy pleaded again for latitude. He knew that after this blunder, his illustrious career would be reduced to this one ugly moment. "Please put something in the record. Don't do this to me—I beg you."

"I think it's plain to see," Zobel began, "that what all of you were saying, after the statement by the witness, is that

Doherty and Troy listen to court proceedings.

you all wished, most sincerely, that the statement had not been introduced!"

In the end, Zobel struck from the record the last statement ("Some of the jewelry was taken from a robbery . . . Labor Day Weekend. Correction: Memorial Day Weekend . . . Depositors Trust in Medford") and instructed the jury to disregard it. Nevertheless, the statement was made in front of a courtroom packed with a who's who of state and federal law enforcement agents who could not strike it from their minds.

A skittish juror named Cook stood and asked to be excused from the trial because he worked at a restaurant in Medford frequented by MDC and Medford police officers, and he realized now that he might be biased toward them.

Wanting to hold the trial together, Judge Zobel instructed Mr. Cook, "If you happen to see any witness that you recognize, tell the jury foreman, Mr. Deveraux, and he will talk to counselors and decide what to do."

Flak asked the judge to allow further cross-examination regarding the jewelry, given that Bangs had full immunity for his testimony. Flak wanted to know if Joey had stolen the jewelry or if someone had given it to him.

Ball objected and was sustained.

"What, Mr. Flak, does that have to do with this case?" Zobel demanded. "The bottom line is that the question of where the witness got the jewelry does not appear to the court to have any relevance to this case whatsoever. Move on!"

Bangs knew, however, that Flak had inside information about one of Bangs' recent armed robberies and would try to find a way to use it against him.

Troy asked if he might sit down to continue his cross-examination—his heart was acting up again, and the steel plate in his leg was putting painful pressure on his knee. Zobel agreed and suggested that Troy arrange for a tall stool to use in the following days. Doherty's heart sank deeper then churned as Troy resumed his cross-examination of Bangs, repeatedly taunting him as a perjurer, questioning his credibility, and threatening to prove that Bangs had killed Bucky Barrett.

Troy tried to regroup, but his best shot was attempting to discredit Bangs by getting him to admit that he and Debbie had smoked cocaine that night while Kelly Ann was in the next room. Together with the fact that Kelly Ann usually lived with her grandparents in Somerville, Troy used the admission to insinuate that Debbie was an unfit mother and that Joey was contributing to the endangerment of a minor.

Bangs remained composed throughout Troy's intense interrogation, flustering Troy with his calm cooperation and politeness. Troy returned to questions about the shooting itself, zeroing in on the moment that Gillen pulled the trigger.

Bangs testified that the office door was locked, and when Troy asked how he knew, Joey stated that he attempted to turn the knob. Bangs had initially told Medford policemen Lee and O'Riordan that he saw Doherty standing behind Gillen in the office, but he later said he only heard Doherty's raspy voice telling him to enter. Gillen shot him from inside the office, and Doherty was there to make sure it happened. Either that or Jackie Gillen was one hell of a ventriloquist.

When he first testified to police, Bangs was worried he was going to die and his assailants would walk because of a technicality, especially Doherty, so he made sure to place him at the scene as clearly as possible, stating that he saw Doherty standing behind Gillen with a chrome-plated revolver. (It was, however, actually stainless steel.) When Joey realized he was going to survive, he made the necessary adjustment to his story. Ball argued that the difference in stories was due simply to Bangs' state of mind; Zobel agreed and instructed Troy to stop pressing the point and move on.

Troy assailed the jurors' perception of Bangs by asking him about the cocaine trade and the practice of smoking cocaine instead of snorting it. Bangs described the process in vivid detail: for instance, mixing it with water and baking soda and cooking it over a flame removed all impurities. Troy also attacked Bangs' memory and interpretation of events and other discrepancies between the accounts he had given.

Was he shot while approaching the stairs, on the stairs, or in the small corridor between the first and second door? Was the weapon Doherty held stainless steel or chrome-plated? Why did he make conflicting statements to troopers Flynn and Lisano during his turbulent two-month stay in the state's witness protection program?

In most cases, the statements varied minimally, and Bangs was able to explain away the discrepancies easily.

Did he actually tell Lieutenant O'Riordan, Sergeant Longo, or Patrolman Lee, in the presence of a doctor, that he had fallen down the stairs and that Doherty and Gillen had jumped over him as they ran out the door and Roberts followed?

Absolutely not, Bangs answered. The detail Joey wanted to add was that many of the Medford cops were indebted to Doherty in one way or another—and were inclined to protect him. But he decided not to open another can of worms at this moment.

As the day wound down, Zobel instructed the exhausted jury members not to listen to anything on the radio or television or to read any reports about the trial and to leave their notebooks with the court officers.

Gillen   Roberts   Doherty

Joey Bangs' Testimony – Day 2

THURSDAY, AUGUST 8, 1985

Now seated on his stool next to the witness box, Tommy Troy picked up where he left off the previous day, testing Bangs' stories for weaknesses and insinuating that Bangs had violent personality traits and little credibility. Once again, Zobel grew tired of the mudslinging:

"So he's beaten up some people!" the judge railed. "How is that relevant to this case? After all, your client allegedly tried to kill someone!"

Troy attempted to make another case for mistrial, noting that in the short time since Bangs had mentioned the Depositors Trust robbery, news outlets had already dug up hundreds of articles released in the five years previous, including features in national magazines, and published dozens of fresh stories. Such a barrage of prejudicial material would undoubtedly taint the jury, Troy argued. Zobel marked the articles for identification and accepted them into the mounds of evidence, but ultimately denied the request for a mistrial.

Troy changed tack and returned to Bangs' drug use, asking him what effect cocaine had on him. Bangs answered that it relaxed him. Troy informed Judge Zobel that he had consulted overnight with a cocaine hotline and learned cocaine does not relax users but rather tends to create paranoia and disorientation—and in some instances makes people violent. Troy then asked Judge Zobel in a sidebar to add to the witness list a physician who specialized in the effects of cocaine. He also sought permission to ask Bangs whether he had ever beaten someone up while under the influence of cocaine.

"How are these points relevant?" queried Zobel.

"I intend to show violent tendencies in a violent character," Troy replied confidently.

"I take it by the way Ms. Ball is looking at me that she objects," Zobel noted. "Denied."

Troy tried next to discredit Bangs by asking the judge to add several neighbors as witnesses who would testify that Joey constantly harassed Doherty, but Zobel determined that the point might be relevant in a civil case, but not in the present trial.

Troy next fell back on asking again for a mistrial, the tactic he resorted to whenever his latest strategy fell short. He asked the judge to rule again on the threatening calls he was receiving at night from someone who claimed to be Bangs.

"I will leave that appropriate investigation elsewhere. I am not encouraging it or discouraging it," Zobel replied.

"Well, Your Honor, if he does it again tonight, I'm going down there to make him identify himself to me as a citizen."

"Mr. Troy," the judge answered flatly, "what you do in your off-hours is entirely up to you, to the extent that you're not serving a sentence for contempt! As it is, the court will note we are all smiling. Anything else, Mr. Troy?"

Tail between his legs, Troy nodded and smiled. He was intelligent enough to know when to leave it alone. The fact is that when Bangs called to harass Troy, Troy told him that he too used to be in the military, a Marine, a boxer, and a cop, just like Joey.

"And that's the difference, pal," Bangs snapped. "You used to play, but I'm still in the game."

Even though he denied objections and motions from the defense more frequently than from the prosecution, Zobel did allow evidence about how cocaine was freebased and what effects its long-term use tended to create in an individual's personality and behavior. Zobel also allowed Troy to demonstrate that Bangs freebased cocaine on a regular basis during the period in question. In fact, Bangs himself admitted to smoking cocaine at least a few days a week for six months before the shooting incident and intermittently for nearly two years prior to that.

Troy asked Bangs whether he ever became disoriented or spoke rapidly or became violent while smoking cocaine, and Joey answered honestly—*no*. Troy asked if Bangs knew Jimmy McGaffigan or Butch Adair or Jay Mitchelson or Joseph Cacio* or Vanessa Bourgeois, all of whom, Troy insinuated, were either pistol-whipped or assaulted by Bangs at one time or another.

Troy followed by asking whether Bangs knew Anthony or Steven Bardara, owners of Richards Motors. Apparently, Debbie had had dinner

---

* Mitchelson was Debbie O'Malley's former boyfriend. Cacio had rented the condo in Pompano Beach, Florida, to Bangs.

with Steven while Joey was out of town on business one evening, and Tommy Doherty spotted Bardara dropping Debbie off in front of #2 Pleasant Street Court. Doherty approached Bardara's vehicle, presented his badge, identified himself as a Medford police lieutenant, and asked Bardara for his license. Doherty pocketed the license and informed Bardara that Debbie's boyfriend—Bangs—would deliver it promptly upon his return.

Troy also claimed that Bangs had gone to Jay Mitchelson's job site, accused him of having sexual relations with Debbie, and pistol-whipped him in front of his friends, who were now too afraid to testify. Bangs denied striking Mitchelson but admitted to sticking a loaded revolver to his chest.

Troy's plan seemed to work: each story struck a nerve with Joey and weakened his resolve ever so slightly. It wasn't much, but Troy took it.

Troy returned next to the champagne-colored 1984 Cadillac Seville that Bangs had purchased in Atlantic City for $25,000 cash. The state police had located the bill of sale, dated June 1984, in the brown vinyl travel bag stashed in the trunk.

The bag also contained a small, amber glass vial containing cocaine residue. Hoping to catch Joey in a lie, Troy asserted that the vial was Bangs' and that only individuals who snorted cocaine, not smoked it, used this type of vial. Ball objected, clarifying that Bangs had already testified he didn't snort coke and that he often gave such items to friends.

Troy next asked if there was any paraphernalia for cutting cocaine in the green Chevrolet. Bangs again answered no, and Troy sensed he was losing whatever little momentum he had perceived.

Desperate, Troy approached the witness stand and began firing questions at Bangs. Ball objected to the hostility, and Zobel called the attorneys to a sidebar.

"There are two judicial prerogatives here," Zobel explained. "One: confess your error." He addressed Ball directly. "Ms. Ball, I apologize for the sexist remark the other day about 'sweeping' the court room. It was a poor attempt at humor—what can I say? Two: the judge gets the final word. Mr. Troy, to save us time, we'll skip option one, and I'll give the final word: proceed, with kid gloves, without yelling at the witness, regardless of what you may consider to be your individual style."

Troy returned to his questioning with a calmer demeanor, but every time he brought up personal issues, mainly Joey's drug use, Ball objected strenuously. In most cases, she was overruled, but she always pressed the matter, no matter how many times the judge overruled. Even though Bangs wasn't on trial, Ball tirelessly protected him—her prized weapon—for three grueling days.

Judge Zobel finally reached a point where he himself challenged Troy's repeated charges that smoking cocaine made Bangs violent.

"Mr. Troy, if you have anyone who has seen the witness ingest cocaine and can testify to the witness's behavior afterwards, we will gladly hear that testimony. Otherwise, move on." Troy, of course, moved on.

Troy turned his attention to the airline tickets discovered in the Cadillac's trunk, issued under Joey's favorite aliases—"J. Fisher" and "Dr. Robert Taylor."

Some of the tickets were issued to Debbie O'Malley for a round-trip flight between Boston and Ft. Lauderdale scheduled for September 2-6, 1984—just after a big argument she and Joey had in Las Vegas, an incident Troy used to characterize their relationship as a high-energy tryst fueled by drugs and violence.

Bangs also answered numerous questions about the Pompano Beach, Florida, condominium he had rented from the Cacio family, who later claimed in an affidavit that during Joey's non-stop partying, he had broken a mirror, shattered a mirrored wall, and shot bullets into another wall, where it appeared he had fired at a coat rack with a hat on top. In all, the damage totaled $4,500. Bangs, however, stated matter-of-factly that the condo was damaged before he arrived, adding in jest that maybe he had thought the hat was someone lying in wait for him.

Troy also introduced statements from a doctor who had leased Bangs a beautiful, beachfront home in St. Petersburg, while Bangs was in protective custody. Technically, the lease didn't expire until December 15, 1985, but the owner learned that Bangs was smoking cocaine and damaging the home during his infamous shindigs and terminated the agreement. Bangs insisted he had not smoked cocaine since.

Once again, Troy wanted both to convince the jury that Bangs became violent when he hit the cocaine pipe and to establish whether Bangs understood and was telling the truth about his behavior under the influence of cocaine. Bangs readily admitted to smoking a few grams during a one-year period in Florida but denied all the claims of misbehavior. At this point, Troy introduced photos that he said depicted the substantial damage done to both condominiums.

And the harder Troy pushed, the more fiercely Ball pushed back in what Zobel later referred to as "a marvelous duet that should be set to music and staged at the Metropolitan Opera."

▾ ▾ ▾

After an extended lunch break, Gillen's attorney, Joe Flak, took the floor for further cross-examination. Out of the gate, Bangs stood up in the witness box, eyed Flak, and warned: "You better not ask any bullshit personal questions about drugs. You've done more shit than anyone in the courtroom."

Titters flitted across the courtroom, and Zobel banged the gavel, again warning Bangs to refrain from any further outbursts. Little did the judge know that on numerous occasions Bangs had phoned Flak in the evening and threatened his life, just as he had done to Troy.

Flak figured that this was his one good chance to stick it to Joey with impunity, and he elaborated to the judge and jury how he believed that Bangs was suffering from severe paranoia and an array of other personality disorders. Ball objected—Flak was not, of course, qualified to comment professionally on Joey's mental state—and the comments were dismissed.

Flak zeroed in on questions about Bangs' weapons and accessories. Bangs conceded that he owned a variety of handguns and holsters, including a belt holster, a double-shoulder holster, a leg holster and an ankle holster.

Flak asked if Bangs possessed a sawed-off shotgun at the time of the shooting, and Bangs explained that he had in fact owned a .410, but it didn't use ammunition like the pellets that had injured him. Double-ought buckshot—the type of projectile that struck Bangs—was used in a twelve-gauge shotgun, not in the smaller .410 weapon; therefore, the defense's question was irrelevant. In addition, Bangs had stolen this particular gun during a home invasion robbery in Rhode Island, and state police recovered it on the Mystic River Bridge on December 26, 1984.

Flak could see the question was getting away from him fast, so he cut Bangs off and asked Judge Zobel to instruct Joey to answer questions with a simple "yes" or "no."

The shotgun thus became a crucial piece of evidence once Ball recounted Joey's testimony to show the jury that it was indisputably not the weapon used in the Bangs shooting. Ball also made it clear during a sidebar that she intended to have the state troopers who discovered Bangs' .410 shotgun explain its differences from the more powerful twelve-gauge shotgun, like the one used against Bangs.

Flak quickly backed off the weapon discussion and returned instead to Joey's drug use on the evening of October 16, 1984. As before, Bangs candidly admitted he smoked cocaine with Debbie before going to Doherty's garage. He also explained that he didn't snort cocaine because he had a deviated septum and snorting coke gave him a speedy, hyper feeling that he didn't enjoy, whereas smoking cocaine had a relaxing effect on him.

Bangs admitted further that on occasion he had smoked cocaine throughout the night and sometimes became irritable when coming down from a freebase binge before growing fatigued and crashing for two or three days. Flak asked Bangs if he ever became paranoid. Joey laughed off the question and said that if anything, he became more sensitive to loud, startling noises. Nonetheless, Joey held firm in his assertion that he used cocaine to "party" and only in the company of an attractive young woman or two.

Flak took a few more jabs at Bangs: Did he ever feel a heightened sense of worth or become boastful while partying? Did coke enhance any emotions for him? If so, which ones? Bangs responded that cocaine did amplify feelings at times, making him feel more happy or gregarious or even invincible, and occasionally, if he were in a foul mood, he might be more inclined to take things a bit further than usual.

Flak pushed deeper into personal territory and asked Bangs whether he and O'Malley ever smoked cocaine in front of Debbie's daughters. Never, Bangs asserted. Again, Bangs would not let the defense depict Debbie as an unfit mother.

Then Flak went for the jugular: "Mr. Bangs, on the evening of October 16, 1984, while under the influence of cocaine, did you have overwhelming feelings of revenge toward defendant Doherty?"

Bangs adamantly denied the accusation—he had no feelings of animosity or hatred or contempt for Tommy Doherty, or for anyone else. He still liked Tommy at that time; he just didn't trust him anymore. And he wanted to be paid the money Doherty owed him.

Bangs did admit, however, that a week before the shooting, he made three or four threatening calls to Doherty, on a Saturday, between 5 and 6 p.m., and he also had a few face-to-face confrontations concerning the money he was owed.

Like Troy, Flak frequently switched gears in an attempt to catch Bangs off balance. For instance, he explained to the jury that Bangs now had immunity from prosecution in this case and was receiving cash, living expenses, and benefits from the state in exchange for his cooperation. Bangs felt compelled to add that while he was in state custody, the Commonwealth paid him only $500 per week, which he exhausted quickly. Zobel didn't appreciate Flak's characterization of the money and protection provided to Bangs as "district attorney services" instead of witness protection, and he warned Flak to tread carefully.

Undeterred, Flak induced Bangs to testify that he was also receiving nearly $2,000 a month from his MDC police pension for hypertension-related disability, and another couple hundred dollars from the U.S. Army as compensation for injuries sustained in combat. Flak also insinuated that Joey's income included welfare checks from Aid to Families with Dependent Children (AFDC) that Debbie O'Malley received at his address. Bangs responded that he had no idea what AFDC was and had no knowledge of any welfare checks.

In an attempt to confuse Bangs, Flak changed his line of questioning on a whim and got him to admit to owning a twelve-gauge, sawed-off shotgun, the same type of weapon used to shoot him and the same type of weapon the state police were unable to locate. In fact, the weapon Flak was referring to was a shotgun that Jerry Clemente had previously stolen from the State Forestry Department office and given to Bangs as a gift— the same weapon Bangs had dumped into the Charles River just after the Depositors Trust robbery.

As he prodded, Flak followed Troy's lead and criticized Bangs' varying accounts of the shooting, which alternately placed Doherty in collusion with Gillen or pinned the entire act on Gillen alone. By Bangs' calculation, if he didn't finger Doherty in the shooting, there may be just enough reasonable doubt for a jury to let him walk. Joey could then collect his debt, the state statute of limitations would expire on the bank job (the federal time limit had already passed), and Tommy would be out on the street where Joey could conduct his own form of street justice. It was a winning scenario all around as far as Bangs was concerned.

▼ ▼ ▼

Al Roberts

Flak finally took a seat, and Al Roberts' attorney, Anthony Baccari, rose to take his best shot at Bangs. Baccari questioned Bangs about a statement he allegedly made to Sergeant Buster Longo. Joey had said that Roberts was working on a vehicle in the garage when he entered to find Doherty. Joey confirmed. To everyone's surprise, Baccari sat down without asking another question.

Baccari knew that the Commonwealth didn't have much of a case against Al Roberts. During a sidebar, Zobel informed Ball that unless she produced some substantiating evidence against the defendant, he would be compelled to dismiss all charges against him. The best the state could do was to try to construct a conspiracy on Roberts' part to commit murder and obstruct justice. His only definite actions had been to allow Bangs into the garage and deadbolt the door behind him. Since he had never locked the door on Bangs before, the district attorney tried to construe the action as aiding Doherty and Gillen.

Plus, since Roberts was working on the main floor of the garage, near a barrel of Speedi-Dry solution, the prosecutors supposed that he must have tampered with the crime scene by covering the blood evidence. Finally, when the state troopers were unable to locate the weapons used by Gillen and Doherty in either the garage or Doherty's house, prosecutors assumed that Roberts had removed them from the scene in the Monte Carlo. In reality, had Roberts not remained in the garage along with Doherty, Gillen, and Troy after the shooting—if he had been gone by the time state trooper Greg Foley arrived—he probably would not have been arrested and indicted.

Though the Commonwealth had arrested and indicted Roberts on thin evidence, it soon became clear they would probably not win a conviction.

Zobel strongly recommended that the Commonwealth rest its case against Roberts; otherwise, he would be forced to rule on it in front of the impressionable jury. Ball agreed, and the case against Roberts was dismissed.

Ball said she didn't want the jurors to know that Roberts had been acquitted, since it might sway their feelings about the other defendants. Zobel agreed, but the defense fought to keep Roberts visible in the courtroom. In the end, Zobel decided to allow Roberts to attend as an

Doherty (L) and Gillen listen to arguments during the shooting trial.

observer and to keep the details of his case from the jury. He also ordered that scientific evidence only be introduced from the second floor of Doherty's garage, so that testimony from Roberts would not be necessary.

To conclude the second day of Joey's testimony, Ball picked up the questioning and redirected the examination, asking Bangs if he were licensed to carry the many firearms he possessed. Troy objected and was overruled, and Bangs stated that, as a police officer, he was indeed licensed to posses and use the weapons.

With the day winding down, Judge Zobel concluded formalities and dismissed the jury until the following morning.

Joey Bangs' Testimony – Day 3

FRIDAY, AUGUST 9, 1985

As Bangs' third day of testimony began, Carol Ball continued her redirect examination by exploring Joey's statement about seeing Doherty in the office, as he initially reported to Lieutenant O'Riordan, Patrolman Lee, and Lt. Detective Spartichino, in contrast to what he had testified the previous day. Ball clarified for the jury that the seeming differences in

Joey's story reflected his state of mind at different times, and the jury seemed more than convinced.

Although Bangs had earlier remarked that he had testified in hundreds of cases during his fourteen-year career with the Capitol and MDC police, Ball probed his comments to show the jury that in this case, he was not bringing his experience as a "professional" witness to bear.

Ball introduced as evidence Bangs' bloody set of keys, marked exhibit #43. The sight of the enormous key chain elicited chuckles from the courtroom: beneath the blood, everyone could make out a miniature replica of a Disney character. Zobel said for the record that he thought it was Goofy, but Troy corrected him—it was Pluto.

"Pluto, Donald Duck, Mickey Mouse, Goofy, it makes no difference!" the judge bellowed. "Move on!"

Bangs noted that the house key was missing and surmised that some drug-addicted Medford policemen must have stolen it while he was in emergency surgery and ventured back to his apartment to search for cocaine before state police arrived on the scene.

Bangs also reported that while he lay bleeding on his living room floor, Lieutenant Merullo whispered to him, "If you have anything laying around the house you want me to get rid of, just tell me where it is."

Bangs sat up a bit straighter, leaned into Merullo, pulled the lieutenant's ear close to his mouth, and shouted at full voice, "Go fuck yourself!"

Bangs never doubted that Medford police officers tampered with the crime scene—they had an enormous stake in the outcome of the shooting. By this time, Clemente and Doherty had been dealing stolen civil service exams and tampering with scores for eight or nine years, and many of the Medford cops, handpicked by Doherty, had obtained some sort of assistance with their entry or advancement. Naturally, they feared that if Doherty were convicted, he might turn state's evidence against the lot of them in any potential investigation into the exams.

❤ ❤ ❤

After Ball finished her questions, Troy finished the morning session by trying to rile Bangs, pursuing a line of questioning that suggested he was in a cocaine-induced frenzy and had threatened Doherty with bodily harm before crossing the street to the garage on the night of the shooting. Bangs didn't take the bait.

Troy then moved on to a discussion of the condo in Pompano Beach, Florida. Bangs testified that he and Doherty had initially leased a corner penthouse unit from a mutual acquaintance who lived in Stoneham, Massachusetts, and after they grew accustomed to vacationing at the beachfront property, they bought an adjacent penthouse outright. They agreed verbally to pay cash and place the title in Doherty's mother's name, to protect the property from the IRS and other government agencies snooping around their affairs.

▾ ▾ ▾

After the usual mid-morning coffee break, the jury heard Bangs testify that he had spoken with Doherty almost daily from July 1984 until the night of the shooting and had visited Doherty's garage regularly for more than a month prior to the attack.

When probed further about his .410 shotgun, Bangs said that his friend Bobby Spencer had the weapon on the night of the shooting, and that he had had it in his possession from February 1984 until December 23, 1984, the last time Bangs saw Spencer. The men met in the parking lot of Memory Lane in Somerville between 10 p.m. and midnight, and Spencer returned the gun to Bangs, along with a suitcase containing four one-pound blocks of hashish.[*]

Two days later, on Christmas Day, Bangs wiped down the shotgun with alcohol to remove fingerprints and wrapped it in a white sheet and duct tape for disposal. As a holiday present, Joey had bought tickets for a number of his family, including Uncle Eddie, Debbie O'Malley, and her daughters, Kelly Ann and Shauna, to fly to Florida to visit extended family and play at Busch Gardens. Bangs asked his cousin, Ronnie Coiro, to drive him and the girls to the airport, and as they passed over the Mystic River Bridge, Joey tried to toss the shotgun from the window of the car into the murky river. As luck would have it, the weapon hit a guardrail and bounced onto the roadway, out of Joey's reach, where state police recovered it the following day after a motorist reported a metal object in

---

[*] Bangs was later compelled to testify against Spencer because Clemente had witnessed the transaction, and if Bangs had breeched his immunity agreement, he would face life and a day behind bars.

the road. Bangs said he had already discussed this incident in detail with state troopers Jimmy Lane and Greg Foley, as well as with Assistant District Attorney Max Beck, Carol Ball's wingman.

Bangs next testified that in September and October, he had seen Tommy Doherty in his garage office with a twelve-gauge, sawed-off shotgun. He assumed this was the weapon Gillen used in the attack.

Troy pressed: "How do you expected anyone to believe your testimony, whereas you were a police officer who had possession of a sawed-off shotgun, yet you would not lie under oath? You possessed a kilo of cocaine, but you would not dare lie under oath? You lie to other policemen, but you would not lie under oath?"

Bangs explained that he was disposing of the shotgun simply because he didn't need it anymore.

"Okay, but why at night?" Troy asked.

"In the past, I've dumped incriminating evidence at all hours. What difference does it make?"

Ball objected repeatedly to Troy's questioning, and Judge Zobel finally came to Bangs' defense: "Mr. Troy, does inconsistency in the witness's statement equal lies?"

As questioning resumed, Troy and Flak dug into another point of contention between Bangs and Doherty: the night Doherty gave Debbie O'Malley a ride home from Logan airport, provoking Bangs' paranoia and jealousy.

In mid-August, Bangs and O'Malley had a boisterous, physical argument in Las Vegas, and Joey decided he was done—he sent her packing to Boston to clear out of his apartment. Bangs called Doherty and warned him not to pick up O'Malley at the airport. Joey also asked Spencer to let Debbie into the apartment, watch her while she packed, and then take her set of keys when she left.

When Spencer arrived at the apartment around 10 p.m., he saw Debbie get out of Doherty's Lincoln. Doherty spotted Spencer and asked him to help carry Debbie's bags inside. Spencer pulled Doherty aside and explained that Bangs wanted neither him nor Debbie at the apartment. After Doherty left, Spencer went inside and watched as O'Malley crammed all her belongings into large, green garbage bags. Bobby helped

Debbie move the bags out, and then, per Bangs' request, he took her keys and locked the apartment—and she was gone.

Bangs returned to Boston a few days later and didn't speak to O'Malley for another two days. He softened over the following days and invited O'Malley and Doherty to his Pleasant Street Court apartment. Even though Spencer had filled in Bangs concerning O'Malley's return from the airport, Joey wanted to suss out the situation for himself.

After the trio started smoking cocaine, Bangs told Doherty that Debbie said he had picked her up at the airport. Doherty denied the accusation, and Bangs played along, ignoring O'Malley's protestations. Doherty's lying drove Bangs mad, but he took it out on Debbie, hitting her several times in the following days. When Doherty saw Bangs' reaction, he egged Joey on, telling him to get rid of O'Malley for good if she were going to lie about something so trivial and cause him trouble.

Troy passed the baton to Flak, who asked Bangs if he knew that Doherty and O'Malley had stopped at the Silver Fox Café for a cocktail. *So what*, Bangs scoffed. The restaurant was owned by one of Debbie's former boyfriends, a man she had dated a decade before.

"Why didn't Doherty come clean about the ride to begin with?" Flak queried.

"He didn't have the balls," Bangs snorted, "until the trial began, when he believed he'd have protection."

"Was there some reason to believe that perhaps Tommy and Debbie had had sex that night?" Bangs laughed.

"So you mean to tell me," Flak persisted, "that you verbally abused Ms. O'Malley, slapped her around, broke up with her, and threw her out of the apartment, all because defendant Doherty picked her up at the airport?"

"That is correct," Joey quipped, "It was the principle of the thing."

Bangs wasn't about to let Flak rattle his cage. He knew that Doherty had lied, that he had let Debbie take the fall, and that he had no honor as either a man or a thief. All their years of friendship and crime—the trust it took to put your life in someone's hands and to hide their darkest secrets and deeds—now counted for nothing.

Bangs reasoned that perhaps Doherty thought the couple would break up before he discovered the truth, or perhaps Tommy actually had his eye on Debbie all along and figured he could edge Joey out. Whatever the case, Bangs knew Flak wanted to paint him as a jilted, coked-out lover bent on doing violence to Doherty, who was only defending himself.

"I still liked Tom Doherty as of October 16, 1984. No hatred, no revenge, no animosity," Joey answered Flak. "I just didn't trust him anymore. I forgave him, but I didn't trust him."

Debbie O'Malley's Testimony – Part 1

FRIDAY, AUGUST 9, 1985

Carol Ball knew that Troy and Flak would do everything legal to attack Bangs by bringing down Debbie O'Malley. If they could build a case that she had betrayed Joey, they could argue that his jealousy led to violence. If they could portray her as the catalyst that incited his erratic behavior, they could show that her presence in the months leading up to the shooting altered for the worse the friendship between Joey and Tommy. If they could find any way to taint her, they could taint Joey by association.

Ball put to rest the notion that O'Malley and Doherty were involved in any sort of dalliance—Debbie's hearty laughter at the suggestion that she had had sex with Tommy ended that conversation.

Ball then asked Debbie about her family life, in particular about her daughters, Kelly Ann and Shauna Lee, who were now fifteen and fourteen, respectively. The girls lived primarily with Debbie's parents, the Hills. O'Malley had her own residence at #32 Newbern Avenue in Medford, but frequently stayed with Bangs, unless he was traveling, which was more often than not.

Ball led O'Malley to lay out the history of her relationship with Bangs: first meeting Doherty around March, 1984, about seven months before the shooting; being introduced to Joey at one of Doherty's house parties a few months later; settling into a committed, if somewhat turbulent, relationship with Joey by August. She then chronicled the events of October 16, corroborating Joey's entire account.

Debbie O'Malley

❤ ❤ ❤

Troy stepped forward to cross-examine. O'Malley reported that she had taken four trips with Bangs in the short time they dated and admitted that she and Bangs had had four or five significant altercations in Doherty's presence between August and September.

Troy sensed that Debbie was anxious—he wanted her completely off balance. He badgered her during every answer to speak louder and complained to Judge Zobel that she was murmuring and needed to speak up. The microphone didn't really amplify her voice, he said. It was just an aid for the court reporter. Debbie apologized and sat forward awkwardly to reach the mic.

Troy asked about Bangs' demeanor at Memory Lane lounge. He was fine, she said. At Kelley's Restaurant for dinner? Fine. When he left for Doherty's garage? Fine.

Troy pressed harder: "When you say you're in a 'committed relationship' with Mr. Bangs, does that also include sexual intercourse?"

"Objection!" Ball snapped.

"Withdrawn."

"Do you know that Joey Bangs is a married man?"

"Yes."

"And do you live with him?"

"Yes."

"As a probationary period, to see if you'll work out, while your children remain with their grandmother?"

"Yes."

"Ms. O'Malley, do you know that, in the Biblical sense, if you and Mr. Bangs were to have sexual relations, that would be considered adultery?"

"Objection!"

"Sustained! As a miner might say, Mr. Troy, you're at the end of that vein."

"Yes, but there are a few arteries left, your honor."

Troy turned to O'Malley's account of the night of the shooting and her admission that she had smoked cocaine with Bangs before he went to Doherty's garage. He reminded Debbie that she didn't have immunity and could be arrested. Feeling she knew the law, O'Malley begged to differ, claiming that she needed to be caught in possession of the substance. Troy disagreed: if she picked up an illegal substance to smoke it, she was in fact in possession. He threatened to file a criminal complaint against her based on her testimony. His attempts to rattle Debbie were working. And he had made his point: O'Malley would do anything for Bangs, even incriminate herself. If O'Malley could do that, he argued, she could certainly tell a lie.

Troy next wanted to know why O'Malley referred to Ms. Ball as "Carol"—what was the nature of their relationship? Ball objected furiously and claimed that Troy was badgering the witness, but Zobel overruled her.

Troy pounded question after question, bullying and flustering O'Malley until Judge Zobel finally acknowledged Ball's repeated objections and warned Troy to tone it down.

Troy asked Debbie if she had ever done cocaine in front of her daughters. No, she replied quickly. Troy then explained that freebasing cocaine gives off a peculiar odor and posited that her daughters could easily have been affected by secondhand smoke if they were sleeping in the next room. O'Malley denied the possibility and reiterated that she was a good mother.

Troy had one more point he wanted to make, one more trap he wanted to lead Debbie into. He asked whether Debbie ever went into the trunk of Joey's Cadillac. No, she replied, except for hauling the occasional load of groceries.

Troy showed her a photo of Joey's brown briefcase. Yes, she had seen it in the car but thought nothing of it.

He displayed photos of the jewelry and other items found in the trunk. She recognized some of the things, in particular the diamond Rolex watch and the gold ring with the diamond "J" in the center.

Then Troy again took O'Malley all the way to the beginning of the evening, at Memory Lane Lounge. Debbie said she had been running late for the 6 p.m. rendezvous. Her makeup wasn't quite done, and she had forgotten her earrings. After drinks, she took a moment to finish her makeup, and, yes, she did remember Joey going into the trunk of the Cadillac because he handed her and Kelly Ann each a pair of diamond-studded earrings. That must have been the moment, Debbie reasoned, that Joey transferred items from the Chevrolet.

O'Malley testified that after she returned home from the hospital in the wee hours of the morning, she discovered state troopers Greg Foley and Billy Flynn searching the apartment. She added that the troopers discovered and confiscated $2,000 cash in hundred-dollar bills, hidden behind the picture of a naked woman.

O'Malley also testified that the troopers refused to allow her to move the Cadillac from the property. According to the troopers' report, O'Malley lurked about the apartment while the officers searched the premises, and they asked her to leave several times. O'Malley claimed, however, that they asked her only once.

When the troopers had finished their search, they secured the apartment and locked out O'Malley, whose keys had already been collected as evidence. O'Malley pleaded with Trooper Foley to let her gather a few personal items—it would be okay to break a window or door, she said—but Foley denied her access and sent Debbie away empty-handed.

Troy finally quizzed O'Malley on Joey's cocaine use and got her to admit that she knew where he kept a small amount of the substance and pipes used to smoke it—in fact, the troopers had found the evidence in the exact location she described. At this moment, it seemed plausible to everyone that Debbie had returned either to destroy drug evidence for Joey or to steal the goods for herself.

Kelly Ann O'Malley's Testimony

MONDAY, AUGUST 12, 1985

After a weekend of much needed rest, Debbie and Kelly Ann O'Malley arrived at the courthouse early Monday for Kelly Ann's day on the witness stand. Kelly Ann had taken Carol Ball's advice and toned down her provocative attire, removing most of the gold jewelry she usually wore, all of it given to her by Joey, who maintained, by the way, that it was legitimately purchased.

Ball met Debbie and Kelly Ann at the courthouse entrance and took them to a private office where they could wait until the session began.

Kelly Ann was anxious yet game for the challenge. She had answered questions for the grand jury, but she knew this trial would be different.

Kelly Ann's confidence melted as she was led past reporters and into the crowded chamber, where a sea of stoic faces watched her march to the witness stand. The bailiff swore her in, and Ball gave her a reassuring smile before walking her through a series of simple questions about the events of the night of October 16.

Troy decided to pass on questioning Kelly Ann, allowing Flak to take the tricky task. Troy knew there was no upside for him: Kelly Ann didn't have any new information, and he would only come across as a bully if he tried to put the squeeze on a teenage witness, especially a girl.

Flak went through the paces, trying now and again to tease out some new insight from Kelly Ann's distracted answers. It was obvious she wanted to be anywhere but there.

Nevertheless, Kelly Ann's testimony offered the defense a few specks of useful information. She didn't recall, for instance, that Bangs gave either her or Debbie earrings outside of Memory Lane lounge. Flak also pressed her about Al Roberts so he could try to criticize Debbie and Joey's judgment in allowing Roberts to babysit Kelly Ann. The earrings proved a dead end, and maligning Roberts was a non-starter: Debbie and Kelly Ann had known Al for years and both felt comfortable around him.

Debbie's and Kelly Ann's statements conflicted in several other points as well: Debbie testified that after the shooting, she awakened Kelly Ann and told her to get dressed, while Kelly Ann said she awoke to Debbie's screaming and went downstairs on her own to assist Joey, before changing her clothes. Also, Debbie stated that Kelly Ann had helped her make emergency phone calls, but Kelly Ann was positive she didn't place any calls that night.

Kelly Ann said that while she was certainly anxious and afraid, her mother was in a state of sheer panic, frantically casting about the house trying to find Joey's handgun. Flak asked if she had ever seen Bangs with a gun, and surprisingly, she answered no. It was difficult to believe that anyone who had been in Joey's company for any length of time would not have seen one of the two guns he carried with him, but Flak let it pass. He followed up by asking Kelly Ann if she was sure that her mother was looking for a gun and not trying to hide drugs or other key evidence. Kelly

Ann was sure—Debbie was running back and forth from the phone to Joey and various places where Joey might have hidden a weapon. And Kelly Ann testified that she overheard Bangs say that Doherty and Gillen had shot him.

After Kelly Ann finished testifying, the state police returned her to her grandfather's cottage on Cape Cod, where she and Shauna remained for a time under the protection of the state, although the girls never tired of breaking the rules and ignoring the curfew that the state troopers tried to impose.

Additional Witnesses

FRIDAY, AUGUST 16, 1985

Following Kelly Ann O'Malley, Ball had planned to call her final witnesses, but since the defense didn't contest either witness's sworn statement, Judge Zobel felt there was no need to have them testify.

The emergency room doctor who operated on Bangs, Dr. Haefitz, testified in his deposition about the amount of plastic wadding inside Bangs' wounds. The defense claimed that Bangs had picked up the weapons and fled the garage without difficulty. The doctor's testimony, however, proved that Joey would have had great difficulty simply opening a door.

Ball also presented a report from a state police ballistician, Jimmy McGuiness, which showed that the shotgun had been fired from less than three or four feet away, given that the wadding from a shotgun shell would not have traveled any further. McGuiness also stated that the .38 slugs he removed from the garage door had not been fired from any of Bangs' weapons.

Judge Zobel also struck from the schedule the testimony of Medford Police Captain Paul Murphy and first responders Eddie Lee and Buster Longo.

The defense then reported that Doherty's mother-in-law—who was also Gillen's mother-in-law and who had lived with Doherty and his wife for many years—had passed away over the weekend. The funeral was scheduled for the following morning at eleven o'clock. Zobel adjourned court that morning and left it to the discretion of U.S. marshals whether to allow Gillen to attend the service, since he was under federal supervision for his conviction in the Maine marijuana bust.

In addition, on Tuesday afternoon after the funeral, the court arranged a field trip to the crime scene, where the jurors were allowed to view Doherty's garage and Bangs' apartment.

When court reconvened on Wednesday, August 14, state trooper Greg Foley testified that he was assigned to the Middlesex County district attorney's office to conduct murder investigations, an assignment he had held for more than three years. Foley testified that he, Lt. Detective Spartichino, and state trooper Flynn arrived at #59 Pleasant Street at 1:15 a.m., where they met with Captain Murphy and acting Chief of Police Jake Keating, who advised them of what had taken place. After surveying the scene, Foley phoned state police headquarters and requested a ballistician, a photographer, and a chemist. Foley, Spartichino, and Flynn then went to Doherty's home and entered the premises through a back door, which led to a cellar outfitted as a bar, where they discovered Troy chatting with Doherty and Gillen, who were immediately taken into custody.

Debbie O'Malley's Testimony – Part 2

During earlier testimony, O'Malley stated that shortly after Bangs left the apartment, she heard a loud bang, which she disregarded because she thought it was a car backfiring. Just a few minutes later, she said, Bangs returned to the apartment from the garage. The sight of Bangs traumatized Debbie, and the events of the evening seemed a surreal blur of blood, noise, fear, and strange faces invading her life. Details of some moments were vivid, others vague.

Troy attacked.

"Ms. O'Malley, could the cocaine have caused you to feel hysterical that evening?"

"No."

"You mean, you didn't do enough to be coked up that night?"

Ball objected; Troy rephrased.

"You mean because it takes a lot for you to get that way, because you do so much?"

Ball again objected to both Troy's question and his attitude, imitating his condescending tone. But Zobel let it play.

"Maybe Mr. Troy hasn't had the stage training some of us have," Zobel remarked, "so his repetition lacked the artistic approach that your rendition of his rendition entertained us with. Overruled! Mr. Troy, you're not winning any points with your style—proceed carefully."

Troy took advantage of the moment to pressure O'Malley by asking her to speak up and to repeat herself, picking away at her confidence in her answers.

O'Malley also testified that her friend, Marie Dailey, later met her at the Medford police station to offer support and give her a ride home.

At this point, O'Malley had difficulty answering certain questions and remarked that she did in fact have a bad memory.

"Because of smoking cocaine?" Troy asked. "Does cocaine affect your memory?"

O'Malley realized she had taken a misstep and quickly backpedaled: "No, not at all. I've always had a bad memory."

Troy's legs began to bother him again, so Flak picked up the re-cross-examination of O'Malley, who had maintained her composure reasonably well so far. Flak asked why O'Malley didn't seem to have difficulty remembering answers to Ball's questions. Had she discussed the case with someone or been coached? Debbie admitted she and Bangs had discussed the case several times. Flak pressed, and eventually O'Malley confessed that she had discussed the case on at least two occasions with ADA Carol Ball, who had "refreshed" her memory on some incidents.

Flak reiterated the question, and Ball again objected. Zobel glared at Flak: "Mr. Flak, I'm told that if one leaves a computer on long enough, it burns the image into the screen." Flak got the message and moved on to new business, drilling into the discrepancies between Debbie's statements and Kelly Ann's testimony, but in the end, the damage was minimal: O'Malley was not on trial, nor was Kelly Ann.

O'Malley admitted she and Bangs had had many verbal and physical confrontations from August to October. On one occasion, she said, Bangs slapped her in front of Doherty and knocked her down, ripped her clothes, and swore at her. Another time, he withdrew a pistol, placed it into her mouth, and threatened to blow her head off. O'Malley acknowledged that Bangs rarely left the apartment without at least two guns on his person, usually one in his ankle holster and another in his waistband. And Bangs had more than once questioned O'Malley about her relationship with Doherty.

But in Debbie's opinion, cocaine did not amplify Bangs' moods. "When it comes to Joey," she said, "it really doesn't matter if he's already aggravated over something or not, when on cocaine."

Flak resumed the questioning and probed further into the airport ride incident from August. O'Malley stated that she called Doherty from Logan Airport and asked him to pick her up. They stopped at Kappy's Liquor Store on the way home so Debbie could buy a bottle of wine— Lancer's Rose, to be exact—before returning to the apartment to collect some clothing and personal items.

O'Malley admitted smoking cocaine with Bangs for two to three days, ten to twelve hours at a time without any sleep. Of course, she also confirmed that she and Joey had smoked cocaine together just ten minutes before Joey went to Doherty's garage on October 16, 1984.

Flak switched gears, fast-forwarding to an incident at the hospital. He asked O'Malley if the ER doctor had covered Bangs with a sheet and allowed her to speak with him after Bangs heard her crying in the hall. Debbie confirmed that she and Joey had a very brief conversation. Flak reported that when a Medford police officer asked her what had happened, O'Malley smugly stated, "Go ask Joe what happened!" O'Malley, however, remembered only that an officer had tried to calm her.

Flak insinuated that O'Malley did a so-called "dry run" statement with Lt. Detective Spartichino on October 17, 1984, while being interviewed at the Medford Police Department, but impugning Spartichino's integrity was a serious miscalculation on Flak's part, since Spartichino was a highly respected state official and masterful law enforcement agent who would never dream of tampering with a case.

Flak returned to Bangs' propensity for violence, especially toward O'Malley's previous boyfriends. He asked O'Malley what her own address was at the time of the shooting: #32 Newbern Avenue, Medford, she replied. Flak pointed out that the property was owned by her former lover, Jimmy McGaffigan, who allowed her to "pay rent" for the second-floor apartment. Flak asked how she paid rent, since she was not working, insinuating that she and McGaffigan must have had some other arrangement. O'Malley adamantly denied the innuendo.

As questioning continued, O'Malley admitted that Bangs had indeed threatened some of her previous love interests—Jay Mitchelson, Butch Adair, Jimmy McGaffigan—and Flak added Doherty's name to the list to suggest that they had had a romantic encounter the night of the infamous airport ride, thus inflaming Bangs' feelings toward Doherty.

Flak then made a considerable issue of Bangs' Cadillac, asking Debbie if she knew whether the car's interior lights shut off automatically. Bangs had previously stated that on the eve of the shooting he stopped at the Caddy to turn off the lights on his way to Doherty's garage. The defense wanted to assert that he had actually stopped at the car to retrieve the sawed-off shotgun used in the attack. O'Malley, of course, said she knew nothing about cars. Flak dropped the matter and had no further questions.

Tommy Doherty's Testimony – Day 1

MONDAY, AUGUST 19, 1985

Tommy Doherty

Forty-three-year-old Thomas Kevin Doherty took the witness stand to answer questions posed by Troy's co-counsel, Eugene McCann. Doherty stared down the prosecution with all the cockiness he could muster, but his legs fidgeted wildly in the witness box.

After the usual introductions and formalities, McCann established that Doherty had been a police officer for nearly two decades and was a hard-working cop who had risen through the ranks from patrolman to lieutenant in a department which had only nine or so lieutenants, five captains, and one chief.

A lifelong resident of the city, Doherty testified that he graduated from Medford High School and later from Northeastern University, with a Bachelor of Science degree in criminal justice. Doherty also tossed out that he was working on his master's degree at the time of the trial, even though he had never been accepted to any graduate program.

Doherty testified that he became a cop in June 1964, after graduating from the state police academy in Framingham, and then worked as a state trooper in Leominster and Orange. Doherty's father was a detective on the Medford police force when he passed away, and his untimely death created a vacancy in the department that Tommy subsequently filled. Doherty received four commendations during his time as a state trooper and many more as a Medford police officer.

When asked how he met Bangs, Doherty stated that the meeting happened during his first vacation to Florida, around Valentine's Day, 1982, a week before school vacation. But Doherty was perjuring himself, whereas the two had obviously met much earlier, since they pulled off the Depositors Trust heist in 1980. Doherty continued to testify—falsely—that his only business dealings with Bangs occurred between 1982 and 1984, when the men considered purchasing a travel agency to run gambling junkets. In reality, Doherty didn't know the first thing about junkets or traveling or even gambling, for that matter.

Doherty denied he had any knowledge of Bangs' drug dealing but admitted he knew Joey used cocaine. Doherty said that although he was never present when Bangs smoked cocaine, he knew when Joey was under the influence because his voice became low and gravelly, his eyes waxed beady, and he grew paranoid, skittish, and vicious, prone to lash out violently at anyone who crossed him in the slightest. Doherty claimed that he often tried to talk Bangs out of doing coke, but that Bangs became extremely upset whenever he did so.

Doherty explained that Bangs moved into his three-family rental property at #59 Pleasant Street—with a side entrance located at #2 Pleasant Street Court—shortly after Christmas in 1983 or the early part of January 1984. The rental property was across the street from Doherty's own home at #50 Pleasant Street, a white house with a pool and the barn-style garage, all surrounded by a white picket fence.

Doherty's mother, Mary, lived at #65 Pleasant Street, and his brother, Brian, lived on the street as well. Doherty added that his brother-in-law and co-defendant, Jackie Gillen, resided directly across the street at #55 Pleasant Street with his wife, who was the sister of Doherty's wife, Carol.

While still under direct-examination by McCann, Doherty stated that he met Ms. O'Malley in March 1984 and noted that she moved into Bangs' apartment shortly thereafter.

Doherty then testified that Bangs always carried at least two guns and sometimes three—a snub-nose .38 Special revolver in his back pocket, a .357 Magnum in his waistband, and a 9mm in an ankle holster. Doherty said he never saw Bangs without at least two weapons.

Troy then launched into an examination of the incidents of August 1984—precipitated by the argument between Bangs and O'Malley in Las Vegas—that changed the course of Doherty and Bangs' relationship and led ultimately to the shooting in October.

Doherty recounted that after O'Malley returned from Las Vegas in August 1984, Bangs called and told him not to do any favors whatsoever for Debbie. According to Bangs, O'Malley had had a romantic encounter with a man by the hotel swimming pool, and, jilted, Joey decided to send her home.

McCann was trying to establish a motive not for lying, but for Bangs' violent actions on the eve of October 16, 1984, and to show that Joey had an ongoing vendetta against Doherty, whom McCann referred to as the only real victim in the case.

Doherty testified that he ignored Bangs' request after receiving an urgent call from O'Malley, who claimed she was stranded at the Eastern Airlines baggage claim at Logan Airport and desperately needed a ride. Doherty also claimed that O'Malley, who reeked of alcohol and was stumbling about, ran to him and gave him a hug, and then begged him to help her straighten things out with Bangs, who seemed to terrify her.

On the ride home, Doherty stopped at Kappy's Liquors in Medford's Wellington Circle and picked up a cheap bottle of wine for the already inebriated O'Malley because, in his words, he'd rather have her pass out than have to put up with what was going on. He then drove straight to #2 Pleasant Street Court and parked on the street because the driveway was reserved for tenants. Pleasant Street Court, Doherty explained, is a private road serving three individual homes.

For instance, Neal Bernard, a young tow truck driver, lived on the narrow and congested street where parking was extremely difficult and limited. In fact, vehicles on the odd side of the street were forced to park on the sidewalk or on the opposite side, with wheels to the curb.

Doherty testified that while he was unloading O'Malley's luggage from his vehicle, Bobby Spencer pulled up and opened Bangs' apartment with his spare key. They all three entered and went upstairs, where Spencer and O'Malley stuffed her clothing into trash bags.

Doherty claimed the telephone rang at this time—it was Joey calling from Vegas. Bangs asked Doherty who was there, and Tommy said that he, Debbie, and Spencer had just arrived. Bangs asked how O'Malley got there. *Taxi*, Doherty said. Bangs asked to speak with Spencer, Doherty handed Bobby the receiver, and the men spoke at length. When O'Malley had finished packing, the men carried the bags out, and Spencer locked the door behind them.

Doherty said he didn't hear from Bangs for three or four days, until Joey showed up at his garage office one night. Tommy used the office for his realty trust company and stayed there most nights to watch the evening news or finish whatever paperwork was urgent. There were several chairs, a desk, a handful of filing cabinets, and a wall of shelves filled with law books.

Joey grilled Tommy about Debbie's ride from the airport. Doherty was concerned—he knew Joey was always armed. After a lengthy interrogation, Bangs stormed from the garage, returning a short time later with Debbie in tow.

"She's saying you picked her up at the airport," Bangs bellowed. Joey wanted the truth, but even more, he wanted peace of mind with regard to Tommy, to know that he could still trust the man he had committed so many crimes with.

Doherty insisted to Joey that he had not given O'Malley a ride. Bangs told Doherty he was going to get to the bottom of the story: he slapped Debbie hard in the face and dragged her out of the office by her hair, his hand reaching for his gun as if he were going to use it.

Doherty also testified that Bangs continued to terrorize him by phone, though he didn't see Bangs again until the latter part of September, when Joey again dragged Debbie up to the office and told Tommy he now believed her version of the story. Even so, according to Doherty, Bangs pistol-whipped O'Malley until she bled, and Debbie refused medical attention when Tommy offered to take her to the hospital.

During the confrontation, Bangs berated Doherty for having lied and threatened to cut his heart out. Doherty believed Bangs had been smoking cocaine, and the moment terrified him: he didn't know whether Bangs was just talking big or was actually unhinged enough to do something crazy.

The worst confrontation occurred on October 14, when Bangs yet again brought O'Malley to the garage office and argued with Doherty about the airport ride. As in past discussions, Doherty denied picking up O'Malley at the airport. Bangs punched Debbie in the face, knocking her to the floor, and kicked her before grabbing her hair and dragging her back to her feet. Doherty stood up and told Bangs to knock it off—he wouldn't allow that kind of behavior on his property. And he was fed up with all the complaints from neighbors about Bangs' disruptive behavior. On a dozen occasions, Doherty testified, he had discussed Bangs' growing reputation for mayhem with the other tenants, most recently just two weeks before with Mr. and Mrs. Boos, the first-floor renters at #59 Pleasant Street. Everyone agreed that Joey was too hot-tempered and prone to fighting. After the incident on October 14, Doherty asked Bangs to vacate the apartment.

Doherty then testified about their third and final confrontation at the garage the very next day, October 15. Doherty said he heard a commotion outside and peeked through a wall peephole to see Bangs on Pleasant Street, leaning into a car window parked in front of his apartment. It appeared that he was talking to a mutual acquaintance, Vanessa Bourgeois. Bangs had a gun in his hand and was tearing off Vanessa's clothing. Vanessa wrestled her way out of the passenger side and ran toward the garage, the irate Bangs in pursuit, laughing maniacally.

Her blouse torn to shreds, Vanessa dashed into the garage, locked the door behind her, flew up the spiral staircase to Doherty's office, and begged for help. Bangs began kicking the overhead door to the garage and shouting that he needed to speak to Vanessa. Doherty got a quick rundown of the story from Vanessa: she had told Debbie about her fling with Joey, and he was beside himself with rage.

Bangs finally discovered an open door and rushed up to the office, where he faced off against Tommy. Vanessa cowered behind Doherty— Tommy asked Joey what the problem was. Bangs ignored Doherty's question and reached past him to punch Vanessa square in the face. As she started to fall, Joey grabbed her and threw her against a wall. Doherty stepped in and shoved him away.

Doherty caught Vanessa's eye and told Bangs she would tell Debbie the "truth" as long as he would act like a gentleman and not hurt her anymore. Doherty again told Bangs he had had it with the erratic behavior and would no longer tolerate such fits on his property. Joey wagged his finger in Tommy's face and calmly declared: "Pay me what you owe me or you're dead." Tommy knew that Joey was serious. He needed no further motivation to do what he felt was necessary.

McCann asked Doherty if anyone else had witnessed Bangs' despicable actions, and Tommy claimed that Jackie Gillen had seen the entire incident. Bangs, however, claimed that Gillen was not present, and that even though he had slapped Vanessa, Doherty had grossly exaggerated everything else about the encounter.

McCann took a moment to review his notes, and then got to the heart of the matter—the events of October 16. Doherty claimed that Bangs phoned him around 5:30 p.m. but didn't seem to have anything specific to talk about. Bangs said he was leaving for dinner in a few minutes and would stop by later.

Doherty testified that he never called Bangs that evening, but that Joey called him around 10:30 p.m. Doherty recognized Bangs' gravelly voice with the first words he heard: "You're dead, you motherfucker." Bangs then launched into a profanity-filled string of incriminations and threats against Doherty and promised to be there soon.

The phone call didn't frighten Doherty, but he had no idea what Joey would do next. Doherty wanted some protection. Rather than call his colleagues at the Medford police station, however, he rang his brother-in-law, Gillen, and asked him to come over, just in case. Bangs called back a little later, Doherty said, to apologize for running late and to tell him he was on his way.

The next thing Tommy knew, he heard the sound of footsteps—those Cuban heels on Joey's fancy loafers—running in his driveway. Doherty testified that at this point, he looked out his window and then heard a door slam and those same shoes click up the metal spiral staircase. Another set of footsteps pounded down the hall, closer to the office—Jackie Gillen then burst through the door and tried to close it behind him.

Bangs and Gillen had arrived at the garage almost simultaneously, and Bangs had chased him upstairs to the office.

McCann next walked Doherty through the shooting: according to Doherty, Bangs wielded a shotgun and somehow managed to wedge its barrel in the door to stop Gillen from shutting it. Gillen held the doorknob with his right hand, leaned all his weight against the door, and reached for the shotgun with his left hand. Doherty ducked behind the desk for cover, leaving Gillen alone to resist Bangs. McCann asked Doherty to diagram on the blackboard the layout of the room at the time he hid—the desk, noted with a D; a B for the fold-away bed often used by Al Roberts; a J for Joey; and a G for Gillen.

Doherty said he heard the blast, a thunderous roar that blew past him, and peered around the desk to see what had happened: Gillen was on the floor with the shotgun in hand. It appeared that Gillen had wrested the weapon from Bangs and fired from the ground, point blank, hitting Joey's upper chest. Doherty heard Bangs' heels popping down the hardwood floor in the hall, fading toward the spiral staircase. He and Gillen started after Bangs, then saw Joey coming at them with a revolver, which Doherty believed was Bangs' Ruger .357.

Bangs raised the gun to fire, Doherty explained, but Gillen beat him to the trigger with another blast from the shotgun that struck Joey and spun him around, sending him tumbling down the staircase until he managed to get himself wedged between the iron rails, about four steps from the bottom.[*]

Doherty said he and Gillen peered down the stairs to make certain the coast was clear and quickly circled down the steps until they came across Bangs, still entangled in the bannister. Doherty claimed that they were forced to walk over Bangs as they scurried past and that Gillen tried to strike him in the head with the empty shotgun in a defensive move, but missed and simply threw the weapon at him. Gillen shouted at Roberts to get out, and Roberts straightaway dropped his tools at the car he was working on and managed to beat Doherty and Gillen out the door.

Gillen followed Roberts, Doherty said, and as he was bringing up the rear, he heard two additional gunshots and turned to see that Bangs had

---

[*] In an interview at his home in Maine in 2008, McCann offered tremendous insight into Doherty's defense and insisted that Doherty—not Gillen—had shot Bangs.

fired his handgun, from his twisted position on the stairs, missing Tommy's head and hitting the door jamb, near a fuse box and umbrella hook. Doherty slipped out and slammed the door behind him.

Gillen and Roberts darted across Pleasant Street to Gillen's home. Doherty tried to leap over the low brick wall between the garage and his home but was so frightened he stumbled and fell to the grass in his backyard, almost rolling into the pool.* Doherty shuffled along the wall toward the house, crouching low for protection as he peered back at the garage to see if Bangs were following. Joey exited the well-lit side door, looked left and right for Doherty and Gillen, and ran to the end of the driveway, where he again scanned the area before crossing the street.

Doherty detailed how he carefully crept into his home and peeked out a kitchen window to track Bangs on Pleasant Street, directly in front of Gillen's home. Doherty instructed his wife, Carol, to retrieve his gun and shut off all the lights.

To Doherty, it appeared that Bangs was carrying both weapons used in the shooting, the shotgun in his left hand and concealed under his jacket, and the handgun tucked under his belt. Doherty said he didn't see any blood, a statement that severely damaged his credibility, given that Bangs was gravely injured and the garage covered with blood evidence. Doherty said that even though Bangs was slightly hunched, he didn't run, but ambled to the sidewalk, scanned up and down the street, and crossed to a green Chevrolet Impala that approached without headlights. Bangs then handed the unidentifiable driver "something"—which Doherty believed to be the guns. As the Impala sped away, Joey stumbled to his apartment, where O'Malley helped him in.

After Bangs disappeared into the home, Doherty came outside and watched from his porch as the lights came on at Joey's apartment. Once Doherty felt the coast was clear, he returned to the garage, locked the door behind him, and searched for attorney Troy's business card, which he never located.

While going between the house and garage, Doherty saw Medford police officers arrive, yet failed to alert them of the incident or warn them about the armed and dangerous Bangs. Instead, he returned home and

---

* Doherty had built the pool with Depositors Trust loot.

went around back to the cellar door, which was locked. Doherty yelled for his wife, Carol, to unlock the door and bring everyone inside the house downstairs, including his mother-in-law and daughter. By this time, an ambulance had arrived at Bangs' residence. Doherty kept the cellar door ajar and watched the activities across the street.

Carol helped Doherty locate Troy's phone number and called him around the same time that Joey was being loaded into the ambulance. Troy arrived at the scene about twenty minutes later. By that time, Gillen and Roberts had joined Doherty in the cellar, and the three men and their attorney then returned to the garage to survey the scene and discuss the night's events.

Sergeant Stone arrived a few minutes later and asked the men to leave, and they headed back to Doherty's basement until Captain Murphy arrived with seven or eight other officers and escorted them to the station for interviews.

Carol Ball tapped her pencil eagerly as Doherty testified—she was champing at the bit to begin cross-examination.

Ball first probed Doherty's reported disability from a work-related back injury just six months prior to the shooting. If the injury were bad enough to merit disability leave, she queried, how was he able to take extended trips to Florida with Joey Bangs? In all, nine trips to Florida—including five to Pompano Beach—and a tenth to Atlantic City, plus additional excursions for an affair with Vanessa.

Doherty testified that Vanessa had traveled to Florida with Bangs on one occasion, but Bangs contended that Doherty and Roberts had hired her to service them and that the party girl had ridden back to Boston with Roberts in a T-Bird in order to score a few more days of pay.

"Have you lived a successful life, Mr. Doherty?" Ball asked.

Judge Zobel jumped in: "Philosophers have battled for centuries, Ms. Ball, to define what a 'successful life' is." Ball acknowledged and moved on.

Ball tried to rile Tommy, continually referring to him in a belittling tone as "*Lieutenant* Doherty." She now dug into his relationship with Al Roberts. Doherty said that Roberts did maintenance on a few of his properties and that it was a "room and board" sort of deal. Doherty also stated that Roberts had his own side business repairing cars out of his Pleasant Street garage, but only for family and friends, since he had no license to offer services publicly. Roberts also used the bathroom in Doherty's basement and often dined with Tommy and his family.

Doherty continued that he and Roberts had traveled together on two occasions, once to Tennessee and later to Mississippi, but he kept the story vague—since neither one had yet been tried for the crimes allegedly committed on those trips—and Ball was left to insinuate that the trips were botched cocaine transactions.

When prodded about his relationship with Bangs, Doherty insisted they had a casual friendship, yet he also admitted that the month before the shooting, he had borrowed a set of repair license plates from Freddie McGovern's Chelsea Towing Company so Bangs could use them to drive to Florida—trips he believed were for cocaine runs.

Ball also led Doherty to admit to purchasing a Chrysler New Yorker and a gold herringbone bracelet worth $1,800 from Bangs just three months prior to the shooting. They were, no doubt, on at least civil terms, Ball contended.*

Doherty also claimed that Bangs held a substantial sum of money in the Depositors Trust Bank—of all places—in the form of savings certificates. In fact, Bangs owned mutual bonds, which carried an interest rate of eighteen percent or better at the time. Doherty related that Bangs spent money as if it grew on trees, buying expensive cars, jewelry, clothing and gifts for his wife and many girlfriends.

Ball picked up the thread. "So even though you were a lieutenant on the Medford police force, it never dawned on you that Joe Bangs might in fact be receiving income from an illegal source such as drug dealing?"

"Sure," Doherty shrugged.

"So why didn't you report Sergeant Bangs to the DEA or state police after you discovered he was an alleged drug dealer or drug addict?"

Doherty hemmed, then smiled and shrugged again. Ball pressed, and Doherty finally admitted to borrowing $15,000 from Bangs in order to purchase a Pompano Beach condo and testified that Bangs later lent him an additional $20,000. Again, Ball zeroed in on why he had never questioned where Bangs got the money.

---

* Bangs later claimed that he had three identical bracelets, all of them loot from the Depositors Trust robbery, and that he had sold one to Jerry Clemente, who was unaware of its provenance.

Doherty claimed he had repaid the loans to Bangs with Western Union wire transfers sent to Las Vegas in July and August 1984. Doherty figured that by testifying he had repaid Bangs, he was covering his ass against a potential civil suit for the balance of the loaned amount following the criminal trial. When Doherty claimed that Bangs had lost more than $200,000 on a gambling spree in a single weekend, Ball again asked why he—a police lieutenant—had not investigated Joey for criminal activity.

Doherty said he learned about Bangs' drug-dealing only after the state police exposed the cocaine found in Joey's trunk—the same trunk, of course, that Tommy had told his colleague Captain Murphy to search—and claimed to be "shocked and appalled" by the discovery. Murphy simply made a mistake while taking his statement, Doherty offered. McCann objected and made a motion for a mistrial, but Zobel denied both counts.

Ball moved on to Doherty's relationship with his unemployed brother-in-law, Jackie Gillen. Tommy defended Jackie: he had been laid off, not fired, because his company—a state-funded agency—had been adversely affected by recent budget cuts.

Ball shifted gears.

"Mr. Doherty, will you tell the jury what the street value of a gram of cocaine is?"

"A hundred dollars," Doherty answered without blinking.

"What about an ounce of cocaine?"

"Two thousand dollars."

"And a pound?"

"About $32,000," Doherty responded without thought.

"And a kilo?"

"$68,000, give or take. For a high concentrate of 74%. Street cocaine is usually only 25% to 35% pure."

While a police officer should undoubtedly know something about illegal trade, Doherty's answers were much too quick and precise—it was obvious he had more than the usual familiarity with the business, even if the prices he quoted were inflated for the current market. In any case, the courtroom got a quick education in discount pricing for volume coke purchases.

Ball asked Doherty to describe the time he had allegedly approached Bangs about his cocaine habit. Doherty stated that he had frequently urged Bangs to stop—every time, in fact, that he saw Joey out of control—but hadn't taken any legal action. The problem had first come to his attention shortly after Debbie O'Malley moved in with Bangs, but Bangs became increasingly aggressive, Doherty asserted, whenever he smoked cocaine. Again, Ball contended, Doherty took no steps to deter Joey's behavior by reporting him to law enforcement and continued to socialize and do business with him.

Ball returned to the evening of October 16. Doherty again denied calling Bangs that night, although the New England Telephone Company had a record to the contrary. The only call Doherty remembered that night was the threatening one Bangs made to him at 10:30 p.m.

Ball questioned why Doherty had apparently just sat and mulled over the situation, rather than calling the police or arming himself or locking the garage and refusing to allow Joey entry. And if he and Gillen knew of Bangs' propensity for violence and that he always carried two guns, why in the world would Gillen have come to the garage unarmed?

Ball asked Doherty to diagram the office and shooting on the chalkboard, and within minutes, she had him so confused he forgot his left from his right and where the shots had struck Bangs.

Ball had Doherty teetering against the ropes now, and she started punching for a knockout. The determined DA got Doherty to claim he didn't see any blood because Bangs was hunched over, but she pointed out that the crime scene was covered with Joey's blood. And how was it possible, she asked, for a highly decorated Vietnam vet and police sergeant armed with two weapons to end up the only one shot?

Fortunately for Doherty, this round in court soon came to an end, and he would have the night to regroup in his corner.

Tommy Doherty's Testimony – Day 2

TUESDAY, AUGUST 20, 1985

The day began with a dilemma for Judge Hiller Zobel. Juror #8, Ms. Russo, had an overseas airline ticket for next day—Wednesday, August 21—and the trial clearly would not conclude during this session. After a brief sidebar, Zobel dismissed Ms. Russo and moved an alternate into her place on the jury. Formidable as ever and relentless in her attack, Ball picked up her cross-examination of Tommy Doherty—a day in court that would soon become legendary in the Commonwealth—with a detailed probe of a number of Doherty's relationships.

Doherty explained first that in 1980 he and a partner had acquired a distressed tool rental business for a song. And in 1984 he sold his share to his partner after they had quadrupled sales and revived the business. At Ball's prodding, Doherty said he sold the business the same month he purchased a Florida condo. In order to make the condo deal work, Doherty had also sold a piece of property at #21 Gibson Street in Medford, purchased at a bank auction for $20,000. A pair of contractors paid $31,000 for the land, yielding Tommy a tidy profit.

Ball abruptly switched topics, pounding Doherty with questions about the shooting. Doherty had stated that when he received the alleged death threat call from Bangs, he was unarmed. Why did he not call police then? Why did he stay at the office, instead of retrieving a weapon from his house next door? Doherty played the question off—Bangs had made idle threats many times, and Tommy expected nothing more than a fistfight. Then why did he summon Gillen to protect him, yet fail to warn Roberts that Bangs was on his way, crazed and intent on mayhem?

"You heard a 'thunderous roar' after you ducked behind the desk?" Ball continued.

"Yes, I did," Tommy replied.

"Yet there's no ballistic evidence to back it up. The weapon was fired facing out of the office, not into it."

Doherty was back on the ropes—Ball hit harder and faster. Why didn't he call police or an ambulance after such a horrific incident? How could he watch from across the street while his police buddies entered the apartment of the armed, injured, and angry Bangs, without warning them of the danger? These were, after all, his brothers in arms on the police force where he had been a respected and commended officer for two decades—they could easily have walked into an ambush. Wasn't he afraid that Bangs might come back? As an officer, he certainly knew how crucial it was to preserve a crime scene, especially if the shooting were simple self-defense. Why had he contaminated the evidence by covering the blood with Speedi-Dry? Why had he, Gillen, Roberts, and Troy even gone back into the garage, an active crime scene?

Or was he just so confident that Bangs would die, she insinuated, that he decided to sit back and watch things play out?—at least until he saw Joey still alive, being loaded into the ambulance, at which point he thought it prudent to call an attorney.

Doherty answered that he didn't know anything about the Speedi-Dry and that he had indeed called Troy, who told him not to speak with anyone.* The jury members' faces revealed that Ball was winning points with each blow.

Almost as an afterthought, Doherty offered that he had asked his wife or mother-in-law to call police, while he called Troy. But Ball pummeled him after this errant swing.

"You mean to say that at a moment as important as this, you can't recall whether you asked your own wife or her mother to make the call?"

Doherty was wobbly now. He tried to explain that after police arrived on the scene and he took his family to the cellar, Lieutenant Merullo phoned him to see if he was all right, but they didn't speak about the incident. Other than that, the only contact he had with police was when he greeted Sergeant Stone and then Patrolman Lanzillo with a simple hello as they surveyed the area. In fact, Doherty claimed, he didn't recognize any of the other cops walking the area. Ball pounced: Medford Police Department is a small, tightknit force where Doherty had worked for twenty years, most recently as lieutenant, and no one in the room was buying that he didn't know every single officer employed at the station.

Ball now sensed that Doherty was so tangled in the ropes that continuing to pound away might actually work against her, so she yielded the floor to the defense.

Although Troy had returned to the proceedings, McCann handled the redirect, asking Doherty first why he had called Troy instead of anyone else. Doherty claimed he knew the situation would look suspicious and reasoned it would be wise to have legal counsel. He then came clean and admitted he had in fact told Captain Murphy about the green Impala and also told him to check the trunk of Bangs' Cadillac.

---

* Doherty later came clean and admitted that Roberts covered the blood with Speedi-Dry, instinctively, without forethought or malice.

Next, McCann addressed several of the financial matters that Ball had broached. He presented Western Union receipts and other financial records, including documentation proving that Doherty had purchased the home at #50 Pleasant Street in December 1970, at a bank auction for a mere $16,000 and sold it to his realty company in 1981 for $30,000. The three-family dwelling now had a $75,000 mortgage. Doherty testified that his police income was approximately $1,300 per month.

Doherty admitted borrowing $35,000 from Bangs in 1983-84 to purchase a condo unit in Pompano Beach, Florida, from the estate of a New Hampshire woman who had recently passed away, but he claimed it was a quick sale that he and his mother concluded, without Bangs' participation.

McCann now began to attack Bangs through Doherty's testimony. Doherty asserted that Bangs had been on a cocaine binge in Vegas and had asked him to wire money on May 27 and 30, 1984. Doherty made a total of three Western Union wire transfers to Bangs: one in the amount of $9,900, sent to "Dr. Robert Taylor," and two others of $7,500 each, sent to the names of Cheryl Fisher and Artie Strahl. As Doherty told it, these payments cleared the loan for the condo. And in the end, Doherty even claimed that Bangs owed money to him. Doherty never explained why his numbers didn't add up—whether he had made other payments or even gotten Joey to write off part of the debt—but McCann moved on to what he thought would be more profitable lines of questioning.

When asked what he knew about Artie Strahl, Doherty said only that he knew Strahl had a gaming license problem with his Cape Cod-based travel agency and that Bangs had taken control of the enterprise.

Within a week of the Vegas transfers, Doherty continued, Bangs asked him to send additional funds to Atlantic City via Federal Express. Joey instructed Tommy to go into his apartment and retrieve a bundle of money wrapped in brown paper and aluminum foil and taped beneath the sink. No questions asked, Doherty placed it in a box and overnighted it to Bangs. Bangs later told him that it was $35,000.

Doherty took further digs at Bangs by claiming he had attempted to wean Joey off cocaine, but that Bangs had told him to mind his own business. Bangs also believed, Doherty testified, that Debbie O'Malley was having an affair with Doherty. Doherty brazenly added that O'Malley threatened to inform the state police of the "side work" Bangs did if he didn't pick her up at Logan Airport in August 1984. That was the only reason he gave her a ride, Doherty claimed.

Doherty admitted he traveled to Atlantic City with Bangs and was amazed at how Joey spent money with abandon, sometimes gambling $50,000 to $60,000 on one hand of cards or roll of the dice. Bangs often purchased casino chips by the rack—$10,000 a pop—and fed his superstitions by playing only black chips. In fact, one time he smashed a champagne bottle over a dealer's head because the young man made a smart remark when Joey refused to play with purple. Doherty finally added that Bangs had purchased the champagne-colored Cadillac Seville on a whim in Atlantic City, paying $25,000 in cash just after he had won $50,000.

Bangs later revealed that he had actually won $80,000 on that trip and that Doherty wasn't present. Bangs had gone for the weekend with Bucky Barrett, Artie Strahl, Jake Rooney, and Vinny D, plus some of the wives and girlfriends. They stayed at the Trump Plaza Hotel and had the time of their lives, especially after winning eighty grand.

Doherty told the court that all told he lent Joey $65,000 to $70,000, usually sent by wire transfer to "Dr. Robert Taylor"—and with the codename "Mickey Mouse," a detail that amused Judge Zobel—at favorite casinos in Las Vegas and Atlantic City. Doherty added that the wires carried fees. For example, a $9,900 transfer actually cost about $10,300, and thus Doherty insinuated that he felt it fair to recover all the fees he had paid. The point was taken, the facts submitted, and the defense yielded once again to the prosecution.

When Ball again picked up questioning Doherty, he reiterated that Joey was nothing more than a casual business associate and tenant residing in one of his many properties; nevertheless, they did all sorts of favors for each another.

Ball asked whether Doherty, as a police officer, had ever become suspicious that Bangs was doing something illegal, given that he was using various assumed names and the code word "Mickey Mouse" for the large money transfers. "Not at all," replied Doherty, feigning dismay.

"And who picked up the money?" shouted Troy. "Pluto?"

Judge Zobel warned Troy about the outburst and banged the gavel to quiet the laughter in the courtroom. Doherty explained that he had signed the Western Union slips "Mr. Doherty" instead of "Thomas Doherty," with an address of Suntaug Estates in Saugus and a phony telephone number, because in his mind, the money got where it needed to go and no one was hurt, so he had done nothing wrong.

When Ball asked if he did any other favors for Bangs, Doherty claimed he paid $20,000 to contractors who were working on Joey's home in Tewksbury. Ball was astounded and asked Doherty how anyone could believe that the men had nothing more than a casual friendship.

Ball then asked Doherty if he were involved in any gambling junkets, and Tommy denied any participation whatsoever.

Ball turned her attention to the Cadillac, asking Doherty why he had told Captain Murphy to look in the trunk, when he hadn't seen Bangs go into the trunk of the car. Doherty lied—he knew perfectly well there was a kilo in the trunk of Bangs' Cadillac, because it was the package he had requested.

At this point, Troy asked for a sidebar and explained that he wanted to call Medford police sergeant Allen Stone to testify, since Al Roberts had made a statement to Officer Lanzillo, part of which Stone had overheard.

"You're not suggesting he was half-stoned, are you?" Zobel quipped.

"Very good, Your Honor," Troy kissed up. He explained that the statement made by Roberts to Lanzillo when they returned to the garage to feed the cats would corroborate a portion of Doherty's testimony. However, Zobel pointed out that Roberts' statement could not be used because Roberts had invoked his Fifth Amendment rights and refused to testify, therefore his statement could not be cross-examined and was not admissible.

Jimmy McGaffigan's Testimony

After a scheduled lunch break, testimony resumed with Jimmy McGaffigan, the retired firefighter who had been Debbie O'Malley's former boyfriend and landlord. Even though he had known Bangs for a short time before the shooting, McGaffigan never liked him, and he didn't hesitate to lay out a negative description of Joey as a jealous and often violent bully.

McGaffigan testified that he had spoken about Bangs to six individuals whom Joey had allegedly pistol-whipped or beaten, and all of them had called Joey a menace to society. Ball objected successfully to the hearsay evidence and asked McGaffigan to identify these individuals: Butch Adair,

Jay Mitchelson, Debbie O'Malley, Jackie Gillen, Tommy Doherty, and himself. Ball asked McGaffigan if he often "spoke to himself" about Bangs' violent tendencies, whereas he had named only five individuals, plus himself. Ball moved to strike McGaffigan's testimony from the record, and Zobel again granted her request. Ball then yielded to Flak, who popped from his seat like a demonic jack-in-the-box and objected. *Overruled!*

McGaffigan detailed the brutal beating he had received from Bangs and recounted everything he knew about Bangs' interaction with the carpenter Jay Mitchelson, who had previously dated O'Malley. McGaffigan explained that the thought of someone else having sex with O'Malley infuriated Bangs to the point of violence. McGaffigan also stated that he had spoken about Bangs' personality flaws to Doherty and Roberts in the garage.

Ball objected, citing the case *The Commonwealth v. Gomez*, in an attempt to have McGaffigan's testimony stricken from the record, but the defense argued that even though the comments were hearsay, they established Bangs' reputation in the community. Zobel ultimately allowed the testimony to stand, and McGaffigan was excused, with instructions to remain close.

Then it happened: realizing they were way behind on points, the defense made a crucial decision and allowed Jackie Gillen to take the witness stand.

Jackie Gillen's Testimony

WEDNESDAY, AUGUST 21, 1985

Jackie Gillen

The following day, Jackie Gillen, then 49, took the stand to undergo direct examination by his longtime friend and attorney, Joe Flak.

Stone-faced, Gillen gave his address as #55 Pleasant Street and laid out the tedious but necessary details: he had bought the property with his wife thirteen years before the incident and lived directly across the street from his brother-in-law and co-defendant, Tommy Doherty. He was a Marine veteran who served honorably during the Korean Conflict from 1952-1956, and he had graduated from Boston Latin High School and Boston University. He was afterwards employed for fifteen years as a social worker, working for an organization called Action for Boston Community Development, located on Trenton Street, and as Director of Intake for an employment center, also located in South Boston.

Gillen testified that he had met Bangs through Doherty in January 1984, but knew him only casually. Nonetheless, he said he was very familiar with Bangs' reputation for violence. He, too, had spoken to six or seven neighbors who all expressed strong concerns about Joey's stability. Plus, Gillen testified, Doherty had told him that Bangs had made at least a dozen threats against Tommy's life in the previous months.

Gillen claimed he had seen Bangs drag Debbie O'Malley out of a cab four or five times while they were arguing. He added that on another occasion, Bangs threatened his former police partner, Bobby Spencer, after O'Malley returned from Las Vegas in August 1984. According to Gillen, Bangs and Spencer were in a heated argument about Debbie in Bangs' driveway. Bangs was shaking his hand, wagging his index finger and screaming profanities at Spencer so loudly the entire neighborhood could hear the altercation.

On another occasion, Gillen said, the battered O'Malley ran from Bangs' apartment, and a concerned motorist stopped to see if he could assist her. Bangs accosted the unidentified man, shoved him to the ground, and began kicking him savagely. At other times, Gillen claimed to have seen Bangs slap O'Malley while dragging her across the driveway by her hair. And yes, Gillen knew Bangs always carried two weapons, one usually in his back pocket.

Gillen asserted that on October 15, 1984, he saw the irate Bangs enter Doherty's garage. Gillen crossed the street to see the commotion and also entered the garage, where he saw that Tommy was trying to help Vanessa, who was struggling with Joey and fending off his slaps and punches.

Gillen added that the next day, on October 16, he received a call from Tommy, who sounded distressed and said he had a problem, or at least, thought he was going to have a problem. Doherty asked Gillen to come to the garage.

Before walking over to Doherty's, Gillen let his two German shepherds into the house from the backyard where they had been frolicking. As he exited his front door and headed toward the garage, he noted Bangs rummaging through the trunk of his Cadillac, just twenty feet away. Gillen quickstepped to the garage, looking back to see Bangs lean into the trunk for something and then slam the lid. Gillen picked up his pace as the footsteps behind him approached.

Gillen turned to face Bangs, who hollered, "And you! I'll take care of you, too, you little motherfucker!"

Flak pressed on with detailed questions, and Gillen said he saw Bangs brandish a shotgun. He dashed into the garage, followed closely by the crazed Bangs. Gillen spotted Al Roberts on the first floor working on an old car engine and told him to watch out, but didn't stop to talk, since Bangs was already at the door.

Gillen stumbled on the spiral staircase when he heard Joey's shoes hit the concrete inside the garage. He ran through the short corridor leading to Doherty's office, grabbed the doorknob, which was on the right hand side, and entered the room. When he tried to close the door, Bangs stuck the shotgun between the door and the frame and wedged it open. Gillen testified that he grabbed the weapon and pushed it away from his face and yelled at Doherty to take cover.

As Gillen struggled with the shotgun, he kicked the door and Bangs lost his grip. Bangs then reached for his .38-caliber revolver, and Gillen fired from the short end of the small stock because he felt his life was in danger. Flak asked what his state of mind was at that point.

"I was excited, nervous, and frightened, all at once." Gillen said.

Gillen explained that he had discharged only a single barrel of the double-barrel shotgun and the recoil had knocked him back three or four feet against a cot at the back of Doherty's office. Gillen heard Bangs running toward the spiral staircase and pursued him so he could warn Roberts, whom he assumed was still downstairs. Gillen cocked the hammer and fired a second blast from the office doorway at Bangs, who had just entered the top of the staircase. Bangs spun to his right with his .38-caliber weapon in hand, then spun left after being hit by the second blast.

Ball remained unusually quiet during the testimony, never objecting. She believed that if she gave the defense enough rope, they would eventually hang themselves.

Gillen said he heard Bangs stumble on the steps, and he raced down the hall to see what had happened. He saw Bangs near the bottom, lying stuck in the rails. At this point, Gillen thought it prudent to leave, so he and Doherty ran down the stairs instead of back to the office because they didn't want to be trapped in the building. Gillen related that as he ran downstairs, he saw that Bangs still had his handgun, so he swung at Joey's head with the empty shotgun.

Once outside, Gillen and Roberts ran for their lives to a yellow house across the street and entered a side entrance leading to the cellar. Gillen locked the basement with a steel bar across the door, and he and Roberts remained there for about fifteen minutes. After catching their breath, Gillen ventured outside to make his way to his own house, where he waited for another twenty minutes until Doherty came across the street to check on him. Gillen claimed he joined Doherty back at his home, where Tommy had gathered his family in the basement's den, including his wife, Carol; his daughter, Diane; and his mother, Mary. Tommy Troy showed up a short time later, and the men returned to the garage office.

Troy questioned Gillen next.

"While you were in the Marines," he asked, "did you have any familiarity with weapons? Are you familiar with a shotgun?"

"Yes. When I was in Korea, I became familiar with the use of firearms under stressful circumstances."

"No further questions at this time, your honor."

Ball rose slowly from her table to cross-examine Gillen.

"How old are you, Mr. Gillen?"

"Almost fifty," Jackie answered proudly.

"How did you and Mr. Doherty meet?"

"We're married to sisters. We met at my wedding fifteen years ago."

Ball then asked Gillen about his financial affairs, and Gillen confessed that he hadn't been employed at all in 1984. Ball fished deeper, trying to establish that Gillen was unable to work because he was under federal indictment for distribution of a controlled substance. Gillen stated that he had no children, and that his wife worked full-time to get them through this "rough patch," as he dubbed it. Ball further ascertained that Gillen didn't actually have a degree in social work, only a social worker's license, which he had earned in 1970.

Gillen explained that he knew Al Roberts because Al was living in Tommy's garage and doing odd jobs for him. Again, he remarked that he had met Bangs in January 1984 and claimed he had no idea Joey was involved in criminal activities.

Ball next returned to Gillen's rendition of the shooting. If the garage's first-floor steel door were ajar when he entered and if Bangs were following him, why did he not simply lock the door behind him so Bangs couldn't get in? She asked how far behind him Joey was, and Jackie estimated ten to fifteen seconds.

Ball produced a stopwatch, flashed it to the jury and started a countdown so everyone could feel the duration of ten seconds.

"Objection!" Flak yelled.

"On what grounds?" asked the judge. "Because it's not a Mickey Mouse watch?"

Once the laughter subsided, Ball withdrew her demonstration. She had made her point.

Ball wanted additional detail about the second-floor incident, however. Gillen stated that he backed into the office and tried to close the door behind him, but Bangs blocked it with the shotgun.

"Will you describe the shotgun?" Ball followed up.

"It was a breechloading, side-by-side, double-barrel," he replied. But that description did not match Bangs' .410 semi-automatic shotgun, which had been entered into evidence.

Gillen then claimed that he grabbed the barrel with his left hand.

"How long was this weapon?" Ball asked.

"About sixteen inches," Gillen replied—ten inches shorter than the average shotgun barrel and much too short for Gillen to have maneuvered it and wrested it from Bangs' grasp.*

When prodded about the time frame, Gillen testified that although he didn't stop to count, this all transpired within a ten- to fifteen-second period, yet seemed like a split second. Gillen also explained that his initial shot hit

---

* In the Commonwealth of Massachusetts, the minimum legal length of a shotgun barrel is in fact eighteen inches.

Bangs in the chest, and the second in the back. Ball rattled Gillen when she informed him that this was contradictory to his earlier statement, when he testified that Bangs was facing him during the second shotgun blast.

Gillen's composure began to melt as he tried to explain how Bangs was four or five feet away during the second blast, pointing a long-barrel .38-caliber handgun at him. Ball asked more about the shotgun—Gillen could only say that he had to cock the hammer before firing. He said Joey had the handgun in his left hand and reached across his body to aim at the office door, where Gillen stood.

Gillen then asserted that as he approached the fallen Bangs on the stairs, he swung at him with the shotgun to try to knock the .38 out of his hand, again contradicting his earlier testimony that he attempted to strike Bangs in the head. Flustered, Gillen offered that he probably threw the shotgun at Bangs as he jumped over his unconscious body. After all this, Gillen testified that Roberts asked to use the maroon Monte Carlo because he needed cigarettes at the store, and Gillen gave him the keys.

Ball reminded the jury that Sergeant Stone went to the office and discovered Gillen, Doherty, and Roberts seated around the desk, having coffee with Tommy Troy in the middle of the bloody crime scene.

When Ball ended her questions, Troy passed on redirect—he felt the moment was gone for this witness. He then announced that his client, Thomas Kevin Doherty, rested his case.

Pursuing Troy's lead, Flak rested Gillen's case, and Ball, who wanted the case in the jury's hands without delay, announced that the Commonwealth also rested. Zobel scheduled closing arguments for the following day, with the prosecution arguing last before jury deliberation.

Closing Arguments

As the attorneys huddled in conference before the jurors arrived for the final court session, Zobel complimented McCann.

"Mr. McCann stood in for you," he said to Troy, "the way Red Smith stood in for Charlie Deere in the 1914 World Series."

"It was a pleasure to work with you, McCann," Ball added.

"Well, I don't know if that's a compliment or not," Zobel quipped.

Nonetheless, Ball meant it sincerely, because McCann had given Doherty as fair a shot at justice as could be expected after Tommy Troy's epic blunder.

Zobel explained to the attorneys his "one-arm rule" for closing arguments: while speaking to the jury, they were to stay within an arm's length of the lectern, but they could place the lectern anywhere they liked. Ball and Troy were famous for their persuasive closing arguments, and McCann couldn't resist getting in one last jab at Ball.

"Your honor, please instruct Ms. Ball not to close by telling the jury to look at the defense table to see 'the finest talent that money can buy.'"

Ball laughed and gave her word that she would refrain from referring to the price of the talent at the defense table.

"Absolutely no personal comments," Zobel added sternly, "flattering or otherwise."

McCann thanked everyone for their kind words and asked to be excused from closing arguments for another commitment—a trip to San Francisco that he and his wife had been planning for months. Zobel graciously released him from the hearing.

⌄ ⌄ ⌄

When closing statements began, Troy took the spotlight first and pulled out his flashiest performance, contending that Bangs lived a "haphazard lifestyle of non-stop cocaine, violence, and jealousy." Flak then blasted Bangs as a "self-serving liar who became growingly violent toward his friends and strangers when it came to live-in girlfriend, Debbie O'Malley." Doherty's picking her up from the airport had set off a horrific chain of events in which Bangs ventured into Doherty's office to kill him but was disarmed and shot with his own weapon. Troy hammered home the idea that after Gillen shot Bangs in self-defense, Bangs ordered O'Malley to call the fire department instead of the police so he could arrange his story.

Assistant District Attorney Carol Ball points to the back of her shoulder, showing the jury how Bangs was hit by the second shotgun blast.

Carol Ball, of course, flipped the characterization to paint the defendants as the unstable, violent actors in the drama, who sought to eliminate Bangs for money and drugs—the shooting was nothing less than a botched assassination attempt. Ball agreed that Bangs was anything but a "proper Bostonian" and even suggested he was a bad man—"an arrogant loudmouth who beat up women." Indeed, he was "no box of chocolates," but he didn't deserve to be gunned down just because he was not a nice guy, and Doherty and Gillen had no justification for taking the law into their own hands.

When Ball concluded, Judge Zobel instructed the jury with detail.

"There is no speed record for fastest verdict," he explained, "nor does the Guinness Book of World Records contain anything on the jury that deliberated the longest time. Therefore, you deliberate for whatever length of time, short or long, it takes to decide these cases. You should decide these cases on the basis of evidence, not speculation, and the government must establish their case beyond a reasonable doubt."

Zobel also explained the difference in various charges as they related to the case. For instance, for "Assault with a Dangerous Weapon with Intent to Murder," the government had to prove beyond a reasonable doubt that the actor in each case was in fact the defendant charged and had used a dangerous weapon, a device capable of inflicting serious bodily harm or death.

In addition, there must be an assault and a threat with a specific attempt to commit murder, defined as the killing of a human being with malice or intent to kill. Otherwise, a simple "Assault by Means of a Dangerous Weapon" would be the proper finding. Even then, the government would have to prove beyond a reasonable doubt that there was a threat to do bodily harm, although not necessarily physical contact. For Doherty and Gillen, this meant that they both fired weapons in a joint venture, that Doherty shared the mental state of the other individual, and that there was actual participation in the crime as a unit.

Zobel ordered the jury to consider each indictment separately, especially since it was never claimed that Doherty actually shot Bangs. Zobel further explained that a finding of self-defense would also need to be proven beyond a reasonable doubt. Finally, Zobel warned the jury not to discuss anything about the cases with anyone outside the court or to read about it or listen to reports on television or the radio. After the courtroom proceedings concluded, the jury deliberated for three hours before retiring at 4 p.m. to spend the night at an undisclosed hotel.

During deliberations, Bangs remained in the cozy confines of the Commonwealth's protective custody, which continued to pay his enormous living expenses. Ultimately, the bill totaled nearly a quarter million dollars in less than a year. The way Bangs calculated it, if the state wanted him alive to testify, they could foot the bill, plus expenses.

▾ ▾ ▾

The jury reconvened the following morning, and to everyone's surprise, concluded a short time later, after less than one full day of deliberation. At that point, the defendants were ordered back to the courtroom: Doherty and Gillen tried to hide their anxiety, but they faced more than twenty years in prison. They fidgeted and fussed with the papers on their table, while sweating out the long minutes until the judge returned to the bench.

The jury took their seats, and the foreman handed the verdict to the court officer, who passed it on to Zobel. The judge read the document and returned it to the jury foreman, who announced the verdict:

"In the case of *The Commonwealth v. Thomas Kevin Doherty and John J. Gillen*, the defendants are hereby found guilty by a jury of their peers of all charges, including assault and battery with a deadly weapon with intent to commit murder."

Zobel revoked Doherty's $5,000 bail and had him placed in state custody until sentencing, which was scheduled for September 5. Tommy blinked slowly, hung his head, and heaved a deep sigh as he was handcuffed and led from the courtroom to the dismay of his family and friends. Gillen was already in the custody of federal marshals and was going nowhere.

Doherty was sentenced to eighteen to twenty years at the correctional institution at Cedar Junction in Walpole, Massachusetts. Flak pleaded for leniency for Gillen, but Zobel remained firm: Gillen received nine to twelve years, to be served subsequent to the prison term he was already serving in the federal penitentiary in Lewisburg, Pennsylvania, for the marijuana bust in Maine.*

Joseph Landolfi, a spokesperson for the Massachusetts Department of Corrections stated, "There are no special precautions being taken to separate Thomas Doherty from the general prison population." Doherty had never busted anyone of note anyway, so he had no real enemies in prison, with the exception of convicts who hated cops on principle.

Doherty's legal troubles continued to mount over the next few years. On the strength of testimony from Joey Bangs and Dick Madden, he was compelled to plead guilty in July 1987 to conspiracy with intent to distribute a controlled substance. The charges stemmed from Bangs and Doherty's plan to have Madden transport two kilos of cocaine from Florida to Massachusetts. Deputy U.S. Attorney Robert Mueller prosecuted the case. As far as Doherty could see, he'd never get law enforcement off his back. Later in 1987, the FBI claimed to have discovered his fingerprint on a vault alarm at the civil service offices. He neither confirmed nor denied the allegation, and the FBI never pursued additional charges—for reasons he never understood.

▾ ▾ ▾

Meanwhile, authorities in Mississippi worked apace to bring Al Roberts and Tommy Doherty to justice for the drug bust. Roberts was easily convicted on April 2, 1985, in the Hinds County Circuit Court in Jackson, Mississippi, presided over by Judge William F. Coleman. During his appeal, Roberts remained free on bail posted by Doherty, but his conviction on conspiracy charges was in time upheld. Roberts and Doherty consequently received the maximum sentence allowed by law—five years in prison and a $5,000 fine.

---

* Doherty served a total of twenty-three years for all his crimes, moving among a number of prisons, including Otisville, New York; Lewisburg, Pennsylvania; Raybrook, New York, with Howie Winters; White Deer (Allenwood), Pennsylvania, with John Houlihan; Cedar Junction; and Concord State Prison in Concord, Massachusetts. Doherty appealed the shooting verdict on October 14, 1986, two years after the botched assassination attempt on Bangs. His request for a new trial was denied and the conviction upheld. Doherty died suddenly on March 23, 2010, not long after being released from prison.

Gillen served a total of approximately fourteen years: six years (of the eight- to twelve-year sentence) for the Maine marijuana bust and eight for the shooting.

▾ ▾ ▾

On August 29, 1985, Assistant District Attorney David Burns confirmed to the media—who couldn't get enough of the rogue cops—that a Middlesex County grand jury had begun a formal investigation of the 1980 Depositors Trust bank heist.

On Wednesday, September 4, 1985, Joey Bangs—still emotionally and physically spent from the shooting trial—appeared before the grand jury and Supreme Court Associate Justice Herbert P. Wilkins. Bangs gave his mailing address as #40 Thorndike Street in Cambridge, and then, without legal counsel, Bangs remained defiant and refused to testify. For well over an hour, Burns grilled Bangs about the Depositor's Trust heist, narcotics trafficking, organized crime, larceny, loan-sharking, arson, assault and battery, home invasions, hijacking, and dozens of other crimes and misdemeanors. However, Bangs continued to invoke the Fifth Amendment until the court was once again compelled to grant him full transactional immunity. A formal grant was made on September 5, 1985, by Associate Justice Herbert P. Wilkins of the Supreme Judicial Court for Suffolk County.

As a result, Bangs was now immune from state prosecution for crimes including breaking and entering; burglary; larceny of various state, county, municipal, and private buildings and dwellings; larceny of civil service entrance and promotional examinations; extortion; loan-sharking; racketeering; forgery; violation of numerous narcotics laws, including possession and distribution of a variety of controlled substances, ten to twelve counts of trafficking marijuana, and twelve to fifteen counts of trafficking cocaine; money laundering; illegal gambling; insurance fraud; various firearms violations; arson; perjury; accessory before and after a crime; and conspiracy—every crime under the sun except for murder.

Bangs appeared before the grand jury on the thirteenth floor of the new courthouse in East Cambridge, on Wednesday, September 11, 1985. When he still refused to testify and was ordered to do so or be found in contempt, he sat motionless and silent.

On the following day, September 12, Bangs appeared again under immunity and declined to testify, much to the consternation of First Assistant District Attorney Thomas Reilly, Assistant District Attorney

David Burns, and the Chief of the Criminal Bureau for the Attorney General's Office, Frederick Riley.

On September 13, Bangs and his attorney, Ralph Champa, entered a crowded courtroom. Bangs was now in contempt. Left no alternative but a lengthy stint in Sing Sing, Bangs finally opened his mouth about the Depositors Trust heist, although he said little of value to the prosecutors during several hours of testimony.

With the ink dry on his immunity paperwork, Bangs called Clemente one final time, just to bust his balls. *Let the cards fall where they may, Jerry.*

During the grand jury hearing, the courthouse hallway swarmed with reporters, politicians, and police, everyone scavenging for tidbits about what was happening and who was going down. Bangs detailed the events surrounding the Memorial Day weekend heist of Depositors Trust Bank and laid out an overview of what had by now become known as "Examscam," the illegal sale of stolen civil service entrance and promotional examinations. Bangs testified that his MDC police captain, Jerry Clemente, had sold him an April 1979 sergeant's promotional examination for $2,500, and that in 1983 Doherty had given him an advance copy of the lieutenant's examination free of charge. Bangs then testified that he saw eight to ten various examinations in the basement of Doherty's home, one of which he understood was for Doherty's son, Michael.

Bangs went on to state that one day Doherty called Michael to the basement and asked Bangs to explain the most efficient way to cheat on the entrance exam. Bangs told Michael to read the exam four or five times and memorize as many of the basic questions as possible. Then, for the longer hypothetical situation questions, rather than waste test time trying to get them right, he should memorize the answers Bangs gave him, or write them on a piece of paper or on his hand.

Bangs concluded that even if Michael were to score a 99%, he would still likely be passed over, since disabled veterans received preferential treatment and needed to achieve only 70% to be appointed to the job before any non-veteran applicant.[*]

---

[*] I legitimately scored a ninety percent on the civil service examination but was passed over around this same time. In retrospect, if I had been offered an advance copy of the exam, I would probably have been mixed up in this shit as well.

Bangs also stated that former MDC Patrolman Freddie LeBert had received a sergeant's promotional examination courtesy of Clemente. However, LeBert was never promoted because he ran into trouble with the ATF for the illegal sale of Mac-10 machine-gun pistols and was eventually fired.

Bangs was also questioned about the botched Jackson, Mississippi, cocaine transaction involving Tommy Doherty. He testified that Doherty was going bad by this time, smoking cocaine day in and day out, and as a result, he and Roberts were later arrested for conspiracy to purchase and distribute a controlled substance.

It was about this time that the court compelled Bangs to take his first of three polygraph tests to prove he was not lying about these alleged incidents, which many observers felt were too outrageous to be true. He failed the tests conducted by the FBI when it came to the questions about homicide and conspiracy to commit homicide. Bangs reasoned that two things affected the results: (1) he had conspired to commit murder and admitted having prior knowledge of murders that took place throughout greater Boston proper; and (2) during his two combat tours in Vietnam, he had seen more than his share of battle, death, and mutilation. Joey figured the polygraph testers should thus cut him a little slack.

❤ ❤ ❤

Concerning Depositors Trust Bank, on October 7, 1985, after a four-week civil trial, a jury found the bank negligent and ordered it to pay $2.6 million in damages to 229 customers, even though the jury found no negligence on behalf of ADT Alarm Systems or the Mosler Safe Company. Thomas Smith, who represented the plaintiffs in the suit, felt that justice had been served on behalf of the individuals who had lost upwards of $100,000, as well as those who had lost $10,000 or less.*

❤ ❤ ❤

During the proceedings against Doherty, Jerry Clemente watched hopelessly from the sidelines as his world unraveled. On Thanksgiving Day, 1985,

---

* As late as August 15, 1988, Bangs was still making court appearances, when he was subpoenaed to the Law Offices of Hale and Dorr at #60 State Street, to give a deposition in Depositors Trust vs. American Telegraph Company (ADT).

Barbara Hickey testified a third time before the Middlesex County grand jury, now under a grant of immunity. Hickey admitted lying for her former lover—perjuring her previous testimony—and her confession sealed Clemente's fate, as far as state prosecutors were concerned. Clemente's defense team contended, however, that Hickey used emotional blackmail to coerce Jerry to get the long-promised divorce—or else. The Depositors Trust bank heist investigation was intensifying.

Pair convicted in
MDC officer murder

Cambridge jury gets Bangs case

2 guilty in MDC police ambush

Medford policeman sentenced to prison

Medford officer, kin found guilty of murder try

Bail revoked for suspended Lt. Doherty

THOMAS DOHERTY
Got 18- to 20-year term

Jail terms for 'botched' police shoot

In prison, Doherty was known as "The Peacemaker."

Doherty and various groups he befriended in prison.
Top: The Pagans. Center: Doherty (far right) with John Houlihan
(2nd from left). Bottom: Doherty with his crew of allies.

Officer's arrest spurs '80 bank robbery probe

1985 — NO. 155   USPS 336-980   MEDFORD, MASSACHUSETTS, THURSDAY, AUGUST 8, 1985   Tel: 321-8000   35 CENTS PER COPY

Bangs says he had bank loot
Provides link to $15M heist

Grand jury probing $15M Medford heist?

Link to $15m heist revealed in testimony

'Ambushed' sgt.: My car held loot from bank heist

Probers crack $15M Medford heist case

BYE, BYE, BOBBY: SPENCER'S DEMISE

JOEY BANGS LOVED, ADMIRED, AND RESPECTED his longtime police partner, Bobby Spencer, as if they were brothers—albeit brothers with a twisted sense of family values.

Bangs and Spencer had last spent time together one evening while Spencer was still on duty. The men picked up two stunning African-American women at a local watering hole in Dorchester and rented a room at the high-rise Howard Johnson off the southeast expressway, where they engaged in all sorts of sexual activity and stoked the cocaine pipes, filling the room with smoke that wafted under the door and throughout the corridor. Their revels came to an abrupt end, however, when the hotel's sprinkler system activated and drenched them with stale, freezing water.

As Bangs and Spencer hurriedly dressed—Bobby in his police uniform—Joey heard sirens and peeked through the curtains to discover that the parking lot was filling with Boston police cruisers and fire trucks, including one that was already extending its ladder toward their fifth-story window. Spencer peered through the peephole in the door and saw police officers pushing their way through the crowd of frantic guests who were scrambling for the elevators or angling for a view of whatever was about to happen. Spencer panicked and deadbolted the door, trying to buy another moment to figure a way out.

The Boston cops and firemen outside yelled and pounded on the door. Joey and Bobby heard the unmistakable crash of a battering ram and flashed each other a look. A second crash cracked the doorjamb, and the men darted toward the window. Bangs smashed the glass with a desk chair. Joey and Bobby thought about climbing down the ladder apparatus and leaving their half-naked and stoned companions to fend for themselves. But chivalry carried the day—they opened the door and simply walked their dates past the firemen and police who just couldn't resist a gibe: "We should have known it was you two assholes."

"Looks like a faulty alarm, right?" Bangs replied. The cops nodded, and Bangs and Spencer slipped out of the hotel with their dates and never looked back.

But the good times would soon fade for the duo when Spencer hit his own run of legal troubles.

❯ ❯ ❯

On September 5, 1985—the day after Bangs first appeared before a grand jury in the Depositors Trust investigation—Spencer, then 38, was ordered off his Boston Esplanade post when a number of paintings were discovered missing from an arts festival—Bobby had been charged with safeguarding the original artworks, worth millions of dollars. MDC Commissioner William Geary was livid when he arrived on the scene to investigate and spotted Spencer lurking about. Spencer was already under investigation by the department and never should have been charged with guarding anything valuable, but he was too slick for the brass and was never arrested for the malfeasance. Most of the stolen pieces were recovered just thirty minutes outside of Boston, with the exception of one painting worth more than ten thousand dollars, which looked magnificent hung over Joey Bangs' fireplace.

An eleven-year veteran of the MDC, Spencer was suspended with pay on September 24, 1985, pending the outcome of the investigation. But his nightmare continued when he was later summoned before a Middlesex County grand jury for questioning about his involvement with narcotics dealing. Spencer invoked his Fifth Amendment privilege and remained suspended pending completion of this second probe.

In November 1985, MDC Police Sergeant Gerry Burke turned up the heat on Spencer by filing disciplinary charges against him and submitting his findings to the U.S. attorney's office, which likewise went after Bobby with a vengeance.

The civil service commission's general counsel conducted a formal hearing on December 3, 1985, and on January 23, 1986, the grand jury returned a secret two-count indictment following its yearlong inquisition.

Although the complaints against Spencer enumerated a variety of offenses, the allegations stemmed from Bangs' testimony during the shooting trial that in February 1984 he had given Bobby the .410 sawed-off shotgun and a tan briefcase containing four one-pound bricks of Turkish hashish, which Spencer had kept stashed in the garage of his Medford home until he returned them to Bangs ten months later, just before Christmas.

During a break in the shooting trial, Bangs had his state trooper escort drive him to Spencer's home. Joey confessed to Bobby that Tommy Troy had caught him off guard with the questions about the shotgun and hash and that in order to protect his transactional immunity, he had no choice but to testify about the exchange. Bobby knew the jig was up anyway, and he unblinkingly told his pal to let it play.

Of course, both men knew these events came to light because Jerry Clemente had informed one of the Tommys—Troy or Doherty—that he was with Bangs in the Memory Lane Lounge parking lot on December 23 when Bobby returned the items to Joey. Clemente didn't actually see the objects, which were safely stowed in a briefcase and gym bag. But Bangs later told him—in a lapse of judgment—what was in them and said he needed to wipe his fingerprints from the shotgun before dumping it. Now, Bangs believed that Clemente couldn't resist the opportunity to get even with him by ratting out Spencer, a move Joey vowed to repay.

Simultaneously, federal and state authorities had initiated a joint probe into the widespread corruption in the MDC Police, including stolen entrance and promotional examinations, and Spencer was snared in that net as well. Bobby's cause suffered further when a man was murdered inside his nightclub, Club Max, an event that ultimately led to the club's demise.

In the end, Spencer was charged with illegal possession of a sawed-off shotgun, possession of hashish, and distribution of hashish (for returning the drugs to Bangs and selling to another man), along with a variety of cocaine distribution charges. Represented by attorneys Anthony M. Traini and Martin S. Leppo, Spencer pled innocent before U.S. Magistrate Lawrence P. Cohen, in U.S. District Court, and was released on a $2,000 bond.

Spencer had been under close scrutiny for narcotics distribution for many months and was allegedly arrested for distributing eight-balls of cocaine from the saddlebags of his police Harley-Davidson. He was desperate for cash to support his pricey lifestyle, faltering nightclub, and growing coke addiction.

Despite all the eyes on Spencer, Bangs believed the real trouble began when Bobby gave cocaine to a niece of MDC detective Leo Papile. Papile was a straight-laced cop with few, if any, vices, and a one-time partner with Joe McCain, whom Bangs considered a "headhunter." When Papile caught wind of Spencer's extracurricular activities, he initiated an intense departmental investigation, and on January 23, 1986, Papile and DEA agents searched Spencer's Medford home and retrieved evidence that led to an indictment within the month.

Spencer was also charged with conspiracy to possess and distribute cocaine between March 1982 and December 1983. The prosecution alleged that Spencer and Bangs possessed and distributed cocaine throughout Florida and Massachusetts during this period. Indeed, for many years, Spencer and other subordinates on the MDC Police had distributed cocaine for Bangs across the greater Boston area, making Joey a very powerful and wealthy man.

▾ ▾ ▾

After the shooting trial and Spencer's subsequent arrest, both the FBI and the district attorney informed Bangs that they wanted him to testify against his loyal partner. The indomitable Mueller told Bangs, "Spencer was not as discreet as you when dealing drugs, and he is going down, with or without your cooperation."

Robert Mueller

Bangs in turn told Mueller he'd have to proceed without his help, regardless of the consequences—the testimony about the shotgun and hashish was all they would get. He also advised the authorities that if they wanted him to continue to cooperate, they should reconsider suspending Spencer without pay until his case had concluded. Joey knew that Bobby was in a financial pinch, and he wanted to help his pal keep the paychecks coming until Bobby could figure out a new gaff. Wanting to placate Bangs—their prime witness—the DA delayed the grand jury indictment so Spencer could continue to receive income for the time being.

Because of Bangs' reluctance to give up Spencer, FBI investigators obtained special approval from the Department of Justice for an additional declaration of immunity for Bangs. "I have to look myself in the mirror every morning when I shave," Bangs told Mueller one day as they passed in the courthouse corridor, but Mueller was not moved by Bangs' loyalty.

After months of discussion, negotiation, and plea-bargaining, Bangs and Spencer were never compelled to testify against each other. Bangs only reiterated the previous statements about the shotgun and hashish, and, on March 25, just four days after resigning from the department, Spencer agreed to a plea deal for distributing narcotics. Mueller would finally be able to make an example of a high-profile cop after all.

Spencer now faced fifteen years in prison and a $250,000 fine. During sentencing on May 20, 1986, Spencer's attorney, Anthony Traini, pled with the unsympathetic U.S. District Court Judge Joseph L. Tauro to consider that Spencer was in fact addicted to cocaine but had been working to turn himself around. Tauro was less than sympathetic and ordered a six-year term in a federal penitentiary, rather than a rehabilitation facility, as previously agreed, and Spencer was led out of the courtroom in shackles by armed marshals. As the door slammed behind Bobby, Joey's empire in law enforcement—years in the making—quaked to its foundation.[*]

If one thing was certain, Joey had to attend to his own burden of legal issues, knowing that now more than ever, his life and freedom lay in the balance.

---

[*] After his release from the federal penitentiary, Spencer did administrative work for a disposal company in Medford. Bangs and Spencer remained best of friends until Bobby's untimely death in December 2007, during the writing of this book.

3 face rap $15M bank heist

suspects' bail

surety as an alternative to cash bail.

The Middlesex County district

Judge
y for

lice captain; Ker
33, of Watertown
O'Leary, 42, of T
rged
y we
dder
ed i
his a

Ex-police captain to go on trial tomorrow in bank break-in case

bail.
vious
cash

to avoid indictment.

"It's not much to suggest that the next step is flight because all else has failed," he said.

was a
nday
A fifth defenda
herty, 45, a form
lice lieutenant, i
bail because he

Opening statements
safe deposit burgla

46 The Boston Herald, Friday, September 13, 1985

Gang rifled bank vault as band played

OUTSIDE the Depositor's Trust Co. on May 26, 1980, patriotic tunes stirred the Memorial

5 nabbed in daring heist

THREE former police officers are expected to be indicted today in connection with the sensational $15-million vault heist from the Depositor's Trust Co. of Medford in 1980, The Herald has learned.

Middlesex County prosecutors yesterday presented evidence to a grand jury suggesting that a six-man gang was responsible for d.

Bank job suspects in $1.5M spending spree

16 heist trial jurors picked

SIXTEEN jurors have been selected for the trial of a former Metropolitan Police captain who is charged

le sus-
ice of-
, safe-
ucky"
been

ne 46

THE BANK ROBBERY TRIAL

ON DECEMBER 9, 1985, JUST SIX MONTHS BEFORE THE EXPIRATION of the state statute of limitations, Middlesex County district attorney Scott Harshbarger, along with FBI Special Agent in Charge James Greenleaf and state police Lt. Detective Robert Long, announced that they had indicted, arrested, and arraigned individuals responsible for the robbery of the Depositors Trust Bank over the Memorial Day weekend in 1980. The pre-dawn arrests earlier that morning had followed secret grand jury hearings that formulated the shocking indictments.*

Greenleaf—a politically smooth leader and handsome gentleman who could have passed for a movie star—ran the FBI's Boston headquarters and oversaw the investigation of the bank heist, offering his expertise to state investigators after the federal statute of limitations expired. Greenleaf never apologized for the FBI's inability to make a timely case against the thieves: he adamantly defended his agents and maintained that they never had enough proof to set forth charges. The FBI also laid the blame for the difficulty squarely on the shoulders of Jerry Clemente, who they asserted was a master at concealing witnesses and evidence, more than the other defendants. His immunity intact, Bangs watched from the sidelines as the drama unfolded.

At 6:30 a.m. that morning, MDC Police Captain Jerry Clemente received the first knock and opened his door to a barrage of flashes from the media mob flanking the state police, who presented Clemente with the indictment and took him into custody. Brother O'Leary and Kenneth "Charlie" Holmes were arrested in quick succession, but with less media hubbub at each stop.

---

* Harshbarger's complete statement is included as an appendix.

Harshbarger (left) and Greenleaf
discuss the arrest of the
bank heist suspects.

Tommy Doherty, who was already serving time at MCI–Walpole for the shooting of Bangs, was then notified as well. Although Bucky Barrett had long since disappeared, he was also formally indicted, in the event he should ever reappear. Whitey Bulger, however, had already sealed Bucky's fate, as it would be revealed years later.

At the arraignment, all four men— Clemente, Doherty, O'Leary, and Holmes—pleaded innocent to charges of breaking and entering, larceny over $100 (a felony), and conspiracy. Bail was initially set at $200,000, and nine days later, it was reduced to $100,000 or a $500,000 double surety bond. Holmes' attorney, Harry Manion, argued for additional reduction to his client's bail, given that Holmes resided in a housing project, owned no property, and had an ill wife at the time—but the court held firm.

The Depositors Trust Company had placed million-dollar liens on the criminals' properties, including Bangs', preventing them from using the homes as collateral. But as early as August, Clemente had sensed something was afoot and had withdrawn $210,000 from his credit union to protect it from seizure and provide cash for bail and attorneys. What peeved Jerry even more than potential legal trouble, however, was having to part with more than $13,000 in early withdrawal penalties.

At Bangs' request, state troopers Billy Flynn, Billy Lisano, and Jimmy Lane early on approached state police Lt. Detective George McGarrity, who was big buddies with Clemente, about helping them broker an immunity deal for Jerry, a "white hat," as they called it. Like so many others, McGarrity was oblivious of Clemente's many illegal activities and refused to believe that his pal had had anything to do with the robbery. Nevertheless, he agreed to present the state's deal to Jerry.

The offer bruised Clemente's outsize ego. Believing he was already two steps ahead of the prosecution, Jerry refused the deal without discussion. He instructed McGarrity to inform the detectives that if they had enough incriminating evidence, they wouldn't need to make a deal.

Clemente, O'Leary, and Holmes spent the next three months in a basement holding cell located in the Middlesex County Courthouse, and it was here that the vengeful trio discussed banding together and plotting their case against Bangs, always whispering to avoid notice by the guards.

Clemente hired criminal defense specialist Marty Weinberg, a partner at Oteri, Weinberg & Lawson, who had masterfully represented many high-profile clients in federal court. Weinberg had at one time defended and befriended Barrett, even going to Atlantic City with Bucky, where they cut loose and had the time of their lives.

Early on, when Clemente first ran afoul of the FBI and MDC brass, Barrett told Bangs to send Jerry to Weinberg so they could attempt to monitor his legal moves. Bangs went one step further and gave Clemente twenty thousand dollars cash in a brown paper bag to cover Weinberg's retainer.

But after Bucky's disappearance, Weinberg felt no loyalty to Bangs or the bank robbery crew—and Marty never betrayed his confidentiality with Clemente, who was blind to Bangs' machinations.

By February 18, 1986, Weinberg had worked his magic and convinced Superior Court Judge Robert A. Barton to try Clemente apart from his co-defendants. The trial was set to begin on March 3. O'Leary and Holmes took the decision in stride, hoping they could glean strategies from Clemente's trial to bolster their own cases.

Tommy Doherty was subpoenaed to testify before a grand jury concerning the burglary, but, ever resourceful, he somehow managed to secure high-priced counsel, who informed the district attorney that Doherty would invoke the Fifth Amendment unless he received full immunity. The DA's office denied the proposal, and, as expected, Doherty asserted his right to avoid self-incrimination.

❧ ❧ ❧

As the trial approached, presiding Judge Barton followed Judge Zobel's precautions and instructed state police to install a metal detector at the courtroom's entrance. Barton also dispatched extra court officers to contend with the media circus that would attend the proceedings. Bangs again had an escort of two armed state troopers assigned to him at all times, and getting into his personal space became next to impossible.

Finally, Barton laid down detailed ground rules for attorneys on both sides, hoping to curtail unnecessary lawyering and tangential proceedings.

On Thursday, March 6, the first day scheduled for testimony, tensions boiled over when, before anyone took the stand, security evacuated the first four floors of the courthouse. As it turned out, the problem was simply malfunctioning elevators. But not to be deterred, the judge wrapped up opening formalities before adjourning the shortened session.

Bank robbery trial defendants (L-R): Jerry Clemente, Kenny Holmes, and Brother O'Leary

Joey Bangs' Testimony – Day 1

FRIDAY, MARCH 7, 1986

Assistant DA Thomas Reilly took the floor, with ADA Frederick Ellis at the table taking notes and reviewing documents. Reilly wasted no time in calling Joey Bangs to the stand as the state's first witness. Bangs had become the celebrity du jour in Boston, and excitement crackled throughout the room as questioning began.

Reilly opened with queries about the Depositors Trust Bank heist and its violent aftermath, including the attempted murder of Bangs and the disappearance of Bucky Barrett. He then plunged into the history of Bangs and Clemente's relationship. Bangs explained that after becoming an MDC patrolman in 1973, he and Brother O'Leary had disposed of Clemente's Cadillac by driving the vehicle into the Boston Harbor, and he regaled the jury with tales about a variety of planned bank jobs and other gaffs, big and small.

As Reilly pounded away, Bangs also admitted to dealing more than fifty kilos of cocaine over a two-year period in 1982-1983 and, he estimated, well over twenty-five thousand pounds of marijuana, netting himself millions of dollars in profit. Bangs also admitted dealing with the infamous Miami "Barrio" during his narcotics tenure.

Joey explained that he often obtained political favors through his Uncle Nick Salerno, owner of the Villanova Lounge and longtime employee of the State House who had serious yank with the governor's office, state senator Dennis McKenna, and distinguished Speaker of the U.S. House of Representatives, Tip O'Neill. *It's not who you know*, Bangs explained, *but rather who you don't know.*

Reilly finally drilled into the Depositors Trust Bank heist. He wanted Bangs to lay out the entire weekend in detail, even though select law enforcement officials knew the whole story by this time.

Bangs testified that on Saturday, the first night of the heist, Clemente was the watch commander at MDC Police Headquarters in Boston and was relieved of duty at 11:30 p.m., when captains traditionally change shift. Bangs explained the events in detail: breaking into the bank and vault, trying to pry open the very first safe deposit box, striking the hinges in frustration with a small sledgehammer, and finally figuring out how to chisel off the faceplate. Then, they were home free.

After the first night in the bank, the men convened at Bangs' house in Tewksbury at about 7 a.m. Joey retrieved glasses, ice trays, and bottles of soda for the thirsty bandits, and they set about dividing the night's loot. The men initially agreed that Clemente would fence the bulk swag—excluding the pink and yellow diamonds—in Florida. Gold and silver would remain at Bangs' home, and Barrett would be responsible for melting and selling the bullion and coins, most of which was accomplished in Boston. The robbers finished that first morning between nine and ten o'clock.

After the others left, Bangs slept until late afternoon and then drove to Brother O'Leary's home on Trull Street in Somerville. The men cruised to the Big Dipper Doughnut Shop on the corner of McGrath Highway and Third Street in East Cambridge, where they used a payphone to call Clemente. Bangs testified that he told Clemente he couldn't sleep because of his excitement and asked the captain to meet them for dinner at Twigs restaurant in Boston's North End at 7 p.m.

After dinner, Bangs and O'Leary returned to Trull Street, and Clemente left to meet Tommy Doherty to make sure the bank breach hadn't been detected. Clemente later joined Joey and Brother back at Trull

Street and told them there had been no reports or inquiries regarding the bank at the Medford Police Station. By the time Clemente returned to Brother's home, Bucky Barrett and Kenny Holmes had arrived, and as they did the night before, the men awaited Doherty's "all-clear" phone call to begin the night's work.

After Doherty's signal, the crew high-tailed it back to Depositors Trust, this time without the heavy tools. Clemente drove Doherty's station wagon and parked the vehicle behind Brigham's Ice Cream, next to the bank. The robbers grabbed the leather duffel bags of small tools, went through the optical shop, and up the stairs into the loft, where Bangs, Barrett, and Holmes dropped back into the vault. Clemente remained on top of the vault in the loft area with the portable radio, which he used to keep in constant contact with outside man Doherty.

The only robbers to handle the radios were Bangs, Clemente, and Doherty, since they were policemen and had experience communicating with police codes and lingo. The "Number One" radio was inside the bank, and "Number Two" was outside.

The robbers looted as many safe deposit boxes as they could before daybreak, as they had the previous night, and at approximately 6 a.m., they made their way back to Brother's home. After again dividing the swag, including sixty to seventy thousand dollars in cash for each man, Bangs took the bulk gold, silver, and jewelry to his home in Tewksbury for safekeeping. Barrett and Holmes returned to their unnamed hotel.

Bangs continued with what appeared to be rehearsed testimony, stating that on the third and final night, Bucky Barrett, who was on federal parole for yet another larceny, notified his fellow bandits that he needed to return to Florida in order to establish his alibi. Barrett had obtained special permission from his parole officer to vacation with his family at Disney World and Busch Gardens. The other men were at first apprehensive about working without Barrett's expertise, but the night went off without incident.

Earlier that night, at 11 p.m., Bangs reported for work at the Upper Basin in Brighton, located on Soldiers Field Road, about fifteen to twenty minutes from the bank. After roll call, he assigned routes and duties to subordinates, before Clemente arrived around 11:40, claiming he needed Bangs' assistance with a "plumbing problem" at his girlfriend Barbara Hickey's home in Revere. Jerry's younger brother, Sergeant Bobby

Clemente, who was on patrol and unaware of the heist, offered to swap positions and cover for Bangs at the station. In the meantime, Clemente broke into the captain's office and stole a pair of portable radios for the job. This baffled Bangs, who testified that Clemente had the key and could have simply unlocked the door, yet opted to pick the lock.

Bangs explained how officers reporting for duty that evening were responsible for gassing up their own police cruisers before the third shift. Gas prices were sky high at the time, and many patrolmen helped themselves to gas for their personal vehicles. Clemente had filled his car that evening, leaving the vehicle at the pump when he went inside to find Bangs. MDC Patrolman Robert Narris, who worked the four to midnight shift, strolled into the police station a while later and asked the off-duty Clemente to move his car so that he could gas up his police cruiser.

Clemente moved his sedan, and after Bangs had finished his duties and set his alibi, the men made their way to Brother's home to await Doherty's call. At Doherty's signal, the robbers returned to Depositors Trust, where Bangs parked on a hill adjacent to Governor's Avenue, which overlooked the bank on High Street.

On this third and final night of the robbery, Bangs testified, he remained outside in full police uniform, radio in hand, while Doherty finally got his hands dirty and entered the building. Although he went inside, Doherty remained in the loft area and acted as radioman, thus compelling Clemente to work in the vault, cracking safe deposit boxes and packing loot.

The next morning, the robbers drove back to Brother's home in Bangs' Cadillac and Doherty's station wagon. O'Leary went in first, carrying the duffel bag of small tools and another with $150,000 cash he had sneaked out, before opening the rear basement door for the others. On his way through the house, however, O'Leary hid the extra cash in his upstairs master bedroom closet—he and Joey had agreed they would split it later. After everyone had entered O'Leary's basement, Bangs made his way back to the Upper Basin Station for final roll call and to be relieved of duty.

Bangs testified that he remained at the station for approximately fifteen minutes, after which he purchased rubber bands to place around the stacks of money and then stopped off at Dunkin' Donuts in Magoun Square in Somerville to purchase coffee and doughnuts for his partners.

Bangs continued his account by stating that when he returned to O'Leary's home, the men divided the money equally, as they had on days prior—except, of course, for the money Brother had stashed upstairs. In the final tally, Bangs and O'Leary received approximately $300,000 each, while their cohorts took home only $200,000 each. The police radio crackled all night with no chatter about the heist, but the following day, when the robbers heard a news broadcast calling the theft the most outrageous crime of all time, the men burst into cheers and laughter.

In the days that followed, the men did everything possible to shore up their alibis. As scheduled, Bangs worked split shifts the entire week following the robbery, Monday through Thursday, four to midnight and midnight to eight. The following weekend, Bangs took his wife, Judy, and their kids, Jody and Joey, Jr., to his aunt's summer cottage in Dennis Port, on Cape Cod.

Bangs testified that while enjoying a cocktail at the Dingy Lounge, he received an urgent call from Clemente, who was on duty, informing him that the FBI had already been to his home asking questions and trying to search the premises without a warrant, which Clemente ultimately refused. The FBI made it clear they were investigating Clemente and Doherty for the bank theft. Bangs testified that Clemente explained in detail how he confided in the FBI agents and told them he had spent eighty to ninety percent of his time over Memorial Day weekend, both on and off duty, with his girlfriend, Barbara Hickey.

Bangs explained that after receiving Clemente's urgent call, he gathered his family and belongings, packed up the family vehicle, and made his way back to Boston, where he met Jerry in the Howard Johnson parking lot located on Montvale Avenue in Woburn. Clemente asked him to get out of the car and go for a walk, because he was afraid his vehicle might have been bugged. Clemente told Bangs the reason he denied the FBI entry into his home was that he was in possession of a stolen television, still in the box.

Clemente also informed Bangs that Gus Gusmini had already tried to shake him down on behalf of La Cosa Nostra. Bangs informed Clemente he had no problem killing Gusmini, but when Jerry balked at the idea, Joey advised, "If he's attempting to extort you, take out a criminal complaint. After all, you're still a cop—more or less." In Bangs' estimation, this simple action would have also thrown off prodding law enforcement, who continued to pressure Clemente.

Rattled by the FBI's snooping, Clemente asked Bangs to come by his home on Fulton Street in Medford to pick up the swag and give it to Barrett, who was in a better position to fence the items. In Clemente's mind, Barrett had less heat on him at this point and would be able to maneuver more easily. As well, the resourceful Barrett would have several secure locations in which to stash the loot until things calmed down.

Bangs testified that during their rendezvous, the brazen Clemente also discussed a real estate investment in Pompano Beach, Florida. Clemente told Bangs how a doctor had passed away and left his condo to his children, who would sell it for a song. Bangs stated that although the venture appeared sound, he expressed concern to Clemente about spreading large sums of money so soon after the heist.

Jerry told him not to worry—he was going to title the property in his father's name. Moreover, if the feds happened to check his father's bank records and questioned whether he could afford such a condo, he'd explain that his father was brought up during the Depression, didn't trust banks, and kept all his savings stuffed in an old mattress, as did his idol, pugilist Rocky Marciano. Bangs and Clemente shared a laugh, and that afternoon around three o'clock, Bangs drove to Clemente's father's home and retrieved the duffel bag crammed with loose diamonds and precious stones. Bangs brought the bag back to his Oxford Street home in Tewksbury and telephoned Brother O'Leary before making his way over to Trull Street.

At O'Leary's home, Joey and Brother snatched a few select diamonds for their own kick, and then Bangs called Barrett to inform him of their new fencing arrangement, issuing a stern warning about what would happen if he fucked up.

Bangs explained that in the aftermath of the heist, the robbers were managing not only stolen goods but also delicate relationships. Bangs expressed to Clemente his concerns about using Barbara Hickey as an alibi and about whether she would be a reliable witness. If she were going to be a weak link, Joey warned Jerry, someone needed to take care of her. Clemente reassured Bangs not to worry: Hickey was all screwed up concerning the hours he was at her home that weekend and now actually believed he was there all along. The men found this statement somewhat amusing, and they agreed to let it play for the time being.

Bangs also recollected that Clemente later approached him just before Hickey was set to testify before a Middlesex County grand jury and asked him to kill her. When Bangs asked why, Clemente stated he feared she might come undone and tell the truth. Bangs asked Clemente whether Hickey knew anything about the robbery itself.

"Absolutely not," Clemente proclaimed.

"Then it's your problem," remarked Bangs.

Of course, it may have been the other way around. Clemente was not a violent person and most likely refused to kill Hickey when presented with the prospect by Bangs—it was likely Bangs who offered to do the honors. However, Bangs denied the accusation and asserted that Clemente did in fact ask him to burn down Hickey's house to send her a message. Bangs claimed he asked Clemente if he were crazy and flatly declined to do it. This sort of action would only bring added attention, Joey stated, and he told Jerry to put the notion out of his mind. What was done was done.

After limited discussion, they agreed that if Barbara Hickey testified against Jerry, he would explain that she was a jilted lover. Clemente had in fact promised Hickey for many years he would leave his wife, Mary—a loving and trusting spouse—and even went so far as to prepare phony separation documents to pacify Barbara, even though he had no intention of going through with the divorce.

Bangs continued to destroy whatever was left of Clemente's credibility when he testified that Jerry had informed him he had planted an illegal listening device on the gutter drainpipe of Hickey's house and had listened to her private conversations for months, through a specific radio tuned to the device. Bangs also testified that he and Clemente often listened to Hickey's telephone conversations from the parking lot of a submarine sandwich shop on the Revere Beach Parkway, in the vicinity of Suffolk Downs horse track. Using equipment Bangs had stolen from Time Warner cobbled together with materials from RadioShack, Clemente rigged the nearby payphone so it rang whenever someone called Hickey's home: Jerry only had to lift and replace the handset on the payphone to engage a transmitter that fed the phone signal to the radio in his vehicle, where he and Joey could sit comfortably and listen in crystal-clear stereo.

Bangs suggested that Clemente became so obsessed with the prospects of a conspiracy that he spent entire days sitting in his car—or even in his police cruiser, if he was on duty—listening to all of Hickey's conversations before eventually concluding she wasn't cooperating with authorities.

Moreover, at Clemente's order, Bangs and Spencer often surveilled Hickey while they were on duty. Bangs described how one weeknight, between 8 and 9 p.m., he and Spencer spotted an unfamiliar vehicle in front of Hickey's residence. After about forty minutes, a tall Caucasian man exited the home and drove off. Bangs and Spencer, who were in an unmarked police car, followed the vehicle to another residence in Revere. Bangs ran the plate number through the Registry of Motor Vehicles, which returned no listing, meaning it was most likely a government vehicle.

Massachusetts state police investigators later ascertained that the house in question belonged to the mother of Assistant Attorney General Frederick Riley. Although this remained speculation, it was a piece of information Clemente would have appreciated during his trial. In addition, Bangs was convinced at the time that the attorney general's office was the source of a major leak that caused the New England underworld much trouble throughout the years.* In fact, after learning that the man leaving Hickey's home was Riley, Bangs refused to have any discussions with the attorney general's office for a time and avoided them like the plague.

Bangs continued to pound away at Clemente with damaging testimony. He explained that just two days after being critically injured in the shooting at Doherty's garage, he received a visit from Clemente in the ICU at Lawrence Memorial Hospital. Bangs informed Clemente that his cooperation with law enforcement would remain limited to the night of the shooting—"not the day before, not the day after"—just the facts pertaining to the events of October 16, 1984. This of course came about after Clemente thoroughly questioned Bangs regarding the status of the bank job.

Bangs stated that the only reason he discussed bits and pieces of the shooting with police was that he believed he was going to die and didn't want his assailants to go unpunished.

Bangs testified that during their brief discussion in the hospital, Clemente reminded him that the five-year federal statute of limitations was

---

* In later years, it came to light that the actual source of intel was informants Whitey Bulger and Steve Flemmi, both protected by the FBI.

set to expire in just seven months, and the state statute in nineteen months. Bangs in turn informed Clemente that all he wanted was the money Doherty owed him—he would exact his revenge later. Bangs and Clemente tentatively agreed that Bangs would point the finger at the actual shooter—Gillen—and exonerate Doherty, so long as Tommy agreed to pay his debt. Being the hothead he was, Bangs surmised he would take care of business later—Doherty wasn't going anywhere, except maybe to jail. In the end, Clemente agreed to act as a conduit between Bangs and Doherty in order to help keep the peace and mend the fence between the friends-turned-bitter-enemies.

Because Doherty was so screwed up on drugs, it was difficult for Clemente to hold Tommy to his word. For instance, Doherty promised Clemente he would fake a heart attack so the shooting trial would be postponed until after May 1986, when the state statute of limitations for the bank robbery expired, but Tommy never followed through with the con. Doherty also promised repeatedly to pay Bangs the money he owed, but didn't produce all the funds. At one point, Doherty also agreed to have his mother sign a quitclaim deed to give Bangs sole ownership of the Pompano Beach condo, but once again Tommy reneged.

Assistant DA Tom Reilly next pursued a line of questioning about the stolen civil service entrance and promotional examinations. Bangs testified that Doherty said he was going to take care of his son Michael on an upcoming police entrance exam, but Bangs admitted he never saw Tommy give his boy the document. Having now testified about the events, Bangs' immunity became effective for his active participation in Examscam, thus laying the foundation for another sensational trial to follow.

Reilly turned again to the shooting, and Bangs recounted that in May 1985, only months after he was released from the hospital and shortly before the shooting trial was scheduled to commence, another pivotal exchange took place with Clemente, this time at the Embassy Lounge in Somerville. Bangs said that Brother O'Leary accompanied him to the lounge for the sit-down, given that he also had a vested interest in the outcome of the discussion.

Bangs, Clemente, and O'Leary agreed that if Doherty was found guilty, he might roll over, and thus they talked extensively about killing him. Bangs suggested that he and O'Leary begin staking out Doherty's home, but Tommy was so messed up on cocaine, he never left the garage.

Bangs detailed for the court a run-in he had at the lounge that night with a tipsy old man named Dick Vining, a close friend of Doherty's who owned Vining Disposal Company in Medford. Although not proud of his actions, Bangs reasoned it would be better to tell the court about the encounter before Clemente had the chance to do so.

Vining overheard the conversation among Bangs, O'Leary, and Clemente and began talking out of school. Even though Bangs was still recovering from this shotgun wounds, he was not in the mood for bullshit and felt he needed to straighten out the loudmouth, who was twenty years his senior. Vining continued with obscenities and verbal insults, before challenging Bangs to a fistfight. Bangs obliged and hit Vining with a single slap that sent him reeling. The lopsided altercation was quickly broken up but not before Bangs reminded Vining, "Next time, mind your own business."

After a final cocktail, Bangs, Clemente, and O'Leary left in firm agreement that Doherty had to go, but Bangs never did get a crack at him.

▼ ▼ ▼

After Bangs' initial testimony, Reilly ceded the floor to Martin Weinberg, Clemente's prestigious counselor, for cross-examination. Thus far, the trial had been uneventful and much less turbulent than the frenzied proceedings for Doherty and Gillen's attempted murder charges. In fact, when questioning Bangs, the astute Weinberg, who had learned from Troy's missteps, took a less aggressive approach. Weinberg prodded Bangs and asked if he would be inclined to commit perjury to protect himself.

Attorney Martin Weinberg, left, and Jerry Clemente listen to court proceedings.

"I will be prosecuted to the full extent of the law," Bangs answered. "In other words, whether I give information or not, I would be prosecuted for these cases rather than receive immunity myself."

Three former policemen boasted of

Ex-officer 'mastermind' of bank heist: DA

Heist 'neighbor' testifies
Medford merchant 'impressed'

Ex-officer details plan for 'big score'

Three days of easy pickings

By ERIC FEHRNSTROM

THE Depositor's Trust bery was pulled off successive ni of crooks the ba riches

police officer kept watch to make sure no one would interrupt the an estimated $1.5 million stune in jewelry

Ex-policeman suggested Medford heist, prosecutor says

Bank looted over holiday weekend

the High Street bank in the early-morning hours of May 25, the first day of a three-day holiday weekend.

The burglars slipped into the building through an optical shop

for the Middlesex County district attorney, said the men returned to the bank over the next two nights, carting away the loot.

At one point, Thomas Doherty, then a sergeant with the Med-

"Doherty, on duty and in uni-form. walked to the store and asked him what he was doing there and when he w ay ing." said Rel

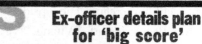

Heist witness 'kept drug biz'
Defendant wanted girlfriend silenced

The Boston Herald, Wednesday, March 12, 1986

Ex-lover links defendant to bank heist
Admits lying to protect former MDC officer

Witness in bank case testifies
he was asked to kill woman

14.

Weinberg was impressed with Bangs' studiousness, especially when he discovered that Joey had represented himself during earlier grand jury proceedings and had negotiated his own terms of transactional immunity with federal and state prosecutors. In fact, Weinberg went so far as to read a portion of the immunity papers to the court and was taken aback to see that Bangs—a "professional witness," as he referred to him—had even waived his right to counsel in doing so.

Although Bangs was compelled to rely on his own experience and criminal justice education, he was also obligated to trust the advice of the district attorney—not an easy task when faced with life in prison, three times over. In addition, Bangs explained how First Assistant U.S. Attorney Robert Mueller had continually harassed and threatened him with a minimum of "three hundred years in prison." However, this did little to faze Bangs, who knew that without his testimony, federal and state prosecutors had absolutely nothing.

Bangs did his best dog-and-pony show, given the strained circumstances. He knew that after receiving a grant of immunity, he either had to talk or sit in jail until he decided to cooperate—neither of which were motivating prospects.

During cross-examination, Weinberg went heavy on the fact that the court-savvy Bangs must have been coached in his testimony. But Bangs countered that he had picked up a thing or two while studying for bachelor's and master's degrees in criminal justice, not to mention that during a fourteen-year career as a police officer, he had made hundreds of arrests and testified in the trials that followed.

As Bangs gained momentum, Weinberg increased the pressure by commenting on Bangs' armed escort, saying, "Your protection here is being provided based on the determination by these officers that your life may be in jeopardy by reason of your cooperation with law enforcement."

However, Weinberg did not initially want to make mention of this or allude to the fact that Bangs was being considered for the Federal Witness Protection Program, because he knew it would make his non-violent defendant, Jerry Clemente, appear to be a potentially dangerous person as well—birds of a feather.

Weinberg returned to the topic he referred to as "rehearsed testimony." In fact, Bangs admitted he had had over fifty conferences with various members of the Middlesex County district attorney's office during the months prior to the trial. Seeing that he was unable to rattle Bangs, Weinberg asked him to break down the man-hours, person by person, to show how he had become a cooperative and "professional" witness.

Bangs testified that he had spent about one hundred hours with Tom Reilly, fifteen or so with Carol Ball, five to ten with ADA Max Beck, another ten with ADA Ellis, twenty-five with ADA Burns, and ten with Fred Riley. Bangs also admitted to spending between ten and twenty hours with Robert Mueller, not to mention another twenty to thirty hours with various other FBI and DEA agents and countless hours with the state police. In all, Bangs admitted to hundreds of hours fielding thousands of questions and formulating in advance his answers to those queries— nothing came as a surprise on the witness stand. Hoping to land a final solid blow, Weinberg informed the jury that Bangs had refused to be interviewed by him or anyone else from his esteemed office before the trial, insinuating that Bangs had something to hide. Joey, however, still remained unfazed.

Weinberg redirected his questioning to the kilo of cocaine discovered in the trunk of Bangs' Cadillac—and to the money that must have passed through Joey's hands. Weinberg asked Bangs how much money he made while working as an MDC police sergeant in 1983. Thirty to forty thousand dollars, Bangs answered honestly. How much had he saved from the sale of narcotics over the years? None, Joey replied, although he added that he had grossed millions of dollars from trafficking cocaine and marijuana.

Thinking he had cornered Bangs, Weinberg asked him if he expected to be prosecuted, now that he had openly admitted he owed money to the Internal Revenue Service: by filing tax returns each year under penalty of perjury and not declaring his drug income, Weinberg explained, he was now subject to arrest.

"I could be, sir, yes," Bangs shrugged, adding that he had neglected to file his taxes for several years.*

The prosecution objected to Weinberg's questions on wealth and character and the hearsay evidence against Bangs. Judge Barton then advised jurors that regardless of how Bangs answered any question, if

---

* For the record, Bangs was never pursued by the IRS for any of his drug-related income.

there was no evidence to support the question, it was as if the question were never asked at all. In addition, Judge Barton instructed the jury not to draw any inferences from any question if the answer was "no."

Weinberg then questioned Bangs about the jewelry discovered in the trunk. Again, Bangs acknowledged that all items seized by state police were subsequently returned to him, with the exception of two watches—a gold Piaget and a gold-and-diamond Rolex—which had been identified by their serial numbers as items lost in the Depositors Trust robbery.

Perplexed, Weinberg continued to grill Bangs and brought light to the fact that his Cadillac was returned to him even though a kilo of cocaine had been discovered in the trunk and seized by state investigators. Bangs explained that the Caddy was returned for two reasons: the illegal search and seizure of the vehicle in the first place, and the immunity agreement signed on November 1, 1984.

Through Weinberg's persistence, it was also ascertained that Bangs had purchased the .357 Magnum and 9mm discovered in the trunk of his Seville from local gun dealer and former MDC patrolman, Freddie LeBert, who was by this time serving a lengthy federal prison term.

Bangs also admitted to using a variety of aliases while he and various mistresses flew abroad and checked into hotels, but only to avoid detection by his probing wife, Judy, not to hide any other crimes—a confession that elicited laughs from the courtroom and garnered Bangs points for candor.

The more Weinberg attempted to discredit Bangs, the more Bangs proudly admitted to his many misdeeds. In fact, while on the witness stand, Joey confessed to every crime that Clemente, O'Leary, or Doherty had any knowledge of. For instance, when questioned about his illegal, unregistered, sawed-off .410 shotgun, Joey shrugged it off as if it were no big deal.

Clemente listened quietly and took notes as his esteemed attorney established that MDC police sergeant Joseph Bangs had committed hundreds of illegal acts, including but definitely not limited to breaking and entering, which carried a maximum prison term of twenty years. Weinberg also established that Bangs was responsible for numerous counts of assault and battery, coercion, and collections of illegal loans, which were all punishable, he said, by three years in state prison. Bangs got Weinberg's goat when he corrected the attorney and explained that the foregoing crimes were each punishable by at least *five* years in prison. It was at this point in the trial that all hope seemed to vanish for Clemente.

But Weinberg refused to take Bangs' zeal lying down, and he asserted that Bangs had committed ten to twelve separate acts of marijuana trafficking of two to ten thousand pounds, which was at the time punishable by five to fifteen years in prison. Weinberg also got Bangs to admit that he had committed twelve to fifteen acts of cocaine trafficking of two hundred grams or more, between 1982-1984. If convicted, each count would have carried a ten- to fifteen-year prison term.

However, the kicker came when Weinberg got Bangs to admit running a fabulously lucrative illicit drug trade even while in state custody in 1985. The courtroom gasped, and titters echoed through the chamber. After the distractions subsided, Judge Barton asked Bangs if he had told the district attorney or U.S. attorney that he was selling cocaine. *No*, Bangs answered. When Barton pressed and asked why not, Bangs replied simply: *They didn't ask.*

This was the first time the district attorney's office caught wind of Bangs' extracurricular activity. Nevertheless, Bangs covered both his and the DA's asses by explaining that the DA never completed a comprehensive list of his many malfeasances—just not enough time in the day. Bangs continued that if district attorney Reilly or U.S. Attorney Mueller had questioned him, he would have answered them truthfully, and he went on to explain that he only told the district and U.S. attorneys about the so-called "big ones."

Weinberg reminded Bangs about the RICO Act and how racketeering could mean twenty years in federal prison and forfeiture of any proceeds from drug trafficking, if it were not for his immunity deal. Bangs reminded Weinberg that the DEA and FBI had not yet concluded their investigation and that this is why he didn't tell them about dealing cocaine while in custody and under a grant of immunity. A lame excuse to say the least, but if Judge Barton would buy it, Bangs wouldn't refuse the protection that he won by testifying.

The frustrated judge had by now had enough of Weinberg's badgering and accusations, and he informed the attorney, "Bad acts do not necessarily establish any evidence of bad character for purpose of interrogation." Barton ordered Weinberg to move on to a different line of questioning.

After the session ended on Friday, Bangs and O'Malley holed up in a suite at the nearby Hotel Sonesta, guarded closely throughout the weekend before his testimony continued the following week.

Joey Bangs' Testimony – Day 2

MONDAY, MARCH 10, 1986

Bangs listens to proceedings.

As soon as the court session opened at 10 a.m., Weinberg resumed cross-examination by getting Bangs to admit to cocaine trafficking once again. Joey sensed, however, that Weinberg was out of his groove, so, hoping to unnerve him further, he continually asked Weinberg to speak clearly, causing Weinberg to begin stammering and repeating his questions in a desperate, low voice.

Bangs' testimony rose above and beyond any of Weinberg's expectations, and it was becoming apparent to everyone that Joey was wearing Weinberg down, as evidenced by the hopeless expression on Jerry Clemente's face. Bangs was shameless in his testimony and delivered the raw, unvarnished truth. So Weinberg decided to cut his losses and move on to a line of questioning regarding the bank robbery itself.

Weinberg asked Bangs to start from the beginning and explain how the job developed. Joey admitted that his reason for participating in the bank job was pure, unadulterated greed and that Red Delaney, owner of the Red Carpet Lounge and an uncle through marriage, had set him onto the gig by introducing him to Bucky Barrett.

Bangs testified how alibis were established for each individual, including the missing and presumed dead Bucky Barrett, who flew to Florida and back on May 25, 1980, the first night of the robbery and again on the last night, in order to check out of his hotel and round out his cover story.

Bangs added that Barrett, the only true professional, didn't want a bulky box truck parked behind the bank and opted for a station wagon. So Clemente acquired Doherty's vehicle to move the heavy equipment needed for the break-in. As he did throughout the trial, Weinberg took a different approach in an attempt to entangle Bangs in a fabrication—he asked him about his relationship with the recently convicted Tommy Doherty.

Bangs testified that the disgraced Medford police lieutenant still owed him a substantial amount of money for a condominium, including the expensive furniture within. Bangs wanted the furniture in the condo returned, but Doherty told him—through Clemente—to go buy new furniture. When asked if he was angry about Doherty's stalling the sale of the property, Bangs replied, "Stalling, no. Swindling, yes." Bangs also testified that Doherty owed him additional money for cocaine.

When asked if his significant other had any idea how he put food on the table, Bangs testified that he concealed his drug use and dealings from his wife, Judy, as well as from his one-time girlfriend, Cheryl Fisher. Bangs also explained how he concealed his cocaine use and dealings from select old-school cops and all of the state's top investigators.

Weinberg feigned ignorance when he suggested he knew cocaine was a white, powdery substance but had never seen it in rock form, and he asked Bangs to explain the process of freebasing. Bangs obliged, explaining that freebasing involves mixing pure cocaine with baking soda and water and bringing it to a boil over a direct flame, after which the cocaine transforms into an oily liquid that, when it cools, becomes a rock-hard substance that can be smoked and enjoyed with friends.

Weinberg made it clear to the court that Doherty was currently under indictment for the Travel Act, that is, traveling across state lines in the commission of a crime, namely, the Mississippi fiasco. Weinberg also brought it to the jury's attention that on August 24, 1984, Bangs had given money for the cocaine transaction for which Doherty had been convicted to Tommy's son Michael, who had it wired to Tommy by former peace officer Michael Fouchette. Weinberg also declared to the jury that Bangs had informed Clemente he was concerned Doherty may testify against him for being indirectly involved in the botched Mississippi cocaine deal, as well as the Depositors Trust Bank robbery, and would keep the money he was owed, even after attempting to kill him.

When asked if this statement was an accurate account, Bangs nonchalantly agreed, yet made it known that by the time of the Doherty shooting trial, he had not spoken to Clemente for four or five weeks. They had spoken by phone on numerous occasions in May and June until Clemente stopped answering Joey's verbally abusive calls.

"When Clemente stopped taking your telephone calls," Weinberg pressed Bangs, "did it make you angry?"

"Not angry, but rather concerned," Bangs retorted.

In fact, Bangs was extremely concerned that Clemente would do exactly what he did when he sided with the drug-addled Doherty. At the end of the day, Bangs was afraid both Tom and Jerry would turn state's evidence to save themselves, and he thought he had no option but to flip himself when Tommy Troy asked the "question heard around the world."

Troy's insistence, not Bangs' initiative, had blown the cover off the DTB robbery. Bangs figured he would beat his former friends to the punch and do what he felt he had to do, realizing he was ultimately on his own and facing multiple life terms behind bars.

Bangs stated that he also felt betrayed when his childhood friend Brother O'Leary called to threaten Cheryl Fisher just before the start of the shooting trial. Clemente had attempted a more subtle approach by inviting Cheryl out for brunch to try to manipulate her to testify against Bangs. But Bangs also believed that Clemente's motives may have included more than just business and that he actually wanted to date Fisher—by this time Jerry had a growing reputation for bedding friends' girlfriends and wives, as Joey had observed with Clemente and Freddie LeBert's wife, Maria.

At Weinberg's prodding, Bangs proudly admitted leaving numerous verbally abusive messages on Clemente's answering machine. Clemente did however pick up one of Bangs' calls, and the men had a lengthy, obscenity-filled conversation. When Weinberg insinuated that a tape of the conversation might exist, Judge Barton advised the attorney, "If there are any illegal wiretaps which would subject Mr. Clemente to further prosecution, those, at least at the moment, have not been used or offered by the defense counsel!"

Weinberg got the message and changed his line of questioning. Bangs testified that he left his final message for Jerry with Clemente's son, Barry, warning, "If you don't get in touch with your father, he'll be going to jail with me for the rest of his life." When Bangs still didn't hear from Clemente, he called Jerry's wife, Mary, and said that her beloved husband was sleeping with Freddie LeBert's wife, Maria. Of course, rather than come clean to Mary, Jerry downplayed the story and blamed it on Joey's vicious temper and vindictive nature.

Weinberg again changed tack and got Bangs to admit that while he was in state custody, he met with Clemente at Logan Airport, where Clemente brought him cocaine and money while acting as a liaison for Doherty. Bangs said he always flew into Logan Airport on one airline and took a taxi to another where he would have Clemente or O'Leary pick him up—he had to stay vigilant when traveling to Boston, he maintained, because "Your enemies will get you either coming or going."

Bangs added that Clemente brought him much less than the promised kilo of cocaine, even when accounting for three separate deliveries—twice with one hundred grams and a third time with three hundred grams, the latter meeting taking place on Somerville Avenue. Bangs testified that these attempts at mediation all happened in May and June of 1985. By this time, Clemente was deathly afraid of drugs and didn't want to be involved in any transaction whatsoever. However, whereas Doherty didn't have the funds to

Jurors tour the premises of the Depositors Trust Bank in Medford.

pay his debt to Bangs, Clemente was forced to meet with Joey and turn over product, which was as useful to Bangs as cash in those days; better, in fact, if the cocaine were pure enough that Joey could cut it and sell it for even more profit.

During the now-infamous meeting at the airport, in an attempt to screw with poor Jerry, Joey told him that a person seated at an adjacent table in the terminal lounge was in fact a state trooper who had witnessed the entire transaction.

Weinberg realized he was getting nowhere fast and again reasoned it was time to move on, since Bangs' brutal candor had left him perplexed and at a loss for further questioning. Weinberg did manage to get Bangs to admit he turned against Clemente simply for not answering his phone calls, but the exchange ended weakly, and Weinberg quickly yielded the witness to Reilly for re-direct.

▼ ▼ ▼

Bangs in court

As Reilly picked up the questioning, he wanted to address earlier accusations that Joey Bangs was a self-serving professional witness. He made it clear that from the beginning Bangs had been a reluctant witness and that the state had forced him to testify. Reilly explained that after his shooting, Bangs was compelled to discuss only the events of the evening of October 16, 1984, and this was the extent of his initial grant of immunity. Reilly also brought up the fact that the Commonwealth was under extreme time pressure to prosecute Clemente and his cohorts before the statute of limitations expired and that they needed Bangs' complete cooperation in order to do so.

When prodded by Reilly, Bangs testified that in fact he, Doherty, and Clemente had initially agreed Tommy would find a way to stall the trial until the statute of limitations expired. However, as Bangs made clear, Doherty double-crossed the men and could no longer be trusted. This is why Bangs became concerned about Clemente's not answering his telephone calls. It was plain to see that Bangs feared a triple-cross and could envision himself holding the bag if this should occur.

Concerning the substantial amount of money Doherty owed Bangs, Joey offered that he thought Clemente was just stalling his efforts to reconcile Bangs and Doherty until the statute of limitations expired. Bangs testified that this also made him suspicious. Bangs believed all along that Doherty would blow the whistle about the bank robbery, in order to work out a deal because of the Mississippi narcotics debacle.

In answer to Reilly's well-constructed queries, Bangs testified that he was in protective custody for five weeks and on his own from the latter part of November 1984 until July 1985, engaged in a serious "toot," having party after party at a rented beach house in St. Petersburg, Florida. While Gillen remained in a federal penitentiary and defendants Doherty and Roberts were out on bail, fighting for their lives, Joey was living large. Bangs testified that during his legendary exploits in Florida, he spoke to Clemente once or twice a week and occasionally met with him when he returned to Massachusetts for hearings or other pressing business.

In May 1985, Bangs testified, he told Clemente to warn Doherty to settle up or expect two things to happen: Tommy's son Michael would lose his job as a Medford police officer, and his girlfriend Nancy would be charged with welfare fraud. As much as those threats concerned Doherty, he never made good on the debt with either cash or cocaine. Bangs could no longer be trusted to keep his word, he believed, and in fact Joey still owed Tommy and the other robbers a substantial cut of the fenced bank loot.

When Reilly presented Bangs with the term "double-cross," Bangs explained how he realized Doherty and Clemente had betrayed him when he received a summons to appear in court for the shooting trial before the state statute of limitations on the bank heist had expired. Bangs added that at this point he knew it was just a matter of time before the bank case came to light, so he took the initiative when questioned.

During a court recess, Bangs—even though surrounded by a slew of state police—launched into a vulgar tirade against Clemente, punctuated by *You don't know what the fuck you're doing, Jerry!*

During Bangs' three days on the stand, Judge Barton repeatedly scolded him for his disruptive behavior. But Bangs had learned a bit from the shooting trial, and he limited his outbursts to breaks and recesses. After this most recent outburst, Reilly announced he had no further questions, hoping to avoid another confrontation that would put his star witness in contempt of court. With Bangs having the final word, Judge Barton adjourned court for the day.

Barbara Hickey's Testimony

TUESDAY, MARCH 11, 1986

Barbara Hickey

After being sworn in, Barbara Hickey indicated that she worked as a court officer—it was obvious to many that it was a gig she had won for cooperation with the present matter.

Hickey admitted to having an affair with Clemente, boldly testifying that he had asked her to commit perjury concerning his whereabouts on Memorial Day weekend, 1980. As she had done previously, on Thanksgiving Day 1985, Hickey admitted lying for one-time lover Clemente because she cared for him.

But now Barbara tore Clemente's defense to pieces, and Jerry grimaced as she pounded away on his perfidy. Following Reilly's well-crafted line of questioning, Weinberg slumped as he watched his legal options evaporate, and by the conclusion of Hickey's testimony, he decided to cut his losses and keep Clemente off the witness stand. Jerry's fate would rest in the hands of twelve strangers, who by this time felt as though they knew the defendant better than he knew himself.

❯ ❯ ❯

In Weinberg's closing statement, he made the jury aware that retired MDC police sergeant Joey Bangs was an extremely bright yet manipulative human being. In addition, Weinberg claimed that Barbara Hickey had by her own admission, "Soiled her oath before God to tell the truth."

After the prosecution's final comments, the jury deliberated from March 14 to March 18 before finding Clemente guilty on all five counts. Jury foreman Lynda Brawn, a teacher from Reading, quietly announced the decision to court clerk Jack Dunn, who read the verdict.

Judge Barton needed no additional time to prepare for sentencing. In what many people considered a political maneuver to make an example of the disgraced police captain, Barton handed Clemente a sentence of thirty to forty years in MCI–Cedar Junction state prison in Walpole for a simple burglary charge—an absurd, unprecedented sentence for a non-violent crime. Even Bangs later agreed that "Jerry got fucked," as he so eloquently put it.

Jurors examine the hole in the ceiling above the vault and the safe deposit boxes at Depositors Trust Bank.

But the fact remained that federal and state authorities desperately needed Clemente's cooperation with the ensuing Examscam case, and only the hope of gaining a reprieve from such a sentence would pressure Clemente enough to garner his cooperation. At a minimum, Clemente would do ten years in a maximum-security prison. Jerry had earlier refused immunity for the bank heist—prosecutors now had him exactly where they wanted him.

After the trial ended, statements flew fast and furious. Judge Barton called Clemente "a disgrace to every hard-working, honest, and decent police officer in the state." ADA Reilly stated, "In my career, I have never seen a more deplorable situation, and I have prosecuted murder, rape, and other crimes. But until today, I have never seen a situation where someone had perverted his sworn duty, whereas his idea of a nightshift was a license to steal. It is a shame that the maximum period to which he could be sentenced is not longer."

When questioned about Bangs, Reilly stated, "Joseph Bangs cooperated with the district attorney because his future—indeed his life—was in danger, and he can never rest easy."

In discussing the outcome of the trial, DA Scott Harshbarger expressed the opinion that "This is the most shocking case of public corruption I have ever seen, and this conviction will begin the return of integrity to law enforcement in Middlesex County." As far as Bangs' credibility was concerned, Harshbarger stated, "When you deal with conspiracy, the only way we will break a case is with some cooperation. We try to use it as rarely as possible, and it is a mistake to think Jerry Clemente is being punished, and Joey Bangs is free."

Jurors Brian A. Simpson, a Melrose salesman, and David Moloney, a Reading computer programmer, stated simply, "We considered all the evidence and tried to investigate what happened from the evidence we had presented to us."

Weinberg later declared that his client was "disappointed but disciplined." Clemente had expected the worst in any case, and for the time being, he took the verdict in stride. Weinberg took it upon himself to call state corrections officials to see that his client was housed in a segregated unit in Concord State Prison, instead of alongside the hardened criminals at MCI–Cedar Junction. Officials promptly informed Weinberg there would be no preferential treatment for the disgraced police captain.

▾ ▾ ▾

Before the onset of the trial, the DA had also offered deals to Brother O'Leary and Kenny Holmes, who now exerted every effort to secure an agreement. After pleading the Fifth Amendment during his only grand jury appearance, Brother O'Leary was indicted and subsequently arrested for the robbery. Having witnessed the outcome of Clemente's trial, O'Leary had Geoffrey Packard—his court-appointed attorney—enter a guilty plea and agree to a twelve- to fifteen-year term in state prison. O'Leary was paroled after serving approximately four years, the majority of the time at the Gardner, Massachusetts, minimum-security facility.

Kenny Holmes also changed his plea to guilty, and during his unceremonious sentencing, the school teacher of one of his four children testified on his behalf, informing Judge Barton that Holmes was a model parent who regularly attended PTA meetings. Holmes' attorney, Harry Manion, also made a strong case for leniency, but Judge Barton informed Holmes, "You have tremendous skills and brains that corporate America could use to learn about protecting banks. However, this was no piggy bank operation." And there was no mercy in court that day—Holmes received a nine- to twelve-year sentence at MCI–Cedar Junction, but served approximately three. For his part, Bangs liked and respected Kenny Holmes, and although he did not know him well, he enjoyed the few occasions they partied with cousin Bucky Barrett.

On March 27, 1986, Tommy Doherty had his day in court for the bank heist, and, as expected, he pled guilty to his role in the caper. Doherty received eighteen to twenty years in state prison to be served concurrently with his eighteen- to twenty-year sentence for the attempted murder of Joey Bangs, with no eligibility for parole for twelve years. However, this sentence did not include time he had received for the narcotics charge in Mississippi or for the upcoming Examscam trial. Although Doherty didn't receive additional prison time for the bank caper, Bangs felt justice had been served.

On December 16, 1985, fifty-three-year-old Capitol police officer Dick Madden was arrested at his Pompano Beach, Florida, condo, the final man prosecuted in connection with the Depositors Trust bank robbery. Madden waived his extradition hearing and returned to Massachusetts with a state police escort, and on December 18, he was arraigned on charges of receiving stolen property. The Depositors Trust Company filed a lien against Madden's Florida condo, but Dick's attorney, Joseph P. McParland, argued that the property was in dispute because of a pending divorce.

The charges against Madden arose from a trip Dick took in 1981, when he was going through some financial difficulties and agreed to drive a car to Florida for Clemente in order to make a few extra bucks. Madden ran a part-time transport service out of his home, and he enjoyed the solitude of the long ride, even if the hours in the car took their toll on his health. Stashed in the trunk of Clemente's car were watches from the Depositors Trust heist, which Jerry claimed that Dick—a pocket watch collector—had agreed to sell, possibly to fellow timepiece enthusiasts. But under oath Madden asserted that he had no knowledge of any such items and that Clemente's accusations were hearsay.

Already on leave from the Capitol Police, Madden spent four months in jail before he was set free after district attorney spokesperson, Thomas Samoluk, announced that exculpatory evidence had come to light as part of the ongoing investigation. On June 2, 1986, Judge Barton dismissed all criminal charges against Madden.

▾ ▾ ▾

As far as restitution was concerned, on December 9, 1985, shortly after the successful arrests of the robbery suspects, 229 customers of Depositors Trust Company filed liens with the Middlesex Superior Court on the homes and properties of the alleged robbers. When unable to reach a settlement, the plaintiffs filed a civil suit for two million dollars against the convicts on September 6, 1986, in the name of Marilyn J. Newton, of Wakefield, Massachusetts.

In a separate civil action later filed in Middlesex Superior Court, the plaintiffs also sued the Depositors Trust Bank for two million dollars, claiming the depository was negligent in failing to carry liability insurance to satisfy judgments against them. After a timely decision, Depositors Trust Company was ordered to compensate their customers. Attorney Earle Cooley and Kevin Glynn from Hale & Dorr Law Office, appealed the judgment, claiming that the bank was as much a victim of the burglars as were the depositors. Mosler Safe Company of Hamilton, Ohio, was also named in the lawsuit.

ADT, the New York-based alarm manufacturer, later hired attorney Stephen Oleskey, who, on behalf of the plaintiffs, also attempted to sue the thieves in a civil action and filed for a motion for approval of *ex parte*, a real estate attachment on the thieves' homes. However, by the time Oleskey placed the liens, many of the properties had already been sold or transferred into family trusts.

In a monumental decision announced on November 20, 1987, Middlesex Superior Court Judge James J. Nixon granted the Depositors Trust Company the right to recoup damages from the robbers in the amount of two million dollars, plus $500,000 in interest, the catch being that the bank was the sole party responsible for collecting the debt. The bank, however, never recouped a dime. Brother O'Leary transferred his Tewksbury home to his wife, Margie, just in the nick of time. Tommy

Doherty transferred all of his property into a family trust, making it virtually untouchable. Finally, Kenny Holmes had nothing to offer the bank to begin with, and they wrote him off as a loss. Bangs sold his property in Tewksbury without a hitch in 1992, assuming that the lien had already been lifted.

After all was done, the plaintiffs never recouped any funds from the bandits, and none of the loot from the heist—with the exception of three watches—was ever recovered. Two watches were discovered in Bangs' Cadillac, and the third, a Movado, was discovered at Holmes' dwelling and later identified by the owner.

Jury deliberations start in case of ex-officer accused of bank heist

15-year term for Medford bank-heist accomplice

Being witness didn't change life of crime

BOSTON — Taxpayers have spent a lot of money to prevent Joseph Bangs from becoming the victi... serv... adm... crimes himself while under police protection

Bo... gove... imm...ty from any crime he has committed -- and his criminal resume is a long one -- except for mur... lege... least...

Th... serg... Civil... has broken the law on numerous occasions since he was first immunized by the Middlesex County Dist... His... fickl...

Bangs' relationship with investigators began after John Gillen s... form... mas...

Since then, Bangs' living and relocation expenses have been paid by the D... Gen... offic...

Th... ney, has indicated through his questions that the District Attorney's office has spent about $250,000 on Bangs. That figure...

In all, Bangs has received at least $4,000 a month from various government agencies on a tax-free...

The witness also said he plans to start a new job soon.

...Cocaine to him three times in the spring of 1985 while he was in protective custody.

...and suspected that a State Police trooper saw the transaction. Bangs testified that he told Cle... he lied to Clemente. On a third occasion, Clemente gave him 100...

Bangs testified that he "gave the cocaine to a friend named Ed,...

"Did you, in fact, sell cocaine while immunized?" Bangs replied, "Uh, yes I did, your honor." He also said that investigators...

troopers about his illegal entry "right after I did it."

The witness also admitted that...ented...da-mage to a house that a state trooper rented for him in...

The now...ages and back rent in connection with the damage allegedly done to the...

...enue g to P.

...arrest of Everett.

In the course of three weeks, Farese said, damage was done to ...oom...the bathroom. There were urination stains, he added. It was consistent un... ...neth King, who is in charge of inspectors, said that neighbors ...bout the... od.

They were out being loud, screeching tires," he said. Bangs was supposed to have stayed there until the end of August, but left on...

Bangs: In hiding, still working the angles

Joe Bangs: Key cop crime witness is marked man

Bangs wanted police job for esteem, and the legitimacy it could provide

Joe Bangs: His life in fast lane fueled by drugs

Bangs got his kicks from criminal capers

Shots fired year ago today echoing still

O'Leary with the champion weightlifting team from the MCI facility at Shirley.

EXAMSCAM

JOEY BANGS SAT NAKED ON THE RICKETY COT, flipping through a ream of documents while he waited for the marshals to arrive. It was about 5:00 a.m. on January 5, 1986. Flakes from the light snowfall the night before swirled outside the poorly sealed window above the bed, and a jet of cold air whistled through the small room—no better than a glorified prison cell—in the federal courthouse. This was Joey's home for the time being, while he was providing information to authorities concerning "Examscam," as this scandal had been dubbed.

The room had an outdated radio-alarm clock and a TV/VCR combo unit that Bangs used to watch *The Verdict* on a loop, and Joey's books, magazines, and legal documents cluttered the area. He had his choice of take-out, but he was not allowed to leave except to shower in the locker room three floors below. Each morning at about this time, Joey padded shoeless through the halls, wearing only a threadbare towel around his waist and a tattered, oversized bulletproof vest flung across his bare shoulders to pacify the overprotective marshals who escorted him to the shower. Today, he'd take a little longer in the shower so he could shave and make his decision. The marshals could wait for breakfast.

Three days earlier, Bangs was offered updated immunity deals from state and federal agencies, approved by Attorney General Francis X. Bellotti, Assistant Attorney General and Chief of Criminal Bureau Frederick W. Riley, Middlesex County First Assistant District Attorney Thomas Reilly, and First Assistant U.S. Attorney Robert S. Mueller, III.* Massachusetts Governor Michael Dukakis also reviewed the documentation, dismayed at the disturbing allegations of police corruption facing not only the city of Boston but also the entire state.

In exchange for his testimony, state and federal authorities agreed not to prosecute Bangs for any previous crimes he testified to, with the exception of murder, of course. If Bangs withheld information or lied about his activities, he could still be prosecuted to the full extent of the law for any such malfeasance. The feds also offered Joey and his family the services of the Witness Protection Program, as well as living expenses—a deal they knew he'd be hard-pressed to refuse.

As he dried and dressed, Joey thought through the ramifications of cooperating—or not—playing out the consequence of each succeeding choice, testing the branches of those trees, looking for the fruit at the end of the bough. Apples and oranges—and he didn't like either. But the chill in the air made Joey think about his grandfather's garden, and the story he told about snakes in the grass and fruit on a tree of knowledge of good and evil. He'd go with the devil—he'd take the deal.

Over the next five and a half months, prosecutors put Bangs through the wringer, interrogating him repeatedly and submitting him to frequent polygraph tests as they pieced together their case. Finally, on June 19, at One Post Office Square in downtown Boston, Mueller and Special U.S. Attorney Carmen Picknally opened a federal grand jury probe into Examscam, with Joey Bangs as the star witness—now talking freely under yet another grant of transactional immunity.

As much as he wanted to believe he had a choice, there was no other way out for Bangs—if convicted of the potential charges against him, he'd go away for life and a day. On the other hand, there wasn't much Clemente or Doherty could do to him now, and he knew that the testimony he'd give was hearsay—or he could present it as such—so he personally would bring no real harm to others.

---

* The notoriety of the triad of trials involving Bangs—for the shooting, the bank robbery, and Examscam—boosted the careers of prosecutors and defense attorneys alike. For example, Middlesex County DA Thomas Reilly went on to become Massachusetts Attorney General. Mueller also benefitted from the high-profile cases: he transferred to Washington, DC, in 1989 to work as an assistant to U.S. Attorney General Dick Thornburgh. In 1998, Mueller became the Attorney General for the Northern District of California and was later appointed Director of the FBI by George W. Bush in 2001.

The dominos were set, and once Joey nudged the first—Jerry Clemente—the rest would topple with dazzling speed, revealing a criminal design beyond anyone's imagination. Bangs was primed to lay out the fabulous tale of a joke that became a half-baked idea to make some extra scratch and grew quickly into a racketeering enterprise that would speed the demise of the century-old Metropolitan District Commission police force, land more than a dozen high-profile officials in prison, and ruin the lives of scores of families.

▾ ▾ ▾

Examscam was conceived while Bangs worked on the Capitol Police in the early 1970s. He and Clemente scoured the State House to locate the stash of civil service entrance and promotional examinations, believing they could make a mint selling them to cops across the state—and earn favors in the process.

After Bangs transferred to the MDC Police, Clemente and Doherty continued the search in the State House—and later the John W. McCormack Building—finally locating the right office a few years later. They used a key given to them by Capitol police officer Dick Madden to break into the third-floor suite of the personnel administration through a side entrance, allowing them to steal hundreds of police and fire department exams. Even if they had been caught in the act, they knew all the Capitol police on duty and trusted that their colleagues would turn a blind eye.

Although they were usually reluctant to bring in additional manpower on their schemes, Bangs and Clemente knew there was one colleague who could help put this gaff over the top—their buddy, MDC Police captain Sonny Barner.

Barner resided in Norwood, Massachusetts, at the time. He was a good-looking fellow and sharp dresser, medium in build, and undoubtedly the bookworm of the three. Sonny worked at the MDC Blue Hills Station for most of his illustrious career, and as Bangs described him, he was the poster boy for the Metropolitan Police. Barner was a damn smart gentleman who graduated cum laude from Northeastern University and made perfect scores on all of his tests, including the stolen captain's promotional exam he took in 1979. A legitimate criminal justice brainiac, Barner eventually became the Acting Superintendent of the entire MDC Police.

Selling copies of the exams would make them a profit, even more if they sold the exams with answers, at a premium. Once in possession of the exams—usually no more than two or three days before the test was to be administered—Bangs, Clemente, and Barner studied them with zeal, researching hundreds of questions, and then took the tests separately at home and compared their results by phone to compile answer keys.

Of course, Bangs suspected that Clemente wasn't actually pulling his weight on this task: the best Joey could tell, Jerry kept Joey on one line and Sonny on the other, jotting down the answers they gave, agreeing with whichever seemed better. Joey decided it didn't matter—it would have just taken more time to discuss Jerry's answers as well. Besides, Clemente didn't have the native smarts Barner did, and after five years of taking the tests, including the exam for chief of police, Bangs had seen it all. No one could legitimately match his scores—there was simply too much information posed in too many different questions.

But with answers in hand, Clemente found plenty of ready buyers, given the little time they had to cram for the test. Plus, Jerry offered an iron-clad guarantee: if the applicant who bought a test was a complete idiot and scored too low, even with the answer sheet, Jerry would break into the administration office and change the grade to an above-average mark.

∨ ∨ ∨

Once the inquisition began, Joey laid out the story of April 23, 1983: Doherty passed Bangs a free copy of the lieutenant's promotional examination in a manila envelope, while the two shared pleasantries at Doherty's Pleasant Street home in the wee hours of the morning. Bangs and Doherty subsequently took the exam and passed with flying colors.

A passing score on the lieutenant's exam was seventy percent, and the average score was around eighty. For their testing group, Bangs and Doherty were two of just five police sergeants from a field of 173 who emerged with a score of ninety percent or better, and the other three had close ties to the Bangs–Clemente–Doherty triumvirate.

But Joey never let himself celebrate. From the start, he had that gnawing feeling that this gaff could go awry at any moment. As early as October 23, 1983—just six months after that late-night exchange with Doherty—Bangs became aware that a massive federal and state investigation into the sergeant's promotional exam had been launched. Four of the five candidates who made perfect scores were identified as members of the Revere Police Department. Local newspaper and television reporters swarmed the Revere station and broke the story wide open by the beginning of 1984.

Clemente was baffled. Bangs calculated that if Jerry had sold an advance copy of the exam to their mutual acquaintance, Freddie McGovern, McGovern in turn had tried to recoup his $2,500—and make a grand or two profit for himself in the process—by reselling copies to the rogue Revere cops who met him after hours in Chelsea barrooms or at the tow yard.

Selling exams had become big business as more people learned about the availability of the tests and as Clemente and crew became bolder in their marketing efforts. The secondary black market had expanded to fill demand for those who didn't have the cash to buy from the source. The vast majority of the candidates who acquired a promotional exam from Clemente—at a price of $2,500 to $3,000, depending on the strength of their friendship with Jerry—would memorize the answers and later resell the test to another potential cop candidate in an attempt to recoup a portion of their hard-earned money. Bangs, however, always refused to provide exams to married men with children; he didn't want an innocent family to go down if—or when—the cheating came to light.

And now Bangs found himself on the witness stand, laying out the entire scheme. In addition to implicating Doherty and Clemente—who then gave up the rest—Bangs testified against Doherty's son, Michael, who had taken and passed the police entrance exam on October 1, 1983, and was subsequently appointed to the Medford Police Department.

Bangs also asserted that Doherty gave his partner in the tool rental business a copy of the entrance examination, which led to another successful score. Bangs next put the finger on former MDC Patrolman Freddie LeBert, who had already been fired, tried, and convicted on unrelated weapons charges.

Even though Doherty had told Bangs about giving exams to many of his crooked cop cronies, Joey's testimony was inconclusive, since he had not actually seen Doherty give the exams to anyone, including Tommy's son, Michael, who was eventually acquitted of the original charges.

As Bangs had planned, the rest of his testimony was also deemed hearsay, and with the exception of Clemente and Doherty, no one suffered from the information Joey provided—or withheld, as the case may be. Nevertheless, the transcripts from the grand jury and federal trials were impounded by the FBI, to avoid any further embarrassment, but Joey was able to obtain carbon copies—fuck their embarrassment—before he was excused.

▾ ▾ ▾

Investigations and lawsuits choked the courts as facts and allegations came to light—some less factual than others. And investigators pulled together stories that reached back well into the 1970s, implicating among others one of the best cops on the force, Frank Thorpe.

MDC Police Sergeant Francis P. Thorpe
"Frank" or "The Crazy Indian" / Age 47 / From Malden

It all began with Frank—ironically, one of the finest cops ever to pin on the tin.

In the 1970s, Thorpe was the supervising sergeant at the Upper Basin in Brighton, where he presided over a patrol officer named David McCue, who always seemed envious of Thorpe's success in cracking cases and the respect it won him from his colleagues. After retiring from his tenure at the Upper Basin, Thorpe allegedly attempted to sell a stolen sergeant's promotional exam to McCue, who had since relocated to the police department in Wilmington, a small town just north of Boston.

Clemente had hounded his hunting buddy Frank for months to offer the test to various patrolmen, such as McCue. Thorpe finally caved to the pressure and approached McCue with the asking price of $4,000. He claimed that he had obtained the test and answers from a girl he knew who worked at the civil service department—the same story that everyone told potential test-buyers.

Unbeknownst to Thorpe, Clemente had allegedly already duped McCue by lowering his test results to make room for some of his preferred clients, who had also purchased the sergeant's promotional examination. In 1978, McCue scored 82 percent on the exam, a solid score, but not enough to receive the promotion, especially being on Clemente's shit list.

David McCue

So when Thorpe initially approached McCue with an exam for sale, McCue became suspicious. At the urging of top MDC officials, McCue taped numerous phone conversations with Thorpe, and in October 1978 he got wired up for a meeting with Frank in the parking lot at a Lawrence doughnut shop.

Petrified, McCue inched toward Frank's classic black 1956 T-Bird convertible, which idled in the corner of the empty lot. McCue reached into his coat pocket and grasped the roll of cash tightly—four thousand dollars in marked bills. McCue knew Thorpe was a serious man, a former ironworker with a sturdy frame raised on the unforgiving streets of Jamaica Plain. Frank was intensely guarded and secretive, and he never gave a clue about what he was thinking or what he'd do next.

McCue was wearing a microphone taped beneath his armpit, part of the sting operation now coordinated by the attorney general's office, which had become involved after the diffident McCue went over the head of MDC brass and reported Thorpe's overture to state officials. The AG had instructed McCue to complete the transaction and arrest the unsuspecting Thorpe. That was the rub for McCue in this moment: like his pal Joey Bangs, Thorpe always carried two guns, and they were always locked and loaded.

McCue also feared that an experienced cop like Thorpe would want to pat him down, so he kept a safe compass when Frank told him to get into the passenger side. McCue refused, staying several feet back from the car, and asked Thorpe if he had something for him.

"Yeah," Frank nodded. "Let's go for a ride."

McCue bowed out: "That's not part of the deal. Show it to me."

Thorpe knew the score—he told McCue, *See ya later,* and sped away with the exam hidden safely in an empty antifreeze container behind the backseat. The sting flopped, and because of the perspiration under McCue's arm, the microphone failed as well. The state's investigation hit a wall, for the moment.

Finally, in 1979, Thorpe was the first cop indicted for attempting to sell an exam, due in large part to the tapped phone conversations McCue made during the long-running undercover investigation he conducted for the attorney general's office.

Under a grant of immunity, Thorpe originally told a federal grand jury that trying to sell the promotional exam to McCue was a practical joke, but he later recanted his story while under cross-examination by his defense lawyer, Richard M. Egbert.* Thorpe explained that he had acted as an intermediary between McCue and Clemente, who had nagged him incessantly to help with the transaction, and had fabricated the first story merely to protect his longtime hunting pal.

"If I lied," added Thorpe, "so did the Commonwealth. I'll lie if I have to, just as I was taught by the Commonwealth. Besides, I owed it to the other cops—the guys busting their humps with me out on the streets. I gave my word, and that's golden."

Thorpe also admitted that in the mid to late 1970s Clemente had provided him with answers to the lieutenant detective's exam and that he had written answers on his shirt cuff, as did many officers who took the exams. Clemente, of course, adamantly denied providing Thorpe with answers.

After passing the lieutenant detective's examination, Thorpe was appointed to the state police, but three months later, a work-related injury forced him to return to the MDC and his original rank of sergeant. Shortly thereafter, in 1975, Thorpe was forced to retire when his injury did not heal and his chronic heart condition worsened.

As Thorpe's trial proceeded, Attorney General Bellotti's office agreed to a plea bargain promoted by a judge concerned about Thorpe's deteriorating heart condition. Thorpe received a one-year suspended sentence and a $1,000 fine for attempting to sell McCue the test and answers to the sergeant's examination—a simple misdemeanor. Upon review, federal court Judge Paul G. Garrity reduced the sentence to probation.

---

* Egbert also represented Revere Police Chief John A. DeLeire, Jr. ("Jake"), in his case.

▼ ▼ ▼

With Bangs' and Thorpe's stories bookending nearly a decade of scandal, prosecutors pushed the investigation relentlessly, and a federal grand jury churned out indictments like a fine-tuned printing press. During the next few years at least ten police departments and two fire departments were implicated in Examscam, including stations in Somerville, Medford, Revere, Malden, Plymouth, Newton, Cambridge, and Arlington. Ten high-ranking law enforcement officials—a former acting MDC police superintendent and three police chiefs among them—plus a state senate aide, soon found themselves standing tall before a federal judge.

No one escaped scrutiny, but Joey Bangs knew that hundreds of cops got away with it. A reluctant witness, Doherty remained tight-lipped, and prosecutors were unable to indict any of his corrupt colleagues. But in an election year, politically motivated authorities really just wanted to make an example of some high-profile offenders. In any case, Bangs quipped that if they had pressed the issue, half the Medford Police Department would have been terminated.

Jury selection for Examscam started on January 9, 1987, and testimony began shortly thereafter. By this time, Clemente had tasted prison life and decided to cooperate, since he had already received an unprecedented sentence for the bank robbery. He hoped for clemency at best, a reduced sentence at worst.

Clemente turned out to be the biggest blabbermouth of all. Over the next ten weeks Jerry spent eighteen grueling days in the witness box, pointing fingers at everyone he could. He testified that he collected approximately $50,000 for stolen exams over a six-year period and that he, Bangs, and Doherty had maneuvered to fill key positions with certain individuals who would later be loyal to them and protect their other illegal activities, including drug dealing, while they built their shadow empire in law enforcement.

U.S. District Judge William G. Young was selected to hear the cases of eleven individuals, ten of whom were respected police officers. The assistant U.S. attorney prosecuting Examscam was the young, eager, and aggressive A. John Pappalardo, whom Bangs referred to regularly as a first-class prick. Examscam served as a springboard for the law-enforcement and political careers of Pappalardo and many other young bucks who succeeded in winning indictments and convictions for the following high-profile offenders.

MDC Police Captain Gerald W. Clemente

"Jerry" / Age 53 / From Medford

While Jerry Clemente was serving prison time for the Depositors Trust bank heist, he came under indictment in July 1986 for allegedly masterminding Examscam along with Bangs and Doherty. Facing up to twenty years in prison and a $250,000 fine if convicted, Clemente initially pleaded innocent to the racketeering charges, but FBI special agent Jim Akers backed him into a corner. Akers locked Clemente in an office, tossed Bangs' grand jury transcript on the desk, and put the screws to Jerry. Facing a lifetime behind bars, Clemente had no choice but to cooperate—and cooperate he did.

Clemente attempted to strike a deal with federal prosecutors, led by Pappalardo and U.S. Attorney William Weld, but the best he could manage was an agreement that if he were to plead guilty, his sentence would run concurrently with his thirty- to forty-year sentence for the bank robbery, which many still considered unreasonable. In exchange for Jerry's invaluable testimony, Pappalardo also agreed to lobby for a reduction in the larceny sentence and even solicited the pension board on Clemente's behalf.

Charles E. Chase and former federal prosecutor Richard E. Bachman represented Clemente in the case and strongly advised him to admit stealing the March 3, 1979, captain's promotional examination. On October 14, 1986, Clemente became the first to plead guilty in Examscam. Clemente then blew the whistle on at least eleven colleagues, including his own brother, MDC police lieutenant Bobby Clemente.

Nevertheless, in the end Jerry got no consideration from Judge Young, who referred to Clemente in a ten-page decision as "a disgrace to all the hard-working men and women who wear a badge." Young rejected arguments for both concurrent prison terms and reduced sentences. On June 19, 1987,

Young sentenced Clemente to fifteen years in the custody of the U.S. Attorney General—three quarters of the maximum sentence allowed by law—and a $250,000 fine. On January 29, 1990, Clemente also lost his appeal to have the sentences run concurrently. Once again, Jerry got fucked.

Clemente's legal troubles continued to mount when he was brought up on conspiracy charges for attempting to conceal five Mac-10 machine gun pistols that he had purchased from Freddie LeBert. LeBert was licensed to sell firearms, but not machine guns, and illegal possession of machine guns carried a life sentence in Massachusetts. Clemente was facing an additional fifteen years in prison and a $20,000 fine if convicted of conspiracy. LeBert sold each machine gun with a case and silencer, and Bangs and Clemente often enjoyed firing the weapons from Jerry's kitchen window into the dense foliage in his backyard.

The purchase in question came to light after LeBert sold a Mac-10 to another Met cop he met while shooting the weapon at a police firing range. The cop turned in the unsuspecting LeBert to the ATF, and LeBert was discharged from the Metropolitan Police in 1983 and sentenced to five years in federal prison.

At the time, Clemente was carrying on a reckless affair with LeBert's wife, Maria. Bangs had caught Clemente "knuckling" Maria at one of his safe-house apartments in Magoun Square in Somerville. Jerry never tried to hide the tryst from Joey—who didn't like the dalliance—even though Jerry had tried to convince him it was just a "one-time fling." After LeBert entered prison, his marriage to Maria ended.

▼ ▼ ▼

During Clemente's tenure as MDC police captain, he constantly peppered Bangs with questions about who would make good prospective buyers, that is, who could be trusted to receive a stolen exam and keep his mouth shut if the scheme was discovered. Bangs would give the exam to almost anyone who could return the favor, but knowing the gig wouldn't last forever, he also made sure to avoid those he thought might not withstand the pressure of an investigation.

For his part, Doherty tossed aside his scruples and worked the scheme to his advantage. Before becoming a lieutenant, Doherty often joked that he sold exams to Medford cops who would make the easiest bosses: "I'm just a sergeant," Tommy whined, "so if I have to work for a lieutenant or captain, I want to pick my own!"

Based on Clemente's testimony, the following suspects were arrested and arraigned on a variety of crimes related to Examscam, ranging from mail fraud to perjury to conspiracy.

In the end, Clemente gave up only the following handful of names, and despite the statewide reach of the corruption, authorities were never able to amass enough evidence to convict the many other suspects.[*]

MDC Police Sergeant Frank Ray
Age 55 / From Somerville

As the dominos toppled, the next officer indicted was MDC police sergeant Frank Ray, who had worked for many years under Clemente at Revere Beach and become fast friends with Jerry. Clemente implicated Ray based on Ray's acting as an intermediary during an illegal transaction and delivering a chief's examination to Somerville Police Captain Arthur J. Pino. Ray's indictment also alleged that he had earlier provided Pino with a captain's exam from Clemente. In addition, it was alleged that Clemente altered Pino's score to reflect a higher grade that would ensure he didn't miss the cut—better safe than sorry, Clemente reasoned.

Following Clemente's lead, Ray pleaded guilty to mail fraud on October 8, 1986, and was sentenced on November 20, 1986. The government recommended three years for Ray, since he had acted merely as a go-between for Clemente and Pino, but Ray served only three months of a one-year sentence, the remainder being suspended upon his release.

Frank Ray has since passed away.

---

[*] Before he retired in 1993, Tommy Spartichino sent word to Bangs that he needed to talk. Bangs arrived at the appointment to find a solemn Spartichino, who said that he couldn't retire and go to his grave not knowing how many men he had missed in the Examscam case. Spartichino knew that the only convictions prosecutors had won were for those officers that Clemente had testified against, although Spartichino had strong suspicions about many others. In the end, Bangs refused to put the finger on any other cheating cops. Before he died, Spartichino expressed his disgust when he informed my dad and me that the Medford police force was without a doubt "the most corrupt department in the Commonwealth."

Somerville Police Chief Arthur J. Pino
"Artie" / Age 50 / From Somerville

Pino had been designated acting police chief, pending his formal appointment to the position. But he would never receive the promotion. Jerry testified that Artie was a "handyman" to whom he had given a captain's promotional exam—in exchange for new Formica in his kitchen. The personal relationship between the men came to an abrupt end when Pino was arrested and convicted in Examscam and sentenced to a four-year prison term on June 12, 1987.

Capitol Police Officer Richard Madden
"Dick" / Age 54 / From Hyde Park

Madden had wanted to leave the force, but like so many others, he reasoned that a higher rank would generate supplemental income for his family. So on October 17, 1981, he purchased a copy of the sergeant's promotional examination scheduled to be given on October 21. He subsequently scored a 92.5%.

On January 7, 1987, in U.S. District Court, Madden pleaded guilty to conspiracy to commit mail fraud. Michael Collora represented Madden, who rightly claimed he was unaware of any co-conspirators in the case. Pappalardo prosecuted the case and made no sentence recommendation for Madden, whereas the mail fraud was inadvertent because the state had no plans to mail the grades that year.

At the time of his plea, Madden had been on leave for four years due to alcoholism, and Judge Young ordered him to be held in the Middlesex Detention Center until his sentencing on February 26. Madden was facing up to five years in prison and a $250,000 fine, but after considering probation, Young sentenced Madden to twelve months, stating that "the year would do him good to sober up."

Dick Madden died of cancer in 1999.

Plymouth Police Chief Richard Nagle
"Dick" / Age 60 / From Manomet

Dick Nagle was a former MDC police detective, a cop's cop and charismatic leader who was very popular with everyone on the force and great friends with Jerry Clemente. Nagle and his longtime partner, Thomas White ("Buzzy"), another solid cop, were a likeable duo who kept spirits high and respected the tradition of the force, even continuing to wear old-fashioned soft hats long after the rest of the officers had started wearing new, contemporary styles.

Despite their long friendship, once the trial began Clemente testified that Nagle agreed to give him a Cadillac in exchange for the December 11, 1976, chief of police promotional examination. However, Jerry settled for $2,000 and a box of Cuban cigars. Clemente also testified that during the exam, he allowed Nagle to sit next to him and copy from his answer sheet.

Nagle was initially suspended without pay over the allegations, and on May 21, 1987, he took a prosecution deal, pleading guilty to mail fraud and perjury, after admitting he initially lied to a federal grand jury.

Clemente and Barner sat for this particular promotional exam only to block a potential fourth candidate from consideration. In fact, Clemente, Barner, and Nagle ranked number one, two, and three on this exam.

Because of a preexisting medical condition, the U.S. attorney's office did not recommend a prison sentence for Nagle, although he faced up to fifteen years and a half a million dollars in fines.

MDC Police Captain Nelson E. Barner
"Sonny" / Age 50 / From South Shore

A 26-year veteran and the highest-ranking member of the 600-man police force, Barner was a cum laude graduate of Northeastern University and a brilliant thinker and leader. He took all the various examinations along with Bangs and Clemente in order to compile answer keys to sell with copies of the tests.

In June 1985, MDC Police Commissioner William J. Geary named Barner successor to retiring MDC Police Superintendent Thomas E.

Keough. On September 9, Geary relieved Keough of his command and installed Barner as Acting Superintendent until Keogh's retirement paperwork became final on December 7. But before Barner's appointment became official, he was swept up in the growing investigation into Examscam, despite Geary's vouching for him.

As more information about Examscam came to light, however, Keough decided not to step down. But when he and Geary became embroiled in a bitter dispute over the sensitive issue, Geary eventually prevailed and forced Keough out of office.

During the U.S. attorney's investigation, Geary remained in constant contact with William Weld, Frank Bellotti, and Scott Harshbarger, who all considered Bangs, Clemente, Doherty, and Barner to be dangerous, renegade cops. By this time, the federal grand jury had subpoenaed personnel records of more than twenty-one current and former MDC police officers, including Keough and Barner.

Barner never received payment for his participation in Examscam, and the charges against him stemmed from his help in preparing answer sheets for the tests. On June 12, 1987, Barner was convicted of mail fraud and perjury, for having lied to a federal grand jury, and sentenced to four years in prison.

MDC Police Lieutenant Robert Clemente, Sr.
"Blackie" or "Bobby" / Age 50 / From Malden

Blackie Clemente was widely described as a good man with a son-of-a-bitch sibling, who fell victim to brother Jerry's wrath and desperation once Examscam broke. But the bad blood between the brothers ran deep—oldest son Jerry always got whatever he wanted, including the family home on Park Avenue in Medford after their father had a life-altering stroke. Jerry later mortgaged the property for $200,000 to pay his hefty legal bills and forged bank documents to withdraw more than $150,000 in cash and other assets from their father's accounts.

Bobby in turn filed a civil lawsuit against Jerry while Jerry was imprisoned for the Depositors Trust robbery. When he heard about the lawsuit, Jerry called their younger brother, Richard, and asked him to deliver a message to Bobby. If Bobby didn't back down, Jerry threatened, he would kill him, his wife, and even his attorney, Thomas Noone, as soon as he was released from prison. Bobby and Noone weren't fazed by the threat, but the next thing Bobby knew, he was under federal indictment.

According to Jerry's testimony, he provided Bobby with a sergeant's exam in April 1979 and a lieutenant's exam in 1983. Although Bobby was no mental giant, he did receive the thirteenth highest score in department history on the sergeant's exam and the second highest on the lieutenant's exam. The only officer to score higher was Dick Nazzaro, and Bangs, coincidentally, scored third.

Bobby Clemente offered the defense that his brother Jerry's allegations were simply retribution for the family lawsuit. Plus, he reasoned, if Jerry were actually doing him a favor, why didn't he offer him better answers on the sergeant's exam? But Jerry was savvy enough to know that if he gave family or friends a perfect score, it would raise suspicions and attract scrutiny. Bobby was eventually convicted and sentenced to four years in prison for his participation in Examscam.

When asked after the trial how he felt about his brother's testifying against him, Bobby exclaimed, "I have no brother! No brother of mine would do what he did to me!"

State Senate Aide Nicholas Salerno
"Uncle Nick" / Age 61 / From Dennis Port

Court Officer William M. Campbell
"Billy" / Age 45 / From Boston

When summoned before a federal grand jury in 1987, Bangs' favorite uncle, Nick Salerno, refused to testify and was subsequently charged with conspiracy to commit mail fraud for buying a copy of the October 1983 sergeant's exam from Jerry Clemente. Salerno obtained the test for Billy Campbell, his friend who worked as a court officer in the Suffolk County Court. Bangs was disappointed to hear about the allegation above all because Nick had gone behind his back—Joey, of course, would have advised Nick to stay away from the exams. For the record, Bangs denied having any knowledge of Nick's obtaining stolen civil service exams from Clemente.

At the time of his arrest, Salerno was working on Capitol Hill as the right-hand man and personal aide to the Democratic state senator from Boston, Michael LoPresti. Nick had worked previously for state senator Dennis L. McKenna (D-Somerville) and knew his way around the halls of power, but now he found himself abandoned by everyone who could have pulled some strings on his behalf.

Even with Salerno under scrutiny for unrelated crimes, Bangs claimed that Clemente and Doherty feared retribution and approached Joey about killing his uncle. After lengthy discussions, Bangs informed the men, "If he has to go, I'll do it, so it gets done right." It's unclear whether Bangs actually planned to go through with the deed or was simply placating his partners as he had done so many times in the past. Nonetheless, once the feds had put the screws to Salerno, they passed along word of Bang's supposed betrayal, and Joey and Uncle Nick have not spoken since.

On June 12, 1987, Salerno was convicted of the mail fraud and conspiracy charges. Judge Young sentenced him to five years in prison and a $10,000 fine, railing against Salerno: "You used your position of public trust for your own personal gain, and you corrupted others for your own benefit!"

Nick later admitted that he had bought from Clemente and disseminated between fifteen and twenty police and fire department entrance and promotional examinations. The recipients of these stolen exams held positions of respect and power and wielded that influence on demand for Bangs, Clemente, and Doherty.

❤ ❤ ❤

Billy Campbell was indicted along with Salerno. In November, after refusing to testify for a federal grand jury—even after being granted full immunity—Campbell found himself in the crosshairs of a stern, no-nonsense judge who sent him to a correctional institution for contempt of court.

In January 1989, after thirteen months of continued silence, Campbell again appeared before the judge, who threatened to send him back to jail for an additional eighteen months unless he cooperated with the investigation. Realizing he no longer had leverage, Campbell followed the advice of his attorney, Harry Manion, III, and testified about his and Salerno's involvement in Examscam.

Campbell recounted that in the beginning, Salerno approached and informed him that exams were available for a price, and Campbell replied that he'd keep his eyes open for potential candidates. Shortly thereafter, Campbell and a Boston municipal court officer, Steven Camerano, sold a sergeant's exam, dated October 22, 1983, to Revere patrolman Robert Nunez for $5,000. Nunez later pleaded guilty to a single count of conspiring to commit mail fraud in connection with the exam.

Campbell further explained that in an attempt to recoup his money, he resold the exam—for a tidy profit—to a female Massachusetts Bay Transit Authority (MBTA) police captain, Dolores Ford-Murphy. Ford-Murphy was the first high-ranking woman on the MBTA force and at the time the wife of Stephen J. Murphy, a former legislative aide to state senate president William Bulger, brother of infamous mobster James "Whitey" Bulger.

According to Campbell, Ford-Murphy paid him $5,000 for the sergeant's exam in 1983 and $5,500 for a lieutenant's exam in 1984. Ford-Murphy was subsequently charged with mail fraud and perjury.

Federal prosecutor Alexandra Leake made the government's case against Ford-Murphy, but when the jury had deliberated for a week without being able to reach a verdict, U.S. District Court Judge Edward F. Harrington acquitted her of all charges on February 6, 1990.

Joey's younger brother, Paul, also took the police entrance examination on October 1, 1983, achieving a perfect score thanks to the answers he had purchased from none other than Uncle Nick. Paul had initially approached Joey about the exam, but Joey knew the end was near and refused to give Paul an advance copy. Thanks primarily to Joey's later guidance and warnings, Paul Bangs was never indicted in Examscam.

Revere Police Chief John A. DeLeire, Jr.
"Jake" / Age 54 / From Melrose

Revere mayor George Colella suspended police chief DeLeire during the lengthy federal and state Examscam investigations and ensuing trial. Clemente testified that as payment for the 1979 police chief's promotional exam, DeLeire promised to find a municipal job for Jerry's girlfriend, Barbara Hickey, and to offer preferential treatment on bail bonds, if the need should arise. Clemente also alleged that DeLeire sold a copy of the lieutenant's exam to Revere police sergeant Salvatore J. Santoro for $3,000. Because it was hearsay evidence, Santoro was later acquitted of all charges.

However, Clemente also said that Revere's acting police chief, Edward Sasso, had bought an exam from him, and the grand jury subpoenaed both Sasso and Lieutenant Carmen J. Maglione. All three men were convicted, but sentencing was delayed for a week when DeLeire's attorney became ill. Federal prosecutor Robert Mueller wanted the men to go directly to jail, but Judge Young rejected Mueller's request and allowed the convicts to report to a federal facility of their choosing.

Medford Police Officer Michael J. Doherty
"Mike" / Age 25 / From Medford

Bangs contended that Tommy's son, Michael, had obtained a copy of the October 1, 1983, police entrance examination and that he himself had coached Michael on how to cheat by memorizing as many answers as possible and writing the others on his hand, cuff, or a crib sheet. With Bangs' mentoring, Michael registered a perfect score on the test. On the strength of this score, Michael obtained an appointment to the Medford Police, joining the department in September 1984.

By December 1985, a federal grand jury had begun investigating allegations that various officers in the Medford Police Department had received advance copies of civil service examinations. In May 1987, Michael Doherty was indicted on three counts: one count of conspiracy to defraud and two counts of perjury. Doherty was subsequently acquitted of these charges and remained on the Medford police force for a time.

But during his testimony, Michael had fibbed about his educational background, claiming he had earned an associate's degree from Bunker Hill Community College. Upon further investigation, another grand jury discovered the inconsistencies in his testimony.

Doherty's attorneys argued that his educational background was not material to the Examscam investigation. The government contended that Doherty's misrepresentation revealed his motive, intent, and credibility.

The grand jury subsequently returned a seven-count indictment— counts one through six charging Michael with mail fraud for using the post to falsely represent his educational background, and count seven accusing him of perjury before the first Examscam federal grand jury. Count seven was ultimately dismissed.

Medford Police Lieutenant Thomas K. Doherty
"Tommy" / Age 44 / From Medford

Doherty—who was housed in Concord State Prison at the time of the Examscam trials—was accused of supplying many officers in the Medford Police Department with stolen entrance and promotional examinations. Doherty's famed attorney, Tommy Troy—who was attempting to redeem his epic blunder in the shooting trial—mounted a fierce defense.

During a pretrial hearing on November 4, 1986, Troy summoned numerous Medford police officers to testify on Doherty's behalf and argued that the examination discovered by the state police in Doherty's Pleasant Street home was seized without a warrant and thus inadmissible as evidence.

But Medford police captain Paul Murphy testified that on the night of Bangs' shooting—at about 1:50 a.m. on October 17—he saw Doherty and Troy at the home and did in fact ask Troy if he could search the premises. Troy asked to be present, and Doherty requested that his personal belongings not be searched. Therefore, state police returned later that morning with a valid warrant for a broader search. Nevertheless, Troy argued that the revised warrant did not specify the exams and should thus be considered illegal.

The judge overruled Troy's argument when federal prosecutors asserted that the exam was in plain sight of state investigators, on a bookshelf in Doherty's garage, where the shooting had taken place.

Doherty was subsequently convicted of racketeering and ordered to pay a $35,000 fine and serve a twenty-year prison term, to run consecutive to his previous sentences—the most severe penalty for any Examscam conviction.

In his sentencing, Judge Young berated Doherty and told him, "You are the co-author of a monstrous evil here, and you and Mr. Gerald Clemente are the source of corruption virtually unparalleled in the history of the Commonwealth."

Although he could have identified scores of other cops involved in Examscam, Doherty never snitched on any of his colleagues at the Medford station, which was arguably one of the most corrupt police forces in the state at the time.

MDC Police Lieutenant Richard A. Nazzaro
"Dick" / Age 44 / From Winchester

On September 2, 1988, Clemente did some additional finger-pointing in federal court—for good measure— this time implicating longtime pal and former MDC police lieutenant Dick Nazzaro. Although Clemente and Nazzaro had once been friends, by this point in time no one was safe from Jerry's wrath. Clemente testified under direct examination for Judge John J. McNaught that he sold an advance copy of the April 1979 sergeant's promotional examination to Nazzaro for $3,000, splitting the profit with Doherty. Bangs, Doherty, and Bobby Clemente also received the test and were all subsequently promoted, along with Nazzaro.

At the time, Clemente also told Bangs he had given exams to a Malden police chief, as well as to a female Newton police sergeant. Of course,

Bangs knew his fellow thieves didn't always tell the whole truth, and in his own testimony he was careful to repeat only what needed to be said.

Bangs had always liked Nazzaro—a hard-working cop and major in the National Guard—whom he had met while working at Revere Beach. Joey almost never accepted money for his role in Examscam—he preferred the cleanness of favors to be repaid—and he knew nothing of any financial transaction with Nazzaro.

Nazzaro received a four-year sentence for participating in the scam but had his sentence postponed during his appeal to the First Circuit Court. In the end, he received a pardon from Bill Clinton upon the president's departure from office in 2001.

The Fallout

After the conclusion of the Examscam trials, a group of hard-working police officers brought a class-action suit against the state for civil rights violations, claiming that the widespread fraud perpetrated by officials had infringed on their opportunities. U.S. District Judge Robert Keeton ultimately dismissed the case on July 11, 1989, calling the grievance frivolous and imposing a $26,273 dollar fine against the attorney who had filed the suit, to deter others from doing the same—another political move to bury the sensitive matter.

The basis of the lawsuit reached all the way back to the aborted transaction between Frank Thorpe and David McCue and the original affidavit signed in 1978 by McCue. McCue roundly criticized the attorney general's handling of the case and resented that Thorpe got off without any jail time. But McCue had failed to obtain the stolen exam in question or provide the AG's office with any other substantiating evidence. Nevertheless, the class-action suit claimed that even as early as 1978 the attorney general should have known civil service exams were being compromised and should have taken appropriate action to put an end to the fraud.

In 1983, McCue scored a failing 69% on the sergeant's exam, a substantial drop from the 82% he had scored in 1978. Failing to secure a promotion, McCue contended that Clemente had tampered with his score, but he was never able to prove the allegation.

Everyone knew that Frank Thorpe was solid and honorable and would have been a tough nut to crack, no matter what the attorney general or district attorney threw at him. Thorpe had not approached McCue with the intent of selling the exam to make a profit. He didn't need supplemental income—he had his pension from the MDC, made rock-solid investments, and owned multiple properties in Malden and New Hampshire.

Thorpe had absolutely nothing to do with Bangs' or Clemente's other criminal exploits, and had he known what was going on, he would have taken matters into his own hands. The simple misfortune of making McCue's acquaintance did not in any way make The Indian a bad person.

McCue made it known that he regretted not taking the Examscam case to the FBI instead of the MDC or attorney general. Federal authorities, who subsequently charged Thorpe with conspiracy to commit mail fraud, later said they believed that if Thorpe had received a stiffer sentence at the outset, he would have flipped. A decade later, McCue called the state's investigation "a hapless comedy of errors barely worth the trouble."

❧ ❧ ❧

Indeed, authorities could have sussed out the scandal before it spread. Well before anyone even imagined Examscam, in 1979, Revere police lieutenant Edward F. Ryan filed a civil suit charging that the attorney general's office knew examinations were being compromised and yet did nothing about it. Ryan claimed he lost the Revere chief of police job because two competitors, DeLeire and Sasso, had received advance copies of the promotional exam and were thus able to achieve perfect scores. However, Clemente later lowered Sasso's score to a 91 percent so that DeLeire, to whom Jerry was partial, ultimately got the appointment. Ryan scored 83 percent. The lawsuit charged that attorney general Francis Bellotti, his assistants, and other civil service officials willfully ignored the ongoing conspiracy and thus facilitated the crime by their inaction.

▼ ▼ ▼

The fallout from Examscam mushroomed as other stories poured from new testimony and old archives, and everyone realized that Massachusetts was no stranger to civil service exam tampering.

For example, in 1978, after a "Spotlight Team" from the Boston *Globe* alleged that a firefighter's entrance exam had been sold from a Revere barroom, roughly fourteen thousand applicants were forced to retake the exam. In 1979, a personnel administration worker was convicted of selling an exam to another employee who was later acquitted of leaking a fire captain's promotional exam and upgrading the score on a firefighter's entrance exam. It thus made sense to authorities that Examscam was an inside job operating in the personnel administration department, and they focused their investigation internally. However, as had happened so many times before, the attorney general's office came up empty.*

Moreover, as early as 1979, officials launched an internal investigation at Doherty's own Medford Police Department when Lieutenant Alan R. MacIsaac noticed irregularities in test scores and took his findings before a grand jury, which was unable to return any indictments.

MacIsaac and Edgar Smith, an African-American reared in West Medford, had been fast friends until they received their scores for the 1979 captain's exam. MacIsaac scored a respectable 86%, but Smith managed a 91% and was made captain in August 1979. MacIsaac was livid and complained that "that nigger" had beaten him unfairly somehow. Smith sued MacIsaac for slander and emotional distress, and MacIsaac launched a personal investigation into the matter.

Although the incident had occurred seven years earlier, testimony in the civil case didn't begin until June 9, 1986. Smith named Jerry Clemente and Tommy Doherty as the men who told him that MacIsaac had used racial slurs and accused him of cheating.

MacIsaac later accosted Bangs in front of Bobby Spencer's home in Medford, ranting about how Doherty and Clemente had "zinged" him. MacIsaac was a well-trained, meticulous policeman, and he refused to believe that Smith could best him in a fair test. Bangs knew that MacIsaac

---

* Bangs and his cohorts got their hands on civil service and firefighter exams, but the men had no time or inclination to study for and take them, so they sold them without answers and let the buyers fend for themselves.

was right; but MacIsaac was also a pain in the ass to work with. Doherty also told Bangs that MacIsaac was too educated in police functions to trust and that Smith would be easier to maneuver. Again, for Doherty, it was all about picking his own boss, regardless of race, color, or creed. In Bangs' assessment, MacIsaac was an honest, hard-working cop, and Joey felt bad that Tom and Jerry had screwed him the way they did.

In a 1983 case, the attorney general's office also investigated allegations of cheating on a police sergeant's promotional examination after 661 officers took the statewide test and five of the top eight finishers were all from Revere. Once again, the attorney general's office stated only that the investigation did not pan out.

Finally, during the time of the grand jury investigation into Examscam, Somerville police sergeant Richard DeSimone levied accusations in a formal complaint with the Civil Service Commission that Frankie Pisani, Jr., had obtained a position as lieutenant that he, DeSimone, rightfully deserved. The matter caused quite a stir in law enforcement circles because Frankie Jr. was the son of Francis P. Pisani, the chief of police in Cambridge, whose wife was also on the Capitol Police at the time.

In his complaint, DeSimone estimated he lost between ten and twelve thousand dollars in wages over two years after being passed over for the promotion. But even though the attorney general's office knew civil service examinations were being compromised, and Middlesex County district attorney Scott Harshbarger supposedly knew the names involved in the ongoing dodge, there was little they could do about it until they had actionable evidence. Bangs, Clemente, and Doherty were just too slick.

❯ ❯ ❯

Because of this and similar allegations, the attorney general's office remained under constant scrutiny for not acting more swiftly on Examscam. After twelve years as attorney general, Bellotti, realizing what was to come, stepped down from the position in January 1986.

As a result, Bellotti's successor, James M. Shannon, defended a class action suit brought against Bellotti and the attorney general's office on December 8, 1987, seeking $150 million in damages—mainly lost wages—for more than one thousand police officers from various cities and townships. The plaintiffs contended that for more than six years, they missed fair access to promotions and raises because Bellotti and his office chose a "conscious course of deliberate indifference toward the Examscam issue." According to the complaint, Bellotti's office had refused to pursue, among other things, prosecution of Frank Thorpe's associates, including Jerry Clemente, who had violated the civil rights of scores of officers and broken numerous provisions of the federal Racketeer Influenced and Corrupt Organizations Act (RICO). As Revere police Lt. Ed Ryan had argued, the plaintiffs claimed that by refusing to take reasonable action to remedy past fraud and prevent future fraud, Bellotti and his staff had actually facilitated conspiracy and criminal activity.

Bellotti, then a partner at the prestigious law firm of Gaston, Snow, Eli & Bartlett, fired back that Examscam had been duly prosecuted by Middlesex County District Attorney Scott Harshbarger and U.S. Attorney William F. Weld—who actually had more firepower with federal law—and declared the accusations outrageous and frivolous.

On January 19, 1988, then-current attorney general James Shannon submitted a 48-page brief asking a federal court judge to dismiss the lawsuit and prevent subsequent actions against the attorney general's office accusing Bellotti and his staff of deliberately refusing to prosecute the 1978 theft and sale of civil service examinations.

Then-current Civil Service Administrator, John J. McDonough, Jr., and Personnel Administrator, David A. Haley, piped up to defend their organizations as well. Haley explained that each year 50,000 people took the state civil service exam and that loss of exams was extremely rare, given the painstaking security precautions used by the administration. In particular, he described the limited access to the production and storage of test materials and explained that there was no single master answer sheet—the reason, in fact, that Bangs, Clemente, and Barner had had to generate answer keys, rather than simply steal them.

Haley also explained that the department administered the test for police sergeants an average of twice a year, usually on a Saturday. On the Friday eight days prior to the test day, the department sent the master copy to the press to begin the print run, making sure that the courier returned the master to the administration offices the same day. By Tuesday, the copies were completed—each booklet with its own tracking number—and delivered by police escort to a vault, where they were bundled, sealed, and prepared for distribution. Early on the morning of the exam, armed couriers transported the packages to test sites. Following the exam, independent monitors collected and resealed the examination booklets, and the armed couriers returned them to Boston.

When questioned further about security measures, Deputy Personnel Administrator Eugene H. Rooney, Jr., declared, "We're not the Pentagon—but then these tests are not Pentagon papers, either."

❮ ❮ ❮

For every cop who had bought an exam, Bangs knew that many others had gotten their hands on them. Hundreds had cheated, though only a handful were arrested and prosecuted as examples and scapegoats. Everyone knew the extent of the corruption, and when Weld was elected Governor of Massachusetts, he endorsed a bill to consolidate the MDC Police, Capitol Police, and Registry Police into a single organization now know as the Massachusetts State Police.

In all, twenty-one members of law enforcement's upper echelon had been indicted in Examscam as of September 1989, but there was no way to prosecute the scores of other perpetrators. The only way to restore the public's trust and silence critics was to dismantle the old departments and reorganize the state's police efforts. This bold action would ultimately put an end to the embarrassment that Bangs, Clemente, and Doherty had inflicted on the Commonwealth and expedite the long and arduous healing process.

Flap over stolen-exam evidence

'Kingpin' details exam scam dirty work

Shooting killed

Clemente: It put ring

'Sold stolen exams only to trusted friends'

Ex-officer tells of raiding vault

Doherty got high mark on 1983 exam

killed exam scam

t put ring out of business

'Almost like playing God'

Scam boss details test revenge

AN EX-POLICEMAN yesterday revealed a vengeful scheme in which he broke into state offices "playing God" by lowering exam

informant last year, is testifying at the federal trial of Doherty, six police officers, and an ex-clerk

ed down a test completed by Carroll earlier that day, Clemente said.

and gave materials he obtained from the group to other officers.

Scam boss torpedoed test scores

he and ex-Medford Police Lt. Thomas Doherty tampered with statewide police tests, his partner boasted: "This is almost

vance copies of exams for $3,000 apiece for about a year when they decide to settle a three-year grudge against then-Somerville Lt. Robert Carroll by

As a result, Carroll scored second highest on the exam for promotion to Somerville Police captain and wasn't promoted.

When asked why he

mente by a civil service worker.

Carroll, who rose to Somerville captain in March 1981 and became chief in 1982, is expected to

THE PROGRAM

AFTER THREE GRUELING TRIALS, BANGS AND O'MALLEY—minus Debbie's two daughters, who remained with her parents—entered the federal Witness Protection Program. Marshals whisked them off to South Miami, where they holed up in an undisclosed hotel. As a condition of his protection, Joey submitted to a weeklong battery of tests and psychological evaluations, which established for the record that though he wasn't entirely insane, he had issues, or at the least, a serious chemical imbalance.

As the days wore on, Bangs grew antsy. He slipped past the marshals one morning to a payphone in the lobby and called a trusted friend in Boston. The next day, an overnight package arrived at the hotel addressed to "Dr. Robert Taylor." Joey went into the bathroom, locked the door behind him, and pulled a worn copy of *War and Peace* from the box. He sat on the john and began leafing through the pages, looking for his spot until he found the gutted-out center of the book that held a fat roll of cash and an ounce of cocaine. Joey sniffed the cash and dipped his finger into the white powder. All would be fine.

Bangs and O'Malley partied each night, and every morning the FBI psychologist struggled to determine whether Bangs would be able to last in their highly structured protection program. At last, he sat Joey and Debbie down to explain the program's regulations.

Rules? Joey thought. *Holy shit!* Although he lived with discipline in his personal activities, Bangs knew from day one that the program was not for him. But before he ditched the feds, he planned to soak them for all he could. An optional identification and new social security number would no doubt prove helpful, as well as whatever funds he could extract. But first, he had to get out of South Miami and back to the beach while he waited for the bureaucrats in Washington, D.C., to process his paperwork.

Ground down by Joey's constant complaining, the marshals eventually found Bangs and O'Malley a plush suite in the expensive Fontainebleu Hilton Hotel in North Miami and gave him a credit card, which they instructed was to be used only for food and necessities. *Fuck that*, Joey thought. He maxed out the card in two days. No worries—another day, another overnight package with a gutted-out novel.

Coincidentally, Bangs happened to be in North Miami on April 11, 1986, during a bank robbery gone horribly wrong. Two FBI agents, Ben Grogan and Jerry Dove, were killed and five other agents injured in a shootout with two perpetrators, William Russell Matix and Michael Lee Platt, who died in a hail of bullets. The event was another embarrassing blunder for the bureau, and for a week, Bangs was lost in the shuffle as all available law enforcement resources focused on the investigation into the bank shootout. Joey was bored to tears, and he reasoned that if the feds could ignore him, he'd ignore their rules—so he flew a few friends in from Boston for the week, and they partied hard.

Once his friends left, Bangs spent two more "quiet" weeks in North Miami before he was brought to the marshals' office in the downtown district. Once there, Joey and Debbie were stripped of all identification and loaded on a private airplane for a flight to Charleston, South Carolina, where they waited for an additional week. They were then shuttled back to the airport without notice or explanation and handed over to another marshal, who loaded them onto a private plane that departed for an unknown destination.

Of all the god-forsaken places they could send me, Joey mused when he stepped out of the aircraft and saw signs for Detroit. He had requested a temperate climate—now he was furious. And how the fuck was a guy like Bangs supposed to stay out of trouble in a shit-hole like Detroit? Yet another marshal met them on the tarmac, packed them and their bags into a small sedan, and headed toward the city without speaking a word.

The marshals knew nothing about the details of the case or of Bangs and O'Malley's identity and history. Joey soon learned, to his dismay, that he was slated to remain in Detroit, with the lead marshal—the uptight asshole in the front seat wearing cheap cologne—as his contact for the foreseeable future.

Instead of driving to Detroit, however, the marshal took them to Southfield, a suburban area about twenty minutes from downtown, and warned Joey not to set foot in the crime-ridden city itself. The marshal checked Bangs and O'Malley into a mediocre, extended-stay hotel, got them a bite to eat, and took them back to the airport for a flight to Indianapolis, where they were debriefed and assigned new identities.

These guys have to be the stupidest motherfuckers on the planet, Joey thought as he sat in a small conference room, listening to all the dos and don'ts the agents recited about his new life. The marshals were courteous, professional and book smart, of course, but in Joey's opinion, they lacked the common sense and street smarts needed to survive a week in the world he knew.

They handed Bangs new identification papers and a new credit card. Again, it was to be used only for food and necessities—Joey chuckled. His spending limit was $500 a week—he exploded in protest. His contact marshal explained that he'd need to make adjustments to his lifestyle in order to make the money last. *Fuck that bullshit,* he thought.

Upon returning to Southfield that night, the marshal dropped Joey and Debbie off at their hotel. The couple walked across the street to a mall lounge to loosen up with a few cocktails and ended up maxing out the card that very night—$2,000 in food and drink they shared with all the new friends they made at the lounge.

Bangs chatted up a friendly bartender named Denise, who joined the couple for a drink after her shift. Joey asked if she knew where they could find a "little shit" (cocaine), and after a quick phone call, they were soon joined by Denise's boyfriend, Danny, who brought along a hefty package of chirping powder. Bangs had once again found his tribe.

When the contact marshal learned that Bangs had exceeded his spending limit, he confiscated the credit card and proceeded to tear Joey a new asshole. Joey would now have to make do with less. And besides, he was informed he'd be allowed only $2,500 to purchase a car. Once again, Bangs pissed and moaned. But tomorrow was another day, and the mail would bring another novel in an overnight package.

After receiving the promised $2,500—for transportation only, the marshal reminded him—Joey made a half-assed attempt to find a clunker, then decided *Fuck it!*, and asked another friend in Boston to send twenty-five grand to the box he had rented at Mail Boxes Etc.

Bangs searched greater Detroit for a champagne-colored Cadillac Seville before settling on a like-new chocolate brown Sedan DeVille. The marshal hounded Joey about the car—*Where did he find it? Whose was it? How did he get it? Where's the registration?* and so on and so forth—and Joey refused to say anything other than he worked a hell of a deal. There was little the marshal could do, but he did harass Joey for weeks to produce a sales receipt, which, of course, Bangs claimed to have lost.

With a new name, social security number, driver's license, and vehicle, Bangs was set to make metropolitan Detroit his new playground. The barmaid and boyfriend introduced Joey and Debbie all over town, and Bangs soon found himself face-to-face with the local riffraff. A player like Bangs can always spot another hustler, and now that he had cash, newfound friends were plentiful.

After Bangs purchased a pricey speedboat at an annual Fourth of July boat show, he and O'Malley received an invitation to an exclusive party at a posh rooftop nightclub in downtown Detroit's Greek Town. Free-flowing booze, fast-acting drugs, and tight bodies prowling the crowd—this was as close to home as Joey was likely to find in Michigan.

Then the crash of a beer bottle and a chorus of shrieks pierced the music. Joey spun to see a tough sort draw an automatic weapon and scan the room for his attacker, beer suds and blood streaming from the gash on his crown. In an instant, nearly everyone else in the room whipped out a weapon from under a coat or vest. Bangs realized he was in the Wild West and wouldn't last long with this kind of temptation to violence. He dropped a handful of cash on the waitress's tray and skirted through the crowd with Debbie in tow. Bangs later learned that eighteen people were murdered in Detroit over that holiday weekend.

Nonetheless, to the dismay of his marshals, Bangs couldn't resist making frequent trips downtown, and he soon made friends with a bar proprietor who went by the name "Sal," a transplant from the Bronx who had obviously left New York for a good reason. Sal asked Joey if he were interested in purchasing a few machine guns. Bangs could smell his way around any city, and this offer carried the whiff of a marshal's ploy to entrap him. Bangs had to know. He found a payphone and dialed the toll-free number that connected him to a hotline in D.C. He entered his personal code, and after a couple of clicks heard his marshal's voice on the other end.

"The jig is up, cocksucker," Joey intoned.

The marshal asked Bangs what the hell he was talking about. Bangs cackled, and the marshal demanded to know where Bangs was.

"Keep the bar owner in sight and don't move!" the marshal ordered.

"Fuck you," Bangs chirped as he hung up the phone. He returned to the bar and made the deal with Sal, scoring a tidy profit when he resold the M-16 machine guns the following week.

About this time, the exasperated marshal informed Bangs that he would need to find gainful employment. Taken aback, Bangs informed the agent that he was retired, in case the man hadn't noticed, and "work" was a filthy four-letter word that didn't exist in his fucking vocabulary. Besides, the only thing Joey knew how to do was be a badass soldier, corrupt cop, bank robber, or drug dealer—or all of the above.

Just for kicks, Joey scribbled out a resume and asked the marshal to review his "qualifications." The agent glanced at the page and then studied Bangs incredulously—a cop? He read further, paying attention now, finally understanding who Joey was. "You're on your own," he mumbled curtly as he handed the paper back to Joey.

The marshal continued pressuring Bangs to produce a sales receipt for the Cadillac—he could feel his influence over Joey waning, and he was grasping at ways to exert control. Bangs realized he couldn't play this game much longer, so he gathered a few personal belongings and piled into the Caddy with Debbie. The marshal ran outside to see where they were going. *Go fuck your mother*, Joey waved, as he sped from the parking lot. And he was gone.

❤ ❤ ❤

Bangs and O'Malley just kept driving and blew through the forbidden city of Boston, continuing to Londonderry, New Hampshire, to visit Joey's Army buddy and longtime pal, John Sullivan, and his beloved wife, Kathy. Joey and Debbie were enchanted by the happy relationship and life of seeming bliss they saw in the Sullivans. A few cocktails later, when Sully and Kathy were in the kitchen checking on dinner, Joey leaned in to Debbie and whispered.

"What do you think?"

Debbie eyed Joey curiously and smiled. Joey winked in accord.

"Hey, Sully!" he yelled. "Get in here." Sully and Kathy scurried back to the living room.

"I need a favor."

"Already done. What is it?"

"Will you two stand in as best man and matron of honor?" Joey asked.

Sully beamed. "Just say when and where!"

"We figure as soon as we get back to Florida, get some things arranged," Joey offered.

"Fuck Florida!" interjected Sully. "There won't be anyone there. You'll do it right here in our house, and I'm footing the bill."

The wedding party packed the Sullivans' modest house, dozens of Joey and Debbie's friends celebrating new marriage and old times, champagne flowing throughout the night to wash clean the tainted memories.

▾ ▾ ▾

After a weekend of revels, Bangs and O'Malley left New Hampshire for his aunt's home in Dennis Port, on Cape Cod, where Joey dug up a stash of swag he had buried in Tupperware containers in her backyard. The packages were still perfectly sealed: Joey peeled the layer of duct tape from the outside, sliced open the superglued lids, and pulled out the rolls of bills and satchels of jewels he had packed with moisture absorbers. He loaded the loot into duffel bags, tossed the empty containers into the trash, and scanned the streets to see if anyone had noticed him. With a nod, he bid farewell to the neighborhood.

Joey and Debbie settled into the Caddy and headed into the sunset, zipping carefree down the Mid-Cape Highway. There was no time now for Boston, and Providence saw only a quick stop for gas and a cup of coffee. Interstate 95 South was Joey's yellow-brick road, and the country clicked by—New York, Philly, Baltimore, DC, Richmond, Raleigh, Florence, Savannah, Jacksonville—as he neared his Emerald City with a trunk full of loot and a smiling wife at his side. The Sunshine State was the land over the rainbow and Miami the place where his dreams would come true. The clouds were now far behind him—or so he thought.

Exonerated of all crimes, Bangs gets back to the business of living. Top left, with his father, Paul. Lower left, his uncle Ed Bangs. Lower right, with his brother, Paul.

Living it up with girlfriend—and later, second wife—Debbie O'Malley

Joey and Debbie, and one of their many homes.

With new friends, after all the old ones landed in prison.

In 2007 with Henry Hill, whose life inspired the film *Goodfellas*.

Bangs outside the Depositors Trust Bank vault, now a dining room
in Salvatore's Italian restaurant, in June 2014.

Bangs inside the converted bank vault, browsing news articles and photos
from the days following the heist, in June 2014.

EPILOGUE

I'VE OFTEN WONDERED WHAT MY FATHER and his hunting buddies thought while peering up at the young, crazed Bangs from the floor of that backwoods cabin as the fireplace exploded with bullets.

Why did my father extend a helping hand to Joey that afternoon at the White Tower? Why did he convince Bangs to take the entrance exam to the police academy? I know my father appreciated the kid's gumption and the strength of his heart, but no crystal ball could have ever foretold that gumption-and-heart would take a human being to the unimaginable places it ended up taking Joey Bangs. I guess everything that was supposed to happen *did happen*, and in some strange way, happened for the best. All things in life, Dad would say, happen for a reason.

In the late 1980s, political and public pressure grew in favor of legislation to consolidate several of the state's police agencies. As a result, on July 1, 1992, Chapter 412 of the Massachusetts Acts of 1991, referred to as the Police Consolidation Bill, went into effect to combine the Metropolitan Police, Capitol Police, Registry of Motor Vehicles Police, and the former Division of State Police into a new force called the Department of State Police.

By this time, the Mets had faithfully served Greater Boston for nearly one hundred years and had become the third largest police agency in New England, under the direction of its final superintendent, William J. Bratton, the former Boston Police Commissioner who would go on to lead the forces in New York and Los Angeles. Many speculated that budgetary issues drove the consolidation, but insiders, including former MDC Police Commissioner John J. Snedeker ("Jack"), viewed the devastating exposure to liability and loss of trust caused by Examscam and the other crimes of Bangs and his cohorts as the primary movers of change.

What still bewilders many Bostonians is how Bangs was able to shroud his exploits for so long from so many experienced law enforcement personnel, people who saw him every day—many of whom were among the state's top investigators—and had no clue that he was lying, stealing, neglecting his duties, working with the mob, terrorizing the city's citizenry, running the largest drug trade in New England, and generally wreaking havoc on the state's storied institutions. Every day that Bangs punched the time clock, the Commonwealth's heart skipped a beat. And when he punched out for the final time, he left in his wake a ward full of crippled and crushed individuals, families, and communities.

David, the State Police gave this to me during Doherty's trial.

Joe

"Has the jury reached a verdict?"

APPENDIX

Depositors Trust Indictment Press Statement

STATEMENT CONCERNING THE DEPOSITORS TRUST BANK
ROBBERY BY SCOTT HARSHBARGER, DISTRICT ATTORNEY
OF MIDDLESEX COUNTY—DECEMBER 9, 1985

"We are here today to announce the indictment, arrest, and arraignment of
five individuals, including three former police officers, who we allege are
responsible for the break-in and robbery of Depositors Trust Bank in
Medford, over the Memorial Day weekend in 1980. Joining me today are
James Greenleaf, Special Agent in Charge of the Boston Office of the
Federal Bureau Of Investigation, and Detective Lieutenant Robert Long,
the Director of the Massachusetts State Police Unit of the District
Attorney's Office. They coordinated and led the investigation which
brought about today's events, under the direction of my First Assistant,
Thomas Reilly, and Assistant District Attorney, David Burns.

"In thirty-six indictments and counts, we allege that these five
individuals broke into the Depositors Trust Bank over Memorial Day
weekend and stole the contents of the bank's safety deposit boxes.
Although at the time of the robbery there was speculation that the amount
taken was in excess of fifteen million, our investigation indicates that the
amount was substantially less, more in the range of one point five million,
plus a substantial amount of jewelry and other valuables. The size and
circumstances of the robbery aside, the most significant aspect of this
crime is that we allege and believe this crime was perpetrated and led by

individuals sworn to uphold the law and to protect the community from crime, and it constitutes a massive violation of that sacred public trust.

"I would specifically like to acknowledge and thank the FBI for their assistance and cooperation in this case. The alleged perpetrators of this crime came very close to exhausting the statute of limitations. In fact, the Federal Statute expired in May of this year. Despite this, the FBI continued to provide advice, information, and assistance crucial to the successful conclusion of this investigation. The State Police Detectives assigned to this office, under the very capable leadership of Lieutenant Robert Long and Sergeant Jim Lange, provided the intensive professional expertise necessary to bring this case forward. I am deeply grateful to each of these men and these law enforcement agencies for their assistance.

"This case is by far the most serious act of public corruption that I have seen in my time as District Attorney. I know that the law enforcement community in this state joins me in my dedication to root out at every juncture, the small minority of public officials who by their violation of public trust call into question the integrity of the government institutions. Therefore, we shall spare no effort or expense to see that justice is done and that those responsible for these, and other related crimes, are made to face the consequences of their actions.

"Thank you, ladies and gentlemen."

PHOTO ACKNOWLEDGMENTS

Photos courtesy of Joey Bangs, Debbie O'Malley, Joey Bangs Jr., Elaine Spencer, Brother O'Leary, Jerry Clemente, Thomas Doherty, the family of Tommy Spartachino, the *Medford Mercury*, the *Malden Observer*, the *Boston Globe*, the *Boston Herald*, the MDC Police Archives, UPI.

Made in United States
North Haven, CT
16 December 2023

46023523R00264